Writing & Grammar 8
for Christian Schools®

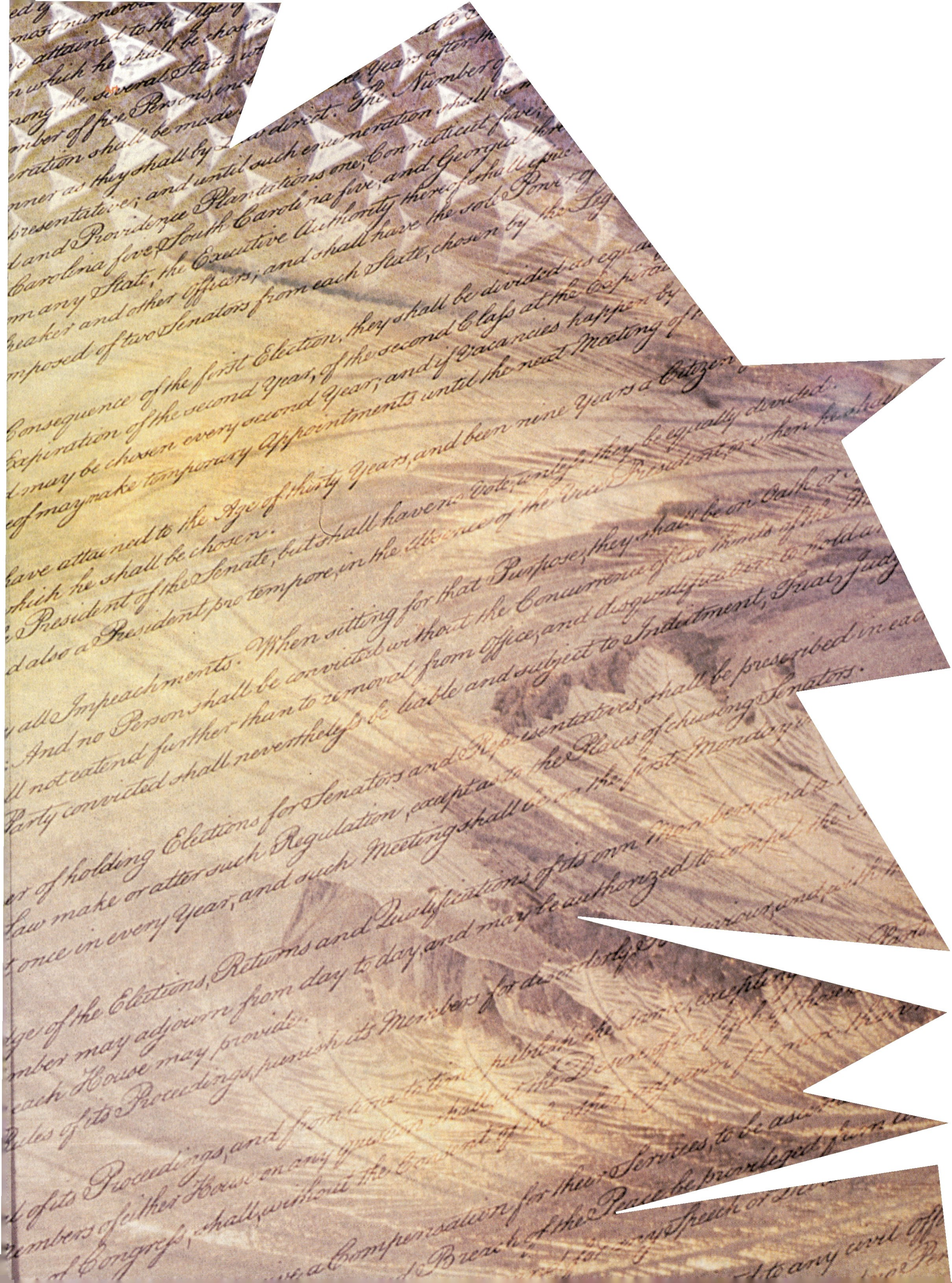

Writing & Grammar 8
for Christian Schools®

June W. Cates
Elizabeth Rose
Kimberly Y. Stegall
Dawn L. Watkins

Bob Jones University Press
Greenville, South Carolina 29614

Second Edition

Note:
The fact that materials produced by other publishers may be referred to in this volume does not constitute an endorsement of the content or theological position of materials produced by such publishers. Any references and ancillary materials are listed as an aid to the student or the teacher and in an attempt to maintain the accepted academic standards of the publishing industry.

WRITING AND GRAMMAR 8 for Christian Schools®
Second Edition

Authors
June W. Cates
Elizabeth Rose, M.Ed.
Kimberly Y. Stegall, M.Ed.
Dawn L. Watkins, M.Ed., M.A.

Designers	**Illustrators**	
Duane A. Nichols	John Bjerk	Tim Banks
John Bjerk	Paula Cheadle	
	Preston Gravely	
Compositor	Jim Hargis	
Nancy C. Lohr	Stefanie Kubina	
	Tami Mehus	
Editors	Asher Parris	
Kelly Cooper	John Roberts	
Rebecca S. Moore	Lynda Slattery	
	Melissa Smith	

Produced in cooperation with the Bob Jones University Division of English Language and Literature of the College of Arts and Science, the School of Education, and Bob Jones Academy.

for Christian Schools is a registered trademark of Bob Jones University Press.

© 2000 Bob Jones University Press
Greenville, South Carolina 29614
First Edition © 1984 Bob Jones University Press

Printed in the United States of America
All rights reserved

ISBN 1-57924-338-X

15 14 13 12 11 10 9 8 7 6 5

Table of Contents

Chapter 1: Sentences

▶ Excerpt from *Shadow of a Bull* 1
   Sentences 2
   Four Types of Sentences 2
   Subjects and Predicates 4
   Inverted Order 6
   Fragments 8
   Fused Sentences and Comma Splices 10
▶ Memories: Describing a Childhood Treasure 15
   Dashing Ahead: Critical Thinking 16

Chapter 2: Nouns

▶ Excerpt from *Little Town on the Prairie* 21
   Nouns 22
   Forms of Nouns 23
     • Spelling the Plural Forms of Nouns 23
     • Forming the Possessive Forms of Nouns 26
   Common and Proper Nouns 29
   Count and Noncount Nouns 30
   Compound Nouns 32
▶ Order at a Glance: Making a Time Line 37
   Stretching Out: The Play's the Thing 39

Chapter 3: Verbs

▶ Excerpt from *Vinegar Boy* 41
   Verbs 42
   Recognizing Verbs 42
   Intransitive and Transitive Verbs 43
   Linking Verbs and Predicate Nouns and Predicate Adjectives 47
   Auxiliaries 52
   Principal Parts of Verbs 55
   Simple Tenses 58
   Perfect Tenses 60
   Progressive Verbs 63
   Active and Passive Voice 66
▶ It's History: Writing an Autobiography 73
   Stretching Out: Doubling Back 75
   Passing the Baton: Writing Across the Curriculum 75

Chapter 4: Pronouns

▶ Excerpt from *But Not Forsaken* 77
   Pronouns and Antecedents 78
   Personal Pronouns 80
   Demonstrative Pronouns 83
   Interrogative Pronouns 83
   Reflexive and Intensive Pronouns 85
   Indefinite Pronouns 87
▶ Destination Decision: Designing a Travel Brochure 90
   Passing the Baton: Writing Across the Curriculum 93
   History of the English Language 93

Chapter 5: Adjectives

- ▶ Excerpt from *Up a Road Slowly* 95
- Adjectives 96
- Comparing with Adjectives 99
- Articles 102
- Possessives 103
- More Adjectives 107
- Proper Adjectives 109
- ▶ All the News: Reporting a Story 111

Chapter 6: Adverbs

- ▶ Excerpt from *Twice Freed* 115
- Adverbs 116
- Positions of Adverbs 120
- Comparing with Adverbs 122
- ▶ How Endings Make Meanings: Finishing a Story 126

Chapter 7: Prepositions, Conjunctions, and Interjections

- ▶ Excerpt from *Twenty Thousand Leagues Under the Sea* ... 129
- Prepositions 130
  - Commonly Used Prepositions 130
  - Prepositional Phrases 132
  - Functions of Prepositional Phrases 135
  - Preposition or Adverb? 137
- Conjunctions 139
  - Coordinating Conjunctions 139
  - Correlative Conjunctions 144
- Interjections 148
- ▶ Someone You Know: Writing a Character Profile 153
- Dashing Ahead: Critical Thinking 154

Chapter 8: Phrases and Clauses

- ▶ "A Will to Learn" 161
- Phrases 162
- Clauses 162
- Simple Sentences 165
- Compound Sentences 166
- Complex Sentences 168
- Adjective Clauses 171
- ▶ For Sale: Writing an Ad for a Table Game 179
- Passing the Baton: Writing Across the Curriculum 180
- Stretching Out: What's in a Name? 181

Chapter 9: Verbals and Verbal Phrases

- ▶ "Two Look at Two" 183
- Verbals and Verbal Phrases 184
  - Participles 184
  - Gerunds 191
  - Infinitives 196
- ▶ Captions with Snap: Writing Photo Captions 204
- Dashing Ahead: Critical Thinking 205

Chapter 10: Subject-Verb Agreement

Subject-Verb Agreement 209
Subject-Verb Agreement with Auxiliaries 211
Agreement with Indefinite Pronouns 214
Agreement with Compound Subjects 216
Intervening Phrases, Predicate Nouns, and Inverted Order 219
▶ A Photo Finish: Creating a Photo Essay 223
History of the English Language 225

Chapter 11: Pronoun-Antecedent Agreement

Agreement with Personal Pronouns 227
Agreement with Indefinite Pronouns 231
▶ Such Talk That Might Have Been: Writing Dialogue for a Painting 236

Chapter 12: Pronoun Usage

Using Subjective and Objective Case Pronouns Correctly 241
Some Pronoun Problems 252
• Possessive Pronouns and Contractions 252
• Courtesy Order 252
• Reflexive and Intensive Pronouns 254
Clear Pronoun Reference 256
• Unclear Antecedent 256
• Indefinite Reference of Personal Pronouns: *They, It, You* ... 260
▶ Think Clearly—Write Clearly: Writing Explanations 265
Stretching Out: The Sky's the Limit 267

Chapter 13: Using Adjectives and Adverbs Correctly

Adjective or Adverb? 269
Double Negatives 273
Adjectives and Adverbs in Comparisons 276
▶ From Both Sides: Scripting a Debate 280

Chapter 14: Using Troublesome Words Correctly

Troublesome Verbs 283
• *Lie/Lay* 283
• *Rise/Raise* 284
• *Sit/Set* 284
More Troublesome Verbs 286
• *May/Can* 286
• *Shall/Will* 286
Other Troublesome Words 287
More Troublesome Words 289
Still More Troublesome Words 292
▶ When Friends Meet Friends: Writing a Book Report 297
Passing the Baton: Writing Across the Curriculum 299

Chapter 15: Capitalization

Proper Nouns: People and Places 301
Proper Nouns: More People and Places (and related terms) 304
Proper Nouns: Cultural and Historical Terms 306
Proper Nouns: Titles 309
First Words and Parts of a Letter 311
Proper Adjectives and Single Letters as Words 313
➤ Aesop Revisited: Writing a Short Fable 316
Passing the Baton: Writing Across the Curriculum 319

Chapter 16: Punctuation

End Marks 322
Other Uses for Periods 323
Commas 325
Semicolons and Colons 332
Quotation Marks 335
Underlining for Italics 337
Apostrophes 340
Hyphens 342
Parentheses 345
➤ Beginning, Middle, End: Writing an Essay Answer 349

Chapter 17: Spelling

Spelling Hints 353
Spelling Singular Present-tense Verbs and Plural Nouns 354
Spelling with *ie* or *ei* 357
Adding Suffixes 358
➤ Minding Your Own Business: Writing a Business Letter 362

Chapter 18: Library Skills

What Can I Find in the Library? 367
How Are the Books Arranged? 367
How Are the Books Labeled? 370
How Do I Use the Card Catalog? 370
How Do I Use the Computer Catalog? 371
How Do I Use the Specific Reference Works? 375

Chapter 19: Study Skills

Developing an Interest 387
Using the Parts of a Book 387
Reading Textbooks 391
Improving Your Study Time 392
Scheduling Your Study Time 392
Using Profitable Memory Techniques 393
Improving Your Reading Comprehension 394
Taking Tests 400
• How to Take Classroom Tests 400
• How to Answer Objective Test Questions 400
• How to Take Standardized Tests 401

Chapter 20 Composition Skills—The Writer's Toolbox

The Writing Process 409
Planning 409
- Choosing a Topic 409
- Narrowing the Topic 411
- Considering Audience and Determining Purpose 412
- Gathering Information 412

Drafting 413
- Paragraphs 413
  - Writing a Topic Sentence 414
  - Developing the Supporting Sentences 415
  - Organizing the Supporting Sentences 416
  - Coming to a Conclusion 418
- Essays 419
  - Writing a Thesis Statement 420
  - Developing Supporting Paragraphs 420
  - Organizing Supporting Paragraphs 421
  - Writing Introduction and Conclusion Paragraphs 422

Revising 423
- Revising for Ideas 423
- Revising for Style 425
- Proofreading 427

Publishing 428

Chapter Reviews

Review 1 431
Review 2 433
Review 3 435
Review 4 439
Review 5 441
Review 6 443
Review 7 445
Review 8 447
Review 9 449
Review 10 451
Review 11 453
Review 12 455
Review 13 457
Review 14 459
Review 15 461
Review 16 463
Review 17 465

Glossary of Terms 467

Index 470

Acknowledgments

A careful effort has been made to trace the ownership of selections included in this textbook in order to secure permission to reprint copyrighted material and to make full acknowledgment of their use. If any error or omission has occurred, it is unintentional and will be corrected in subsequent editions, provided written notification is made to the publisher.

CHAPTER 1
Excerpt from *Shadow of a Bull* by Maia Wojciechowska. Reprinted with the permission of Atheneum Books for Young Readers, an imprint of Simon & Schuster Children's Publishing Division from *Shadow of a Bull* by Maia Wojciechowska. Copyright © 1964 Maia Wojciechowska.

CHAPTER 2
Excerpt from *Little Town on the Prairie* by Laura Ingalls Wilder. Text copyright 1941 by Laura Ingalls Wilder, Copyright © renewed 1969 by Charles F. Lankin, Jr. Used by permission of HarperCollins Publishers.

CHAPTER 3
Excerpt from *Vinegar Boy* by Alberta Hawse. © 1970 Moody Bible Institute of Chicago. Used by permission of Moody Press.

CHAPTER 4
Excerpt from *But Not Forsaken* by Helen Good Brenneman. © 1954 Herald Press. Renewal © 1982 Helen Good Brenneman. Used by permission of Christian Light Publications, Inc., Harrisonburg, VA. All rights reserved.

CHAPTER 5
From *"Up A Road Slowly"* by Irene Hunt. © 1966 by Modern Curriculum Press, Simon & Schuster Education Group. Used by permission.

CHAPTER 6
Excerpt from *Twice Freed* by Patricia St. John. © 1970 Patricia St. John. Used by permission of Moody Press.

CHAPTER 8
Excerpt from *Free Indeed: Heroes of Black Christian History* by Mark Sidwell. © 1995 Bob Jones University Press.

CHAPTER 9
"Two Look at Two" by Robert Frost. From: *The Poetry of Robert Frost,* edited by Edward Connery Lathem, Copyright 1951 by Robert Frost. Copyright 1923, © 1969 by Henry Holt & Company. Reprinted by permission of Henry Holt and Company, Inc.

CHAPTER 18
Page 966 from *The American Heritage Dictionary.* Copyright © 1997 by Houghton Mifflin Company. Reproduced by permission from *The American Heritage College Dictionary, Third Edition.*

Photograph Credits

The following agencies and individuals have furnished materials to meet the photographic needs of this textbook. We wish to express our gratitude to them for their important contribution.

British Information Services
B. W. Carper
George R. Collins
Corel Corporation
Digital Stock
Embassy of Spain
Gerald R. Ford Library
Beulah Hager
LEGO Systems, Inc.
Library of Congress
Missouri Botanical Garden
Colonel Kemp Moore
The Museum of Printing History
National Archives
National Library of Medicine
Nebraska State Historical Society
New Bedford Whaling Museum
Old Dartmouth Historical Society
PhotoDisc, Inc.
Planet Art
The Seeing Eye®
SoundForth
United States Coast Guard
United States Naval Historical Center
United States Navy
Unusual Films
www.arttoday.com
Walker Art Center
Dawn L. Watkins
Frederick R. Weisman
Woodrow Wilson House

Cover
Digital Stock (top right); Unusual Films (left, background script, back cover)

Title Pages
Corel Corporation (background design); Unusual Films (background script)

Chapter 1
PhotoDisc, Inc. 3, 7; Corel Corporation 4; Library of Congress 9; www.arttoday.com 10, 13, 15; Beulah Hager 11

Chapter 2
Library of Congress 22; Solomon D. Butcher Collection, Nebraska State Historical Society 25; www.arttoday.com 28; National Archives 33

Chapter 3
Colonel Kemp Moore 48; Unusual Films 52; Digital Stock 53; PhotoDisc, Inc. 63

Chapter 4
Woodrow Wilson House, Washington, D.C. 78; Corel Corporation 92

Chapter 5
National Archives 97, 111

Chapter 6
www.arttoday.com 119; The Museum of Printing History 121

Chapter 7
George R. Collins 131; Old Dartmouth Historical Society, New Bedford Whaling Museum 138; www.arttoday.com 146, 147, 149; U.S. Naval Historical Center 148; U.S. Navy 152

Chapter 8
B. W. Carper 164; SoundForth 165; British Information Services 169; Library of Congress 170; Unusual Films 173

Chapter 9
PhotoDisc, Inc. 189, 194; photo courtesy of The Seeing Eye® 195; Unusual Films 204(both)

Chapter 10
Digital Stock 208-9, 213(bottom), 220; Corel Corporation 210, 221; PhotoDisc, Inc. 213(top), 217; Unusual Films 223(all); Dawn L. Watkins 224

Chapter 11
PhotoDisc, Inc. 226-27; LEGO Systems, Inc. 230; Unusual Films 236; Planet Art 237, 239

Chapter 12
PhotoDisc, Inc. 240-41; Digital Stock 243, 249; Embassy of Spain 251; Library of Congress 253, 256; www.arttoday.com 262

Chapter 13
Digital Stock 268-69; PhotoDisc, Inc. 270; National Library of Medicine 276; Missouri Botanical Garden 279

Chapter 14
Digital Stock 282-83; Unusual Films 286; Library of Congress 291, 293

Chapter 15
Digital Stock 300-301; United States Coast Guard 314

Chapter 16
PhotoDisc, Inc. 320-21; Gerald R. Ford Library 329; Collection Walker Art Center, Minneapolis, 1988 gift of Frederick R. Weisman in honor of his parents, William and Mary Weisman 338

Chapter 17
Digital Stock 352-53

Chapter 18
Digital Stock 366-67; Unusual Films 368, 371, 382

Chapter 19
Digital Stock 386-87; Unusual Films 393

Chapter 20
PhotoDisc, Inc. 408-9; www.arttoday.com 418

To the Student

Why do we study English? We learn how to understand and how to speak English while we are very young. Why, then, do we spend so much of the rest of our lives studying something we already know?

English is a living language. It changes—constantly. New words appear; obsolete words fade away as they are no longer needed. Usage patterns change; even rules occasionally change. We need to learn to speak and to write so that others can understand. Without a thorough understanding of English, we cannot communicate effectively.

English is also a flexible language. We use different levels of formality for different audiences. We speak to our friends differently than we speak to our pastor or teacher. We use one style for a letter home from camp and another style for a research paper to be graded by a teacher.

WRITING AND GRAMMAR 8 for Christian Schools, Second Edition, will help you learn to communicate in English more effectively. The first step toward the goal of better speaking and writing is to acquaint yourself with the text. Take a few minutes to look through the book and become familiar with these features:

- **Flags** in the margin point you to other pages in the text with more information about the topic.
- **Etymology** notes tell you the histories and definitions of certain English words.
- **ESL** boxes explain in detail concepts that can be difficult for students from another language background *(ESL* is an abbreviation for *English as a Second Language).* Every student can learn more about English from these helpful explanations.
- **Passing the Baton: Writing Across the Curriculum** brings your writing skills into contact with other areas of study, such as geography, history, and science.
- **Stretching Out** offers tips for improving your writing style.
- **Dashing Ahead: Critical Thinking** develops your critical thinking skills as you try to solve the mysteries that confront Inspector Jameson and Officer Bell.
- **History of the English Language** explains how our language developed over the years.
- **The Glossary** is a collection of definitions of the terms used throughout the book.

The personal satisfaction of becoming an effective communicator is a good feeling to have—just like crossing the finish line first. As Hebrews 12:1 instructs us, "Let us run with patience the race that is set before us."

Chapter 1

Sentences

Shadow of a Bull
by Maia Wojciechowska

Grammar

"*"Great son of the Juan Olivar, won't you sit down?" The man pointed to an old upholstered chair that dominated the otherwise almost empty room.

"No, thank you. I just came to see your son, Juan."

"What possible business could you have with my idiot son?"

"It's rather private, and I would very much like to see him right away."

"He's still asleep. He has been to Seville. He caped some bulls in someone's pasture; and I believe," the man laughed bitterly, "he got hurt somewhat. But then, Juan does not get invited to tientas. But enough about him! You look exactly as your great father looked at your age. Are you too going to be the greatest torero Spain has ever seen?"

Manolo did not like being mocked by the man, and he did not know how he should answer him.

"Father, let him go to see Juan," Jaime said.

"Not yet! Not before we have our little talk," the man said turning to Manolo and pointing to the chair again. "Sit down, and I'll tell you a story."

Manolo did as he was told, more to humor the man than to hear what he had to say. He felt very uneasy; if it had not been for Jaime who remained in the room, he would have fled."

- *Whom would you rather talk with, Juan's father or Manolo? Why?*
- *Why do you think Juan's father treats Manolo the way he does?*

The types of sentences in the dialogue help characterize Juan's father and Manolo. Declarative sentences give an impression of restraint; exclamatory and imperative sentences usually reveal stronger emotions. The author has used sentence types carefully to reveal the personalities of her characters.

In this chapter you will learn more about imperatives, interrogatives, and the other types of sentences.

Sentences

What is a sentence? A good definition of a sentence will include at least four characteristics.

- A sentence begins with a capital letter.
- It ends with a period, question mark, or exclamation point.
- It includes both a subject and a predicate.
- It expresses a complete thought.

>Spain's influence on other countries has been extensive.
>The Spanish Empire included territory in both North America and South America.

Sentences are important because they convey meaning. We use sentences in both speech and writing to get our ideas across to other people—our listeners and readers. This chapter will help you learn more about this important element of our language.

Four Types of Sentences

One way to classify a sentence is to identify its function, or purpose. Sentences have four functions in English: to declare, to question, to command, and to exclaim. These functions give us the names we use to classify the four types of sentences. In addition, the sentence function will determine which type of punctuation we should place at the end of that sentence.

A **declarative sentence** makes a statement, usually a fact, and ends with a period.

>Our visit to Spain will last five days.

An **interrogative sentence** asks a question and ends with a question mark.

>Where is your ticket?

Interrogative is a combination of the Latin words *inter,* "between," and *rogare,* "ask." The word *interrogate* means "to question formally."

An **imperative sentence** gives a command or makes a request and ends with a period or, occasionally, an exclamation point.

>Please help me with this luggage.
>Don't drop that suitcase!

Imperative comes from two Latin words that mean "to prepare against." The phrase later came to mean a command or an order to prepare.

An **exclamatory sentence** expresses strong emotion and ends with an exclamation point.

>I can't wait to arrive in Madrid!

In English, one of the major differences in the types of sentences is the rising and falling of pitch, called the *intonation*. Intonation of a sentence can be a hint as to what type the sentence is.
1. Declarative sentences have falling intonation at the end.
2. Many interrogative sentences have rising intonation at the end.
3. Imperative sentences have falling intonation at the end.
4. Exclamatory sentences are stated at a higher pitch than other sentences or with a greater difference between the high and the low pitches.

ETYMOLOGY

Intonation comes from two Latin words: *in*, meaning "in," and *tonus*, meaning "a musical sound." To intone, then, is to give words a musical sound.

IN SUMMARY

A **declarative sentence** makes a statement and ends with a period.

An **interrogative sentence** asks a question and ends with a question mark.

An **imperative sentence** gives a command or makes a request and ends with a period or an exclamation point.

An **exclamatory sentence** expresses strong emotion and ends with an exclamation point.

Chapter 16: End Marks
p. 321

1-1 PRACTICE THE SKILL

Identify each sentence as declarative, exclamatory, imperative, or interrogative. Write the appropriate punctuation mark at the end of each sentence.

interrogative 1. Do you know anything about matadors?

declarative 2. A matador is a man who fights a bull in a special contest.

interrogative 3. Would you want to have a matador's job?

exclamatory 4. I definitely would not!

declarative 5. A *matador de toros* is a highly skilled matador.

imperative 6. Open your books to page 28.

declarative 7. That page shows a picture of a matador.

interrogative 8. Do you like his brightly colored costume?

Sentences 3

exclamatory 9. Wow! This is really interesting!

imperative 10. Tell your friend about what you learned today.

1-2 Review the Skill

Identify each sentence as declarative, exclamatory, imperative, or interrogative. Write the appropriate punctuation mark at the end of each sentence.

declarative 1. Piñatas are made with papier-mâché and contain small gifts and candy.

exclamatory 2. The piñata is beautiful!

interrogative 3. Have you ever seen a piñata at a birthday party?

declarative 4. Spanish children try to break the piñata to get the candy inside.

interrogative 5. Have you ever broken a piñata?

imperative 6. Move out of the way!

exclamatory 7. That boy just broke the piñata!

declarative 8. Now start picking up the candy.

declarative 9. There is enough candy for everyone.

interrogative 10. Did you enjoy trying to break a piñata?

Subjects and Predicates

Every sentence includes two main parts, a **subject** and a **predicate.** The subject names the person, place, thing, or idea that the sentence discusses. The predicate makes a statement about the subject.

The subject usually comes at or near the beginning of the sentence. The **simple subject** is the main noun or pronoun in the sentence. The **complete subject** includes the simple subject and its modifiers.

*The largest coastal **city** in Spain* is Barcelona.
*Spain's Mediterranean **coastline*** stretches from Cape Creus to the Strait of Gibraltar.

ETYMOLOGY *Predicate* comes from two Latin words meaning "to say in public" or "to proclaim." A predicate in a sentence makes some "proclamation" about the subject.

4   Chapter 1

The predicate usually follows the subject. The **simple predicate** is the main verb in the sentence. The simple predicate may include two or more verbs working together. The **complete predicate** includes the simple predicate and its modifiers, objects, or other completers.

Madrid ***is*** *Spain's capital and its largest city.*
My cousin ***has traveled*** *in Spain three times.*
Tourists from all over the world ***visit*** *Spain every year.*

Both subjects and predicates can be compound. A **compound subject** is two or more nouns or pronouns functioning as subjects joined by a conjunction. A **compound predicate** is two or more verbs joined by a conjunction.

Mexico and *Panama* are two countries influenced by Spain.
Spanish sailors *explored* and *settled* many other countries too.

Most imperative sentences seem to have only a predicate. Because these sentences are commands, we understand that the subject is *you*. Only an imperative sentence can have understood *you* as its subject.

   S   P
(You) Tell me about your trip to Seville.

   S   P
(You) Please find Granada on this map.

Word Order
In English, unlike some other languages, the subject almost always comes before the verb.
    S P
1. John played basketball with Philip.
    S P
2. Philip was quicker than John.
    S   P   S   P
3. John said, "(You) Throw me the ball."

In Summary

The **simple subject** is the main noun or pronoun in a sentence.

The **complete subject** includes the simple subject and its modifiers.

A **compound subject** is two or more nouns or pronouns joined by a conjunction.

The **simple predicate** is the main verb in the sentence.

The **complete predicate** includes the simple predicate and its modifiers, objects, or other completers.

A **compound predicate** is two or more verbs joined by a conjunction.

Some **imperative sentences** have understood *you* as the subject.

Chapter 3: Recognizing Verbs
p. 42

Chapter 10: Subject-Verb Agreement with Compound Subjects
pp. 216-17

Chapter 7: Conjunctions
pp. 139-40

1-3 PRACTICE THE SKILL

Draw a vertical line between the complete subject and the complete predicate. Underline the simple subject(s) once and the simple predicate(s) twice. If the subject is understood *you*, draw a line before the simple predicate.

1. The Alcazar in Segovia, Spain, appears as a lofty and noble bulwark.
2. This castle rests on a rocky cliff.
3. Segovia's Alcazar is a rather long castle.
4. However, many photographs and drawings reveal only part of the castle's length.
5. Look at the beautiful silhouette.
6. Another famous Spanish castle and tourist attraction in Grenada is the Alhambra.
7. The Alhambra was built by the Moors between 1248 and 1354.
8. Observe and examine the twenty-three towers on the wall.
9. Alhambra means "red" in Arabic.
10. The Alhambra is one of the most important examples of Islamic architecture.

1-4 REVIEW THE SKILL

Draw a vertical line between the complete subject and the complete predicate. Underline the simple subject(s) once and the simple predicate(s) twice. If the subject is understood *you*, draw a line before the simple predicate.

1. Spain consists of fifty provinces.
2. This picturesque country borders France and Portugal.
3. Millions travel to Spain each year.
4. Notice all of the historical landmarks.
5. The tourists visit the castles along the countryside.
6. However, an avid sports fan or visitor may choose a soccer game instead.
7. Soccer is called football in Spain.
8. Most Spaniards enjoy old folk songs.
9. Their traditional costumes are always bright and colorful.
10. Explore and enjoy this beautiful country.

Inverted Order

In most sentences, the subject comes before the predicate. However, some sentences are in **inverted order,** with the subject coming after the predicate or between the two parts of the predicate. Many interrogative sentences are in inverted order.

> *Was* the **Spanish Armada** a failure?
> There *were* 130 **ships** in the fleet.
> *Did* **Philip II** *overestimate* the Armada's ability?

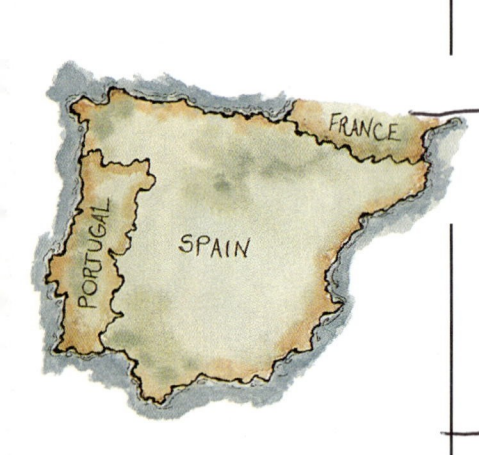

Chapter 10: Subject-Verb Agreement with Inverted Order
p. 220

You can rearrange inverted sentences to make sure you have found the subject and the predicate.

The **Spanish Armada** *was* a failure.
One hundred thirty **ships** *were* in the fleet.
Philip II *did overestimate* the Armada's ability.

In Summary

Inverted order occurs when the subject comes after the predicate or between two parts of the predicate.

1-5 Practice the Skill

Underline the simple subject(s) once and the simple predicate(s) twice.

1. Are chinchillas native to North America?
2. A chinchilla is a small South American rodent.
3. There are chinchilla ranches in Europe, North America, and South Africa today.
4. After whom are they named?
5. The Spanish named them after the Chincha Indians and sold the fur in Europe.
6. The Chincha Indians and Inca Indians ate chinchillas.
7. Chinchillas eat roots and grasses.
8. Here is a book on chinchillas.
9. Do you know their weight at birth?
10. They weigh slightly more than an ounce.

1-6 Review the Skill

Underline the simple subject(s) once and the simple predicate(s) twice.

1. Where <u><u>is</u></u> the <u>town</u> of Seville?
2. <u>Seville</u> <u><u>is</u></u> a seaport in southern Spain.
3. There <u><u>are</u></u> many famous <u>stories</u> about Seville.
4. Do <u>you</u> <u><u>know</u></u> any of the stories?
5. <u><u>Was</u></u> <u>Don Quixote</u> born in Seville?
6. There <u><u>is</u></u> a famous bell <u>tower</u> in Seville.
7. What activities do <u>people</u> <u><u>enjoy</u></u> in Seville?
8. There <u><u>are</u></u> festivals and bullfights in the <u>city</u>.
9. <u>Bullfights</u> <u><u>must be</u></u> very exciting.
10. There <u><u>are</u></u> few <u>cities</u> as beautiful and attractive as Seville.

Fragments

A **fragment** is a group of words wrongly capitalized and punctuated as though it were a sentence. Unlike a sentence, a fragment fails to express a complete thought.

There are two types of fragments. The first type lacks either a subject or a predicate. The other type has both a subject and a predicate but also includes a word that makes the fragment unable to stand alone as a sentence.

> The famous Alhambra in Granada.
> Although the Moors were defeated in 1492.

You can correct a fragment by supplying the missing information or by joining it to another fragment or a sentence that completes the thought.

> The famous Alhambra in Granada is a Moorish palace.
> Although the Moors were defeated in 1492, their influence on Spanish architecture survived.

Chapter 8: Dependent Clauses
p. 162

In Summary

A **fragment** is a group of words wrongly capitalized and punctuated as though it were a sentence. A fragment can be corrected by adding the missing subject or verb or by joining it to a complete sentence.

1-7 Practice the Skill

Label each group of words *S* (sentence) or *F* (fragment).

S   1. Isabella I reigned as queen from 1474-1504.

F   2. The region of Castile.

S   3. She gained control of the throne.

___F___ 4. After Henry IV's death in 1474.

___S___ 5. Isabella I married Ferdinand of Aragon in 1469.

___F___ 6. Through this marriage.

___S___ 7. She received rights as consort in Aragon.

___S___ 8. Even today many people know about Isabella and Ferdinand.

___S___ 9. Because they gave Christopher Columbus financial support.

___F___ 10. For his voyage of exploration.

Christopher Columbus at the Court of Ferdinand and Isabella

1-8 REVIEW THE SKILL

A. Label each group of words S (sentence) or F (fragment).

___S___ 1. The Rock of Gibraltar is an impressive picture of power and protection.

___F___ 2. On a small peninsula in southeastern Spain.

___S___ 3. The land area of Gibraltar is only 2.5 square miles.

___F___ 4. Because Gibraltar is controlled by Britain.

___S___ 5. The people commonly speak both English and Spanish.

___S___ 6. Gibraltar is the location of the famous Gorham's Cave.

___S___ 7. An exciting cave with stalactites and mysterious passageways.

___F___ 8. Because there are historic fortresses and castles.

___S___ 9. Millions of tourists visit Gibraltar each year.

___F___ 10. To see the breathtaking Rock of Gibraltar.

B. Rewrite the fragments from Part A, making them complete sentences. You may combine groups of words. If a group of words is already a sentence, write *sentence* in the blank.

1. ___Sentence___

2. ___The Rock of Gibraltar lies on a small peninsula in southeastern Spain.___

Sentences   9

3. _Sentance_

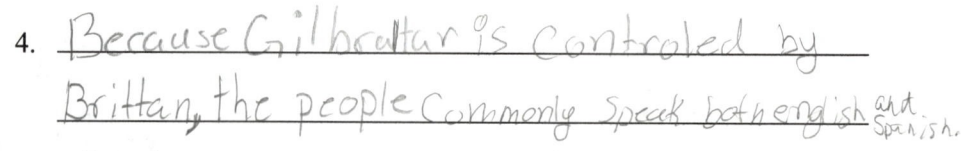

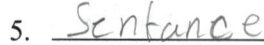

4. _Because Gilbraltar is controled by Brittan, the people commonly speak both english and Spanish._

5. _Sentance_

6. _Sentance_

7. _Sentance_

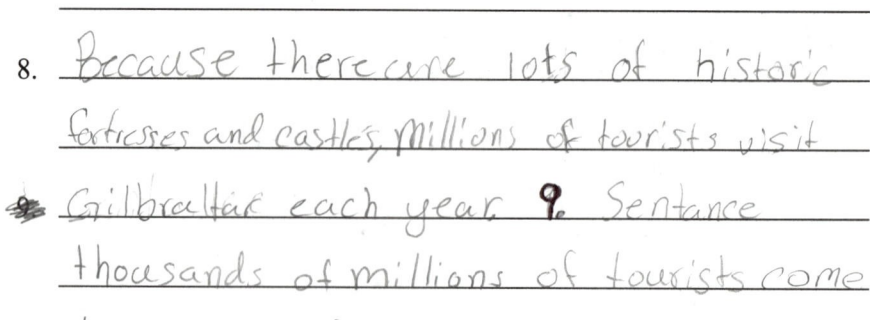

8. _Because there are lots of historic fortresses and castles, millions of tourists visit Gilbraltar each year._ 9. _Sentance_

10. _thousands of millions of tourists come to Spain to see the wonderous Rock of Gilbrattar._

Fused Sentences and Comma Splices

A **fused sentence** consists of two sentences incorrectly joined without any punctuation. A fused sentence does not show clearly where one idea ends and another begins.

> **Wrong:** Many different invaders have settled Spain over the years the Romans were only one group to conquer Spain.
>
> **Wrong:** Roman soldiers first invaded Spain more than two hundred years before Christ's birth they eventually ruled both Spain and Portugal.

A **comma splice** consists of two sentences incorrectly joined by only a comma. Like a fused sentence, a comma splice does not clearly separate the two sentences.

> **Wrong:** The Romans built many roads and bridges in Spain, their most impressive structures may be the aqueducts.
>
> **Wrong:** The Romans' language was Latin, Spanish developed from Latin over a period of several centuries.

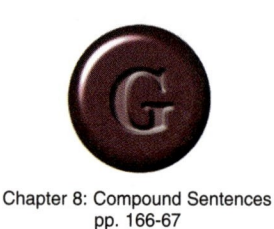

Chapter 8: Compound Sentences
pp. 166–67

You can correct a fused sentence or a comma splice by separating the two sentences or by joining them correctly. If you separate the sentences with an end mark, remember to begin the second sentence with a capital letter. If you choose to join them, use either a comma and a coordinating conjunction or a semicolon.

Right: Many different invaders have settled Spain over the years. The Romans were only one group to conquer Spain.

Right: The Romans built many roads and bridges in Spain, but their most impressive structures may be the aqueducts.

Right: The Romans' language was Latin; Spanish developed from Latin over a period of several centuries.

Chapter 16: Commas; Semicolons pp. 326, 332

Chapter 7: Conjunctions pp. 139-40

IN SUMMARY

A **fused sentence** consists of two sentences incorrectly joined without any punctuation.

A **comma splice** consists of two sentences incorrectly joined by just a comma.

1-9 PRACTICE THE SKILL

Label each group of words *S* (sentence), *FS* (fused sentence), or *CS* (comma splice).

__S__ 1. Spanish culture differs greatly from American culture, it is not merely a difference of language.

__FS__ 2. The Spanish typically transact business on a more personal level than Americans sometimes people will stop by a store for a social visit rather than for business purposes.

__S__ 3. In fact, the American straightforward approach may appear rude to a Spanish person.

__FS__ 4. Each business owner sets his own hours some owners close for an afternoon siesta and reopen a few hours later.

__CS__ 5. Many Spanish people choose July and August for their vacations, business hours during these two months are especially diverse.

Sentences 11

___S___ 6. Table manners also differ in Spanish cultures people may rest their hands, elbows, and arms on the edge of the table rather than in their laps.

___S___ 7. They always leave a little food on their plates.

___S___ 8. This practice signals the end of your meal, otherwise the hostess may serve you another helping.

___CS___ 9. A Spanish meal consists of many courses each person may eat at his own pace, however.

___S___ 10. Most Spanish cafés are small, they serve as meeting places more for the local neighbors than for the general public.

1-10 REVIEW THE SKILL

A. Label each group of words *S* (sentence), *FS* (fused sentence), or *CS* (comma splice).

___S___ 1. Díaz de Vivar, a famous Spanish soldier, is commonly known as the Cid.

___S___ 2. Beginning in 1086, several Spanish cities did not want to be conquered by King Alfonso VI they asked the Muslim Almoravids to help them.

___S___ 3. The Almoravids conquered much of Spain, Seville fell in 1091.

___FS___ 4. Many other cities were conquered Valencia did not fall to the Almoravids.

___S___ 5. The Valencians rebelled against their ruler, and the Cid decided to take control of the city.

___S___ 6. The Valencians did not want him as their ruler, he blockaded the city for twenty months.

___S___ 7. The Valencians faced starvation no one could take food into the city.

___CS___ 8. The city surrendered on June 17, 1094, the Cid allowed the people to own property and to choose their own religions.

___S___ 9. The Cid ruled the city until his death in 1099.

___S___ 10. The Cid is now considered a national hero, many stories about him are myths, however.

B. Rewrite each fused sentence or comma splice from Part A to make it a correct sentence. If a group of words is already a sentence, write *sentence* in the blank.

1. ___Sentance___

2. ___Sentance___

3. Sentance

4. Many other cities were conquered. However, Valencia did not fall to the Almoravids.

5. Sentance

6. Sentance

7. Sentance

8. The city surrendered on June 17, 1094. The Cid allowed the people to own property and choose thier own religions.

9. Sentance

10. Sentance

1-11 USE THE SKILL

Rewrite the following paragraph, revising each fragment, fused sentence, or comma splice to make it a correct sentence. There are five errors.

A famous Spanish national hero is the Cid his real name was Rodrigo Díaz de Vivar. The name *the Cid* comes from the Arabic *El Sayyid*. He was born near Burgos, Spain. The Cid served in Sancho II's and Alfonso VI's armies, He was a famous warrior, An unjust accusation of disloyalty in 1081. This accusation caused the Cid's banishment from Alfonso's army, the armies suffered without this great warrior. The Cid paid men for his own personal army. His army gave him great power, he also had vast wealth. The Cid captured Valencia from the Moors and became a great legend. *The Poem of the Cid* commemorates the Cid.

[Student handwritten response:]

A famous Spanish national hero is the Cid. His real name was Rodrigo Diaz de Vivar. The name The Cid comes from the Arabic El Sayyid. He was born near Burgos, Spain. The Cid served in Sancho II's and Alfonso VI's armies. He was a famous warrior, although, there was an unjust accusation of disloyalty in 1081. This accusation caused the Cid's banishment from Alfonso's army. The armies suffered without this great warrior. The Cid paid men for his own personal army. His army gave him great power, he also had vast wealth. The Cid captured Valencia from the Moors and became a great land. The Poem of the Cid commemorates the Cid.

POLE VAULTING

Read the excerpt from *The Shadow of a Bull* again, noticing the types of sentences the characters use when they speak.

- *How does the author's use of declarative sentences make Manolo seem polite, controlled, and confident?*
- *How does she use sentence types to make the father less polished and controlled?*

Memories: Describing a Childhood Treasure

What makes something valuable?

Would you be more apt to pick up a penny that was bright and shiny or one that was dull and worn and looked as if it had been run over several times? Would you choose a rare foreign postage stamp over a string of pearls? Would you be more excited to find a baseball card of a Hall of Fame player or an old version of a computer game at a discounted price?

You have heard the saying "One person's junk is another's treasure." An object's value to us is not necessarily based on its monetary worth but on our likes and dislikes.

One person may be delighted with something that would have no appeal for someone else. Your mom might get excited over a recipe for fish and lentil stew that would make your little brother turn up his nose. You might see nothing special in the scuffed, cracked-leather golf bag that your dad prizes as an antique. But chances are you and your little brother have "treasures" of your own that your mom or dad would not value.

Did you have a treasure as a child? Maybe it was an unusual object from nature, like a bird's nest or a seashell. Or maybe it was a keepsake, like a photograph of your great-grandfather or the hood ornament from your uncle's '57 Chevy.

Perhaps your treasure had sentimental value that only you knew about. Maybe you kept a lock of mane from the horse your family had to sell when you moved to the city. Or perhaps you have saved a piece of ordinary wrapping paper or ribbon for years because it had been attached to a special present. Your childhood treasure could be common or rare, new or old, quirky or classy. Its value depends on you.

Here's one student's description of her childhood treasure:

My Grandma's Button Jar

When I was six or seven, my grandma gave me her button jar while I was visiting at her house. It was a little glass jar, about six inches tall, full of buttons of all different shapes, colors, and styles. She had collected the buttons over the years and thought that I might like to play with them or add to the collection.

I kept the button jar under my bed, and whenever I was in the mood to look at it, I pulled it out. I liked to pour the buttons out and feel them falling through my fingers. Sometimes I sorted them by color or made up little games and played them with my friend Trina. I think one reason that I liked the buttons so much was that they were all so different. They made me think about all the different kinds of things God has created and how each one is special in its own way.

Now that I'm older, I've started adding some buttons of my own to the collection. Sometimes when I lose a button, I find one in the jar to replace it. I plan to keep the jar with me until I can give it to my own daughter some day.

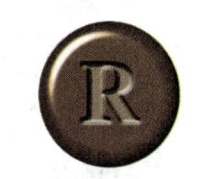

Chapter 20: Choosing a Topic
pp. 409-10

Your Turn: Displaying Your Treasure

Write two or three paragraphs describing your own childhood treasure. See whether you can answer each of the following questions in your description:
- What did it look like?
- How did you get it?
- Where did you keep it?
- Why did you consider it a treasure?
- Where is it today?

DASHING AHEAD!
CRITICAL THINKING

The Case of the Stolen Champ

It was nearly dawn when Inspector Jameson and Officer Bell arrived at the crime scene. Inspector Jameson could just barely see extensive gardens overflowing with flowers. The first rays of sunrise gave a peaceful glow to the surroundings; however, almost all the lights on the ground level of the large house were on, hinting of the trouble within.

Inside, the inspector found the members of the household gathered in the library discussing the events that had occurred earlier that morning. Mr. Mort stepped forward and introduced himself. "Inspector Jameson, I am Reginald Alwin Mort. Thank you for coming."

"Not at all, Mr. Mort. Please explain what happened."

"Early this morning we were awakened by the sound of shattering glass."

"Who are 'we,' Mr. Mort?" interrupted Inspector Jameson.

"This is my wife, Edwina. Here is my daughter, Jessica."

Both women were thin, pale, and nervous looking. Mrs. Mort nodded as she was introduced; Jessica glanced briefly at the inspector and then looked away.

Reginald continued. "This is my nephew, Ronald Albert Mort. He lives here. Almost like a son to me."

Ronald gave Jameson a slight smile and stifled a yawn. "Nice to meet you, I'm sure—although not under these circumstances," he said.

"And this is Red Herring, our gardener, whom I hired last week."

Herring extended his hand and clasped Jameson's firmly. "Pleased to meet you, sir!"

"All right, Mr. Mort, please continue with the events as they happened."

"Please don't touch that!" Mr. Mort exclaimed suddenly. He was across the room in two steps, pulling Officer Bell back from a display case. "Don't you know not to touch evidence at the scene of a crime?"

"Mr. Mort, I wasn't touching it," Bell said, slightly irritated. "I was merely examining the evidence."

"I apologize," said Mr. Mort. "I know I'm jumpy this morning, but it seems we could be doing more than merely standing around talking!"

"Once we have all the details, we'll do what we can to solve this mystery," Jameson said.

Reginald Mort cleared his throat. "Well, we were awakened by the sound of shattering glass about 4:15 A.M. I should have had better security for my prized collection of baseball cards! Now the most valuable one is gone!" He paused. "Let's see, where was I? Well, we all rushed downstairs. The thief must have used a brick or something huge—"

"Or perhaps this fireplace poker," Bell said, pointing to it. It stood in a rack on the hearth with several other fireplace tools. But it was slightly bent and had bits of mud clinging to it. It was also a little damp, perhaps from dew.

"It really doesn't matter what he used, does it?" Mr. Mort said. "Anyway, when we heard the crash, we all came down here quickly. Even Ronald, who's usually a sound sleeper, was awakened. He was the first one down and met Red, who was already in the hallway. Red's room is right off the kitchen, you know, on this floor. I followed Ronald, and Jessica and my wife were right behind me. By the time we reached this room, everyone was together. Glass from the window had littered the floor, as you can see. The window had been broken, the latch flipped, and the window raised. You can see for yourself how he came in. Ronald phoned the police right away so as to catch the thief, who was no doubt only seconds away in his escape back through the window."

"Which phone did Ronald call from?" asked Jameson.

"That one right there," Mort said, pointing across the room.

"What possible difference can it make which phone I used, Inspector?" Ronald asked.

Jameson shrugged. "Probably none at all. Just need to re-create the scene in my mind."

Inspector Jameson noted the open window and shattered glass on the otherwise clean green carpeting. He leaned out the window and in the early morning light saw footprints in the muddy soil of the flower bed underneath the window. He looked over the garden outside as well. "Yes, Mr. Mort. Someone definitely was out there."

Reginald threw his arms upward. "Of course someone was out there! We're wasting time! Look at my display case." Grabbing the Inspector's sleeve, he pulled him across the room. "It's been pried open and my 1920 Guy Champ rookie card is missing! Please get busy and find the person who stole it!"

"All in good time," said the observant inspector as he examined the case of neatly displayed cards. Only one had been taken, disturbing the symmetry of the display. "It's interesting to me that only one card, your most valuable, was taken."

"Why's that interesting? Of course a thief would take the most valuable item!"

"But you have many others here that appear valuable as well."

Officer Bell peeked between the two men. "Oh yes! Here's a 1932 Reuben Thwackbatt. And a 1954 Byron Swartz!" He let out a whistle. Officer Jameson and Reginald Mort both gave him a long, level look. "Uh . . . sorry!" he said, backing away.

Sentences

Officer Jameson and Reginald Mort both gave him a long, level look. "Uh . . . sorry!" he said, backing away.

Jameson turned around and looked over the members of the household. Reginald tapped one slippered foot impatiently. Red shifted from foot to foot, smiling ingratiatingly at Jameson. Ronald yawned. Jessica's face was white with fear. As the sound of a doorbell startled her into action, Mrs. Mort turned to leave the room. As she left, she mumbled, "That must be Connie, my day help. I'd better explain things to her. Strangers crashing through windows, ransacking our whole house! Such random violence these days! What is this world coming to?"

"Others will be arriving soon, Inspector, and the thief is getting more of a head start. Can we get on with it?" Reginald said impatiently.

"Others?" asked Bell. "Are you planning on company today?"

"Yes, we're planning for quite a large luncheon today. Within a few hours this whole place will be overrun with guests and hired help. How can we have a party in just a few hours when my card is probably being hocked at a pawn shop as we speak?"

"Has anyone other than Mrs. Mort left this room since you all rushed down here this morning?"

Reginald Mort frowned, considering a moment. "No. Why?"

"Officer Bell, would you please call Mrs. Mort back into the room?" Jameson asked.

Bell hurried out to obey and quickly returned with Mrs. Mort, who asked, "Is this going to take long? I need to prepare for the luncheon."

"I don't think it will take long, Mrs. Mort." He walked over and shut the library door, closing them all in together. "I don't think it will take long at all. You see, I believe the guilty person—and probably the stolen card—are both in this room right now!"

Before you finish the story—

- *What clues has Jameson noticed that point to its being "an inside job"? Reread if necessary.*
- *If Jameson is right and the thief is in the room, who do you think it is? Why?*

"What!" Mr. Mort exclaimed. "You would dare to blame a member of my own household?"

"Yes, I'm afraid so. Please, everyone, sit down and let me explain." The Morts and Red Herring did so. "First, as Officer Bell pointed out, the weapon used was no doubt the fireplace poker. It was neatly replaced after the window was broken."

Mrs. Mort spoke up. "I hardly think, Inspector, that someone placing a fireplace poker in its proper place proves that he—or she—lives in this house. Anybody could see that that's where it belongs."

"Yes, but how did the thief obtain it in the first place? Does it make sense that a thief would somehow gain access to this room, take the poker, go outside, smash the window, enter, and then replace the poker?"

The Morts and Mr. Herring began looking at each other with suspicion.

"Also, there's some evidence that should be here but isn't."

"What on earth do you mean by that?" Reginald Mort said, exasperated.

"While there is glass all over the carpet, there is no mud on the carpet. Any thief coming in from outside would have left muddy footprints from the window to the case and back again. Curiously, they're not there."

"Good catch, sir," Bell said. "I didn't think of that!"

"So precisely what is your theory—and whom are you accusing, Inspector?" Ronald asked.

"I think it's quite clear what happened. Someone in this room took the card early this morning, prying open the case and merely sticking the card in a pocket. Unlike a thief unfamiliar with the collection, this member of the household knew exactly which card to take. The thief then picked up the poker, went outside, trampled the flowers, smashed the window, and then ran inside again, removing his or her shoes. He replaced the poker, banking on the fact that it would take the family a few moments to be fully aroused, put on dressing gowns, and come downstairs."

"It was you!" Mrs. Mort suddenly cried out, pointing at Red Herring. "You are the only one whose room is downstairs! I should have known better than to let you stay in the house, you . . . you thief!"

Red looked horrified. "No, no! I didn't do it! I didn't!"

Inspector Jameson continued calmly. "I didn't accuse you, Mr. Herring. In fact, I think I can prove right now who the thief is." All eyes were on him as he slipped on a pair of latex gloves and walked over to the phone table. He flipped quickly through the pages of the phone book and removed something from it, lifting it in the air for all to see.

Mr. Mort was on his feet in an instant. "My card! You've found it!" Then the realization hit him. "Ronald, you were the only one to use that phone this morning! How could you—how could you, when I've taken you in and treated you as a son?"

Ronald's face twisted into a rude sneer. "Because the measly little allowance you give me isn't enough to live on. Because I get sick of hearing you talk on and on about your precious baseball card collection."

Jessica spoke for the first time since the detectives' arrival. "Why don't you admit the truth, Ronald?" she asked. Then she turned to Inspector Jameson. "Ronald has run up huge debts on his credit cards. He told me, but he asked me not to tell Mother or Father. He probably hid the card there, knowing he could sneak it out of the house during the luncheon today. No doubt he wanted to sell the card to help pay his debts. Is that right, Ronald?"

Ronald crossed his arms and glared at her.

"All you would have had to do was ask me for financial help, Ronald, and I would have given it!" Reginald said. Then he turned back to Jameson. "Well, the good news is that the card is back." He reached out to take it from the inspector.

"Ah-ah-ah!" said Officer Bell. "Don't you know not to touch evidence at the scene of a crime?"

- *Were you right in your guess at who the guilty party was? If not, why not?*
- *What three clues made it clear to Jameson that someone in the room was guilty?*

Sentences 19

Chapter 2

Nouns

Little Town on the Prairie
by Laura Ingalls Wilder

Grammar

> The corn was taller than Laura now, a lavish sight to see, with its long leaves rustling thickly and its nodding tasseled tops. As Laura went in between the rows, a great black swirl of birds rose up and whirled above her. The noise of their wings was louder than the rustling of all the long leaves. The birds were so many that they made a shadow like a cloud. It passed swiftly over the corn tops and the crowd of birds settled again.
>
> The ears of corn were plentiful. Nearly every stalk had two ears on it, some had three. The tassels were dry, only a little pollen was still flying, and the cornsilks hung like thick, green hair from the tips of the green cornhusks. Here and there a tuft of cornsilk was turning brown, and the ear felt full in the husk when Laura gently pinched it. To make sure, before she tore it from the stalk, she parted the husks to see the rows of milky kernels.
>
> Blackbirds kept flying up around her. Suddenly she stood stock-still. The blackbirds were eating the corn!
>
> Here and there she saw bare tips of ears. The husks were stripped back, and kernels were gone from the cobs. While she stood there, blackbirds settled around her. Their claws clung to the ears, their sharp beaks ripped away the husks, and quickly pecking they swallowed the kernels.
>
> Silently, desperately, Laura ran at them. She felt as if she were screaming. She beat at the birds with her sunbonnet. They rose up swirling on noisy wings and settled again to the corn, before her, behind her, all around her. They swung clinging to the ears, ripping away the husks, swallowing the corn crop. She could do nothing against so many.

- *Which words help give you the setting of the story?*
- *What do those words tell you about the place and time?*

Many of the words you have chosen are probably nouns. Words like *leaves* and *birds* tell us that the scene is outside. Words like *cornhusks, stalk,* and *crop* indicate a country setting. The words *tassels, kernels,* and *cobs* let us know the season of the year—late summer. What does the word *sunbonnet* contribute to our understanding of the time period?

This chapter will tell you more about this basic equipment of any writer. Knowing how to choose words well is as important to a writer as good shoes are to a runner.

An "ear of corn" is the edible, seed-bearing part of the plant.

ESL

Nouns

Nouns make up the largest group of words in the English language. Nouns identify someone or something. They name persons, places, things, and ideas.

Persons: carpenter, Mrs. Radford
Places: cornfield, Wrigley Field
Things: snow, blackbird
Ideas: friendship, emotion

IN SUMMARY

A **noun** names a person, place, thing, or idea.

2-1 PRACTICE THE SKILL

Underline five nouns in the paragraph. Above each underlined noun, label it *person, place, thing,* or *idea.* Try to find an example of each type of noun.

Annie Oakley possessed a phenomenal ability with firearms. She hunted to help her family survive after her father died. As she became famous, she competed in Ohio with Frank Butler, a celebrated marksman. Though he lost the competition, he later married Annie. Annie's fame spread through both America and Europe. She was able to hit a dime in the air and also could hit the edge of a card.

2-2 REVIEW THE SKILL

Underline the fifteen nouns.

When the government opened Oklahoma for settlement, the settlers were not allowed to stake a claim until noon on a certain day. The people waited with enthusiasm to race for the land. At noon, the people furiously hurried to their desired land. The new pioneers were called "Boomers."

ESL

"To stake a claim" means "to claim as one's own" (usually land).

22   Chapter 2

Forms of Nouns

Most nouns can appear in four forms: **singular, singular possessive, plural,** and **plural possessive.** If a word can appear in these four forms, it can function as a noun.

Singular:	The North American *prairie* stretches from Texas to southern Canada.
Singular possessive:	One of the *prairie's* nicknames is "sea of grass."
Plural:	Many former *prairies* have become cornfields.
Plural possessive:	These *prairies'* inhabitants included rabbits, bison, foxes, and blackbirds.

Spelling the Plural Forms of Nouns

A singular noun indicates that there is only one person, place, thing, or idea. A plural noun indicates that there are two or more persons, places, things, or ideas. Most nouns follow a regular pattern in the spelling of their plural form. Some nouns, however, have irregular spellings for their plural form. These rules below will help you spell plural forms correctly. Remember to consult your dictionary if you are unsure of the correct spelling.

Regular Plural Formation

Add *s* to the singular form of most nouns to form the plural.

pitcher	pitchers
idea	ideas

Add *es* to singular nouns ending with *s, x, z, ch,* and *sh.*

guess	guesses
ax	axes
buzz	buzzes
torch	torches
sash	sashes

If a noun ends with a consonant followed by *y,* change the *y* to *i* and add *es.*

trophy	trophies

If a noun ends with a vowel followed by *y,* add only *s.*

day	days

If a noun ends in *f* or *fe,* consult your dictionary. For some nouns, add *s;* for others, change the *f* to *v* and add *es.*

bluff	bluffs
loaf	loaves
fife	fifes
knife	knives

Chapter 17: Spelling Plural Nouns
pp. 354-55

If a noun ends in *o,* consult your dictionary. For some nouns, add *s;* for others, add *es.*

   patio   patios
   concerto   concertos
   tornado   tornadoes

Irregular Plural Formation

Change the spelling of the noun.

   child   children
   tooth   teeth
   mouse   mice
   ox   oxen

Change nothing.

   moose   moose
   trousers   trousers

Add *'s* to letters being discussed.

  one *q,* many *q's*

Add only *s* to numbers being discussed.

  1600, the 1600s

Pronunciation of Plurals and Possessives:

English has three different pronunciations for its plural (and possessive) noun forms.

1. Plurals after *s, x, z, ch,* and *sh* sounds are pronounced /ez/. Examples: foxes, bushes, quizzes, watches, misses.
2. Plurals after *b, d, g, l, m, n, r, v, w,* or vowel sounds are pronounced /z/. Examples: chairs, tables, claims, bugs, doves, eyes.
3. Plurals after *f, k, p,* or *t* sounds are pronounced /s/. Examples: rocks, plants, caps, coughs.

In Summary

A **singular noun** indicates that there is only one person, place, thing, or idea.

A **plural noun** indicates that there are two or more persons, places, things, or ideas.

Add *s* or *es* to form the plural of most singular nouns.

Some nouns have irregular plural forms.

2-3 PRACTICE THE SKILL

In the blank write the correct plural form of the italicized singular noun.

homes 1. The *house* found on the frontier differed from today's dwellings.

_1800s_ 2. The frontiersmen in the *1800* built with the materials offered by the environment.

churchs 3. Prairie homes often were made from sod because lumber was rare; in wooded areas, however, homes and other buildings, such as the frontier *church,* often were made of logs.

families 4. Log cabins soon were the dominant form of architecture for the frontier *family*.

chimneys 5. Sticks plastered with mud mortar created the *chimney*.

roofs 6. The *roof* consisted of split timber and mud, which was used to close the gaps.

homes 7. Inside features of the early pioneer *home* were just as simple as the exterior characteristics.

buffaloes 8. Some settlers used hides from the American *buffalo* for bedding and made the floor serve as a bed at night.

deer 9. A gun rack might be a set of antlers from the forest *deer*.

shelves 10. More refined items such as pewter and china sat on the *shelf* and helped settlers remember their former homes in the East.

2-4 REVIEW THE SKILL

In the blank write the correct plural form of the italicized singular noun.

settlers 1. The early American *settler* faced many dangers.

quantities 2. The flat land and wind stirred up a huge *quantity* of dust and caused harmful erosion.

leaves 3. In the 1870s, many crops were completely destroyed by large swarms of locusts that ate wood, grass, *leaf,* and even leather.

fires 4. Because of the dry weather, prairie *fire* was not uncommon.

wimen 5. The whole family would work to put out the fire, including the *woman* and children.

Nouns 25

tornadoes   6. Another imminent danger was the *tornado*.

thieves   7. The settlers also had to fear a wild animal and a *thief*.

foxes   8. Wild animals included coyote and *fox*.

anxieties   9. Cruel hailstorms that destroyed crops and homes often caused *anxiety*.

heroes   10. A family who bravely endured all of these hardships was the *hero* of the West.

Forming the Possessive Forms of Nouns

Possessive nouns show ownership or belonging. They tell who or what owns a thing. All possessive nouns have apostrophes.

To form the singular possessive, add *'s* to the singular form of the noun (even if the noun already ends in *s*).

    clock   clock's face
    Charles   Charles's opinion

Traditionally, add only *'* to the proper names *Jesus* and *Moses*.

    Jesus   Jesus' love

To form the plural possessive, add only *'* to a plural noun that already ends in *s*.

    governors   governors' luncheon
    the Smiths   the Smiths' dog

If a plural noun does not end in *s*, add *'s* to form the plural possessive.

    mice   mice's nest

IN SUMMARY

Possessive nouns show ownership or belonging.
To form the singular possessive, add *'s* to the singular noun.
To form the plural possessive, add *'* or *'s* to the plural noun.

2-5 PRACTICE THE SKILL

In the blank rewrite the italicized phrase as an equivalent phrase containing a possessive noun.

1. John Chapman was one of *the famous pioneers of the Ohio frontier*.

   the famous pioneers' of the Ohio frontier

2. Although he was part of *the population of Massachusetts* by birth, John Chapman spent most of his life in the Ohio region.

   the population of Massachusetts'

Chapter 5: Possessives p. 103

Chapter 16: Apostrophe p. 340

3. *The name of the frontiersmen* for John Chapman was Johnny Appleseed.

   The name of the frontiersmen's

4. Johnny Appleseed earned his name because he traveled throughout *northern and central parts of the Ohio wilderness* planting young trees and apple seeds.

   northern and central parts of the Ohio's wilderness

5. As reimbursement for his seedlings and apple seeds, Johnny Appleseed would accept *the money of the people* or other items the pioneers offered.

   the money of the people's

6. *The wanderings of Johnny Appleseed* made him famous.

   The wanderings of Johnny Appleseed's

7. We know that he was not forgotten in *the memories of the pioneers*.

   the memories of the pioneers'

8. Johnny Appleseed helped meet *the needs of the settlers* by acting as a physician using herbal medicine.

   The needs of the settlers'

9. Also, during the War of 1812, Johnny Appleseed functioned as one of *the messengers of the frontier area*.

   The messengers of the frontier's area

10. Johnny Appleseed was best known for his work with apple trees; these plants contributed to *the strength of the farming business* in Indiana and Ohio.

    the strength of the farming's business

2-6 Review the Skill

In the blank rewrite each phrase as an equivalent phrase containing a possessive noun.

1. the horse of the cowboy — the cowboy's horse
2. the soddie of the family — the family's soddie
3. the stalls of the horses — the horses' stall
4. the squawk of the goose — the gooses' squawk
5. the flight of the geese — the geese's flight
6. the wagon of the Davises — the Davises' wagon

7. the pond of the fish — the fish's pond
8. the antlers of the deer — the deer's antlers
9. the games of the boys — the boys' games
10. the letter of the girl — the girl's letter

2-7 Review the Skill

In the blank write the correct singular possessive, plural, or plural possessive form of the word in parentheses.

Coyote's — 1. The _?_ howl, carried on the air of the prairie, is a reminder of the days of the frontier. *(coyote)*

wolves — 2. Coyotes, though small in comparison, look remarkably like _?_. *(wolf)*

Coyotes' — 3. Like wolves, coyotes are predators; however, _?_ prey typically consists of small animals such as mice, gophers, and rabbits. *(coyote)*

elk — 4. Coyotes also eat larger mammals such as _?_ and antelope. *(elk)*

Carcasses — 5. Since coyotes also scavenge for their food, it is not always correct to blame a coyote for a large _?_ presence. *(carcass)*

Shifts — 6. Coyotes sometimes run in _?_ while pursuing larger prey in order to exhaust quarry that a single coyote would not be able to catch. *(shift)*

Sheepman's — 7. As farmers began to raise sheep in the West, coyotes became the _?_ enemies because coyotes sometimes prey on defenseless sheep. *(sheepman)*

rancher's — 8. Many coyotes died from poisoning as a result of official efforts to ensure the _?_ economic welfare. *(rancher)*

1970s — 9. Although the law stopped the poisoning on public territory in the _?_, coyotes still encounter danger from both human and natural sources. *(1970)*

America's — 10. The coyote has appeared in _?_ eastern regions as well, perhaps migrating to avoid danger. *(America)*

28 Chapter 2

Common and Proper Nouns

All nouns are either common or proper. A **common noun** names a general person, place, thing, or idea. A **proper noun** names a specific person, place, thing, or idea. Proper nouns are always capitalized.

	Common Nouns	Proper Nouns
Persons	daughter	Georjean
	carpenter	Ralph Radford
Places	park	Banff National Park
	zoo	San Diego Zoo
	city	Tulsa
	state	Oklahoma
Things	drama	*As You Like It*
	cereal	Quaker Oats
Ideas	philosophy	Stoicism
	freedom	Classicism

In Summary

A **common noun** names a general person, place, thing, or idea.
A **proper noun** names a specific person, place, thing, or idea. Proper nouns are always capitalized.

2-8 Practice the Skill

Imagine that the narrator of the following sentences lived on the western frontier during the mid-1800s. In the blank write a proper noun to replace the italicized word or phrase.

Richmond 1. My family and I used to live in *a state* in New England.

September 2. Last *month* we moved here.

Sophia 3. I miss our old house and *my neighbor*.

Kaity 4. I also miss *my dog*.

Lisa 5. I met *a new friend* in school today.

Richford 6. I hope to find some new friends among the students at *school*.

Camas 7. My father is going to pastor the new church in *town*.

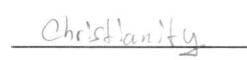

Christianity 8. Now that more settlers are coming to our town, we will be able to teach many people *religious truth*.

Chapter 5: Proper Adjectives p. 109

Chapter 15: Capitalization pp. 301–11

Nouns 29

Rancher 9. I like the beautiful scenery here in the West, especially the *mountains*.

Bob 10. *My uncle* plans to move here with his family next year.

2-9 REVIEW THE SKILL

Imagine that the narrator of the following sentences is describing an attack on a frontier stagecoach. In the blank write a noun that completes the sentence. Use a variety of common and proper nouns.

frontier's 1. Last week, bandits tried to rob the _?_ stagecoach.

Washoagal 2. The coach was traveling from Weston to _?_.

letters 3. The driver and his companion were transporting two mail _?_ and some silver from the bank in Weston.

bandits 4. As the coach approached Farson Crossing, four _?_ with masks rode down from the surrounding rocks.

guns 5. The _?_ from the robbers frightened the coach's horses.

Frank 6. Fortunately, _?_ and his deputies were also approaching the area.

across 7. Hearing gunshots and knowing the stagecoach was due to pass _?_ at Farson Crossing, the sheriff's party hurried into position.

Leon 8. The driver, _?_, put a small distance between his coach and the attackers.

Bandits 9. As soon as the coach rushed through the pass, the sheriff's men moved behind the coach, separating the _?_ from their target.

Johnson 10. Although two of the robbers escaped, the others were caught by Deputy _?_ and the sheriff.

Count and Noncount Nouns

Every noun is either a **count noun** or a **noncount noun.** Count nouns can be singular or plural in form. Noncount nouns are always singular in form. Only common nouns can be count or noncount.

Normally we make distinctions between count and noncount nouns automatically. If you are unsure whether a singular noun is count or noncount, try this test. A count noun can be introduced by a number word, such as *a, an,* or *one.* A noncount noun cannot be introduced by a number word.

Count Nouns	Noncount Nouns
a leaf	dirt
two glasses	milk
many answers	knowledge

Count and Noncount Nouns

1. Use *many* with plural count nouns and *much* with noncount nouns. (We saw *many* fish and *much* water at the aquarium.)
2. Use *a few* with plural count nouns and *a little* with noncount nouns. (Yesterday morning I drank *a few* cups of coffee with *a little* cream and sugar.)
3. Do not put an *s* on the end of a noncount noun. (*Incorrect:* My report contains many informations. Many waters are in the ocean. *Correct:* My report contains much information. Much water is in the ocean.)

IN SUMMARY

Count nouns can be either singular or plural in form.
Noncount nouns are always singular in form.

2-10 PRACTICE THE SKILL

Label each italicized word *count* or *noncount*.

Count 1. The Conestoga wagon is a famous *symbol* of the American frontier.

Count 2. Conestoga, Pennsylvania, was the *birthplace* of this covered wagon.

Noncount 3. These wagons with high sides served as a means of moving large quantities of *freight*.

Count 4. The *floor* of a Conestoga wagon was curved so that its cargo would be unlikely to shift.

noncount 5. Conestoga wagons had wide-rimmed wheels to help them move through the *mud*.

Count 6. The front and back of Conestoga wagons were higher than the middle; the wheels came off so that the wagon could serve as a *boat*.

noncount 7. The canvas top of the Conestoga allowed the wagon to be used in inclement *weather*.

noncount 8. The Conestoga wagon was the product of Pennsylvania Dutch inventors, who used the wagon to transport *produce* and other goods.

Count   9. Conestoga wagons helped the frontier remain connected with places of *commerce* in the East.

Count   10. The *design* of the prairie schooner, named for its top that resembled a ship's sails, was based on the earlier design of the Conestoga.

2-11 REVIEW THE SKILL

Label each italicized word *count* or *noncount*.

noncount   1. People today owe much of their *knowledge* of the Old West to William Frederick Cody.

count   2. Cody is often better known by his *nickname* Buffalo Bill.

count   3. He earned this nickname hunting *buffalo* in Kansas to feed railroad workers.

count   4. As a young man, Cody rode for the *pony express*.

count   5. Later he acted as a *scout* for the U.S. Army in several conflicts with the Indians.

noncount   6. His *fame* grew as many people read dime novels about his adventures.

count   7. He organized a Wild West *show* to demonstrate life on the frontier.

count   8. People as far away as Europe could see an attack on a *stagecoach* or a cowboy riding a bucking bronco.

count   9. One *year* Cody persuaded Sitting Bull to tour with his group.

count   10. Cody worked hard to create an *image* of the West as a rough, exciting place to visit.

Compound Nouns

Some nouns are formed by combining two or more other words. These nouns are **compound nouns.** The meaning of a compound word is often a special combination of the meanings of the two original words. Compound nouns can be written as one word, one hyphenated word, or two words.

To form the plural of a compound noun, change the most important word into its plural form. If you are unsure which part of the compound noun should be made plural, check a dictionary for the correct form.

Chapter 18: Dictionaries
p. 375

> Compound nouns in English have their main stress (loudest syllable) in the first part of the compound: *high*chair, *basket*ball, *red*head, *son*-in-law. However, when an adjective modifies a noun, the noun has the main stress: a high *chair,* a red *head.*

ESL

Original Words	Compound Noun	Plural Compound Noun
book + shelf	bookshelf	bookshelves
snow + man	snowman	snowmen
great + aunt	great-aunt	great-aunts
father + in + law	father-in-law	fathers-in-law
milk + shake	milk shake	milk shakes
attorney + general	attorney general	attorneys general

In Summary

Compound nouns are formed by combining two or more other words.

2-12 Practice the Skill

Underline the singular compound noun in each sentence. In the blank write the correct plural form of the underlined compound noun.

Cowboys 1. The legendary <u>cowboy</u> of the American western frontier originated as the cattle business developed.

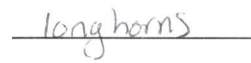

longhorns 2. Ranchers in Texas raised cattle such as the famous Texas <u>longhorn.</u>

Cattlemen 3. Many practices of America's western <u>cattleman</u> have changed.

Nouns 33

Cow Ponies 4. Cowboys herded cattle on animals called cow pony.

Grasslands 5. These men guarded cattle as the animals grazed on the prairie grassland.

six shooters 6. Many men carried guns, such as the famous six-shooter.

railroads 7. The rigorous cattle drives conveyed cattle to the railroad.

old-timers' 8. The men would share stories around the fire or play pranks, with the new man perhaps being the target of the old-timer's practical joke.

Cowboys 9. A cowboy hat protected a man from the sun and the dust.

bronco busters 10. The original broncobuster faded into history shortly after the use of fences became common.

2-13 REVIEW THE SKILL

Underline the singular compound noun (omit *pony express*) in each sentence. In the blank write the correct plural form of the underlined compound noun.

Mailmen 1. The pony express provided mail service for the West in the early 1860s with a different sort of mailman.

businessmen 2. The businessman William Russell, Alexander Majors, and William Waddell operated that mail experiment, which carried messages through a relay of riders.

Stage coachs 3. The pony express horses were much faster than the stagecoach.

daredevils 4. A pony express rider might be a daredevil willing to ride through deserts and over mountains while facing wild animals and storms.

Bride-to-bes 5. Lonely young men in the West could now send notes quickly to their bride-to-be in the East.

Passerbys 6. In order to keep the mail safe from thieves, pony express riders had to watch out for the suspicious passerby.

sons-in-laws 7. For $3.50, a man in St. Joseph, Missouri, could send a message of ten words that would be received in just over ten days by his son-in-law in Sacramento, California.

___mail___ 8. Even the middle class could afford to send mail quickly through the pony express.

___wild west shows___ 9. Wild Bill Cody, who was famous for his Wild West Show, was a former pony express rider.

___telegraphs___ 10. The pony express was replaced after only sixteen months by the telegraph, which could send messages at the touch of a fingertip.

2-14 USE THE SKILL

Underline each incorrect plural or possessive noun form. Write the words correctly on the lines below. There are ten errors.

The Indians of the Great Plain's represent much of the frontiers history. The Indians depended upon bisons for necessitys such as shelter, food, clothing, weapones, and tools. Originally, hunters had to pursue their game on foot. One of the hunters' tactics was to chase bisons over high cliffs. The frontiersmens' move to the West irrevocably changed the Indians's way of life. Skirmishs erupted between the Indians and the settlers, and full-fledged battles often ensued. One famous battle was the Battle of Little Bighorn, which pitted Custers' troops against the Sioux. Custer and all his troops died, and the American army's loss gave the Indians a new hope of regaining their land. Eventually, the settlers took over the Indian's territory. Today many Indians live on reservations, and many still preserve their traditions and customes.

___Plains, frontier's, bison, weapons, hunters, frontiersmen's, Indians', skirmish, Custer's, army___

2-15 Cumulative Review

Rewrite the following paragraph correctly on the lines below. Correct the ten errors in these categories: fragments, comma splices, fused sentences, incorrect plural noun forms, and incorrect possessive noun forms.

Ghost towns intrigue the imagination with thoughts of the people and activitys that might have filled the area. A ghost town once had many inhabitants, it now has few or no people living in it. Although ghost towns exist all over the world, Most of these villages are in Americas' western states. The Southwest has an especially large number of deserted towns the remaines of buildings survive in the regions dry climate. Some towns were shipping stations for crops or cattle, but more were mining centers where gold or other precious metals had been found. As soon as the metals ran out, the miners and shopskeeper in the town left too. Today those once-busy towns lie silent and empty, a few decrepit structures remind the towns's visitors of what once was.

Ghost towns, intrigue the imagenation with thoughts of the people, and activitys that might have filled the area. A ghost town once had many inhabitants, it now has fewer or no people living in it. Although, ghost towns exist all over the world, most of these villages are in America's western states. The Southwest has an especially large number of deserted towns, the remaines of buildings survive in the regions dry climate. Some towns were shipping stations for crops or cattle, but more were mining centers where gold, or other precious metal had been found. As soon as the metals ran out, the minors and shopskeepers in the town left too. Today those once-busy towns lie silent and empty, a few decrepit structures remind the towns' visitors of what it once was.

Chapter 2

POLE VAULTING

Look again at the excerpt from *Little Town on the Prairie*. Notice the singular and plural nouns.

- *How does the author's use of plural nouns intensify Laura's predicament?*
- *What singular nouns help add to the impression that Laura's battle is too big for her?*

Order at a Glance: Making a Time Line

Does your family ever have conversations like this one?

"Now, let's see. How many years ago did our car break down on the way to California? Was that the summer of '94?"

"No, I had already gotten my driver's license, Dad, so it had to be '95 at least."

"But wasn't '95 the year we went to see the Pelzers in Michigan instead of going to California?"

"No, that was '94 because it was also the year that Kyle got thrown from the motorcycle and broke his arm. And we sold the motorcycle in '94."

"Yeah, and '95 was the year that Aunt Lucy had her baby, which was why we were dying to go to California. Remember?"

Do you ever wish for a way to organize important events in your family history so that you can see them in their correct order at a glance?

A time line lets you organize events by years. Years are marked at regular intervals along a horizontal line, and events are placed wherever they fall between those markings. Some time lines are divided into intervals of five years, some of ten, and so on. It takes only a moment to understand a time line's structure; thus, a time line allows you a glimpse of the "big picture" right away. Then you are free to absorb the details at your leisure. Here's how you can show the order of the important events in your life.

- Make a list of events you would like to include on your time line.

    Ask yourself these questions:
    - What events brought significant changes to my life?
    - What events come up often in family discussions?
    - What events do I like to remember?

    Narrow your list to eight to twelve events that you will include on your time line.

- Decide how you will divide your time line.

    Choose your time line divisions according to what will present most clearly the events you have chosen. If the events are spread out over several years, you might want divisions at every two years. If the events are close together, or if you have several occurring in the same year, consider dividing your time line into half-years to allow you more space.

Chapter 20: Making a List
p. 409

Nouns   37

- Draw your line and then mark and label the correct divisions.

Tape several sheets of paper together to make your time line long enough. Use a ruler to keep your line straight and your dividing marks perpendicular to the line. Measure to make sure the divisions are evenly spaced along the line.

- Place the events you have chosen at the appropriate spots along the line.

Keep your captions short and to the point.

- Write a few sentences of explanation under the line, beneath each captioned event.

These short paragraphs will be the "meat" of your time line. Include your feelings and special memories about each of the events shown on your line. When you finish, read these paragraphs together as a sort of mini-history of your life. You might even be surprised to see how earlier events affected later ones.

Here is what one student chose to include on her time line:

1992   Moved to Nebraska from Colorado
We moved so that Dad could take over as pastor of a church in a small Nebraska town. I don't remember much about the move except that I missed seeing the mountains, and I missed having a tree right outside my bedroom window.

1993   Caleb born
My brother Daniel and I were so excited to have a new baby brother. I remember that when Mom brought him home I thought something was wrong with his face because it was so red.

1994   Started school
I had never had so many kids my own age to play with before. I loved my teacher, Mrs. Rineheart, and wanted to be just like her when I grew up. I made friends with Cindy and Kaitlin the first day of school, and we are all still good friends.

1997   Mom's surgery
I remember visiting Mom in the hospital the night before and Dad praying by her bed. I had never been so scared, but seeing Dad pray helped me feel safe. Grandma stayed with my brothers and me while Mom recovered. I'm glad God gave her a successful recovery.

1998   Started piano lessons
Mrs. Moseley, our church pianist, offered to teach me piano. I had my first lesson the afternoon of my first day of fourth grade.

1999   Saved at camp
I had heard Dad preach about salvation so many times that it didn't seem quite real to me. But hearing the evangelist at camp talk about it was different. For the first time, I realized what a sinner I was. I asked God to save me that night with the guidance of my counselor, Anna.

2000   Misty came
Dad decided we could keep the stray dog that had been hanging

around our house. We had all fallen in love with her by that time, and she's still an important part of our family. I named her Misty because she's white and her eyes always look kind of sad and misty, like she's about to cry.

2001   Baptism
Dad baptized me at church. Afterwards the choir sang "Saved by the Blood of the Crucified One," and I remember feeling so glad I was saved that I could hardly keep from crying.

2002   Played first church special
I was so nervous, but Mrs. Moseley really wanted me to play. She accompanied me on the organ, but there was one part that I had to play by myself. Mom and Dad told me it had gone well, and Dad made homemade ice cream when we got home from church that night.

Your Turn: Putting Your Life in Order
Follow the steps listed above to make your own time line.

STRETCHING OUT

The Play's the Thing

Have you ever seen something in your "mind's eye"? Have you ever heard someone say "there is method in my madness"? Most English speakers would be surprised to know how often they quote Shakespeare. Both phrases quoted above come from the play *Hamlet*. Over the years, such statements change as they are borrowed again and again. "Method in my madness" comes from an observation made about Hamlet when Hamlet was pretending to be insane: "Though this be madness, yet there is method in't." Today we use this phrase to explain any unusual thing we are doing for a good reason.

It is always good to know how phrases were used originally. Before you hand someone a box of candy and say, "Sweets to the sweet," you might want to know why someone standing beside a grave said those words in *Hamlet*.

Chapter 3

Verbs

Vinegar Boy
by Alberta Hawse

Grammar

"But the boy broke loose and ran toward the tree. "Salome! Salome!" he yelled. "John wants you to come down to the garden."

Salome leaned into the wind trying to hear. Magdalene heard. "No, we will not leave. John should be up here with us."

"He says there is going to be a very bad storm."

"No. Salome, you can't go." She grabbed at the older woman's arm. "We cannot leave Him alone."

"John wants all of you to come. Straightway, he said." The boy was urgent.

"No!" Magdalene screamed. "You cannot leave our Lord."

Salome put her free arm about the smaller woman. "I must do what John says. Come, Mary."

"I will not go. I will not!"

"Stay then," Salome said without anger, "but we are going." The other woman went without argument.

"Go!" Magdalene shrieked. The wind lifted her words and threw them back at her. "Be like all the others. Leave Him to die alone like a fox in the field!"

Vinegar Boy watched wide-eyed as lightning cracked the walls of heaven. Straight up and down from the center of the vault above them to the valley floor below the lightning glowed as the sunlight had glowed through the crack in the walls of the alley.

Behind the lightning the thunder came in a deafening blast. The hill trembled. Rubicon, the centurion's horse, screamed. The old tree bent in agony like a woman caught in the pangs of birth. A branch whipped loose and struck Magdalene across the shoulders. As if the branch had been a whip used on a stubborn child, she gathered up her skirts and ran after Salome. She stopped once, with the wind pushing her relentlessly, and threw a look at Jesus. Then the wind seemed to lift her from her feet and shove her on."

- *Would you say that this scene is peaceful or disturbing? What words make you feel that way?*

Most of the words in this passage create drama, but especially the verbs. How would the mood be different if the last sentence used the word *move* in place of *shove*? Now read the biblical account of this event in Matthew 27:35-52. Can you see where the author of *Vinegar Boy* got a sense of the intensity of the events she writes about? Do you think that much of the energy comes from the verbs Matthew uses?

Verbs

Verbs energize sentences. Without them, sentences would carry no action or meaning. Imagine a group of words like "The boy the cross." The boy did what? Saw? Built? Lifted? Watched? Each verb infuses the other words with purpose. A verb gives the subject movement or states the existence of the subject. Learning about verbs of different types will help you to make your writing vivid.

Recognizing Verbs

Verbs express action (what someone or something does) or state of being (what someone or something is like). Some **action verbs** name actions we can see; other action verbs convey internal action.

> The boy *carried* the cross.
> The boy *thought* about the cross.

State-of-being verbs describe a state or a condition.

> The cross *was* heavy.
> It *seemed* too much to bear.
> The scene *had* an air of mystery.

The most common state-of-being verb is the verb *be,* which has eight forms.

| am | is | are | was | were | be | being | been |

Because a verb acts as the main word in the predicate, it is important to know how to find verbs in sentences. Nearly every verb can have *s* or *ing* added to it without changing the verb's meaning. Any word that fits into the following test frames can be a verb.

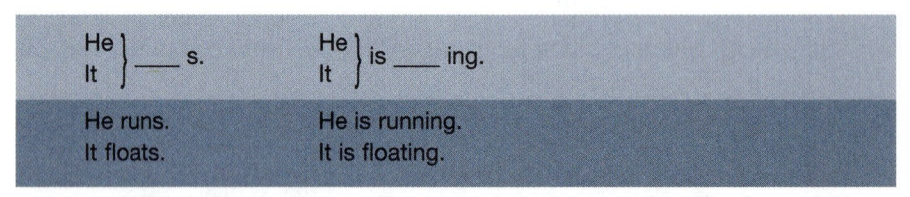

> He ⎫
> It ⎭ ___ s.
>
> He ⎫
> It ⎭ is ___ ing.
>
> He runs.
> It floats.
>
> He is running.
> It is floating.

Chapter 10: Special Forms of the Verb *Be* p. 212

IN SUMMARY

Verbs express action or state of being. An **action verb** shows what the subject of the sentence does. A **state-of-being verb** describes a state or a condition.

3-1 PRACTICE THE SKILL

Underline the verbs.

1. The Hebrew language <u>is</u> one of the oldest languages in the world.
2. The Hebrew alphabet <u>consists</u> of twenty-two letters.
3. One <u>writes</u> Hebrew from right to left, unlike English with its left-to-right movement.
4. Hebrew <u>is</u> the language of some of the oldest and best works of literature.

42   Chapter 3

5. The Old Testament is the only remaining example of ancient Hebrew.
6. The Jews revived the language after their reunification in Israel.
7. About three million Israelis speak Hebrew today.
8. Hebrew speakers throughout the world pronounce the Hebrew language differently from each other.
9. Modern Hebrew literature includes novels about important current issues.
10. Mastery of classical Hebrew remains a popular goal among many modern scholars.

3-2 Review the Skill

Underline the verbs. Label each verb *action* or *state-of-being*.

action   1. Hannah dedicated her son to God.

action   2. As a child Samuel lived at the temple.

state-of-being   3. Eli was the high priest at this time.

action   4. One night a strange voice woke Samuel.

action   5. Samuel ran into Eli's room.

action   6. Samuel listened to Eli's advice.

action   7. The Lord called Samuel again.

state-of-being   8. This time Samuel is ready.

state-of-being   9. "Lord, here am I."

action   10. Now Samuel has a message for Eli.

Intransitive and Transitive Verbs

Intransitive Verbs

In some sentences the verb expresses an idea without needing anything to complete it. These verbs are called **intransitive verbs** (InV). Intransitive verbs do not send their action toward any receiver. The sentence pattern for an intransitive verb is **S-InV.**

      S   InV
The violets bloomed.

      S   InV
The violets bloomed abundantly.

Here is the diagram for S-InV: **The violets bloomed abundantly.**

violets	bloomed

Verbs   43

Transitive Verbs and Direct Objects

Unlike intransitive verbs, some verbs need another word to complete the idea. These verbs are called **transitive verbs** (TrV) because they transfer their action to receivers called **direct objects** (DO). In the sentence "The boy dropped the glass," the noun *glass* receives the action of the verb *dropped*. The direct object is a noun or pronoun that follows the verb, receives the action of the verb, and answers the question *whom?* or *what?* after the verb.

```
      S     TrV      DO
George opened the hood.

      S     TrV       DO
George repaired the car.
```

Car is the direct object of the verb *repaired*. *Car* follows the verb *repaired*, receives the repairing, and tells what George repaired. To identify the direct object, first find the subject and the verb; then ask *whom?* or *what?* If more than one word answers this question, the direct object is compound. Remember, direct objects do not tell *how, when,* or *where.*

```
      S     TrV       DO        DO
George repaired the car and the boat.
```

Sentences containing a transitive verb and a direct object follow the pattern **S-TrV-DO**. Notice the diagrams: **George repaired the car.**

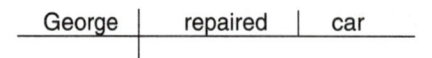

| George | repaired | car |

George repaired the car and the boat.

| George | repaired | car / and / boat |

ETYMOLOGY
Transitive comes from the Latin word *transire*, "to go over or across." The action of a transitive verb goes across to a receiver.

Notice that verbs are intransitive or transitive depending on the context of the sentence. The same verb could be intransitive in one sentence and transitive in another sentence.

Intransitive: Shelley wrote daily for one hour.
Transitive: Shelley wrote an essay for history class.

Remember that even intransitive verbs can be followed by nouns and pronouns. However, these nouns and pronouns are not direct objects because they do not receive the action of the verb and they do not answer the question *whom?* or *what?* about the verb. For example, the noun *hour* in the sentence above tells *when* Shelley wrote; it does not tell *what* Shelley wrote.

Transitive Verbs and Indirect Objects

Sentences that have a transitive verb and a direct object sometimes also contain an **indirect object** (IO). The indirect object is a noun or pronoun that answers the question *to whom?* or *for whom?* after the direct object and tells who or what was affected by the action of the verb. The indirect object goes right after the verb but before the direct object.

      S   TrV   IO   DO
Marjorie gave her *mother* a gift.

In the example, *mother* is the indirect object. The noun *mother* tells to whom Marjorie gave a gift. To identify the indirect object, find the simple subject, the verb, and the direct object; then ask *to whom?* or *for whom?* the action was done. Of course, if more than one word answers the questions, the sentence contains a compound indirect object.

      S   TrV   IO   IO   DO
Marjorie gave her *mother* and *father* an anniversary gift.

This new sentence pattern is **S-TrV-IO-DO.** Sentences with indirect objects are diagrammed similarly to sentences with the sentence pattern S-TrV-DO: **Marjorie gave her mother a gift.**

Marjorie gave her mother and father an anniversary gift.

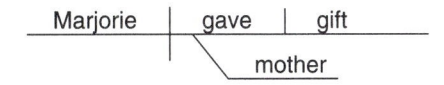

Chapter 1: Finding Subjects and Predicates
pp. 4-5

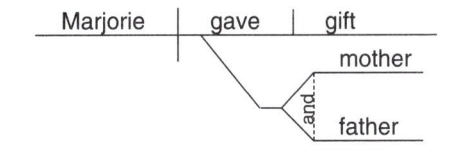

IN SUMMARY

- An **intransitive verb** does not need a direct object to receive its action.
- A **transitive verb** needs a direct object to receive its action.
- A **direct object** is a noun or pronoun that receives the action of a transitive verb.
- An **indirect object** is a noun or pronoun that tells to whom or for whom the verb's action was done.

Verbs

3-3 Practice the Skill

Label the sentence patterns *S-InV*, *S-TrV-DO*, or *S-TrV-IO-DO*. Above each word of the sentence pattern, write its label.

1. [S] God [IO] created Adam [IO] and Eve [InV] on the sixth day.
2. [S] God [TrV] granted [IO] Adam [IO] and Eve [DO] authority over all of the animals.
3. [S] Adam [InV] named the animals.
4. [S] God [InV] visited with [IO] Adam [IO] and Eve in the garden.
5. [S] God [TrV] gave [IO] Adam [DO] a warning about the tree of knowledge of good and evil.
6. [S] Adam and Eve still [InV] sinned against God.
7. [S] They [TrV] forfeited [DO] their home in the Garden of Eden.
8. [S] God [TrV] gave [IO] them [DO] clothes from animal skins.
9. [S] Then He [TrV] sent [IO] them [DO] out of the garden.
10. [S] Disobedience results in punishment.

not sure how to layble

3-4 Review the Skill

Label the sentence patterns *S-InV*, *S-TrV-DO*, or *S-TrV-IO-DO*. Above each word of the sentence pattern, write its label.

1. [S] Sin [TrV] brings [DO] separation from God.
2. [S] Old Testament saints [TrV] needed [DO] a priest for representation before God.
3. [S] The priests [TrV] inherited [DO] no land from God.
4. Instead, [S] God [TrV] called [DO] them to ministry.
5. [S] The people [TrV] brought the priests [IO] animals [DO] for sacrifice on the altar.
6. Once a year [S] the high priest [TrV] entered [DO] the holy of holies.
7. [S] There he [TrV] sprinkled [DO] blood on the mercy seat.
8. At the cross, [S] the need for an earthly high priest [TrV] [DO] [InV] ceased.
9. [S] God [TrV] sent [IO] us [DO] Jesus as our High Priest.
10. Today [S] Jesus Christ [TrV] [InV] intercedes for us in heaven.

Linking Verbs and Predicate Nouns and Predicate Adjectives

Some verbs link the subject with a word or phrase in the predicate. We call these verbs **linking verbs.** A linking verb is almost like an equal sign, linking the subject with something in the predicate that renames or describes the subject.

        S   LV
Mr. Patterson *is* a teacher.
Mr. Patterson = teacher

The word *teacher* renames the subject *Mr. Patterson*. The linking verb *is* links *Mr. Patterson* to *teacher*. A noun or pronoun in the complete predicate that renames the subject is a **predicate noun;** therefore, *teacher* is a predicate noun. The verb before a predicate noun is a linking verb. This sentence follows the pattern **S-LV-PN.**

Sometimes the most important word in the complete predicate is an adjective. A **predicate adjective** is an adjective in the complete predicate that describes the subject; the verb before a predicate adjective is a linking verb.

        S   LV   PA
Mr. Patterson *seems* compassionate.

In this sentence, *compassionate* is a predicate adjective. This sentence follows the pattern **S-LV-PA.**

Both the S-LV-PN and S-LV-PA sentence patterns can contain compound parts.

        S   LV   PN   PN
Mr. Patterson is a *teacher* and *coach*.

        S   LV   PA   PA
Mr. Patterson seems *compassionate* and *fair*.

The two sentence patterns S-LV-PN and S-LV-PA are diagrammed the same way: **Mr. Patterson is a teacher.**

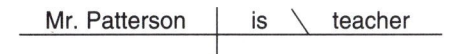

    Mr. Patterson | is \ teacher

Mr. Patterson seems compassionate and fair.

    Mr. Patterson | seems \ compassionate / and / fair

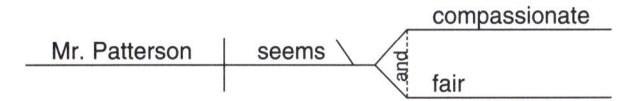

In Summary

- A **linking verb** links the subject of a sentence to a word that renames or describes the subject.
- A **predicate noun** is a noun in the complete predicate that follows a linking verb and renames the subject.
- A **predicate adjective** is an adjective in the complete predicate that follows a linking verb and describes the subject.

Chapter 5: Adjectives
p. 96

3-5 PRACTICE THE SKILL

Label the sentence patterns *S-LV-PN* or *S-LV-PA*. Above each word of the sentence pattern, write its label.

1. Israel is the Jews' homeland. [S LV PN]
2. The land of Israel is not very large. [S LV PA]
3. Its lack of natural harbors was a protection against invaders from the sea. [S LV PN]
4. The coastal plain was very open and fertile. [S LV PA PA]
5. The central range was the site of Israel's most important cities. [S LV PN]
6. Hazor became Palestine's largest city during the biblical period. [S LV PA]
7. The terrain in Judea is very rugged. [S LV PA]
8. The Jordan Valley is a small part of a fault from Africa to Asia. [S LV PA]
9. The Dead Sea is very salty. [S LV PA]
10. Woodlands and pasture were abundant in the territory of Gilead. [S LV PA]

3-6 PRACTICE THE SKILL

Label the sentence patterns *S-LV-PN* or *S-LV-PA*. Above each word of the sentence pattern, write its label.

1. Nehemiah is an example of a motivational leader.
2. He was responsible for the repair of the walls of Jerusalem.
3. Nehemiah became very sad about the broken walls.
4. Nehemiah was the cupbearer for King Artaxerxes.
5. The king was supportive of Nehemiah's plan.
6. Sanballat and Tobiah were opponents of the project.
7. During the work, many people were watchful of opponents.
8. Nehemiah was confident of God's protection.
9. After the walls' repair, the people were hungry for God's Word.
10. Ezra was the priest during that time.

48   Chapter 3

3-7 Review the Skill

Underline the verbs. Label each verb *transitive* or *linking*.

transitive 1. The New Testament <u>mentions</u> Luke three times.

linking 2. Luke <u>was</u> a physician and a writer.

transitive 3. He probably <u>received</u> his education at Tarsus.

transitive 4. Tarsus <u>contained</u> a famous medical school.

linking 5. Luke <u>became</u> the author of the books of Luke and Acts.

linking 6. He <u>was</u> Paul's friend and companion.

transitive 7. He <u>accompanied</u> Paul on the second and third missionary journeys.

linking 8. Luke's character traits <u>were</u> loyalty, humility, and faithfulness.

transitive 9. Luke <u>used</u> his talents for the gospel.

linking 10. He <u>is</u> one of the prominent heroes of the faith.

Other Linking Verbs

So far the linking verbs we have seen in S-LV-PN and S-LV-PA sentences have included forms of *be, seem,* and *become.* However, several other words can function as linking verbs as well, depending on the sentences in which they are used. Some of these words are not always linking verbs. Look at the verb and the words that come after the verb to determine whether it is a linking verb, a transitive verb, or an intransitive verb. Here are some of the verbs most often used as linking verbs.

appear	look	sound	become
remain	stay	feel	seem
taste	grow	smell	

The fabric *feels* soft. *(linking)*
The seamstress *feels* all sorts of fabrics before choosing one. *(transitive)*

The meal *smells* delicious. *(linking)*
I *smell* lasagna. *(transitive)*

The new church *looks* lovely. *(linking)*
The members *look* for neighbors to invite. *(intransitive)*

It is important to distinguish between nouns used as predicate nouns and nouns used as direct objects. Remember that predicate nouns follow linking verbs and rename the subject. They are "equal to" the subject.

Dr. Healey is a dentist.
Dr. Healey = dentist

On the other hand, direct objects follow transitive verbs. The direct object is the receiver of the action. Direct objects do not rename the subject.

Cole batted the ball.
Cole batted *what?* (the ball)

No verb can be both transitive and linking at the same time in the same sentence.

In Summary

The verbs most often used as linking verbs are *be, become, remain, stay, grow, seem, appear, smell, sound, feel, taste,* and *look*.

A **predicate noun** renames the subject.

A **direct object** receives the action of the verb.

3-8 Practice the Skill

Underline each verb. Label each verb *linking, transitive,* or *intransitive*.

intransitive 1. Jochebed hid her son from Pharaoh's men.
Linking 2. Miriam stayed with her brother.
Linking 3. An Egyptian princess appeared at the river.
transitive 4. She discovered Moses' hiding place.
~~Linking~~ transitive 5. The princess looked into the basket.
Linking 6. The baby ~~looked~~ healthy.
Linking 7. The princess seemed compassionate.
intransitive 8. Miriam ran for her mother.
transitive 9. Pharaoh's daughter adopted the baby as her own son.
Linking 10. Moses became a great leader of Israel.

3-9 Review the Skill

Underline each verb. For the sentences with linking verbs, circle the predicate noun or predicate adjective and identify it as *PN* or *PA*.

_____ 1. Nicodemus was a Pharisee.

_____ 2. The Pharisees seemed very religious.

50   Chapter 3

_____ 3. The Pharisees studied the Old Testament.

_____ 4. Nicodemus knew much about the Messiah.

_____ 5. The Pharisees doubted Jesus' words.

_____ 6. Nicodemus was afraid.

_____ 7. He went to Jesus at night.

_____ 8. Jesus gave Nicodemus the answer to his questions.

_____ 9. He told Nicodemus of his need.

_____ 10. Nicodemus accepted Jesus as his Savior.

3-10 Practice the Skill

Label the sentence patterns *S-LV-PN* or *S-TrV-DO*. Above each word of the sentence pattern, write its label.

1. According to some scholars, Egypt's Queen Hatshepsut was probably Moses' adoptive mother.
2. She was a strong leader with a powerful personality.
3. Hatshepsut married two different pharaohs.
4. She exercised much control over both of them.
5. Thutmose III became Hatshepsut's second husband.
6. He was probably Egypt's greatest pharaoh.
7. Hatshepsut and Thutmose III ruled Egypt for over twenty years as coregents.
8. Eventually Hatshepsut lost her power and influence.
9. Thutmose III assumed full power in his twenty-second year of rule.
10. Hatshepsut may have been the rescuer of the future leader of God's people.

3-11 Review the Skill

Label the sentence patterns *S-InV, S-TrV-DO, S-TrV-IO-DO, S-LV-PN,* or *S-LV-PA*. Above each word of the sentence pattern, write its label.

1. On his deathbed, Elisha called King Joash to his side.
2. With great love for Elisha, the king wept over him.
3. Elisha was a wise counselor for Israel.
4. Elisha gave Joash an assignment.
5. "Strike the ground with the arrows."
6. The arrows were symbols of God's deliverance.
7. After only three blows, the king became still.
8. The prophet's response sounded angry.
9. "Now you have only three deliverances from the Lord!"
10. The victories of Israel were incomplete because of the king's lack of determination.

Auxiliaries

Often words are added to the main verb in a sentence to give special meaning or emphasis or to express time. These words are called **auxiliaries** (sometimes called helping verbs). The following is a list of common auxiliaries.

- am, is, are, was, were, be, being, been
- have, has, had
- do, does, did
- will, would, shall, should, can, could, may, might, must

Together the auxiliary and the main verb form the **complete verb**. A complete verb may be a single verb (with no auxiliaries) or several auxiliaries and the main verb.

> Jesus possibly *built* wooden items in Joseph's carpenter shop.
> He probably *had worked* with Joseph many times.
>
> By the time Mary and Joseph discovered that Jesus was missing, they *had been traveling* home for one day.

For diagramming, be sure to include the main verb and all auxiliaries as the complete verb: **He probably had worked with Joseph many times.**

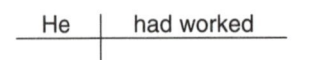

| He | had worked |

Gerard van Honthorst, *The Holy Family in the Carpenter Shop*, The Bob Jones University Collection.

Note that some words can be used either as auxiliaries or alone as main verbs. *Be* can act as a linking verb. *Have* and *do* can also be main verbs. Also note that other types of words sometimes separate the auxiliary and the main verb.

> The secretary *is trying* to reach her boss by phone. *(auxiliary + main)*
>
> She *is* patient. *(main)*
>
> She *has* already *tried* his home phone and his car phone. *(auxiliary + main)*
>
> The boss *has* a pager. *(main)*
>
> Sometimes he *does* not *remember* to wear the pager. *(auxiliary + main)*
>
> The secretary *does* her work well. *(main)*

ETYMOLOGY

Auxiliary comes from the Latin word *auxilium,* meaning "help."

IN SUMMARY

Auxiliaries are added to the main verb in the sentence to give special meaning or emphasis or to express time.

The auxiliary and the main verb combine to form the **complete verb**.

Be, have, and **do** are verbs that can be either auxiliaries or main verbs.

3-12 PRACTICE THE SKILL

Underline the complete verb in each sentence. Write *aux* over any auxiliary.

1. Paul uses a footrace as an example in his first letter to the Corinthians.
2. The Corinthians must have *(aux)* been familiar with this sport.
3. Races probably were *(aux)* held at the Olympic games in Greece.
4. Roman sports were more violent than Greek sports.
5. Men would *(aux)* fight each other to the death.
6. At other times they might place criminals, slaves, and even Christians in an arena with wild animals.
7. Often, the contestants did not *(aux)* have any weapons for protection.

8. The contestants could not survive the brutal attacks. [aux over "could not"]

9. Many people had been killed in the Roman arenas by the end of this era. [aux over "had been"]

10. The Romans did many disgusting things merely for entertainment. [aux over "did"]

3-13 REVIEW THE SKILL

Underline the complete verb in each sentence. Write *aux* over any auxiliary. Some sentences may not contain an auxiliary.

1. Tents have long been the homes of nomads.

2. They were the homes of Old Testament heroes such as Abraham, Isaac, and Jacob.

3. Many nomads are still living in tents today.

4. Tents are different shapes and sizes.

5. The women do most of the work for the arrangement of the tent.

6. Mats and rugs cover the floors.

7. Food is usually kept in goat-hair bags.

8. Normally one camel or donkey can carry one family's gear.

9. Abraham must have had many tents for all of his family, servants, and guests.

10. They would have needed several animals for all of their possessions.

3-14 REVIEW THE SKILL

Label the sentence patterns *S-InV, S-TrV-DO, S-TrV-IO-DO, S-LV-PN,* or *S-LV-PA.* Above each word of the sentence pattern, write its label.

1. Publicans [S] were usually wealthy Romans [TrV DO] in charge of tax collection in specific cities.

2. Several local Jews [S] became tax collectors. [LV InV]

3. The Romans [S] paid [TrV] the Jews [IO] much money [DO] for their work.

4. The Jewish tax collectors [S] seemed [InV] treacherous to their kinsmen.

5. Every male over fourteen [S] and every female over twelve [S] paid [TrV] the poll tax. [DO]

54   Chapter 3

6. Merchants would pay the tax collectors a fee on all imports and exports.
7. Tax collectors also collected tolls on roads and bridges.
8. Most Jews hated tax collectors.
9. Tax collectors were often unkind to other Jews.
10. Jesus was the friend of tax collectors.

Principal Parts of Verbs

Verbs in English have just three basic forms. These are called the principal parts of the verb. (*Principal* here means "main.") The first principal part is called the **present,** the second is called the **past,** and the third is called the **past participle.** The past participle is the form that is used after some form of the auxiliary *have.* As you study tenses, you will learn how to use these principal parts.

The difference between regular and irregular verbs is the way they form the second and third principal parts. **Regular verbs** form the past and the past participle by adding *d* or *ed* to the present.

>climb, climbed, (have) climbed
>hope, hoped, (have) hoped

Irregular verbs form the past and the past participle in various ways. Look at these examples.

Some irregular verbs have three different principal parts:

>begin, began, (have) begun
>take, took, (have) taken

For some irregular verbs the second and third principal parts are alike:

>bring, brought, (have) brought
>lead, led, (have) led

A few irregular verbs have all three principal parts the same:

>burst, burst, (have) burst
>set, set, (have) set

Learning the principal parts will help you avoid mistakes in usage. A dictionary lists the principal parts of any verb right after the pronunciation guides. The chart below lists the principal parts for some troublesome verbs.

Present	Past	Past Participle
bring	brought	brought
burst	burst	burst
choose	chose	chosen
climb	climbed	climbed
come	came	come
do	did	done

Present	Past	Past Participle
drag	dragged	dragged
draw	drew	drawn
drink	drank	drunk
drive	drove	driven
drown	drowned	drowned
eat	ate	eaten
fall	fell	fallen
feed	fed	fed
get	got	got, gotten
give	gave	given
go	went	gone
grow	grew	grown
hang	hanged	hanged
hang	hung	hung
keep	kept	kept
lay	laid	laid
lead	led	led
lie	lay	lain
ride	rode	ridden
ring	rang	rung
rise	rose	risen
run	ran	run
see	saw	seen
set	set	set
shine	shined	shined
shine	shone	shone
shrink	shrank, shrunk	shrunk, shrunken
sing	sang, sung	sung
sit	sat	sat
slay	slew	slain
sneak	sneaked	sneaked
speak	spoke	spoken
steal	stole	stolen
swim	swam	swum
take	took	taken
throw	threw	thrown

IN SUMMARY

The three principal parts of the verb are the **present, past,** and **past participle.**

The past participle is the form that is used after some form of the auxiliary *have*.

3-15 PRACTICE THE SKILL

Underline the correct verb from the choices in parentheses. Be sure to check for any auxiliaries before you choose the verb.

1. After Jesus' death, His friends *(took, taken)* His body to the tomb.
2. On the first day of the week, several women *(went, gone)* to the sepulchre.
3. An angel *(sit, sat)* at the tomb's entrance.
4. In the garden, Mary had *(saw, seen)* Jesus.
5. Jesus *(spoke, spoken)* Mary's name.
6. She *(fell, fallen)* at Jesus' feet.
7. The two disciples had *(ran, run)* to the empty tomb.
8. Jesus *(slew, slain)* death.
9. He had *(rose, risen)* from the dead.
10. The time had *(come, came)* for Jesus to return to heaven.

3-16 REVIEW THE SKILL

In the blank write the correct past or past participle form of the verb in parentheses.

(wrote) 1. The historian Josephus *(write)* about the destruction of Jerusalem.

(grew) 2. In the early first century, tension *(grow)* between the Jews and the Romans.

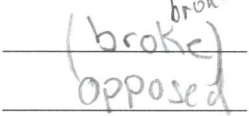

(broke) broken 3. By A.D. 66 fighting had *(break)* out.

opposed 4. The High Priest Ananias had *(oppose)* the revolt.

slew 5. The Jewish rebels quickly *(slay)* him.

distroyed 6. In A.D. 70 the Romans *(destroy)* Jerusalem.

carried 7. They *(carry)* off the golden candlesticks, the trumpets, and other valuable pieces from the temple.

resistED 8. A few small groups of Jews *(resist)* for three more years.

fell 9. Masada *(fall)* to the Roman army in A.D. 73.

Conquered 10. The Romans had *(conquer)* the Jews.

Verbs   57

Simple Tenses

Most verbs change their form to indicate time: present, past, or future. We call these verb forms **tenses.** Tense helps differentiate what happened yesterday from what is happening today and from what will happen tomorrow. We make all tenses from the principal parts discussed earlier.

There are three simple tenses. They are the simple **present,** the simple **past,** and the simple **future.** The present and past tenses are formed with a single word. The future tense requires the auxiliary *will* or *shall* with the main verb.

Tense comes from the Latin word *tempus*, meaning "time."

Present Tense

The present tense form of a verb is the same as the verb's first principal part. The present tense sometimes makes a statement about something that is true right now.

> God *loves* us.
> He *sees* all our actions.

Sometimes the present tense tells what is done habitually or usually.

> We *use* math skills every day.

We add *s* or *es* to the first principal part when a singular noun or a singular third-person pronoun *(it, he,* or *she)* is the subject of a sentence. (This is the same *s* you used in the verb test frame.)

> The runner *sprints* to the finish line.
> He *sprints* to the finish line.

Plural subjects, whether nouns or pronouns, and the singular pronouns *I* and *you* never take the added *s.*

> The fans *cheer* the sprinters on. (**But:** The fan *cheers* the sprinters on.)
> We *cheer* for some of the same people.

> I *cheer* for my favorite athletes.
> (**But:** He *cheers* for his favorite athletes.)
> You *cheer* for your friends too.

Past Tense

The past principal part is used by itself for the past tense. The past tense tells what occurred in an earlier time period.

> Brock *moved* the equipment out of the way.
> LaVonne almost *tripped* over a loose cord.

Future Tense

The future tense form of the verb uses the first principal part plus *will* or *shall* to express action or to make a statement about something that will happen in the future. Every verb makes the future tense the same way.

> Anne's friends *will arrive* shortly for the party.
> She *will know* about the surprise soon enough.

Chapter 10: Subject-Verb Agreement
p. 209

Chapter 17: Spelling Singular Present-tense Verbs
pp. 354-55

Chapter 17: Adding Suffixes
pp. 358-59

IN SUMMARY

The **present tense** shows action or makes a statement about something that is occurring right now.

The **past tense** tells what occurred in an earlier time period.

The **future tense,** formed by the first principle part plus the auxiliaries *will* or *shall,* expresses action or makes a statement about something that will happen in the future.

3-17 PRACTICE THE SKILL

Underline each verb. Label its tense *present, past,* or *future.*

Present — 1. Philippi <u>gets</u> its name from Philip of Macedon, Alexander the Great's father.

Past — 2. Philip <u>conquered</u> the city in 360 B.C.

Past — 3. Paul first <u>introduced</u> the gospel to Philippi three hundred years later in A.D. 49-50.

Past — 4. At Philippi Paul <u>saw</u> his first European converts.

Past — 5. These converts <u>included</u> Lydia and a jailer.

Past — 6. The Philippian Christians <u>remained</u> loyal to Paul even during his imprisonment.

Past — 7. Paul <u>wrote</u> the book of Philippians from his Roman prison cell.

Present — 8. In it he <u>warns</u> the Philippians of the dangers of disunity and pride.

Present — 9. He <u>instructs</u> them in the joys of servanthood.

future — 10. This book will <u>encourage</u> readers in times of trial.

3-18 REVIEW THE SKILL

In the blank write the correct form of the verb in parentheses.

is — 1. Jerusalem _?_ a very old city with a rich history. *(be, present)*

controlled — 2. In ancient times it _?_ important trade routes. *(control, past)*

Provided — 3. It also _?_ a strategic military stronghold for the nation who controlled it. *(provide, past)*

made — 4. The Bible _?_ the earliest recorded mention of Jerusalem in Genesis 14:18. *(make, present)*

Verbs 59

greets 5. In this passage Melchizedek, king of Salem (Jerusalem), _?_ Abraham after Abraham's conquest of neighboring kings. *(greet, present)*

saw 6. King David _?_ the central location of the city of Jerusalem. *(see, past)*

made 7. As a result, he _?_ Jerusalem the capital of the united kingdom of Israel. *(make, past)*

passed 8. After Rome destroyed Jerusalem in A.D. 70, control of the city _?_ into the hands of many different nations. *(pass, past)*

will exist 9. Tensions between Arabs and Jews regarding control of Jerusalem _?_ until the Rapture. *(exist, future)*

shall stand 10. Jerusalem _?_ as a reminder of God's provision for His people in the past and a promise of His kingdom still to come. *(stand, future)*

Perfect Tenses

Perfect tenses tell about actions that are "perfected" or completed. In other words, they are used in conjunction with a reference to some other point in time. The perfect tenses use the same three names as the simple tenses: *present* perfect, *past* perfect, and *future* perfect. Perfect tenses are formed from the third principal part and require a form of the auxiliary *have* to complete them. (Remember that this third principal part is called the past participle.) The names of the perfect tenses come from the form of *have* used with the past participle.

Tense	Auxiliary
Present Perfect	have or has
Past Perfect	had
Future Perfect	will have (or shall have)

Present Perfect Tense

The **present perfect tense** expresses an action or state of being completed during the present time period or one that began in the past and has continued to the present. Present perfect combines the present tense of *have* and the past participle of the main verb. So the present perfect tense of the verb *walk* would be formed as follows:

    have/has   +   *walked*   =   *have/has walked*
  (present tense)   (past participle)   (present perfect tense)

I *have walked* both to and from the park many times.
We *have completed* the CPR course.
She *has walked* to the library.
Sandra *has completed* the requirements for her lifesaving badge.

Past Perfect Tense

The **past perfect tense** expresses an action that was completed (or a state that existed) before a certain time or event in the past. Past perfect combines the past tense of the auxiliary *have (had)* and the past participle of the main verb. Notice that only the tense of *have* changes; the main verb remains the same for all of the perfect tenses.

had + *walked* = *had walked*
(past tense) (past participle) (past perfect tense)

Past perfect tense tells about something that happened before something else happened; both events are in the past. For example,

Florio *had walked* all the way home before his mom arrived.

In this sentence Florio's mother arrived home to find that Florio was already there. Mom's arrival was in the past, and Florio's arrival was even before that.

Future Perfect Tense

The **future perfect tense** tells about an action that will be completed before a future time or before a future event takes place. Future perfect takes the future tense of *have* (*will have* or *shall have*) plus the past participle (the same as for the two previous perfect tenses).

will/shall have + *owned* = *will have owned*
(future tense) (past participle) (future perfect)

By summer we *will have owned* our horse for a year.

In this sentence the action of owning the horse for a year will be completed before the time summer arrives. Notice that like the present perfect and past perfect, the future perfect describes something "perfected" or completed.

In Summary

The three **perfect tenses** use forms of the auxiliary *have* and the past participle of the main verb.

Use the **present perfect tense** to express action completed during the present time period, often up to the present moment.

Use the **past perfect tense** to express action completed before some past time or event.

Use the **future perfect tense** to express action that will be completed before a future time or event.

3-19 Practice the Skill

In the blank write the correct form of the verb in parentheses.

resented 1. The first century Jews _?_ being under Roman rule. *(resent, simple past)*

hoped 2. They _?_ that Christ would deliver them from Roman domination. *(hope, past perfect)* _look_ 3. They still ? forward to the coming of their Messiah. *(look, simple present)*

dead 4. By the time Christ returns, many people ? , still looking for His coming. *(die, future perfect)*

Scatterd 5. When Jerusalem fell in A.D. 70, God's people ? all over the various continents. *(scatter, past perfect)*

endure 6. Since that time, the Jewish people ? much pain and persecution. *(endure, present perfect)*

return 7. Today, many Jews ? to their homeland. *(return, present perfect)*

threaten 8. However, political unrest still ? the nation of Israel. *(threaten, simple present)*

serve 9. By the time they reach middle age, all Israeli men and women ? in the military. *(serve, future perfect)*

comes 10. Peace ? to Israel only when Christ returns. *(come, simple future)*

3-20 REVIEW THE SKILL

Write a sentence using the tense indicated. Use verbs other than *be* verbs wherever possible.

1. Tell about your most enjoyable vacation. *(past)*

   When I was 11, I went to Whales, It had magnifacent castles, and beautiful landskapes

2. Write a sentence about what you think you will do next week. *(future)*

   Next week will probably be the usual week of school work and running.

3. Describe what you had done before your last birthday party ended. *(past perfect)*

   24 hours before April 14, I was getting hyped up on caffine with one of my BFF Alex!

4. Tell about the house you live in now. *(present)*

   Old, Beautiful, Big, those are some lovely words to discribe my present house.

5. Write a sentence about one thing you plan to have accomplished by the time you are seventy. *(future perfect)*

   To stay alive will be a nice acompleshment by the time im 70.

6. Tell about your favorite Christmas tradition. *(present perfect)*

   Christmas means christmas tree, my favorite tradition is decorating the glorious tree.

7. Tell about one broken New Year's resolution. *(past)*

   New Year Resolutions are never broken for me because I forget about it the next Day.

8. Write one sentence about your favorite novel. *(present)*

   Do you like adventurres, Dragons, and enchantments, if you do my favorite book the Chronicals of the Enchanted forest is for you.

9. Write about your favorite household chore. *(present)*

   Chores, my favorite chore is to mow the lawn because you can tell when your done and is outside.

10. Tell about the job you intend to have when you grow up. *(future)*

    In the future I intend to become a FBI Field Agent or Detective, dont tell me no,

Progressive Verbs

You have learned six verb tenses: simple past, simple present, simple future, present perfect, past perfect, and future perfect. These verbs are the most common ways to express action or state of being. However, often we need to express action in progress, action that continues. The **progressive form** of the verb shows that something happens over a period of time.

> Conner *is learning* to walk.
> Theo *was flying* his remote-controlled plane.

The action of Conner's learning to walk is going on over a period of days or weeks; Theo's flying of the plane took up several minutes or hours but was viewed as ongoing.

Each of the six tenses has a progressive form. It is made up of a form of *be* as an auxiliary plus the *ing* form of the verb. This *ing* form is made by adding *ing* to the present (or first) principal part. Without the *ing* form the verb is not progressive.

Verbs 63

Notice that like the perfect tenses, the progressive form takes its name from the form of the auxiliary it uses. The perfect tenses use a form of *have,* and the progressive form uses a form of *be.*

	Forms of *be*	Example with *read + ing*
Present progressive	present tense of *be*	He *is reading* his Bible. I *am reading* my Bible. They *are reading* their Bibles.
Past progressive	past tense of *be*	He *was reading* his Bible. They *were reading* their Bibles.
Future progressive	future tense of *be*	We *will be reading* our Bibles.
Present perfect progressive	present perfect tense of *be*	We *have been reading* our Bibles before the service each Sunday.
Past perfect progressive	past perfect tense of *be*	We *had been reading* until the service began.
Future perfect progressive	future perfect tense of *be*	We *will have been reading* our Bibles for ten minutes when the service begins.

IN SUMMARY

The **progressive form** of the verb shows that something happens over a period of time. The progressive form is made up of a form of *be* as an auxiliary plus the *ing* form of the verb.

3-21 PRACTICE THE SKILL

Underline the complete verb in each sentence. Label the tense of the verb and indicate whether the verb is progressive.

1. In Matthew 10 Jesus is talking to His disciples.

2. Prior to this passage He has been healing the sick and maimed.

3. He was preaching the gospel to them as well.

4. Here He is instructing His disciples in their responsibilities.

5. They will be taking neither money nor extra clothes with them for their journey.

future
__no__ 6. They will <u>rely</u> on God for their needs.
present
__no__ 7. In this passage Jesus <u>warns</u> the disciples about the fear of man.
future
__no__ 8. The Holy Spirit will <u>give</u> them the right words at the right time.
future perfect
__yes__ 9. By the end of the disciples' lives, many people will have been <u>persecuting</u> them for Jesus' sake.
past perfect
__yes__ 10. Ever since His command to His disciples, Christ has been <u>searching</u> for willing and obedient Christians.

3-22 REVIEW THE SKILL

In the blank write the progressive form of each italicized verb. Do not change the tense of the verb.

__are speaking__ 1. The Old Testament Messianic prophecies *speak* of Christ.

__is disclosing__ 2. In these passages, God *discloses* some facts about Christ's coming.

__was promising__ 3. In Genesis 3:15, God *promised* that one day the seed of the woman would crush the serpent.

__is narrowing__ 4. God *narrows* the scope of the promise with the call of Abraham.

__was identifying__ 5. In his prophecy, Jacob *identified* the Messiah as a king.

__be coming__ 6. The Messiah *will come* from King David's line.

__is telling__ 7. In II Samuel 7:12-14 God *tells* David that the Messiah will be God's Son.

__is asserting__ 8. This passage *asserts* Christ's deity.

__were revealing__ 9. As time went by, the prophecies *revealed* Christ to the Old Testament saints.

__be returning__ 10. Someday, Christ *will return* for all of the Old Testament believers who put their faith in the promised Messiah.

Active and Passive Voice

In most sentences the subject *does* something or *is* something. In sentences like these, the verb is **active.** All the basic sentence patterns have active-voice verbs. Look at these examples.

S-LV-PA: The hit *was* good.
S-InV: The crowd *cheered.*
S-TrV-DO: The runner *rounded* the bases.

Any sentence with a transitive verb—that is, any sentence with a direct object—can be rewritten so that the subject is not acting. Instead of acting, the subject is acted upon. In these sentences the verb is **passive.**

active: The baseball *broke* the window.
passive: The window *was broken*.

active: Marcie *found* the ball and glass on the couch.
passive: The ball and glass *were found* on the couch by Marcie.

Notice that in the passive sentences above, the direct objects of the active sentences have become the subjects of the passive sentences. The verb forms in passive sentences have also changed to include a form of the auxiliary *be.* As with the perfect tense and the progressive form, the tense of the passive-voice verb is named for the tense of the auxiliary.

	Active Voice	Passive Voice
Present	choose/chooses	am chosen is chosen are chosen
Past	chose	was chosen were chosen
Future	will choose	will be chosen
Present Perfect	has chosen have chosen	has been chosen have been chosen
Past Perfect	had chosen	had been chosen
Future Perfect	will have chosen	will have been chosen

Often the the word that was the subject of the active sentence is included in a prepositional phrase in the passive sentence (as in *by Marcie* above), or it is left out of the passive sentence entirely (as in the first passive example above).

In Summary

Sentences with **active verbs** show the subject doing something or being something.

Sentences with **passive verbs** show the subject receiving the action. The verb form also changes to include some form of the auxiliary *be.*

3-23 Practice the Skill

Underline the complete verb in each sentence. Label the verb *active* or *passive*.

active 1. Both barley and wheat <u>were grown</u> as main food sources in Palestine during Bible times.

passive 2. Often they <u>were combined</u> into a flour mixture.

active 3. Barley was <u>used</u> mainly as feed for cattle, horses, and mules.

passive 4. However, poor people <u>ate</u> barley as well.

active 5. Wheat was often <u>exported</u> to surrounding nations.

active 6. Barley <u>harvest</u> begins in the spring.

active 7. Wheat <u>harvest</u> usually follows four weeks later.

passive 8. Harvests of both barley and wheat are <u>mentioned</u> in the Bible.

action 9. Ruth <u>returned</u> to Bethlehem at the beginning of barley harvest.

action 10. Gideon was <u>threshing</u> wheat at the time of his call.

3-24 Review the Skill

Rewrite each of the following passive sentences, changing them to active voice. Do not change the tense of the verb.

1. Shadrach, Meshach, and Abednego were captured by the Babylonians.

   Babolonians captured Shadrach, Meshach and Abendigo.

2. The Babylonian people were ruled by Nebuchadnezzar.

   Nebuchadnezzer ruled the Babolonian people.

3. A golden idol was built by Nebuchadnezzar's men.

   Nebuchadnezzer's men built a golden idol.

Verbs 67

4. The idol was worshiped by everyone.

    everyone worshiped the idol

5. The king's command was not followed by Shadrach, Meshach, and Abednego.

    Shadrach, Meshach and Abendego did not follow the King's command.

6. Shadrach, Meshach, and Abednego were thrown into the fiery furnace by the king's men.

    The King's men threw Shadrach, Meshach, and Abendego into the fiery furnace

7. The guards were burned by the flames.

    the flames burned the guards.

8. No fear of death was shown by the three men.

    the three men showed no fear of death.

9. The Son of God was seen with the three men by Nebuchadnezzar.

    Nebuchadnezzer saw The Son of God with the three men.

10. The king's heart was softened by God.

    God Softened the King's heart.

Forming the Passive

Transitive verbs have passive forms for every tense. The passive of each tense is made of a form of the auxiliary *be* plus the past participle. For instance, the passive form of the past tense uses the past tense of the auxiliary *be (was/were)* and past participle. (The past participle, you remember, is also used in the perfect tenses.)

    past active: God *chose* Joshua to lead the Israelites.
    past passive: Joshua *was chosen* by God to lead the Israelites.

68   Chapter 3

The past perfect passive voice uses the past perfect of *be (had been)* and the past participle.

past perfect active: Earlier God *had chosen* Moses.
past perfect passive: Earlier Moses *had been chosen* by God.

IN SUMMARY

The passive of each tense is made of a form of the auxiliary *be* plus the past participle.

3-25 PRACTICE THE SKILL

Write the correct form of the verb as indicated in parentheses.

1. God _is using_ Elisha. *(past active, use)*
   Elisha _was used_ by God. *(past passive, use)*

2. Elisha _is helping_ the widow. *(present active, help)*
   The widow _is helped_ by Elisha. *(present passive, help)*

3. Elisha _is communicating_ God's plan. *(present active, communicate)*
   God's plan _is communicated_ by Elisha. *(present passive, communicate)*

4. The sons _collected_ many empty vessels. *(past active, collect)*
   Many empty vessels _were collected_ by the sons. *(past passive, collect)*

5. The woman _poured_ the oil into the vessels. *(past active, pour)*
   The oil _was poured_ into the vessels by the woman. *(past passive, pour)*

6. God _is giving_ the family more oil. *(present active, give)*
   The family _is given_ more oil by God. *(present passive, give)*

7. The family _is selling_ the oil. *(present active, sell)*
   The oil _is sold_ by the family. *(present passive, sell)*

Vers 69

8. God __Provided__ for the needs of the family. *(past active, provide)*

The needs of the family __were provided__ by God. *(past passive, provide)*

9. God __hears__ our prayers. *(present active, hear)*

Our prayers __are heard__ by God. *(present passive, hear)*

10. God __knows__ our every need. *(present active, know)*

Our every need __is known__ by God. *(present passive, know)*

3-26 REVIEW THE SKILL

In the blank write an appropriate active or passive verb. Refer to the book of Ruth for help in completing these sentences.

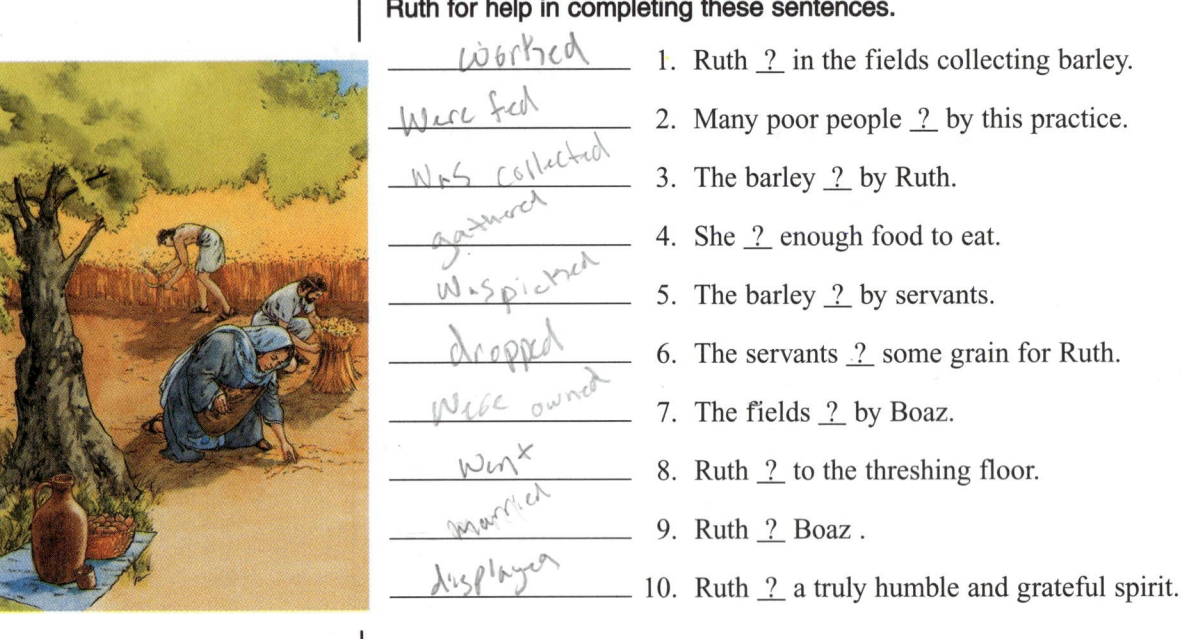

__worked__ 1. Ruth _?_ in the fields collecting barley.

__were fed__ 2. Many poor people _?_ by this practice.

__was collected__ 3. The barley _?_ by Ruth.

__gathered__ 4. She _?_ enough food to eat.

__was picked__ 5. The barley _?_ by servants.

__dropped__ 6. The servants _?_ some grain for Ruth.

__were owned__ 7. The fields _?_ by Boaz.

__went__ 8. Ruth _?_ to the threshing floor.

__married__ 9. Ruth _?_ Boaz.

__displayed__ 10. Ruth _?_ a truly humble and grateful spirit.

3-27 USE THE SKILL

Write a sentence to answer each question. Use the active or passive voice as indicated in parentheses and underline the verb you choose.

Example: What happened when the girl pulled the cat's tail? *(active)*

The outraged cat bit the naughty girl.

1. What happened to the car during the snowstorm? *(active)*

The care drove off the cliff.

2. What happened during the orchestra's concert? *(passive)*
   the orchistra recieved a roar of clapping by the audiance

3. What happened when the family attended the fair? *(active)*
   The kids got lost.

4. What do you do when you get locked out of your house? *(active)*
   Call someone who has a key.

5. What happened when the lightning struck a tree? *(passive)*
   a deer was smashed by the tree.

6. What did the student say when asked where her essay was? *(passive)*
   My papper was ate by my dog.

7. What happened when he bought a new car? *(passive)*
   the car got in an accident.

8. What unusual thing did the teacher tell you? *(active)*
   Dont forgett to do your homework.

9. What happened when the girl went to the amusement park? *(active)*
   She threw up.

10. What happened during the basketball game? *(passive)*
    the hoop fell off the wall.

3-28 CUMULATIVE REVIEW

Rewrite the paragraph correctly on the blanks provided. Correct the ten errors in these categories: fragments, comma splices, fused sentences, incorrect plural noun forms, incorrect possessive noun forms, incorrect verb forms (e.g., *writed* or *had wrote*).

    Christ teached many lessons with parables. The story of the ten bridesmaids teaches us a lesson about Christs' return. No doubt the bride-to-be was eagerly awaiting the arrival of her groom. He could come at any time and she should be ready. The bride with the help of ten bridesmaids. They watched for the imminent arrival of the groom. One night the groom came! Five of the bridesmaid's lamps had oil five of them had none. The five without oil had not be watching diligently for the bridegroom. Christ is our Bridegroom, He will come for us on an unexpected day. Christ is coming very soon, we should watch and be ready!

[Handwritten answer:]

Christ taught many lessons with parables. The story of the ten bridesmaids teaches us a lesson about Christ's return. No doubt the bride-to-be was eagerly awaiting her groom. He could come at anytime, and she would be ready. The bride prepared herself with the help of 10 bridesmaids. They watched for imminent arrivals of the groom. One night the groom came! Five of the bridesmaids' lamps had oil; five of them had none. The five without oil had not been watching diligently for the bridegroom. Christ is our Bridegroom, and He will come for us on an unexpected day. Christ is coming very soon; we should watch and be ready!

POLE VAULTING

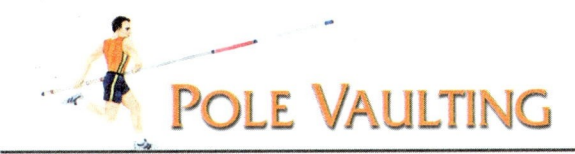

Reread these sentences from the last paragraph of the excerpt from *Vinegar Boy*. Change them from active to passive sentences.

"A branch whipped loose and struck Magdalene across the shoulders."
"She gathered up her skirts."
"She . . . threw a look at Jesus."

- *What did the paragraph lose when the sentences became passive?*
- *Why do you think writers use mainly active verbs?*
- *Find a book you really like. Open it to the first chapter and check out the verbs. Which type predominates—active or passive? How does the verb choice help create a mood?*

It's History: Writing an Autobiography

Have you ever heard from a third party about a funny or exciting experience your friend had? Probably the next time you saw your friend, you asked him about the experience. You probably said something like this: "I've already heard about it from So-and-so, but I want to hear you tell about it."

A telling of your own life's story is an autobiography. Someone else's telling of it is a biography. Which do you think is more impartial? Which is more personal?

Reading a person's autobiography often makes you feel as if you know that person better—not only what he did but also what he thought and how he felt about what he did. Popular kinds of autobiographies include stories of missionaries, stories of people in interesting professions, and stories of people who have made great accomplishments. But anyone can write an autobiography.

What makes your own life interesting to other people? People are interested in *unique experiences*. They like to read about things they have never done and probably never will do. They like to get outside their own limited world and into someone else's—just for a little while. But even more important, people are interested in *universal emotions*. They may have never done the thing you have done, but they would like to relate to your feelings about doing that thing. If you write well about an experience, the emotion will come through without your having to state specifically how you felt.

Let's say that you are reading the autobiography of someone who climbed Mount Everest. The uniqueness of that mountain-climbing experience is what made you pick up the book in the first place. But if the author has done his job well, you can see the universality of that experience. Although you may not know exactly what it feels like to be hanging from a rope against a sheer cliff thousands of feet above sea level, you have experienced feelings of fear or triumph before. You can relate to the sensations of fear or triumph that would come with being so high above the rest of the world.

Verbs

Chapter 20: Choosing a Topic, Paragraphs
pp. 409-11; 413-14

Your Turn: Writing Your Own Life Story

It is often harder to write about yourself than about someone else. Here's a list of questions to help you as you begin.

- What are the unusual experiences in my life?
  - What things have I done that most other people have not done or have not done in the same way?
  - What things have I done that make me the person I am, that make me different from everyone else?
- What are the universal emotions of those experiences?
  - How did I feel while I was doing those things or after they happened?
  - How can I convey those feelings, perhaps without stating them specifically?

Limit your autobiography to three paragraphs. Here is a student example to help get your train of thought rolling.

unique experiences

universal emotions

I was born in Los Angeles, but my family moved to a small town in the desert when I was seven. The town seemed so empty to me after living in a big city. Everything seemed lonely, especially at school. Because I was shy, it took me a little while to make new friends. But then I met Heather, who is still my best friend today. Since that time, Heather has come over at least once a week to go horseback riding with me.

When I was eight, my brother was bitten by a snake, and I was afraid he was going to die. That started me thinking about death. I knew I didn't want to die, because I wasn't sure what would happen to me. I talked to my mom about it, and she showed me verses in the Bible about how I could be saved. That was when I made the most important decision of my life and asked Jesus to save me.

Last summer my family took a trip to visit my cousins in Ohio. I spent a lot of time with my nine-year-old cousin Philip, who is paralyzed from the waist down. I was amazed at how much he could do even in his wheelchair. Watching Aunt Cindy work with Philip made me really want to help children like him. I decided that I might like to be a physical therapist someday.

STRETCHING OUT

Doubling Back

Does *wind up* mean to get ready or to finish something? That depends on whether you're talking about a pitcher with a baseball cocked beside his ear or a speaker getting to his last point in a lecture.

Why do people drive on a parkway and park on a driveway? Why are things sent by ship called "cargo" while things sent by car are called "shipments"? The word *cleave* means "to separate" in a butcher's shop, but it means "to join permanently" in a marriage ceremony. Can you imagine how difficult it would be to learn a language so full of contradictions? Just when you thought you were a "smash" at it, you would find you were in for a "smash."

Passing the Baton
WRITING ACROSS THE CURRICULUM

Business

Think about a job, career, or business in which you may be particularly interested. Interview a person in the area of your interest either by letter or personal visit. Keep your questions brief, taking no more than five or ten minutes of the person's time. Remember to thank the person for his help.

Include questions about the following topics: (1) educational requirements or special training, (2) reasons for choosing the job or career, (3) a typical day's experiences, and/or (4) an unusual work-related experience.

After you have completed your interview, adapt the information into a script. State the date, the time and place of the interview, and the person's name. Use the format below.

Interviewer: Were there any special educational requirements or training for your job as veterinarian?

Dr. Stanford: Yes, besides the medical training, I had a few courses in animal psychology.

After you have finished your script, perhaps you would like to send a copy to the person you interviewed.

Verbs 75

Chapter 4

Pronouns

But Not Forsaken
by Helen Good Brenneman

Grammar

"Penner—Maria, Hansie, and Rosie. Please tell us your name, too, Grandma. You are so kind. You—you don't know what this means to us."

"I think I do. My name is Erna Maier and my husband is Wilhelm Maier. He is upstairs looking at our supply of wood. He will be surprised."

Maria took off her shoes, moved closer to the fire, and sank farther into her chair. "Then we will call you Grandma Maier, if that's all right."

Her eyes followed the new friend around as Grandma tried to hustle her old body to get their meal. The children watched too, with interest. Grandma Maier was supple for her age. She was dressed in a dark, long-sleeved dress and a large, print apron, patched colorfully.

"Mamma, I'm afraid I'll have to replenish the wood supply. I don't believe it's going to last." They had been hearing heavy footsteps in the room above the kitchen, and now a tottering old man appeared in the stair door beside the stove. Rosie, not yet at ease, gave a startled little cry.

Grandma Maier's face crinkled into a smile.

"It is only Father, child. Father!" She lifted her voice and her words came forth with a new resonance. Apparently the old man was somewhat deaf.

He glanced in surprise around the kitchen and then looked questioningly at his wife, who begged him with her eyes to understand.

"They had no place to spend the night and no food, Father," she explained, and the knife in her hand trembled. "Is it all right?"

He stroked his beard and looked thoughtful, first at one and then the other. Finally, his eyes rested on young Hans and filled with tears.

Forgetting to acknowledge the introductions which his wife had hurriedly made, Father searched Grandma Maier's face.

"Did you notice?"

"Yes, I did. And the girl, too."

He looked at Rosie for a long moment. "Yesssssss," he finally agreed. Remembering his manners, he shook hands solemnly with each member of the family.

"Of course they may stay, Mamma," he replied benevolently. "Have I ever been one to send a child out into the night?"

When supper was almost ready, Grandma poured some hot water from a dilapidated teakettle into a washbasin.

"You will all want to wash now, and perhaps bathe sometime before you leave again in the morning." She hesitated. "Or whenever you decide to leave; there is no hurry."

And then they ate, Grandfather helping the children to their food, and Grandma obviously enjoying her bustling for the sake of these new friends.

Maria did not know whether the old couple would have bowed their heads in thanksgiving or not, had she not instantaneously done so. Limping along from one meal to the next, Maria knew how to be thankful. It was a lesson she could never forget.

- *Do you think the Maiers are the children's real grandparents? What gives you your impression?*
- *What do you think the Maiers notice about Rosie and Hans?*
- *What is unusual about the way the Maiers talk to each other?*

In a scene where there are many characters and where one character can go by different names, a writer must take care that the reader always knows who is talking or being talked about. Pronouns serve much the same purpose as place cards at a dinner table. They help the reader keep track of characters.

Pronouns and Antecedents

Pro means "in place of." What does *pronoun* mean?

ETYMOLOGY

Pronouns are words that substitute for nouns. Pronouns allow us to simplify our writing and speaking.

The **antecedent** is the noun or other pronoun that the pronoun replaces. An antecedent usually appears before the pronoun that replaces it.

Commuters in California depend on **their** vast freeway system.
The first *freeway* in California opened in 1940; **it** covered six miles from Pasadena to Los Angeles.
Nobody then realized how quickly the freeway system would grow.

In Summary

Pronouns are words that substitute for nouns.

The **antecedent** is the noun or other pronoun that the pronoun replaces.

4-1 Practice the Skill

Underline each pronoun. In the blank write its antecedent.

_____ 1. Although the League of Nations assembled in 1920 to prevent aggression between countries, the rising dictators and their threat to world peace continued.

_____ 2. Japan began its defiance of the League of Nations by taking Manchuria from China.

_____ 3. Because no country was willing to stop the aggression, Japanese troops continued their invasion of China in 1937.

_____ 4. The Italian dictator Mussolini defied the League when he led an invasion of Ethiopia in 1935.

_____ 5. The League still did not use military force, but it imposed sanctions on Italy instead.

_____ 6. Adolf Hitler also desired a powerful empire, so he pulled Germany out of the League of Nations.

Chapter 11: Pronoun-Antecedent Agreement pp. 227-32

Chapter 12: Pronoun Usage pp. 256-61

League of Nations, Geneva, 1925

78 Chapter 4

_____ 7. In attempts to acquire more land, Hitler and his troops invaded Poland in September 1939.

_____ 8. Because Britain and France supported Poland, they declared war on Germany two days later.

_____ 9. While Germany invaded Poland on the west, Russian troops made their assault on Poland from the east.

_____ 10. By the end of the 1930s, Germany and its forces appeared indestructible.

4-2 Review the Skill

In the blank write a pronoun to replace the italicized word or phrase.

_____ 1. Keith, did *Keith* know that the Allied retreat from Dunkirk was a miracle?

_____ 2. Most Americans know only part of the story. *Americans* all can be thankful to God for the outcome.

_____ 3. Many British and French men escaped with *the men's* lives because of a German military error.

_____ 4. Hitler normally receives the blame, but *Hitler* was only partly to blame.

_____ 5. Runstedt, a high-ranking German military official, called for *Runstedt's* soldiers to cease all front-line activity.

_____ 6. The Germans knew that *the Germans* must follow the authority of their leaders.

_____ 7. Because the port at Dunkirk was small, *the port* could not hold many troops.

_____ 8. Operation Dynamo was unique because many fishermen used *the fishermen's* own boats to rescue the soldiers.

_____ 9. *The rescue* became one of the most famous rescues of World War II.

_____ 10. The soldiers were brave; we salute *the soldiers*.

Personal Pronouns

Personal pronouns are the most commonly used type of pronoun. All personal pronouns have four characteristics: **person, number, gender,** and **case.**

Singular	Subjective	Objective	Possessive
First Person	I	me	my, mine
Second Person	you	you	your, yours
Third Person			
neuter	it	it	its
masculine	he	him	his
feminine	she	her	her, hers

Plural	Subjective	Objective	Possessive
First Person	we	us	our, ours
Second Person	you	you	your, yours
Third Person	they	them	their, theirs

Person tells whether the personal pronoun refers to the speaker, the person(s) spoken to, or another person or thing.

First person: *My* cousins live in South Dakota.
Second person: Have *you* ever visited Mount Rushmore National Memorial?
Third person: *It* is a popular tourist attraction.

Number tells whether the personal pronoun is singular or plural.

Singular: Gutzon Borglum and *his* son Lincoln chiseled the memorial.
Plural: *They* were talented sculptors.

Gender tells whether the personal pronoun is neuter, masculine, or feminine. Only the third-person singular pronouns show a difference of gender.

Neuter: *Its* construction took fourteen years from 1927 until 1941.
Masculine: Gutzon Borglum died before seeing *his* masterpiece completed.
Feminine: Mrs. Borglum must have been proud of *her* family's work.

Case is the form of the pronoun that tells how it is used in a sentence. Subjective case pronouns usually function as subjects and predicate nouns; objective case pronouns function as objects; and possessive case pronouns often function as adjectives.

Subjective: Before Borglum began work on Mount Rushmore, *he* designed the carvings for Stone Mountain in Georgia.
Objective: Today, people remember *him* as a master craftsman.
Possessive: Mount Rushmore is *his* best-known sculpture.

IN SUMMARY

Personal pronouns reflect **person** (first, second, third), **number** (singular, plural), **gender** (masculine, feminine, neuter), and **case** (subjective, objective, possessive).

4-3 PRACTICE THE SKILL

Underline the personal pronouns in each sentence.

1. Jean Henri Dunant presented his idea for the Red Cross in *A Memory of Solferino* after he saw the wounded from the Austro-Sardinian War.

2. In this pamphlet Dunant requested aid for the wounded regardless of their nationality.

3. Delegates discussed his idea in 1864, which led to the agreement known as the First Geneva Convention; yet they did not all agree with him.

4. Clara Barton learned of the Geneva Convention while in Switzerland. Her efforts led to the beginning of the American Red Cross.

5. She wrote many stirring letters that increased support for the International Committee of the Red Cross (ICRC).

6. During World War II, soldiers relied on the ICRC to forward letters to them from their families.

7. The ICRC promoted the use of capture cards, which each prisoner sent to his family to let them know where he was.

8. Unfortunately, not all prisoners received these cards nor were all of them forwarded to their respective families.

9. Because many prisoners did not receive proper care during the war, the ICRC also sent them relief parcels, which helped them survive.

10. After the war, many Americans credited it for keeping our soldiers alive.

4-4 Review the Skill

Write ten sentences using the correct personal pronouns as indicated in the parentheses. Use the pronoun chart whenever necessary.

Example: Write a sentence about a friend. *(third person singular, feminine, subjective case)*

She is an encouragement at all times.

1. Write a sentence about soldiers. *(third person plural, objective case)*

2. Describe your history book. *(first person plural, possessive case)*

3. Tell about a leader in World War II. *(third person singular, masculine, subjective case)*

4. Ask someone what his most memorable battle is. *(second person singular, possessive case)*

5. Write a sentence about a nurse's work. *(third person singular, feminine, subjective case)*

6. Describe the campground with hundreds of soldiers. *(first person plural, subjective case)*

7. Tell about the first night in a foreign country. *(first person singular, objective case)*

8. Describe a doctor's night in a field hospital. *(third person plural, objective case)*

   _____

   _____

9. Ask someone about the most important battle in World War II. *(second person singular, subjective case)*

   _____

   _____

10. Tell about the trip home from the war. *(third person singular, objective case)*

    _____

    _____

Demonstrative Pronouns

The **demonstrative pronouns** *this, these, that,* and *those* point out persons, places, things, or ideas being discussed. *This* (singular) and *these* (plural) point to things that are near, and *that* (singular) and *those* (plural) point to things that are farther away.

> *This* is a fascinating story about Allied storage of wartime supplies.
> The Allies need *that* to prepare for the invasion of Normandy.
> Munitions, vehicles, and chewing gum—all of *these* were stored in the British countryside.
> *Those* were vital to the success of Operation Overlord.

Interrogative Pronouns

The **interrogative pronouns,** *who, whom, what, whose,* and *which,* like interrogative sentences, are used to ask questions.

> *Who* first suggested an underwater pipeline?
> Admiral Mountbatten's suggestion benefitted *whom?*
> For *what* did the Allies use the pipeline?
> *Whose* was the idea for the acronym PLUTO ("Pipeline Under the Ocean")?
> *Which* of the European countries were connected by PLUTO?

Chapter 12: Using *Who* and *Whom* Correctly
p. 250

Chapter 12: Possessive Pronouns and Contractions
p. 252

IN SUMMARY

Demonstrative pronouns *(this, that, these,* and *those)* point out persons, places, things, or ideas.

Interrogative pronouns *(who, whom, what, whose,* and *which)* are used to ask questions.

Pronouns   83

4-5 Practice the Skill

Underline the demonstrative and interrogative pronouns in the following sentences. Label the pronoun *D* (demonstrative) or *I* (interrogative).

_____ 1. What was the name of the German air force?

_____ 2. The name of that was the Luftwaffe.

_____ 3. This says *Luftwaffe* means "air weapon."

_____ 4. In World War II the command of the German forces was whose?

_____ 5. Reich Marshal Hermann Goering led some of these during the war.

_____ 6. The honor of top-scoring fighter ace in the war was given to whom?

_____ 7. Erich Hartmann received this after 352 victories.

_____ 8. Which of his relatives was also a pilot? His mother was an accomplished pilot and taught Hartmann to fly.

_____ 9. Who were some of the other pilots in the Luftwaffe?

_____ 10. One of those was First Lieutenant Bruno Dilley. The tough pilots made the Luftwaffe hard to defeat.

4-6 Review the Skill

In the blank write an appropriate demonstrative or interrogative pronoun to complete the sentence.

_____ 1. ? bombers did the Germans use during World War II?

_____ 2. One of ? was the Heinkel He 111.

_____ 3. ? had the fastest planes during World War II?

_____ 4. ? flew faster than any Allied interceptors?

_____ 5. The Arado AR 234 B-2 could do ?. However, Germany did not make many of them during the war.

_____ 6. ? was nicknamed the Blitz because of its great speed.

_____ 7. Of all the planes, ? were the hardest to shoot down.

_____ 8. ? was Germany's strategy?

_____ 9. The idea to use these planes to destroy Britain's Royal Air Force was ??

_____ 10. ? caused the defeat of the German Luftwaffe because Britain's Royal Air Force was better equipped.

84   Chapter 4

Reflexive and Intensive Pronouns

The **reflexive pronouns** and **intensive pronouns** look the same but function differently. Both types are made by adding *self* or *selves* to certain pronouns.

	Singular	Plural
First Person	myself	ourselves
Second Person	yourself	yourselves
Third Person		
neuter	itself	themselves
masculine	himself	
feminine	herself	

A reflexive pronoun always refers to the same person or thing as the subject of a sentence. Therefore, the subject is the antecedent. Reflexive pronouns function as direct objects, indirect objects, and objects of prepositions.

> During the 1940s, many men removed *themselves* from the work force to enter military service.
> Women then gave *themselves* the responsibility of filling jobs in defense factories.
> A working woman earned the nickname "Rosie the Riveter" for *herself.*

An intensive pronoun emphasizes its antecedent, a noun or pronoun already used in the sentence. Because an intensive pronoun does not function as part of the sentence pattern, it can be removed without changing the basic meaning of the sentence.

> Norman Rockwell *himself* popularized the image of Rosie the Riveter with a magazine cover illustration.
> Popular songs also mentioned Rosie *herself.*
> The phenomenon of women in the workplace outlasted the war *itself.*

Chapter 12: Reflexive and Intensive Pronouns
pp. 254-55

IN SUMMARY

A **reflexive pronoun** is used as an object and refers to the same person or thing as the subject of the sentence.

An **intensive pronoun** emphasizes a noun or pronoun already used in the sentence.

4-7 Practice the Skill

Underline the reflexive pronouns and intensive pronouns. Label each underlined pronoun *I* (intensive) or *R* (reflexive).

_____ 1. A kamikaze sacrificed himself in suicide missions during World War II.

_____ 2. The kamikazes themselves flew their explosive-filled planes into targets.

_____ 3. The pilots earned themselves the name *kamikazes*.

_____ 4. However, the plane itself was also called a kamikaze.

_____ 5. More than a thousand kamikazes gave themselves in the defense of Okinawa in 1945.

_____ 6. A kamikaze pilot would have a funeral for himself before flying on his mission.

_____ 7. The kamikaze pilot himself made the decision to sacrifice everything for the Japanese cause.

_____ 8. The pilot's mother herself must have experienced incredible emotional strain.

_____ 9. The strategy itself worked very well; many English and American soldiers died as a result.

_____ 10. You can read about it for yourself in this article.

4-8 Review the Skill

In the blank write an appropriate reflexive or intensive pronoun to complete the sentence.

_____ 1. Jeremy found _?_ in a precarious situation.

_____ 2. Leah _?_ carried the medicine into the hospital.

_____ 3. The gun seemed to get dirty all by _?_.

_____ 4. We found _?_ unprepared for battle.

_____ 5. Have you _?_ ever seen the general?

_____ 6. Fred and Jose wrote the battle strategies _?_.

_____ 7. Michelle rebuked _?_ for not writing Tom a letter.

_____ 8. Stephen _?_ flew the plane faster than anyone else.

_____ 9. Sara asked _?_ when Lance would be back from across the sea.

_____ 10. Justin _?_ lived in France for two years.

Indefinite Pronouns

Unlike other pronouns, **indefinite pronouns** usually do not refer to specific persons or things. Indefinite pronouns often do not have obvious antecedents. Most indefinite pronouns are singular; some are plural; and some can be either singular or plural depending on how they are used.

Singular				
another	each	everything	neither	one
anybody	either	little	nobody	somebody
anyone	everybody	less	no one	someone
anything	everyone	much	nothing	something

Plural				
both	few	fewer	many	several

Singular or Plural				
all	any	more	most	none / some

Everyone was affected by food shortages during wartime.
Victory gardens provided vegetables for *many*.
All were careful not to waste scarce foods.

> While *few* means "not many," *a few* means "some" or "several."
> *Little* means "not much," but *a little* means "some." *Few* and *little* have a more negative meaning than *a few* and *a little*.
> 1. Although few people shop early in the morning, a few people like to shop after breakfast.
> 2. There is little rain during a drought. It rained a little this week.

Chapter 10: Subject-Verb Agreement with Indefinite Pronouns p. 214

Chapter 11: Pronoun-Antecedent Agreement with Indefinite Pronouns pp. 231-32

IN SUMMARY

Indefinite pronouns usually do not refer to specific persons or things, nor do they usually have antecedents.

4-9 PRACTICE THE SKILL

Underline the indefinite pronouns.

1. The atom bomb is one of the nuclear weapons available in war.
2. All of these weapons receive their power from the changing of atoms into energy.
3. Torpedoes, missiles, and mines make up a few of these weapons.
4. Both of the bombs dropped in August 1945 caused mass destruction.

5. Because the bomb dropped on Hiroshima killed over seventy thousand people, many disapproved of its use.
6. However, everyone rejoiced when the war ended.
7. Since that time, no one has used nuclear weapons in battle.
8. Most of the world believes that the threat of nuclear war has kept peace among the strong nations.
9. Some believe that nuclear weapons will eventually destroy the world.
10. Even though the countries with nuclear weapons have the advantage, nobody has used these weapons recently.

4-10 Review the Skill

In the blank write an appropriate indefinite pronoun to complete the sentence.

_____ 1. _?_ of my friends sleep late on Saturdays.

_____ 2. My brother and I get up early on Saturdays. _?_ of us work around the house.

_____ 3. _?_ of us ever misses our mother's great breakfasts.

_____ 4. Later in the day, _?_ comes to our house.

_____ 5. Every week _?_ invents a new game.

_____ 6. Horsenappers, Pickle, and Foursquare are _?_ of our games.

_____ 7. _?_ remembers all of our games.

_____ 8. I still know _?_ of the rules to my favorite games by heart.

_____ 9. Almost _?_ was enthusiastically accepted.

_____ 10. _?_ loves Saturday afternoons at our house.

4-11 Use the Skill

In the blank write an appropriate pronoun as indicated in parentheses.

_____ 1. *(Interrogative)* was one of the most influential generals of World War II?

_____ 2. *(Demonstrative)* was Erwin Rommel.

_____ 3. Because of *(personal)* command of the troops in the North African desert, Rommel earned the nickname "Desert Fox."

_____ 4. *(Personal)* led the German defense of Normandy against the Allies.

_____ 5. He became *(indefinite)* of the most famous generals of World War II. Implicated in the plot to assassinate Hitler, Rommel chose death by poison instead of a trial.

_____ 6. He decided this by *(reflexive)*.

_____ 7. *(Demonstrative)* was probably Rommel's most difficult decision.

_____ 8. Hitler *(intensive)* ordered a day of mourning for Rommel.

_____ 9. *(Indefinite)* in Germany mourned his death.

_____ 10. *(Personal)* was buried with full German military honors.

4-12 Cumulative Review

Underline each pronoun. Then rewrite the paragraph, correcting the five errors of these types: fragments, comma splices, fused sentences, incorrect noun plural forms, incorrect noun possessive forms, incorrect verb forms (e.g., *writed* or *had wrote*).

A secret war occurred throughout World War II between the German and the British spies. Britain had an advantage it deciphered some of Germanys' secret codes. The code-cracking instrument named Ultra was an invaluable resource. For all of the Allied forces. Britain's new information revealed the location of the next Luftwaffe attack, the leaders themselves carefully hid the success from the Germans' discovery. The British spys belonged to a secret organization, the Special Operations Executive. Many gained necessary information for the Allied forces.

POLE VAULTING

Well-chosen pronouns keep writing from sounding choppy and redundant. Imagine trying to talk to your friends all day without using the pronoun *you*. They would soon tire of hearing their own names. Just as place cards relieve the hostess from calling everyone by name to the table, pronouns let writers refer to characters without constant repetition of their names.

- *Read the second paragraph of the excerpt, substituting* Erna Maier *for each* I *and* Wilhelm Maier *for each* he. *Rather ruins the flow, doesn't it?*

Destination Decision: Designing a Travel Brochure

"The Rockies: Come experience the majesty!"

"Open a door to the past in Williamsburg . . ."

"Antigua: a Caribbean paradise"

"A royal welcome awaits you in London."

Expressions like these are the kind you might read on the front of travel brochures. Which one seems most attractive to you? Which one makes you want to visit the place it names? What types of pictures might be included on each brochure?

The goal of a travel brochure designer is to entice you to visit a certain place. The place might be another country, a city, a recreational spot, or even the local historic home in your neighborhood. You may not have to travel thousands of miles to get there. Wherever the place is, the designer has to give it enough appeal to make you willing to spend money and to travel if necessary in order to experience it.

Travel brochures use two different means of persuasion—words and pictures. The pictures really do most of the work. But the words add meaning to the pictures and give additional information about the place, such as its geographic location, its historical background, its most popular sights, its recreational activities, and its best sources of food and lodging. What additional information might you find inside the four brochures quoted above?

If you were to design a travel brochure, what place would you choose to picture? How would you start? It would probably work best to start with pictures. Do you have actual photos of the place? If not, could you use someone else's? Or could you cut out photos from magazines or old calendars? (Of course, if you were actually going to publish your brochure, you would need to get special permission to use photos that are not your own.) If no photos of the place are available, you might consider drawing your own pictures.

Chapter 20: Precise Words
p. 425

Once you have decided which photos or pictures to use, you are ready to lay out your brochure.

- Fold a piece of paper into thirds, arranging them so that the left third is on top and the right third in the middle.
- Choose your most interesting picture for Panel 1 of the brochure. Remember that the front of the brochure is what will attract your reader first. Choose a photo that will make him take the brochure from the rack in the travel agency and open it.
- Choose your second most interesting picture for Panel 2. You will want one that draws the reader to spread out the complete brochure and find out more.
- Open your brochure completely and arrange your remaining pictures on the three inside panels. You can put a picture or two on the back of the brochure (Panel 6) if necessary. Once you have your pictures in place, you will know how much room you have left for words, or copy.

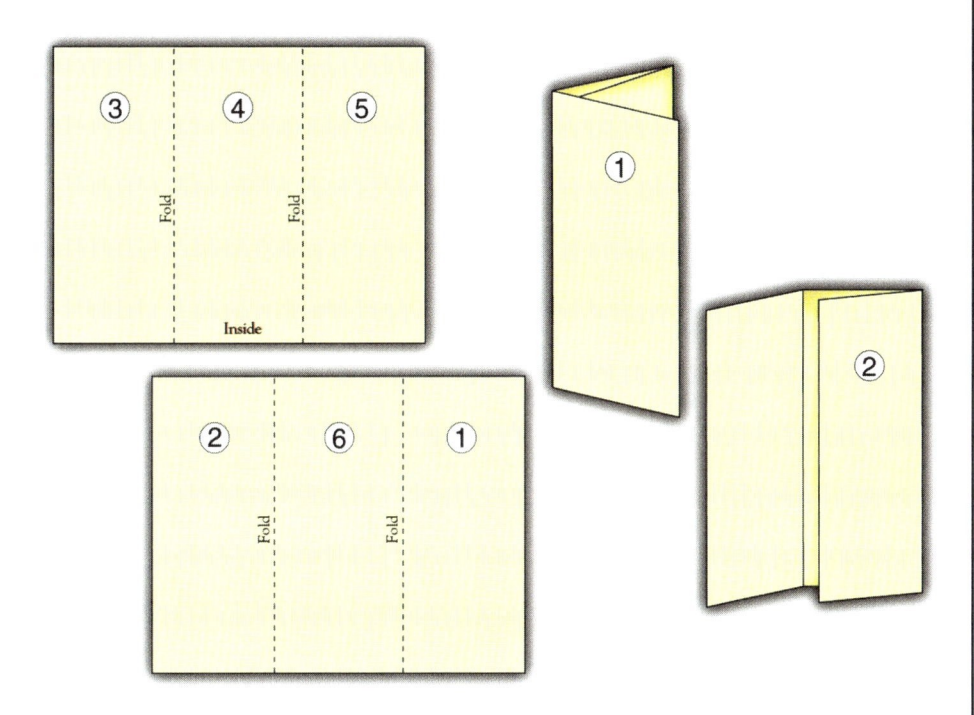

Now you are ready to write the copy to accompany the pictures. Remember that the words in a brochure add meaning to the pictures and give additional information.

- What will you say on the front of your brochure? Make your statement something that is brief, something that goes well with the picture, and something that attracts your reader's curiosity or imagination.
- Now continue your copy on Panel 2 and the three inside panels. Include the kind of additional information discussed above, and try to state it in a bright and interesting way.

Pronouns   91

Here's how one student designed his travel brochure:

Panel 1: Lake Samoset: A Place for Summer Fun!
(photo of boy water-skiing)

Panel 2: Lake Samoset is more than just a lake.
(photo of family hiking a trail near the lake)

Panel 3: Bring your whole family to Lake Samoset National Park off Highway 70, just south of Lakeville. Lake Samoset has been one of the South's most popular recreation spots for more than a century. *(small map of highway, showing Lake Samoset National Park)*

Panel 4: Lake Samoset offers a variety of recreational activities. Rent canoes, paddle-boats, and pontoon boats or bring your own boat. Enjoy water sports like skiing and tubing. Take advantage of some of the best bass and trout fishing anywhere. Explore some of the hiking trails around the lake. Or just relax and enjoy the sun and the scenery. *(photos of children canoeing, a man fishing)*

Panel 5: The Lodge, located near the entrance to the park, is a great place to find out all about the wildlife in the park. Maps are available for each of the trails. Meals and snacks are also available at the Lodge—just in case you forgot the picnic basket. *(photos of Lodge, inside and outside)*

Panel 6: So come to Lake Samoset and stay all day. Don't forget to stick around for the evening's feature presentation— the sunset. *(photo of sunset over Lake Samoset)*

Your Turn: Going Places

Choose one of these assignments.

1. Trip Down Memory Lane—Design a brochure for a place you have actually visited.

2. Dream Vacation—Design a brochure for a place you have never been but have learned or read about and would like to visit someday.

3. Flight of Fancy—Design a brochure for a fictional place or a place that would be impossible to visit (such as the planet Saturn or King Arthur's castle).

Passing the Baton
Writing Across the Curriculum

Earth Science

How often do you think about the weather? Do you think only about how it might affect your plans for the day, or do you think of it so often that your friends think you'll become a meteorologist?

Describe the weather where you live. What is the average temperature in the summer? In the winter? How much rain falls in your area? Do floods, hurricanes, or tornadoes occur where you live? Does your school give special safety training sessions for these weather events? Think about how the weather affects you personally. Have you recently had to cancel an activity because of weather? Would you say that the weather occasionally affects your personality?

HISTORY OF THE ENGLISH LANGUAGE

Early Modern English

The King James Version of the Bible was produced during the Early Modern English period (approximately A.D. 1500-1660). This edition contains archaic word forms such as *saith, goest, thee,* and *thine*. Learning these word forms can help us to understand the Bible and to appreciate the dignity and beauty of our language as it was in earlier times.

Chapter 5

Adjectives

Up a Road Slowly
by Irene Hunt

Grammar

"My stepmother came to her classes each day beautifully groomed, poised, alert, and with a sweet-sour quality to her comments that made them palatable in spite of an occasional sting. I was quite proud of her, really, although for a long time the memory of Laura's room and of my lonely, bewildered feeling that morning in the breakfast nook tinged my feeling for her ever so slightly. But I couldn't deny the fact that she was a charming person and an exceptionally fine teacher. There was no loafing in Mrs. Trelling's classes; we had to dig ideas out of our own minds instead of reference books; we were treated to no pablum feedings of "true-false" or "fill-in-the-blank" tests. And our themes were not devoted to accounts of a vacation trip or a résumé of *Silas Marner*. Alicia liked originality and independence of thinking; sometimes, however, she had considerable difficulty in discovering either among the adolescents who sat before her.

I remember how fresh and radiant she looked that morning, her blue eyes cool and smiling under her smooth black brows. It occurred to me that my father's wife was still very happy after almost three years, and I envied her a little."

- *What is your opinion of the stepmother after reading this excerpt? What words give you this impression?*
- *What is your opinion of the speaker? What words convey her attitude?*

Probably most of the words you chose were adjectives. Words like *bewildered*, *poised*, *radiant*, *cool*, and *charming* add a great deal to your understanding of the characters. Describe someone you really admire. Did you use adjectives? It is almost impossible to describe anything without them.

Adjectives

In Chapter 1 you read that a sentence is a group of words that contains essential parts, such as the subject and the verb, and that expresses a complete thought. Sentences can be structured in such a way that all they contain are the subject and the verb. In fact, when you were learning how to read, you probably read a lot of these kinds of sentences: John ran; Sue sang; Spot barked. Now those sentences seem boring and uninteresting to you. You want to read sentences that have excitement and more detail. One way to create more exciting sentences is to add adjectives.

An **adjective** is a word that modifies a noun or pronoun. Adjectives give information and details that make a noun's meaning clear. Adjectives often answer the questions *which one? what kind? how many?* and *whose?* about the words they modify.

Which one? Shelby chose *this* topic.
What kind? She will research *frontier* teachers and classrooms.
How many? Mr. Gladstone will require *five* sources for *the* paper.
Whose? *His* class is *Shelby's favorite* class.

The adjectives *this, frontier, five, the, his, Shelby's,* and *favorite* help to create a better picture of the topic, the teachers, the classrooms, the sources, and the class.

Most adjectives come just before the nouns they modify. Some adjectives come after a linking verb; these adjectives are called **predicate adjectives**. A predicate adjective always describes the subject of the sentence.

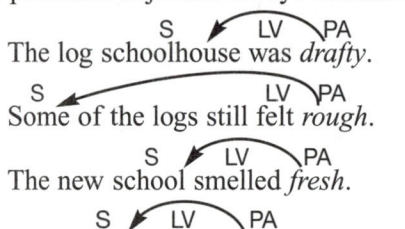

The log schoolhouse was *drafty*.
Some of the logs still felt *rough*.
The new school smelled *fresh*.
The children were *thankful* for a place to learn.

To determine whether a word is an adjective, ask yourself the adjective questions or use the adjective test frame. Any word that will fit into the frame can be used as an adjective. However, not all adjectives will fit the frame. For example, the words *a, an,* and *the* do not fit the test frame but are considered adjectives. Ultimately, if a word modifies a noun, it is an adjective.

The _____ thing (or person) is very _____.

The *cold* water is very *cold*.

The *kind* boy is very *kind*.

To diagram an adjective, write it on a slanted line beneath the word it modifies. Look at the diagram for the following sentence: **The substitute teacher asked several difficult questions.**

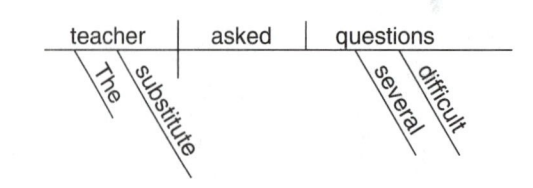

Chapter 3: Linking Verbs, Predicate Adjectives
p. 47

Chapter 7: Prepositional Phrases
p. 135

96   Chapter 5

ETYMOLOGY

Modificare, "to make a measurement," is the source for the verb *modify*. A modifier is a word that modifies, measures, or limits the meaning of the word modified.

IN SUMMARY

Adjectives modify nouns and usually tell which one, what kind, how many, or whose. Most adjectives will fit the adjective test frame.

5-1 PRACTICE THE SKILL

Underline the adjectives. Draw an arrow from each adjective to the noun it modifies.

1. Modern schools are different from earlier schools.
2. America's first students did not have nutritious meals at school.
3. Sometimes three age groups shared a classroom.
4. Early schools lacked elaborate playgrounds for children.
5. The first students in American schools often traveled great distances to school.
6. Many schools now provide bus transportation.
7. This transportation protects students from harsh weather.
8. Some modern schools use air conditioners during warm weather.
9. Classrooms may have two computers for students' use.
10. Schools' equipment have changed.

5-2 REVIEW THE SKILL

Underline the fifteen adjectives. Draw an arrow from each adjective to the noun it modifies.

Example: The old jalopy jerked down the bumpy street.

Anne Mansfield Sullivan provides an excellent illustration of the commitment that teachers need. In 1887 Sullivan began educating deaf and blind Helen Keller. Since previous experiences had allowed her to learn the manual alphabet, Sullivan seemed a likely candidate for tutor. Before beginning to teach Helen, Sullivan earned an exemplary record in school and faced painful surgeries to re-establish sight in her weak eyes.

5-3 Practice the Skill

Write an appropriate adjective to answer the question in parentheses.

_____ 1. There are ? people in my English class. *(how many?)*

_____ 2. English class is ? . *(what kind?)*

_____ 3. In class I sit in the ? row. *(which one?)*

_____ 4. My ? friends and I worked on a research paper together. *(how many?)*

_____ 5. We wrote a(n) ? paper about Charles Dickens. *(what kind?)*

_____ 6. We went to ? house to work on the project. *(whose?)*

_____ 7. For ? hours we worked on the paper. *(how many?)*

_____ 8. We realized that we needed ? material. *(how much?)*

_____ 9. The ? page was finally finished. *(which one?)*

_____ 10. It was worth all the hard work when we all received a(n) ? grade. *(what kind?)*

5-4 Review the Skill

Write an appropriate adjective to answer the question in parentheses.

_____ 1. After school Jason and ? friends play basketball. *(whose?)*

_____ 2. On days without much homework, they have ? time for sports. *(how much?)*

_____ 3. Joe is the ? basketball player. *(which one?)*

_____ 4. Basketball is Jeremy's ? game. *(which one?)*

_____ 5. Dan makes ? baskets during the game. *(how many?)*

_____ 6. Jason is a(n) ? player. Sometimes he guards Dan. *(what kind?)*

_____ 7. Then Dan makes ? baskets. *(how many?)*

_____ 8. Jeremy is ? competitive than Jason or Dan. He plays just for fun. *(how much?)*

_____ 9. After the game, the ? boys need a break. *(what kind?)*

_____ 10. The boys take ? minutes for rest before time for homework. *(how many?)*

Comparing with Adjectives

Sometimes the need arises to compare two or more nouns. We make comparisons by changing the form of the adjectives. Adjectives that can be compared answer the question *what kind?* and come just before the nouns they modify. They have **positive, comparative,** and **superlative** forms. The positive form is the stem form of the adjective. The comparative form is used when we compare two people or things, and the superlative form is used when we compare three or more people or things. Most **regular adjectives** add *er* to the positive form to make the comparative form and *est* to the positive to make the superlative form. For adjectives that would sound awkward with *er* or *est,* we use *more* and *most* before the adjectives.

Positive	Comparative	Superlative
fresh	fresher	freshest
friendly	friendlier	friendliest
amazing	more amazing	most amazing

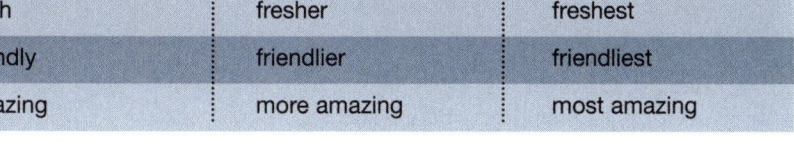

Chapter 13: Adjectives and Adverbs in Comparisons p. 276

June is hot in Georgia. July is hotter, but August is the hottest month of all.

Alana was busy with her homework in her room. Mother was busier cooking supper in the kitchen. However, the baby was the busiest: he was unraveling a quilt in the den.

Mrs. Hall's lemon chess pie was delicious, and Cammie's coconut bars were even more delicious. But Mom's chocolate cake was the most delicious dessert at the church picnic.

Some adjectives cannot be compared by adding *er/est* or *more/most* to the stem form. These are **irregular adjectives.**

ETYMOLOGY
Irregular is from the Latin prefix *in,* meaning "not," and *regula,* meaning "rule." If something is irregular, it does not go by the rule.

Unfortunately, irregular adjectives do not follow simple rules for forming the comparative and superlative. These adjectives often have entirely different forms to show comparison, or they may not change at all.

Positive	Comparative	Superlative
good	better	best
well	better	best
bad	worse	worst

Adjectives that can be compared (descriptive adjectives) will always fit the test frame. However, be sure to use the positive form of the word when using the test frame. Failure to use the stem form can result in an illogical sentence.

Wrong: The *weariest* person is very *weariest*.
Right: The *weary* person is very *weary*.

Remember to consult a dictionary whenever you are in doubt about the correct form or correct spelling.

Some adjectives cannot be compared. For example, the word *dead* means "no longer alive." A thing or person is either alive or not alive; it cannot be less alive than something else; therefore, it cannot be *deader* or *deadest*. Other words that cannot be compared are *unique, perfect, eternal,* and *round*.

In Summary

Regular adjectives show comparison by adding *er/est* or *more/most* to the stem form of the adjective.

Irregular adjectives may have entirely different forms to show comparison.

5-5 Practice the Skill

Underline the correct form of the adjective in parentheses.

1. The Ivy League was formed because of a desire for a *(big, biggest)* football league.
2. The reputation of Ivy League schools is *(prestigious, more prestigious)* than that of other colleges.
3. The *(more famous, most famous)* Ivy League schools are Harvard, Yale, and Princeton.
4. Harvard is the *(older, oldest)* institution of higher learning in the United States.
5. Yale is the second oldest institution of higher learning in the United States, but Yale is *(younger, youngest)* when compared to Harvard.
6. Yale has one of the *(bigger, biggest)* libraries in the world.
7. Yale has a *(small, smaller)* enrollment than most of the other Ivy League schools.

8. The old brick buildings and spacious design make Harvard's campus *(beautiful, most beautiful)*.

9. One of the *(newer, newest)* additions to Princeton's campus is the Plasma Physics Laboratory.

10. Although they are more famous, Ivy League schools are not necessarily *(good, better)* than other schools.

5-6 REVIEW THE SKILL

Write the correct form of the adjective in parentheses.

_____ 1. An ? invention than some of today's teaching equipment, the chalkboard has been an instrument of learning since its first widespread appearance in Europe during the 1600s. *(old, comparative)*

_____ 2. The chalkboard or one of its counterparts exists in nearly every American school, even in the ? of all settings. *(poor, superlative)*

_____ 3. Teachers consider their chalkboards to be ? teaching devices. *(essential, positive)*

_____ 4. Is there a tool ? to a math teacher than the chalkboard? *(helpful, comparative)*

_____ 5. Chalkboards may still be the ? tool used in education. *(popular, superlative)*

_____ 6. The chalkboard is popular because it is ? . *(reliable, positive)*

_____ 7. The chalkboard is ? than other classroom equipment since it functions even during a power loss. *(dependable, comparative)*

_____ 8. The chalkboard is perhaps the ? to maintain of all educational equipment. *(cheap, superlative)*

_____ 9. Traditional chalkboards appear black or green, though some boards may display ? pigments than others. *(dark, comparative)*

_____ 10. Chalkboards are one of the ? classroom inventions of all time. *(good, superlative)*

Adjectives   101

Chapter 14: Other Troublesome Words
p. 287

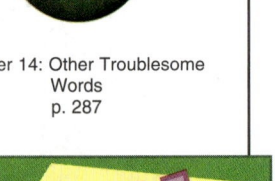

Articles

The words *a*, *an*, and *the* are **articles,** the most common type of adjective. *The* is a **definite article** because it points to specific things. *A* and *an* are **indefinite articles** because they refer to nonspecific things.

Sonny picked up a leaf from the ground. *(any leaf)*
He was looking for an orange one. *(any orange leaf)*
His leaf was from the maple tree in the front yard. *(a specific tree)*

Use *a* before a consonant sound (*b, c, d, f, g,* etc.): Myong bought a new car. Before a vowel sound, *a* changes to *an* (vowels: *a, e, i, o, u*): Hanna purchased an old car.

IN SUMMARY

The **articles** *a, an,* and *the* are the most common adjectives.
A and *an* are indefinite articles.
The is a definite article.

5-7 PRACTICE THE SKILL

Underline the articles.

1. The preeminent example of a master teacher is Jesus Christ.
2. Jesus is an excellent example of a master teacher for several reasons.
3. Perhaps the characteristic that best distinguishes Christ as a master teacher is His omniscience.
4. The best teacher must have complete understanding of his students.
5. Christ possesses the ultimate understanding of His students because He is their Creator.
6. Jesus taught His disciples based on an unlimited knowledge of their innermost thoughts as well as an accurate interpretation of their outward behavior.
7. Other qualities that distinguish Jesus as an extraordinary teacher are His sinlessness and His perfect knowledge of truth.
8. Christ's divine nature keeps Him from making those errors made by an imperfect human teacher.
9. Jesus was never an unfair judge of His students' performances or a poor example for His disciples to follow.
10. Christ's instruction is perfect because He teaches His followers the Word of God.

5-8 Review the Skill

Underline the ten articles.

Some of the earliest textbooks were in the form of wall paintings called murals and picture writings called hieroglyphics. People learned how to write using picture forms such as an upside-down fish or a three-armed man. The number of strange characters representing single words made hieroglyphics a complicated system to remember. Imagine having a writing system composed of thousands of picture symbols. The language studies class would be the longest class of the day!

Possessives

Possessives as Adjectives

A **possessive** is a noun form or a pronoun form that shows ownership. Most often, possessives function as adjectives. A possessive functioning as an adjective answers the question *whose?* about the noun it modifies.

Possessive Pronouns	Singular	Plural
First person	my, mine	our, ours
Second person	your, yours	your, yours
Third person	its, his, her, hers	their, theirs

Possessive nouns and possessive pronouns usually signal that a noun will follow in the sentence.

> *Aaron's* school has a good hockey team.
> *His* school colors are orange and red.
> Sometimes the players tease *their* coach, Mr. Brown, about the colors.
> They call themselves "*Brown's* Clowns."

The possessive noun *Aaron's* modifies the noun *school* to show whose school has a good team. The possessive pronoun *his* modifies the noun *colors* to show whose colors are orange and red. *Their* modifies *coach*, and *Brown's* modifies *Clowns*. Most often possessive nouns and pronouns function as adjectives.

To diagram a possessive used as an adjective, follow the diagram for any other adjective: **Aaron's school has a good hockey team.**

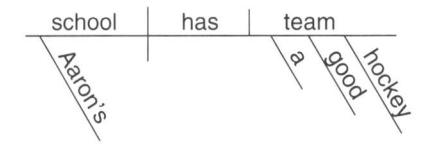

Chapter 2: Forming the Possessives of Nouns
p. 26

Chapter 4: Possessive Pronouns
pp. 80-81

Adjectives 103

If a possessive noun is modified by at least one other adjective, the possessive and its modifier form a possessive phrase. The entire possessive phrase shows possession.

His sister's school plays t-ball instead.
Each parent supplies *his child's* bat and ball.

Notice that *sister's* alone is not the complete possessive. The entire possessive phrase *his sister's* tells us precisely whose school plays t-ball. Likewise, *his child's* is a complete possessive phrase. A possessive phrase is diagrammed in a way slightly different from a single-word possessive used as an adjective. The adjective that precedes the possessive word is attached to the possessive itself rather than to the main noun. Look at the diagram for this sentence: **His sister's school plays t-ball instead.**

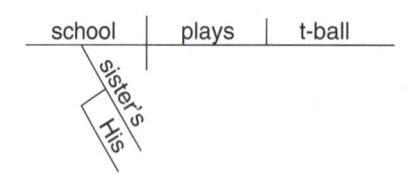

```
  school  |  plays  |  t-ball
    \sister's
      \His
```

5-9 Practice the Skill

Underline the possessive nouns and pronouns functioning as adjectives.

1. Many old schoolhouses had their own pot-bellied stoves.
2. The school's stove was important.
3. The stove was the teacher's responsibility.
4. The little stove provided the room's only warmth.
5. The students' schoolroom chores included several stove duties.
6. Some students chopped the stove's wood.
7. Sometimes the students tended its fire.
8. Others cleaned the schoolhouse's chimney.
9. My school did not have an old pot-bellied stove.
10. Today our schools have central heat.

5-10 Review the Skill

Write an appropriate possessive noun or pronoun.

_____ 1. Each morning, my _?_ alarm clock rings before I am ready to get up.

_____ 2. _?_ mother always knocks on the door to make sure my brother and I are getting ready for school.

_____ 3. After scrambling around to find something suitable to wear, I hurriedly eat some of _?_ favorite cereal.

_____ 4. Today our teacher told us about the _?_ lifestyles in colonial times.

_____   5. In those days the _?_ call at dawn probably woke up the entire farm.

_____   6. Many of the children had to milk all of the _?_ cows before breakfast.

_____   7. Sometimes the _?_ feed had unwanted creatures that needed to be scooped out.

_____   8. Because of the _?_ one room, all of the classes were taught together.

_____   9. The _?_ desks were hard and uncomfortable.

_____   10. Nevertheless _?_ teachers taught them to be thankful.

Independent Possessives

Sometimes, a possessive noun or pronoun can replace an entire noun phrase.

> *His little sister's school* plays t-ball instead.
> *Hers* plays t-ball instead.

In the second sentence above, the possessive pronoun *hers* does not modify any noun in the sentence. Instead, the word *hers* replaces the entire phrase *his little sister's school*. When a possessive acts in place of a noun or a noun phrase, it is called an **independent possessive.** Independent possessives are not adjectives, because they replace nouns instead of modifying them.

> *Sarkis's favorite subject* is math.
> What is *your* favorite?
> *Mine* is science.

In the first sentence, the possessive noun *Sarkis's* is an adjective because it modifies the noun *subject*. In the second sentence, the possessive pronoun *your* is an adjective that modifies *favorite*. In the third sentence, *mine* does not modify a noun. It is an independent possessive functioning as the subject of the sentence.

> One student closed *her desk lid*. *(noun phrase)*
> Another student opened *hers*. *(independent possessive)*
>
> *Their coach* was the best. *(noun phrase)*
> *Theirs* was an excellent teacher and leader. *(independent possessive)*
>
> I can't find *my pencil*. *(noun phrase)*
> Could I borrow *yours*? *(independent possessive)*

Adjectives

Because an independent possessive replaces a noun or pronoun and therefore functions as a noun or pronoun, it should be diagrammed according to the function of the word or phrase it replaces. Look at the following sentence: **Another student opened hers.**

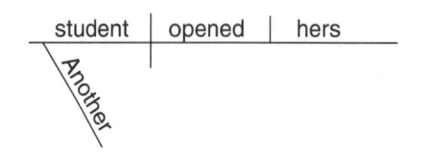

```
  student  |  opened  |  hers
   \
    \Another
```

IN SUMMARY

Possessives are adjectives made from nouns or pronouns to show ownership. They signal that a noun will follow.

Independent possessives are not adjectives; they replace nouns and function as nouns or pronouns.

5-11 PRACTICE THE SKILL

Underline the possessives. Label each underlined word *Adj* (adjective) or *IP* (independent possessive).

1. The stories of many men of faith are recorded in the Bible; however, these men's teachers are not well known.
2. Paul's was Gamaliel.
3. Luke's statement in Acts 5:34 describes Gamaliel as a "doctor of the law."
4. Gamaliel's expertise in the law was widely acknowledged.
5. His was a valued legal opinion.
6. The New Testament's record of Gamaliel shows that he was a man of courage.
7. Gamaliel's speech saved the apostles from death but not from punishment.
8. Theirs was a severe beating.
9. The apostles' delivery of the gospel was able to continue partly because of Gamaliel.
10. Although he did good things, Paul's teacher was probably a lost man.

> **5-12 REVIEW THE SKILL**

Underline the possessive nouns and pronouns functioning as adjectives. Circle the independent possessives.

If your local church holds Sunday school, it is performing a ministry begun largely by Robert Raikes. Raikes was a journalist for the *Gloucester Journal* in England. Raikes's Sunday schools developed from his observations of prisons. England's were full of children. The children laboring in factories had no time for school. If a young girl worked in a factory, her only day off was Sunday. When not at work, these children often created trouble. Raikes knew those children could end up in the prison system. He believed a children's school would lessen their opportunity for mischief. Raikes started the first Sunday school in Sooty Alley, Gloucester, in 1780. The schools offered reading instruction so that children could read the Bible. The schools' curriculum also included morals, manners, and even writing and arithmetic. Though others' attempts at this type of work had failed, Raikes's succeeded and eventually spread to other countries.

More Adjectives

Sometimes nouns and pronouns act like adjectives when they modify another noun. These words are functioning as adjectives only when they modify nouns; therefore, when these words are functioning as subjects, predicate nouns, or objects, they are not adjectives. When you see a word that may be a noun, a pronoun, or an adjective, determine how the word is functioning in the sentence.

  Adjective: Paul attends *this* school.
  Pronoun: *This* is the best local Christian school.

  Adjective: North Park Christian School has a great *debate* program.
  Noun: Both Paul and his brother will participate in the upcoming *debate*.

  Adjective: The brothers will enjoy *that* tournament.
  Pronoun: They will enter the Lincoln-Douglas category; they are good at *that*.

  Adjective: The tournament awards a best *speaker* trophy.
  Noun: Either brother could be named the best *speaker*.

Chapter 4: Demonstrative Pronouns
p. 83

Notice that a noun that functions as an adjective always comes right before the noun that it modifies, after any other adjective that may be there. In English, we would never talk about "a debate great program" or "the speaker best trophy."

5-13 Practice the Skill

Label each underlined word *N* (noun), *P* (pronoun), or *Adj* (adjective).

_____ 1. Elizabeth I's tutor was <u>a</u> man named Roger Ascham.

_____ 2. Ascham was responsible for training the princess to become the <u>queen</u>.

_____ 3. Ascham voiced his <u>educational</u> opinions in the *Schoolmaster*.

_____ 4. The subject of <u>this</u> was the education of the children of the social elite.

_____ 5. <u>One</u> of Ascham's famous topics was how to develop a harmonious individual.

_____ 6. His second book does not discuss <u>education</u>.

_____ 7. *Toxophilus* praises the sport of <u>archery</u>.

_____ 8. <u>Archery</u> fans find his book insightful and amusing.

_____ 9. <u>That</u> was the man who taught the future queen.

_____ 10. Ascham was also <u>secretary</u> to Elizabeth's sister, Queen Mary I.

5-14 Review the Skill

Label each italicized word *N* (noun), *P* (pronoun), or *Adj* (adjective).

_____ 1. Plymouth Plantation is a reconstruction of an early *settler* town.

_____ 2. *Many* students visit it while studying American history.

_____ 3. The people who work there act as though they were the first *settlers*.

_____ 4. They try to speak in the vernacular of two *hundred* years ago.

_____ 5. *That* requires a drastic change in their thought processes.

_____ 6. *Many* ask the actors questions about their kids.

_____ 7. The *actors* will give an answer about their goats and sheep.

_____ 8. Actors portraying *Indians* come into the plantation to sell furs and buy provisions.

_____ 9. Barnyard smells and the aroma of homemade *bread* are overpowering.

_____ 10. Plymouth Plantation is a great place to learn *historical* facts.

Proper Adjectives

Like nouns, which can be common or proper, adjectives can be common or proper. **Proper adjectives** are adjectives that are made from proper nouns. Some proper nouns change form to become adjectives; other proper nouns do not change form. If a word modifies a noun, it is an adjective (even if its form does not change).

> Many *Hawaiian* farmers grow pineapples.
> Fajitas are one of my favorite *Mexican* foods.
> We usually visit my grandparents during *Christmas* vacation.
> Have you heard the saying, "*April* showers bring *May* flowers"?

Chapter 2: Common and Proper Nouns p. 29

Chapter 15: Capitalizing Proper Adjectives p. 313

> Proper adjectives cannot be made plural in English.
> **Wrong:** The Americans students enjoyed learning about other cultures.
> **Right:** The American students enjoyed learning about other cultures.

IN SUMMARY

Proper adjectives are adjectives made from proper nouns.

5-15 PRACTICE THE SKILL

Underline the proper adjectives.

1. American education reflects the influence of many individuals from the past.
2. For instance, some instructors follow the ancient Socratic method of teaching by asking questions.
3. Geometry students learn the principles of Euclidean geometry.
4. They apply the Pythagorean theorem when working with triangles.
5. Physics instructors use the Kelvin scale, a precise means of determining temperature.
6. Most chemistry labs are equipped with Bunsen burners.
7. Many students in literature class have read a Shakespearean sonnet.

8. Their teacher may spend several weeks discussing authors of the Victorian period.
9. Geography or history classes study nations controlled by Marxist thought.
10. Everyone in health class should learn about current Red Cross life-saving techniques.

5-16 REVIEW THE SKILL

Write an appropriate proper adjective.

_____ 1. Education in ? schools often includes studying a foreign language.

_____ 2. Even many ? schools offer more than one language course.

_____ 3. The ? language and the ? language are two common choices for study in America.

_____ 4. In other parts of the world, however, the ? language is the foreign language being studied.

_____ 5. Many ? and ? students study this language.

_____ 6. Some schools consider the ? language an important one to study.

_____ 7. ? or ? knowledge would help any student of the Bible.

_____ 8. Students in the fields of medicine or music often choose to learn German, since ? influence is so strong in those areas.

_____ 9. Foreign language students often experience part of the culture of the country they are studying; for example, a student learning Japanese might try some exotic ? foods.

_____ 10. Many students of a foreign language respond to the ? command to "Go . . . into all the world."

5-17 USE THE SKILL

Look at the picture at the beginning of the chapter. On your own paper, write three sentences about the picture. If any of your sentences have adjectives, underline them and label the kind of adjective (proper, possessive, or an article). If none of your sentences have adjectives, can you find a place to add one?

5-18 CUMULATIVE REVIEW

Label each italicized word N (noun), V (verb), P (pronoun), or Adj (adjective).

_____ 1. Clara Barton is *famous* as a wartime nurse and as founder of the American Red Cross.

_____ 2. However, Clara *was* also a dedicated schoolteacher.

_____ 3. Others encouraged young Clara about opportunities for her as a *teacher*.

_____ 4. Clara studied diligently, and *her* examiners gave her an excellent evaluation.

_____ 5. Clara once *shocked* her students with her unexpected participation in their recess games.

_____ 6. For twenty years, *she* taught school in New England.

_____ 7. At one time, Clara volunteered her services to *a* New Jersey town.

_____ 8. This town started a public school for local children, especially for *some* of the town's boys.

_____ 9. These previously idle youths received an education because of *Clara's* sacrifice.

_____ 10. Certainly, Clara's hard *work* as a teacher also helped her later with her work in the Red Cross.

POLE VAULTING

Look again at the excerpt from *Up a Road Slowly*. Although adjectives are not as crucial to meaning as nouns, verbs, and pronouns, a skillful writer interweaves them so well that they cannot be lifted from the text without the ideas unraveling.

- *What unusual adjectives does Irene Hunt use in this passage?*
- *What does the adjective* sweet-sour *contribute to your impression of the stepmother and of the speaker's opinion of the stepmother?*
- *What is pablum? How does the speaker's using it as an adjective convey her feelings about true-false tests?*

All the News: Reporting a Story

Some people think writing for a newspaper must be all excitement, with late-night car chases and midday bank robberies. Others think that it must be terribly boring, typing out stories in the same format every afternoon and having to start over on a whole new story when the ink on the last one isn't even dry. News writing has its mundane tasks and its moments of high drama, but like all other crafts, it has some basic rules and skills and plenty of room for creativity.

Chapter 20: Drafting
pp. 413-23

News Stories: The Basic Form

Almost any news piece follows the same general outline: it has an opening, called a **lead**; a **body**; and a **conclusion.**

The Lead

The classic lead, a summary, includes the "five Ws" (*who, what, when, where,* and *why*) and sometimes a *how.*

> Last night, Berta Marks was parking her car at her home on Parley Drive during a thunderstorm when lightning struck a large oak tree, causing it to fall through the roof of the garage.

Another kind of opening is the suspended lead, in which the writer holds back some information in order to give the rest of the story an extra flair.

> **Lead:** James Wilson may want to think twice before he calls out the police force again.
>
> **Body:** Last Thursday Wilson called the city police to report that his car had been stolen. When officers arrived, they noticed a car matching the description of Wilson's half a block down the street. Upon investigation, they discovered that it was indeed Wilson's car and that it had crashed into a fence, engine running.
>
> After questioning Wilson and witnesses, police determined that Wilson, having had a heated argument at his office, had gone inside his house to get a bill of sale as proof in his dispute and had left his car running.
>
> **Conclusion:** Wilson was charged with negligence, endangering pedestrians, and destruction of private property.

Can you see how using the summary lead would have diminished the flavor of this piece?

The Body

Bodies of news stories usually need to provide either additional facts or an account of events leading to the main news item.

> **Facts:** Three separate fires downtown last night resulted in two injuries and thousands of dollars in property damage.
>
> The first fire occurred at 10:30 P.M. in the Daniel Building. Tom Jenkins, the night watchman, alerted the fire department and tried to put out the small blaze himself. Officials believe the fire started in a waste container in the basement. Jenkins was treated for minor burns to the hands and wrists and was released.
>
> The second fire started at approximately 1:15 A.M. in the warehouse . . .
>
> **Events:** Jenny Fielding was rescued last evening by an unknown good Samaritan in Edgerton Plaza.

Fielding was walking her two German shepherds at 7:00 P.M. when a cat darted across her path. The normally well-behaved shepherds lunged after the cat, pulling Fielding off the sidewalk into a busy parking lot.

As Fielding tried to control her dogs and extricate herself from entangling leashes, a passing driver threw a hamburger and fries at the dogs. The dogs immediately stopped for the treat, and Fielding got them under control and took them home.

"I don't know who she was," says Fielding, referring to the driver who had helped her, "but she had a bumper sticker that said 'Cats Are People Too.'"

The Conclusion

Conclusions summarize the story and bring it to a single focus. Well-planned conclusions may reflect the leads in some way. For example, in the story about James Wilson, the conclusion puts a slightly comic twist on the lead—calling the police to report a stolen car and getting cited for negligence instead.

Conclusions can offer a clue to possible unknown outcomes. "Police are searching for a man in his late thirties with a crewcut and glasses" implies that there will be more to this story when the police find the man.

The Basic Procedure

Gathering Facts

News writing requires research, both in and out of books. Sometimes interviews with people will provide all a writer needs to fill out his news article. Sometimes he will have to do some old-fashioned library digging to get names and dates and other material crucial to the integrity of his writing.

Planning the Piece

Choosing the best way to present the story will ensure its being clear. For example, using the suspended lead for a piece on the four bills up for a vote in City Council will only leave the reader puzzled when there is no "punch" ending, which such a lead usually signals.

It's also important to have all the information in hand before the writing begins. Sometimes, of course, a vital bit of information will escape the best reporter—but it should never be one of the five Ws.

Writing the Article

Once a writer has collected his material and decided on his approach, he has only to write the rough draft, revise it, and check it for errors. As in any writing, news writing that is correct and clear gains respect and attention.

Your Turn: Getting the Scoop

Find a newsworthy story in your school or neighborhood and become a reporter. Collect information—uphold good manners and ethics at all times!—and choose your format. Perhaps your class would like to produce an entire newspaper. If your school or some local organization already has a newspaper, choose your story with an eye to getting it published.

Chapter 20: Showing, Not Telling
p. 425

Chapter 20: Revising, Proofreading
pp. 423-27

Chapter 20: Publishing
p. 428

Chapter 6

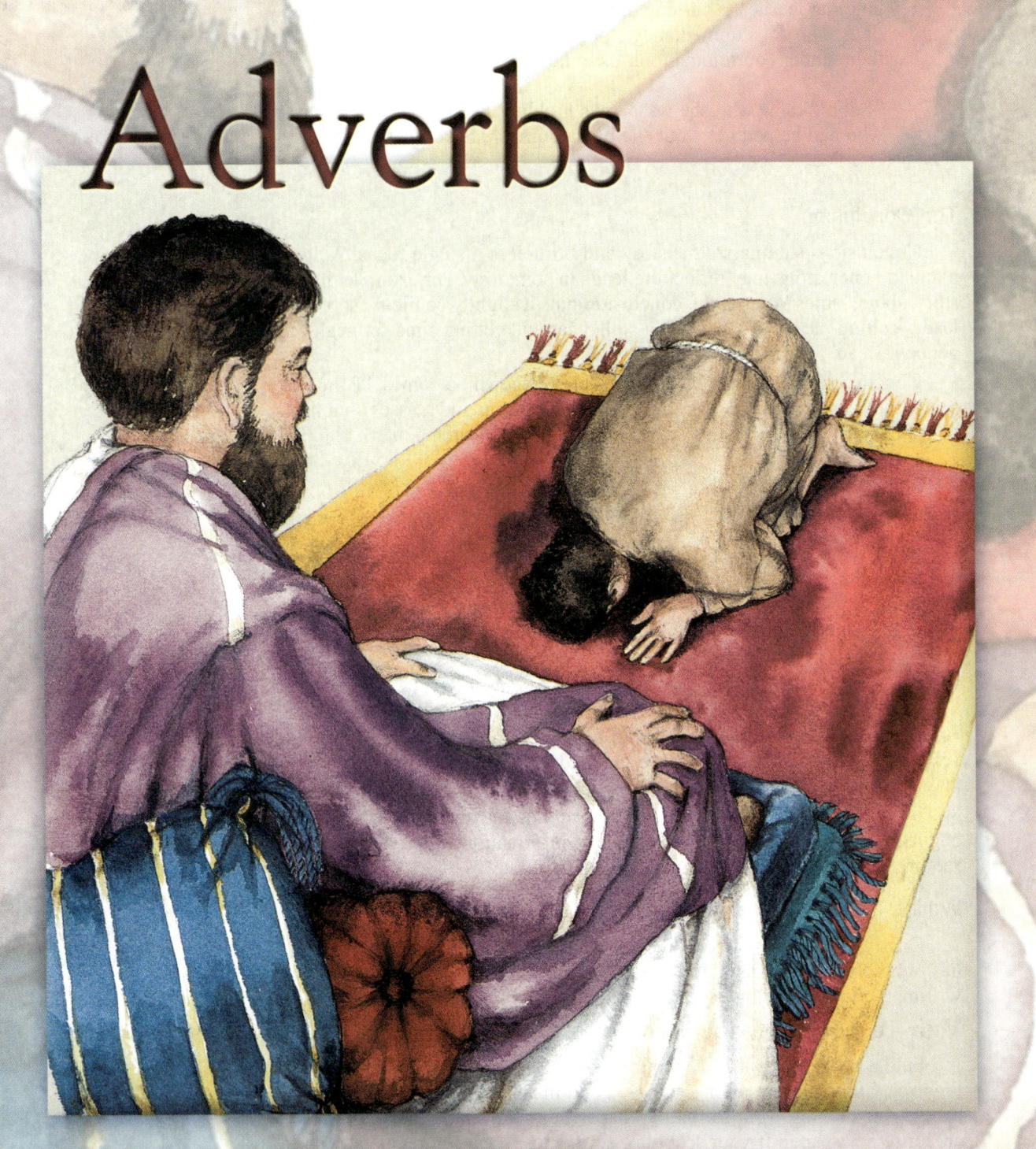

Adverbs

Twice Freed
by Patricia St. John

Grammar

"Gold cannot disappear without hands," said Philemon at last, "and you knew the price. Take him away, Janus, and do it quickly."

Archippus suddenly stepped forward. He did not look at Onesimus but stood in front of his father, hands clasped, pleading.

"Father, Father," he cried, "not branding. He's only young. Father, pardon him. Let him be beaten with rods, but not branding!"

His father hesitated.

Archippus, spurning the old man out of his way with his foot, fell on his knees before Philemon. "Oh, Father, have mercy."

A soft voice at his side made Philemon turn. His beautiful wife, Apphia, had laid her hand on his arm and spoken timidly, for it was not her place to enter into judgment.

"My husband, he is your slave who serves you in front of our guests. Do you want him spoiled and disfigured? As our son says, he is young. Let the rods teach him. If it happens again, he will be branded."

Philemon smiled at her. He never could refuse her anything, and her gentle wishes were the law of the home. He turned back to Onesimus and spoke sternly.

"You are fortunate! Render thanks to the gods for a merciful mistress, and take heed to yourself in the future. Now, go with Janus and be taught by the rods. Silence, Master Goldsmith, and be gone! You shall be given a gold piece to make up for the trouble my slave has caused you."

- *What details in this passage indicate a biblical setting?*
- *Read the passage without using any of the words that end in* ly. *What is lost?*

Contrast the effect when the word *silence* is shouted and when it is whispered. How does the tone of the word change? Adverbs often act as "volume controls" for the actions of characters. How does the word *quickly* function in this passage? How does *timidly* function? A good writer is constantly adjusting the volume of his sentences to get the exact tone he wants.

Adverbs

Adverbs modify verbs, adjectives, and other adverbs and answer certain questions about those words. Adverbs that modify verbs usually tell *when, where,* or *how* about those verbs. Adverbs that modify adjectives and other adverbs tell *to what extent* about those words. Adverbs qualify, strengthen, or weaken the words they modify.

> *Adverb* comes from the Latin *ad-*, meaning "additional," and *verbum*, meaning "word." *Adverb* literally means "additional word."

When? We arrived *later*.

Where? Darcy waited *outside* for the rest of the group.

How? They proceeded *slowly* to the edge of the cliff.

To What Extent? Mark felt *slightly* fatigued after the long trip.

Negative Word *Not*

The word *not* is an adverb. It shows negative meaning and does not answer any of the common adverb questions. Unlike other adverbs, *not* can be connected to the main verb as a whole *(cannot)* or in a contraction *(can't)*.

Gretchen will *not* participate in the upcoming regional debate.

She is *not* able to debate on the assigned topic.

She can*not* be expected to travel.

It is*n't* that she has*n't* prepared—she has broken her leg!

Ly Words

Many adverbs are made from other words. The most common way to form an adverb is to add *ly* to an adjective.

slow + *ly* → slowly
quick + *ly* → quickly
clear + *ly* → clearly
fond + *ly* → fondly

However, not all words ending in *ly* are adverbs. (Words like *lovely* and *friendly,* which are formed from a noun plus *ly,* are adjectives and modify nouns or pronouns.) Be sure to consider the word in the context of the sentence before determining whether it is an adverb.

IN SUMMARY

Adverbs modify verbs, adjectives, and other adverbs.

Adverbs often answer the questions *when? where? how?* or *to what extent?*

The word *not* is an adverb.

6-1 Practice the Skill

Underline the adverbs. Draw an arrow from each adverb to the word it modifies.

1. Onesimus was a slave who <u>wrongly</u> ran away from his master, Philemon.

2. The slave <u>somehow</u> met the apostle Paul.

3. After his salvation, Onesimus <u>quickly</u> recognized his responsibility to his master.

4. Onesimus had become a servant and <u>very</u> close friend of Paul, and Paul did <u>not</u> want to separate from him.

5. The <u>unusually</u> small book of Philemon in the New Testament is Paul's letter to Onesimus's master.

6. Paul <u>lovingly</u> makes an appeal to Philemon for the forgiveness of Onesimus.

7. Paul <u>sacrificially</u> offers to pay any debts of his friend Onesimus.

8. Paul appeals <u>quite</u> <u>humbly</u> to Philemon by reminding him that all saved men are brethren in the Lord.

9. The story of Onesimus demonstrates the forgiveness that we receive <u>freely</u> in Christ.

10. Onesimus may have been <u>graciously</u> pardoned by his earthly master, but <u>certainly</u> his greatest pardon was the forgiveness of his sins in salvation.

6-2 Review the Skill

Underline the adverbs. Draw an arrow from each adverb to the word it modifies.

1. *Treasures of the Snow* <u>clearly</u> demonstrates the consequences of bitterness.

2. Annette blames Lucien <u>somewhat</u> <u>unfairly</u> for her brother's injury.

3. Lucien was <u>partially</u> guilty. His teasing had led to Dani's fall.

Adverbs 117

4. However, Annette does not notice the harmful effect on herself.

5. Very soon she spreads her version of the story to others.

6. A woodcarver befriends Lucien and eventually gives him hope.

7. Annette adamantly refuses Lucien her forgiveness.

8. In fact, she destroys his quite intricate woodcarvings.

9. Eventually she forgives him for his part in Dani's accident.

10. She confesses her bitterness humbly and asks for Lucien's forgiveness.

6-3 Practice the Skill

Underline the adverbs. In the blank write the question that the adverb answers.

_____ 1. Lew Wallace's book *Ben Hur* tells the story of Judah Ben-Hur, a member of an important Jewish family, who unintentionally knocks a tile off the roof of his house onto a Roman leader.

_____ 2. Ben-Hur immediately is sent to row with slaves as punishment, and his mother and sister are imprisoned.

_____ 3. Messala, a Roman who was at one time a very close friend to Ben-Hur, refuses to help his former companion.

_____ 4. When Ben-Hur is providentially rescued from the galleys and placed in the favor of the important Roman Arrius, he determines to find his mother and sister and to have his revenge on Messala.

_____ 5. Ben-Hur completely defeats and humiliates Messala in a chariot race.

_____ 6. He has had his revenge against Messala but is quite bitter toward the Roman government that took his family's freedom.

_____ 7. His mother and sister had spent several years in a miserable prison cell and later had to join a colony of lepers outside the city.

_____ 8. Ben-Hur becomes one of the group that follows Jesus continually in His travels about the countryside in the hope that Jesus will lead the Jews in a fight against the Romans.

_____ 9. Jesus compassionately heals Ben-Hur's mother and sister of their leprosy.

_____ 10. Finally, Ben-Hur realizes after Jesus' death on the cross that true freedom from Rome has to come from within, and he gives up his bitterness.

6-4 Review the Skill

In the blank write an appropriate adverb to answer the question in parentheses. Try to use a variety of adverbs.

Example: __Soon__ ? the king stood. *(when?)*

_____ 1. Many Christians ? misunderstand the concept of forgiveness. *(how?)*

_____ 2. In fact, they substitute a ? weak apology in the place of a request for forgiveness. *(to what extent?)*

_____ 3. God ? explains in His Word what true forgiveness is. *(how?)*

_____ 4. If we rely on our ? unstable emotions, we will not always feel forgiven. *(to what extent?)*

_____ 5. Instead, we must believe I John 1:9. If we confess our sins, God will ? forgive us. *(when?)*

_____ 6. When Christians confess their sin, God puts the sin ? from His thoughts. *(where?)*

_____ 7. Because God ? breaks His promises, He forgives repentant sinners. *(when?)*

_____ 8. Isaiah 43:25 tells us God does ? remember our sins after He forgives us. *(negative)*

_____ 9. Forgiveness does not mean forgetting a hurt, but it does mean ? putting that hurt out of your thoughts. *(to what extent?)*

_____ 10. Based upon His example, Christians should ? forgive one another. *(how?)*

Adverbs

Positions of Adverbs

Adverbs that modify adjectives or other adverbs come just before the word or words they modify.

The water was *somewhat* cool.
The weary hiker drank it *very* quickly.
He was *so* sleepy that he wanted to stop.
After the hike, his muscles were *exceedingly* sore.

Unlike adverbs that modify adjectives and other adverbs, adverbs that modify verbs are usually movable within the sentence. There are five possible positions for this type of adverb:

After the verb: The group will leave *soon.*
After the direct object: The group will leave the campsite *soon.*
After the auxiliary verb: The group will *soon* leave the campsite.
Before the complete verb: The group *soon* will leave the campsite.
At the beginning of the sentence: *Soon* the group will leave the campsite.

Notice that moving the adverb changes the emphasis of the sentence. When you write, be careful to place adverbs where they will best give the emphasis that you want in your sentences.

Diagramming a sentence with an adverb is similar to diagramming one with an adjective. Be sure to attach the adverb line to the word it modifies, regardless of where the adverb occurs in the sentence. Look at the diagram for this sentence: **They will leave the campsite soon.**

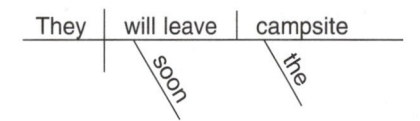

```
They | will leave | campsite
            \soon        \the
```

IN SUMMARY

Adverbs that modify adjectives or other adverbs come just before the word or words they modify.
Adverbs that modify verbs are usually movable within the sentence.

6-5 PRACTICE THE SKILL

In the blank write an appropriate adverb.

_____ 1. Johann Gutenberg is known _?_ for the invention of movable type.

_____ 2. However, not many people know about his _?_ lengthy battle with bitterness.

_____ 3. Gutenberg _?_ needed additional support, so he approached Johann Fust for funds.

_____ 4. Fust _?_ agreed and supported Gutenberg.

_____ 5. Through deceptive methods, Fust _?_ gained control of Gutenberg's shop and printing press.

_____ 6. Upon his deathbed, Fust _?_ begged for a visit from Gutenberg.

_____ 7. Fust admitted his past deception and asked for Gutenberg's forgiveness _?_.

_____ 8. Gutenberg remembered _?_ the words about forgiveness in his Bible.

_____ 9. Though he felt _?_ awkward, he forgave Fust for past injustices.

_____ 10. Gutenberg realized that his forgiveness had _?_ cured his bitterness.

6-6 REVIEW THE SKILL

In each of the following sentences, circle the numbers of the places where the adverb at the left sounds natural. You will circle more than one number for most of the sentences.

Example: *cheerfully* ①The birds ②sang ③in the trees ④

1. *often* ₁ The story of the prodigal son ₂ reminds ₃ us ₄ about forgiveness.

2. *rashly* ₁ In this story the younger son ₂ asks ₃ for his inheritance ₄ from his father.

3. *sadly* ₁ His father ₂ divides ₃ the money ₄, and his son leaves home.

4. *foolishly* ₁ This son ₂ squanders ₃ his money ₄ in riotous living.

5. *soon* ₁ All of his money ₂ is ₃ spent ₄, and he needs food.

6. *eventually* ₁ He ₂ returns ₃ home.

7. *joyfully* ₁ His father ₂ welcomes ₃ him ₄ and forgives him instantly.

8. *seemingly* ₁ The father ₂ forgives ₃ even before his son asks for the forgiveness.

9. *not* ₁ The father ₂ did ₃ scold ₄ but rejoiced at his son's return.

10. *similarly* ₁ God ₂ forgives ₃ us ₄ when we do wrong but are penitent.

Adverbs

Comparing with Adverbs

Like adjectives, many adverbs have comparative and superlative forms. The comparative form is used in comparing two actions or qualities; the superlative is used when comparing three or more. Many short, **regular** adverbs use the suffixes *er* and *est* to form their comparative and superlative forms. Other adverbs, including those that end in *ly*, use the words *more* or *most* to form their comparative and superlative forms. A reliable dictionary will give you the correct forms of any adverb.

Positive	Comparative	Superlative
soon	sooner	soonest
quickly	more quickly	most quickly

Divia practiced *more diligently* than her sister, and she played the *most accurately* of all the piano students.

Other adverbs are **irregular** and form their comparative and superlative forms in different ways.

Positive	Comparative	Superlative
well	better	best
badly	worse	worst

Sheriana performed *well* on the first test, but she did *better* on the next one.

Many adverbs, like some adjectives, are not compared. To make comparisons with these would not make sense. Among others, these include some very common adverbs: *not, daily, now, very, really, almost,* and *here.*

IN SUMMARY

Regular adverbs show comparison by adding *er* and *est* or *more* and *most* to the stem form of the adverb.

Irregular adverbs have entirely different forms to show comparison.

Some adverbs cannot be compared.

Chapter 13: Adjective or Adverb? p. 269

Chapter 13: Adjectives and Adverbs in Comparison p. 276

6-7 Practice the Skill

In the blank write the correct form of the adverb in parentheses.

_____ 1. Any discussion of forgiveness must _?_ include the cross. *(eventually, positive)*

_____ 2. Through His death, Christ demonstrated forgiveness _?_ than anyone else. *(completely, comparative)*

_____ 3. His own people cried _?_ for His death. *(loudly, positive)*

_____ 4. He _?_ endured cruel suffering. *(bravely, positive)*

_____ 5. He suffered _?_ when God the Father turned His back on Him as He carried the sins of the world. *(intensely, superlative)*

_____ 6. Death came _?_ than the crowd expected. *(soon, comparative)*

_____ 7. They would have _?_ witnessed a long ordeal that ended only when a soldier broke the legs of the prisoner. *(eagerly, comparative)*

_____ 8. Before He died, though, Christ asked His Father _?_ for forgiveness for those who had put Him on the cross. *(publicly, positive)*

_____ 9. Christ's love extended _?_ than the people's hatred. *(far, comparative)*

_____ 10. _?_, Christ's death provided the forgiveness of sins that every person needs in order to go to heaven. *(importantly, superlative)*

6-8 Review the Skill

Underline the correct form of the adverb in parentheses.

1. Zacchaeus was one of the *(higher, highest)* ranking publicans in the city of Jericho.

2. He was a wealthy man because of his *(shamefully, more shamefully)* dishonest business practices.

3. When Zacchaeus heard that Jesus was coming through his town, he tried *(earnestly, more earnestly)* than anyone else to see Him.

4. Because Zacchaeus was not very tall, he cleverly climbed a tree so that he could see *(better, best)* than everyone else.

5. Although Zacchaeus was amazed to see Jesus, he was *(more, most)* amazed that Jesus recognized him and called out to him.

Adverbs

6. When Jesus called out, "Zacchaeus, make haste, and come down; for to day I must abide at thy house," it was the *(more, most)* wonderful dinner invitation that Zacchaeus had ever received.

7. Many people were surprised that Jesus would *(gladly, more gladly)* visit the home of a despised sinner.

8. Of all the people who heard Jesus that day, Zacchaeus showed his love *(better, best)* when he promised to restore any stolen money fourfold and to give half of all he owned to the poor.

9. The religious people were even *(more, most)* skeptical when Jesus forgave Zacchaeus and granted him the gift of salvation.

10. Though Christ looks at our outward good works, He looks *(closely, more closely)* at the heart for true repentance like that of Zacchaeus.

6-9 USE THE SKILL

Insert at least one adverb into each sentence. Try to use a variety of adverbs.

1. The Bible relates stories about God's forgiveness of repentant sinners.

   _____

   _____

2. Eve ate the forbidden fruit.

   _____

   _____

3. Abraham told Pharaoh that Sarah was his sister.

   _____

   _____

4. Jacob deceived his father and brother.

   _____

   _____

5. Jonah disobeyed the Lord and sailed toward Tarshish instead of going to Nineveh.

   _____

   _____

6. Zacchaeus stole from the Jews.

7. Peter denied the Lord three times.

8. The thief on the cross was crucified for his sins.

9. Onesimus ran away from his master.

10. God forgave each of these sinners, and He will forgive us when we repent.

6-10 CUMULATIVE REVIEW

Underline the adverbs. Then rewrite the paragraph on the lines below, correcting these kinds of errors: fragments, comma splices, fused sentences, incorrect noun plural forms, incorrect noun possessive forms, incorrect verb forms (e.g., *writed* or *had wrote*). There are five errors.

Paul experienced the compassion and forgiveness of God, Paul unmercifully persecuted and murdered Christians before his miraculous salvation. The Lord speaked to Paul on the road to Damascus, and Pauls conversion thoroughly changed his ways. Paul was used mightily by the Lord. Paul suffered many persecutions and trials he gratefully persevered because of his all-consuming love for Christ. Paul's testimony in I Timothy 1:14-15. "And the grace of our Lord was exceeding abundant with faith and love which is in Christ Jesus. This is a faithful saying, and worthy of all acceptation, that Christ Jesus came into the world to save sinners; of whom I am chief."

Adverbs 125

POLE VAULTING

Not all the adverbs in the excerpt act as volume controls. Writers sometimes use adverbs to completely redirect the sentence.

- *Find the adverbs in the excerpt from* Twice Freed *that do not end in* ly. *Which of these adverbs negate the sentences in which they appear?*

How Endings Make Meanings: Finishing a Story

Nathaniel Hawthorne tells a story ("The Birthmark") about a brilliant scientist who marries a beautiful woman. The lady has a tiny birthmark on her face. Most people think it makes her all the more beautiful. But the scientist is determined to find a way to remove the mark and thereby have a perfect wife.

He works day and night and studies all the science books he can to find a "cure." His patient wife tries all the things he asks her to, but the birthmark never fades.

Then one day, he brings her some medicine to drink, and he tells her that he is sure this is going to take away the mark. Because she loves him and wants him to be happy, she drinks the liquid. Soon the birthmark starts to fade. As it becomes less and less distinct, the beautiful wife begins to grow weak. At the moment the mark is entirely gone and she is perfect, she dies.

What does Hawthorne imply by making the story end that way? One meaning is that man cannot create perfection in an imperfect world and that it is wrong for him to "play God."

How would the meaning of the story change if, instead of dying, the lady lived and became vain about her beauty? Perhaps then the meaning would be that we should be content with what we have and that trying to manipulate things is wrong.

It is the ending of a story that gives the story its meaning. A good story, a story worthy of a Christian's admiration, must have not only good style and interesting characters but also a theme that fits with God's truth about life.

Suppose, for example, that the scientist cures his wife's birthmark and thereby creates a perfect human being. Does this ending fit with God's reality? Not at all. And no matter how artfully the story could be told, it would never be a good story.

A story is one of the most powerful tools in the world. It can move people to good action or bad. It can make them respect truth or yearn for evil. The story writer, then, must be very aware of his craft; and the Christian writer doubly so.

Your Turn: Coming to a Good End

Here is the beginning of a story. You finish it to give it a worthy meaning. Be prepared to explain your meaning to your teacher.

> Sarah, a girl in a small town, wants with all her heart to go to summer art camp. But she has no money, and her family can hardly afford to live on what her father makes since he was injured in an accident at work and was abruptly asked to leave his job. He now works as a librarian at the town's modest library.
>
> Sarah takes a job in the local store, but the wages are low; even if she saves carefully, it will take her months to earn enough money, and there is little time. She nearly gives up hoping that she can ever go to camp.
>
> Then one day she receives a letter. When she opens it, she finds money for a summer at camp and a letter telling her that she can use the money only to go to camp. If she no longer wants to go, she is to return the money to post office box 34. The letter is signed only "a friend of the family."
>
> Sarah shows the letter and the money to her parents, and they decide that she should go to camp. She writes a happy thank-you letter and addresses it to post office box 34.
>
> For several days, Sarah, and sometimes her brother, watch the post office to see who comes to box 34. They never see anyone, but a few days later, Sarah gets a letter that says, "You're quite welcome."
>
> So Sarah goes to camp. She studies hard and does well. In fact, her painting takes first place at the competition. At the end of the summer, Sarah gets a note from her benefactor that says, "If you would like to meet me, I will be sitting in the third seat behind the driver of the bus on your way home."
>
> As Sarah waits at the station, she scans the bus she is taking, quickly counting windows. Her eyes come to the third seat. She draws in her breath as she recognizes the man in the window—he was the man who had unjustly fired her father years before.

How does the story end? What does your ending make the story say?

Chapter 7

Prepositions, Conjunctions, and Interjections

Twenty Thousand Leagues Under the Sea
by Jules Verne

Grammar

"Unfortunately," he continued, "I cannot take you through the Suez Canal; but you will be able to see the long jetty of Port Said after to-morrow, when we shall be in the Mediterranean."

"The Mediterranean!" I exclaimed.

"Yes, sir; does that astonish you?"

"What astonishes me is to think that we shall be there the day after to-morrow."

"Indeed?"

"Yes, Captain, although by this time I ought to have accustomed myself to be surprised at nothing since I have been on board your boat."

"But the cause of this surprise?"

"Well, it is the fearful speed you will have to put the *Nautilus,* if the day after to-morrow she is to be in the Mediterranean, having made the round of Africa, and doubled the Cape of Good Hope!"

"Who told you that she would make the round of Africa, and double the Cape of Good Hope, sir?"

"Well, unless the *Nautilus* sails on dry land, and passes above the isthmus—"

"Or beneath it, M. Aronnax."

"Beneath it?"

"Certainly," replied Captain Nemo, quietly. "A long time ago Nature made under this tongue of land what man has this day made on its surface."

"What! such a passage exists?"

"Yes; a subterranean passage, which I have named the Arabian tunnel. It takes us beneath Suez, and opens into the Gulf of Pelusium."

"But this isthmus is composed of nothing but quicksands?"

"To a certain depth. But at fifty-five yards only, there is a solid layer of rock."

"Did you discover this passage by chance?" I asked, more and more surprised.

"Chance and reasoning, sir; and by reasoning even more than by chance. Not only does this passage exist, but I have profited by it several times."

- *Where in the excerpt do you first realize that the voyage is unusual? What in the passage tells you the story was written before underwater exploration was common?*
- *Why do you think Aronnax is on board the* Nautilus? *What do you think the captain thinks of him? What kind of man do you think the captain is?*
- *Put the captain's last sentence in your own words. What is the reason for the difference between his statement and yours?*

Sometimes there is more to be discovered in a book than the details of the story. A little investigation and deduction with this excerpt, for example, can yield theories about the characters, the plot, the setting, and the writer. You know that the story is set before submarine travel was known because of Aronnax's astonishment at Nemo's calm announcement of his plans to sail beneath the isthmus. What does this tell you about the author?

An 1800s setting does not necessarily mean an 1800s author. But clues in the style of writing reveal that this is not a modern author. When you re-stated the captain's line, it was probably something more like "Oh, it exists all right, and I've used it many times." Your version is less formal. Notice the formal structure and wording of all the dialogue in the passage. Compare it to the dialogue in a modern book you've read.

One means an author has of making dialogue formal or informal is his choice of prepositions, conjunctions, and interjections. After studying this chapter, you will be able to make other deductions about Jules Verne and his *Twenty Thousand Leagues Under the Sea.*

Prepositions

A **preposition** is a word that introduces a prepositional phrase and shows a relationship between its object and some other word in a sentence. The **object of the preposition** is a noun or pronoun that follows the preposition. All prepositions have objects.

Example: We looked *for* the needle *in* the haystack.
We looked *for* the needle *on* the haystack.
We looked *for* the needle *under* the haystack.
We looked *for* the needle *near* the haystack.
We looked *for* the needle *from* the haystack.

In each sentence above, a different preposition links the verb *looked* to the object of the preposition *haystack*. The preposition shows how the verb is related to the object of the preposition. Notice how the change in preposition changes the meaning of the sentence.

Commonly Used Prepositions

about	behind	except	on	to
above	below	for	onto	toward
across	beside	from	out	under
after	between	in	outside	until
against	beyond	inside	over	upon
among	but	into	past	with
around	by	like	since	within
at	down	near	through	without
before	during	of	throughout	

ETYMOLOGY
Preposition (pre + position) literally means something "placed in front of."

IN SUMMARY

A **preposition** is a word that introduces a prepositional phrase and shows a relationship between its object and some other word in the sentence.

The **object of the preposition** is a noun or pronoun that follows the preposition.

130   Chapter 7

7-1 Practice the Skill

Underline the prepositions.

1. The sea level fluctuates <u>with</u> the changing tides.
2. Oceanographers say that sea level is halfway <u>between</u> high and low tide.
3. However, even mean sea level varies <u>around</u> the world.
4. Currents, ocean depth, temperature, and other factors contribute <u>to</u> these differences.
5. The currents are the lifeblood <u>of</u> the ocean.
6. Currents tie together remote regions and carry warmth <u>toward</u> the frigid poles.
7. The deepest recorded part is <u>around</u> eleven thousand feet.
8. The ocean's temperature varies <u>from</u> one place <u>to</u> the next.
9. Oceans cover <u>about</u> 71 percent <u>of</u> the earth.
10. Generally, sea level is increasing <u>by</u> approximately one millimeter each year.

7-2 Review the Skill

Underline the prepositions.

1. <u>In</u> the late 1760s, David Bushnell experimented <u>with</u> underwater explosives.
2. He believed that these explosives could be used <u>against</u> the English navy.
3. Eventually, he formulated the idea <u>of</u> a submarine.
4. A submarine would get the torpedo <u>near</u> its target, so Bushnell began building one.
5. <u>On</u> an August night <u>in</u> 1776, Sergeant Ezra Lee <u>of</u> the Continental army climbed <u>into</u> the world's first submarine.
6. He slipped <u>under</u> the water <u>near</u> Manhattan Island and headed <u>for</u> the *Eagle,* an English blockade ship.
7. The machine functioned perfectly, but the submarine's screw could not break <u>through</u> the *Eagle*'s iron supports.
8. Lee soon gave up and set the torpedo loose <u>beside</u> the ship.
9. The torpedo exploded but only shook the crew <u>of</u> the *Eagle.*
10. <u>Although</u> the first mission was a failure, today David Bushnell is called the father <u>of</u> the submarine.

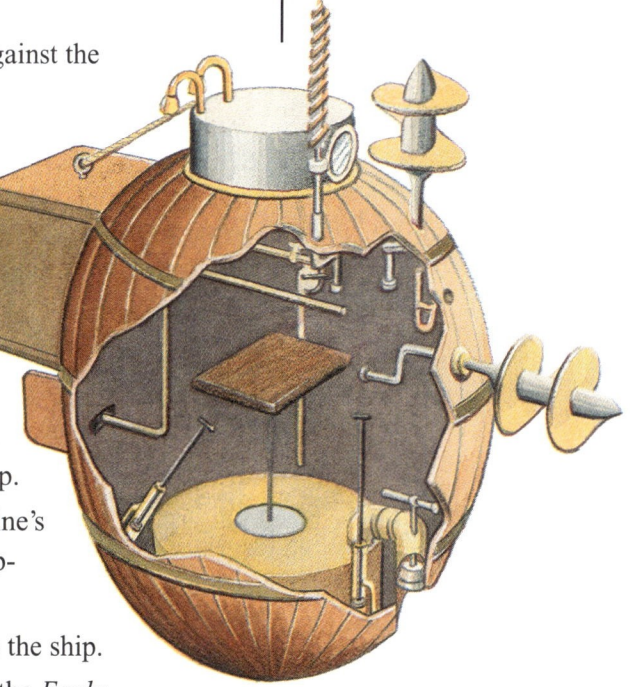

7-3 USE THE SKILL

In the blank write an appropriate preposition to complete each sentence.

_____ 1. Whales live ? the world.

_____ 2. Porpoises and dolphins are part ? the whale family.

_____ 3. Baby whales, called calves, stay close ? their mothers for the first few weeks.

_____ 4. Swimming ? their parent's current helps to minimize the swimming effort for the small whales.

_____ 5. Most whales stay ? groups called schools, but a few whales swim independently of others.

_____ 6. Many whales swim ? the surface of the water because they need the air's oxygen.

_____ 7. Dolphins can jump twenty feet ? the water.

_____ 8. Whales communicate ? their schools in many different ways.

_____ 9. The pitch of some whales' sounds is ? human perception.

_____ 10. ? the past century, scientific research has greatly increased our knowledge about whales, dolphins, and porpoises.

Prepositional Phrases

A preposition and its object together form a **prepositional phrase.** Any modifiers of the object are also included in the phrase. By itself, the object is the simple object of the preposition. The object and its modifiers together are the complete object of the preposition.

> The toy octopus *with only seven arms* was injured *in a battle against the garbage disposal.*

The example above contains three prepositional phrases. Each one consists of a preposition followed by a noun phrase (the object and its modifiers). The preposition *with* links the complete object of the preposition *only seven arms* to the subject *octopus*. The preposition *in* shows the relationship between its object, *a battle,* and the verb, *was injured. Against* links *the garbage disposal* with the previous simple object of the preposition, *battle.*

Some prepositional phrases contain compound objects. In the prepositional phrase *by the wind and sea,* below, both *wind* and *sea* are simple objects of the preposition *by.*

> The boat was tossed *by the wind and sea.*

IN SUMMARY

A **prepositional phrase** consists of the preposition and the complete object of the preposition.

Chapter 10: Agreement with Intervening Phrases
p. 219

7-4 Practice the Skill

Place parentheses around the prepositional phrases. Underline the simple object of each prepositional phrase. Above each word of the sentence pattern, write its label.

1. Fish can live in fresh or salt water.
2. Their body temperatures change with their environment.
3. A fish has sensory organs on its sides.
4. A fish's sense of smell is strong.
5. A female fish releases many eggs during spawning season.
6. Some fish release seven million eggs at one time.
7. Some fish have lived over fifty-five years.
8. A characteristic of all fish is fins.
9. Scientists are still learning about fish's migratory patterns.
10. For almost all fish, the fish's sides are the location of its fins.

7-5 Review the Skill

Place parentheses around the prepositional phrases. Underline the simple object of each prepositional phrase.

1. Beginning in 1998 an underwater exploration team documented eight ancient ships in a fifty-five-mile radius at the bottom of the Mediterranean Sea.
2. Five of the wrecks were of Roman origin, and three were from North Africa.
3. The depth of these shipwrecks has kept them largely undisturbed by storms.
4. Until recent times divers could examine only those ships that were found no deeper than two hundred feet.
5. With the help of a remotely operated vehicle (ROV), archaeologists can uncover artifacts at 2,800 feet.
6. Like a diver, an ROV can map the site of a wreck and retrieve artifacts.
7. An elevator lifts artifacts with its mesh net to the scientists in the boat.
8. The team removed only a few artifacts from six of the ships.
9. They left the rest for further exploration.
10. As technology advances, more ancient time capsules will be discovered beneath the ocean's surface.

7-6 USE THE SKILL

Expand each sentence by adding an appropriate prepositional phrase.

Example: Jonathan visited a state.
Jonathan visited a state near Montana.

1. Cailin smelled the salt water.

2. Cailin had never been out of the country.

3. Cailin had never been on a cruise.

4. Cailin and her parents were traveling.

5. At first, Cailin became sick.

6. Cailin watched the whales.

7. On the third day, storm clouds swirled.

8. The storm raged on and off.

9. Cailin was glad when they finally arrived.

10. Cailin's parents got off the boat.

Functions of Prepositional Phrases

One function of a prepositional phrase is to modify nouns. Because they function like adjectives, these prepositional phrases are called **adjectival prepositional phrases.** They add information about the nouns they modify.

> Tashawna saw the birthday present *on the red table.*
> She noticed the gift *on a desk in the hall.*
> The box *with the ribbon* contains a surprise.

Each of the italicized prepositional phrases in the sentences above modifies the noun that it follows: *on the red table* modifies *present; on a desk* modifies *gift; in the hall* modifies *desk;* and *with the ribbon* modifies *box.* A prepositional phrase that modifies a noun usually comes just after that noun.

Another function of prepositional phrases is to modify verbs. Because they function like adverbs, these phrases are called **adverbial prepositional phrases.** These phrases add information about the verbs they modify.

> Wendy and Felice jumped *into the ball pit.*
> Felice lost her expensive watch *under the balls.*
> *In desperation* the friends searched *among the balls for an hour.*

Each of the prepositional phrases above modifies the verb of the sentence. *Into the ball pit* modifies *jumped,* telling *where* about the verb; *under the balls* modifies *lost* and tells *where* about the verb; *in desperation, among the balls,* and *for an hour* all modify the verb and tell *how, where,* and *how much/to what extent* about *searched.* Notice that adverbial phrases can appear just about anywhere in the sentence: at the beginning, at the end, or next to the words they modify.

The prepositional phrase is always diagrammed under the word it modifies. Look at the diagram for this sentence: **Titus put his wet suit into the back of the truck.**

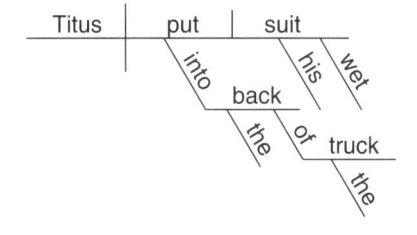

Chapter 5: Adjectives p. 96

Chapter 6: Adverbs p. 116

Prepositions, Conjunctions, and Interjections 135

IN SUMMARY

Prepositional phrases can be used like adjectives to modify nouns or like adverbs to modify verbs.

7-7 Practice the Skill

Label each underlined prepositional phrase *adj* (adjectival prepositional phrase) or *adv* (adverbial prepositional phrase).

_____ 1. In the mid-1800s Queen Victoria hosted an international exposition to celebrate the achievements <u>of Britain and her empire</u>.

_____ 2. The world was sent an invitation <u>by Queen Victoria and Prince Albert</u> to send a yacht to race with the British Royal Squadron at Cowes.

_____ 3. <u>Because of the upcoming race</u>, the New York Yacht Club formed a syndicate and financed a boat.

_____ 4. The *America* was designed and built <u>by George Steers and William H. Brown respectively</u>.

_____ 5. In August of 1851, she was ready <u>at the starting line</u>.

_____ 6. Three hours later the *America* sailed <u>past the onlookers</u> and across the finish line in first place.

_____ 7. The *America* gained the impressive reputation <u>of the fastest yacht</u>.

_____ 8. The *America,* one of the prize-winning exhibitions <u>at Queen Victoria's Great Exhibition</u>, was the centerpiece of a lithograph.

_____ 9. The lithograph portrayed pictures <u>of American inventions</u> ranging from the McCormick reaper to Goodyear's India rubber globe and Colt's repeating pistol.

_____ 10. The *America* was the recipient <u>of the most famous trophy and prestigious prize</u> awarded in the sport of yachting.

7-8 Review the Skill

Place parentheses around each prepositional phrase. Label each prepositional phrase *adj* (adjectival prepositional phrase) or *adv* (adverbial prepositional phrase).

_____ 1. The mystery of the *Mary Celeste* has baffled seamen and land dwellers.

_____ 2. On November 7, 1872, Captain Benjamin Briggs, his family, and a seven-man crew sailed.

_____ 3. All of the crewmen were excellent seamen.

_____ 4. Captain Briggs's wife brought her sewing machine and some toys for their daughter.

_____ 5. A month later, the *Dei Gratia* spotted the *Mary Celeste* between the Azores and Portugal.

_____ 6. The captain of the *Dei Gratia* hailed the *Mary Celeste*.

_____ 7. Not a soul was found on board.

_____ 8. No signs of violence were evident.

_____ 9. Some signs of a quick departure were evident.

_____ 10. Their fate remains a mystery to this day.

Preposition or Adverb?

Some of the same words that are used as prepositions can also be used as adverbs. To determine whether a word in a sentence is a preposition or an adverb, look for an object of the preposition.

> The swimmer swam *around* the buoy.
> The swimmer swam *around* for thirty minutes.

Around is a preposition in the first sentence because it is followed by the object *buoy*. In the second sentence, *around* is an adverb that tells where the swimmer swam, and it has no object. (*For thirty minutes* is itself a prepositional phrase and cannot be the direct object.) Every preposition must have an object.

IN SUMMARY

Some words used as prepositions can also be used as adverbs.

A preposition is followed by an object; an adverb does not have an object.

7-9 PRACTICE THE SKILL

Label each italicized word *prep* (preposition) or *adv* (adverb).

_____ 1. The table toppled *over*.

_____ 2. The rocket shot *over* the moon.

_____ 3. The bird flew *up* in the air.

_____ 4. The smoke curled *up* the chimney.

_____ 5. He was running *in* the rain.

_____ 6. The dog lay *behind* the car.

_____ 7. The jogger fell *behind* in the race.

_____ 8. The camper placed a sweater *around* his shoulders.

_____ 9. The new sailor ran *aboard* the ship.

_____ 10. The mixture was consistent *throughout*.

Chapter 6: Adverbs
p. 116

7-10 REVIEW THE SKILL

Label each underlined word *prep* (preposition) or *adv* (adverb).

_____ 1. In the late 1800s the age of the sail was giving way <u>to</u> the age of the steam-powered boat.

_____ 2. The demand <u>for</u> shipmasters such as Captain Joshua Slocum was waning.

_____ 3. But Captain Slocum had been sailing the sea too long to spend the rest of his life <u>on</u> land.

_____ 4. In 1894 he decided to do what no seaman had done before: sail <u>around</u> the world by himself.

_____ 5. On April 24, 1895, Captain Slocum set <u>off</u> in his little sloop.

_____ 6. Captain Slocum would often lash the helm, set the sail, and go <u>below</u> to read *Life of Columbus*.

_____ 7. Since no one else was <u>around</u>, Slocum would sing a sea chantey to ward off loneliness.

_____ 8. Crossing the Atlantic <u>during</u> the summer was relatively easy compared to what lay ahead.

_____ 9. It took Captain Slocum twice as long to cross the Strait <u>of</u> Magellan as it did to cross the whole Atlantic Ocean.

_____ 10. On June 27, 1898, three years, two months, and two days <u>after</u> the beginning of his journey, Joshua Slocum became the first man to sail around the world alone.

7-11 REVIEW THE SKILL

Find the ten prepositional phrases in the paragraph. On the lines below, write each prepositional phrase and the word it modifies.

    The American school was bigger than my school in France. I found my desk in the back row of the class. The girl on my right folded the pleats of her skirt into a fan. The girl on my left twirled her long blonde braid around her finger. The boy in front pooched out his lips and balanced his pencil on them.

Adapted from *Roses on Baker Street* by Eileen M. Berry, © 1998 Journey Books.

1. _____

2. _____

138   Chapter 7

3. _____

4. _____

5. _____

6. _____

7. _____

8. _____

9. _____

10. _____

Conjunctions

A **conjunction** is a connecting word that joins words or groups of words in a sentence. In this book you will study two types of conjunctions: the coordinating conjunction and the correlative conjunction.

Conjunction comes from the Latin prefix *com-*, meaning "together," and the Latin verb *jungere*, meaning "to join."

Coordinating Conjunctions

One kind of conjunction, the **coordinating conjunction,** connects sentence parts that are the same type. The words or groups of words joined by a coordinating conjunction must have the same function within the sentence. The chart below lists commonly used coordinating conjunctions.

and	but	or
nor	yet	for

Jerrold **and** *Sara* are fishing. *(compound subjects)*

Jerrold *checked* **and** *rechecked* the boat's hull for holes. *(compound verbs)*

He will test the *oars* **or** the *anchor* next. *(compound direct objects)*

Sara's favorite fishing spots are the *cove,* the *canal,* **and** the *middle* of the lake. *(compound predicate nouns)*

Jerrold prefers *calm* **and** *shallow* water. *(compound adjectives)*

They both enjoy fishing *early* **or** *late.* *(compound adverbs)*

Chapter 1: Finding Compound Subjects and Predicates p. 5

In each of the sentences above, the words joined by the coordinating conjunctions have the same function. Coordinating conjunctions must join words that share the same function in the sentence.

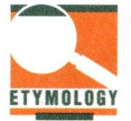

> **ETYMOLOGY** — *Coordinating* comes from our word *coordination*. *Coordination* is from the Latin prefix *co-*, meaning "same," and the Latin noun *ordinatio*, meaning "arrangement." In English, words joined by a coordinating conjunction have the same basic function.

A coordinating conjunction can also join phrases that have the same function.

> *A team of soccer players* **and** *a bunch of volunteers* cleaned up the abandoned field. *(compound complete subject)*

> The group *collected trash* **and** *mowed the grass. (compound complete predicate)*

> It was *after lunch time* **but** *before supper time* that they finished the job. *(compound prepositional phrases)*

> Two of the volunteers were *the junior high principal* **and** *the high school dramatics coach. (compound complete predicate noun)*

Compound parts are diagrammed in the same general way that single parts are diagrammed. The line is split into two lines, and the parts of the compound are written on the lines. The conjunction is written on a broken line joining the two lines. Look at the diagram for this sentence: **Jerrold and Sara are fishing.**

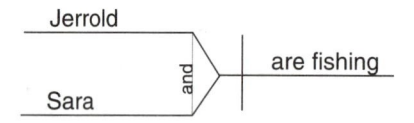

When diagramming a compound part made of phrases, be sure to include all parts of the phrase on the correct line: **The group collected trash and mowed the grass.**

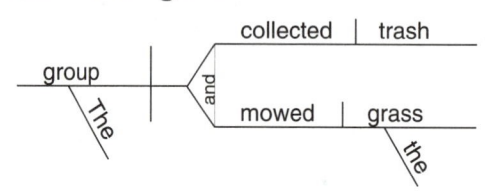

Since coordinating conjunctions join grammatical parts of equal rank, a comma and one of these conjunctions can also join two clauses.

> *Jan and Joanie tried out for cheerleading,* **but** *Jan did not make the squad.*

> *Horace and Marilyn snorkeled in the bay offshore,* **and** *they saw many exotic fish.*

> *The Scripture commands us to love the sinner,* **yet** *we are not to love the sin.*

Chapter 8: Compound Sentences
p. 166

Chapter 8: Phrases and Clauses
p. 162

Clauses that are joined by coordinating conjunctions can be diagrammed: **Horace and Marilyn snorkeled in the bay offshore, and they saw many exotic fish.**

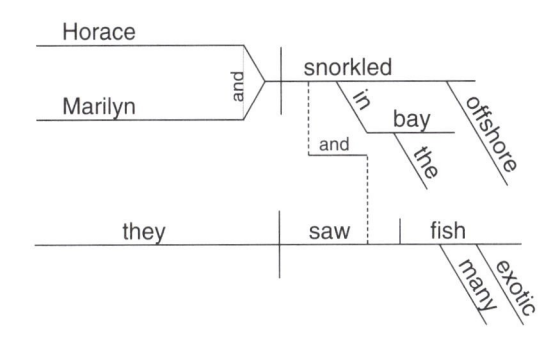

In Summary

- A **conjunction** is a connecting word that joins words or groups of words in a sentence.
- A **coordinating conjunction** joins sentence parts of the same type.
- The parts of a sentence joined by a coordinating conjunction make up a compound part of the sentence.

7-12 Practice the Skill

Circle the coordinating conjunctions.

1. The oceans and the seas are awe-inspiring parts of Creation.
2. Man had not witnessed the full power or the destructive ability of water until the Flood.
3. "The waters prevailed, and were increased greatly upon the earth" (Genesis 7:18).
4. God protected the Israelites but not the Egyptians from the waters of the Red Sea.
5. "The horse and his rider hath he thrown into the sea" (Exodus 15:1).
6. Jonah tried to run from God, but he found it impossible.
7. The sailors took Jonah and cast him into the sea.
8. We may call God the Creator of the seas or the Master of the seas.
9. "What manner of man is this, that even the wind and the sea obey him?" (Mark 4:41)
10. "Worship him that made heaven, and earth, and the sea, and the fountains of waters" (Revelation 14:7).

Chapter 16: Commas p. 326

7-13 REVIEW THE SKILL

Circle the coordinating conjunctions and underline the words, phrases, or clauses joined by the coordinating conjunctions. Label the function of the compound part *S* (subject), *Pred* (predicate), *DO* (direct object), *PN* (predicate noun), *PA* (predicate adjective), *Adj* (adjective), *Adv* (adverb), *OP* (object of the preposition), or *Cl* (clause).

_____ 1. The octopus is the coral reef's largest and most formidable predator.

_____ 2. In different situations, an octopus can be harmless or dangerous.

_____ 3. Eight arms or tentacles give the octopus an ominous appearance.

_____ 4. Its rubbery body has no shell or backbone.

_____ 5. The octopus is an exceptional hunter with intelligence and long arms.

_____ 6. The octopus's usual food is fish and crustaceans.

_____ 7. The octopus gives its victim an injection, and it crushes the victim with its mouth.

_____ 8. The octopus usually hunts at night and hides from its enemies during the day.

_____ 9. The octopus can change its color from chocolate brown to milky white to a brilliant red or green.

_____ 10. An octopus can quickly and easily squeeze into a very narrow crevice.

7-14 USE THE SKILL

Combine a word from the first sentence with a word from the second sentence to make a compound sentence part joined by a coordinating conjunction. In the blank write the new sentence.

Example: Odalis was a supportive teacher. Odalis was a sensitive teacher.
Odalis was a supportive and sensitive teacher.

1. Frederick Tudor was a man of single-mindedness. Frederick Tudor was a man of determination.

_____

_____

2. He came up with the idea of shipping ice to the tropics. He came up with the idea of shipping ice to other temperate regions.

_____

_____

3. Tudor had difficulty hiring a crew for his ship because people thought that the ice would melt. Tudor had difficulty hiring a crew for his ship because people thought that the ice would sink the ship.

4. He also had difficulty finding buyers for his cold cargo. He also had difficulty finding buyers for his unfamiliar cargo.

5. Finally he persuaded the owner of an amusement park to let him freeze ice cream. Finally he persuaded the owner of an amusement park to let him sell ice cream.

6. This venture was successful. This venture was profitable.

7. He discovered that sawdust was the best packing material for shipping ice. He discovered that sawdust was the best insulating material for shipping ice.

8. He planned ice houses at ports around the world. He built ice houses at ports around the world.

9. By the 1830s Tudor was shipping ice halfway around the world. By the 1830s Tudor was shipping ice across the equator.

10. The ice trade lasted until the late nineteenth century when mechanical refrigeration made it unnecessary. The ice trade lasted until the late nineteenth century when electrical refrigeration made it unnecessary.

Prepositions, Conjunctions, and Interjections   **143**

Correlative Conjunctions

Correlative conjunctions are conjunctions that are used in **pairs.** They also join sentence parts of the same grammatical type. The correlative conjunctions are divided in the sentence, but they work together to relate the two sentence parts. These are the most common pairs of correlative conjunctions.

both . . . and	either . . . or
neither . . . nor	not only . . . but also

Compound *subject:*   **Both** *Kathy* **and** *Joe* have done their homework.
Compound *verb:*   My sister **neither** *likes* **nor** *wants* surprises.
Compound *adjectives:*   We want **not only** *strawberry* **but also** *pineapple* toppings for the ice cream.

In the examples above, the correlative conjunctions join single words. Like coordinating conjunctions, correlative conjunctions can also join phrases or complete clauses. When *not only . . . but also* joins clauses, the subject of the second clause may come between the words *but* and *also*.

Compound *complete subject:*   **Neither** *my aunt* **nor** *my sisters* are here now.
Compound *object of the preposition:*   They have gone to **either** *the park* **or** *the mall*.
Compound *sentence:*   **Not only** *did they leave the house,* **but** *they* **also** *took the car.*

ETYMOLOGY *Correlative* comes from the Latin prefix *com-*, meaning "together" and the Latin noun *relatio*, meaning "relation." Correlative conjunctions work together to relate two things.

Correlative conjunctions joining compound parts are diagrammed in the same way that coordinating conjunctions are diagrammed. The pair of words is written on the broken line joining the two parts.

She won not only the math award but also the spelling award.

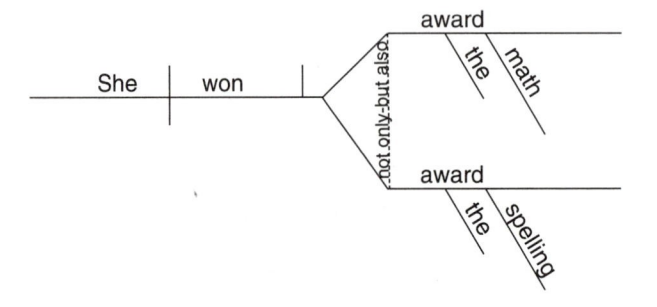

Either Mina or John-Paul will sing for chapel.

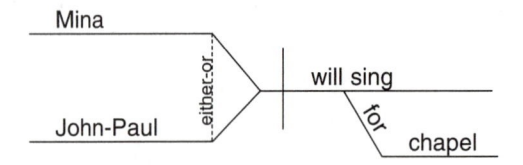

IN SUMMARY

Correlative conjunctions are joining words that are used in pairs to join sentence parts of equal rank.

7-15 PRACTICE THE SKILL

Circle the correlative conjunctions.

1. The story of the *Titanic* is both fascinating and sobering.
2. When the ship sailed from England in 1912, neither the ship's crew nor the passengers suspected that the ship might sink.
3. Several warnings were sent to the ship concerning an iceberg, but they were either unnoticed or ignored.
4. By the time the iceberg was sighted from the ship, not only was the *Titanic* approaching the iceberg, but it also was too late to turn around.
5. Some passengers neither believed the fatal announcement nor agreed to cease their frivolous activities.
6. On the dark night of April 14, the *Titanic* not only struck an iceberg but also sank into the cold, black ocean less than three hours later.
7. The ship's crew had neither adequately learned how to employ the lifeboats nor trained the passengers how to use them.
8. About 1,500 people died, both men and women, both rich and poor, both cowardly and brave.
9. Research teams from both England and France discovered the remains of the *Titanic* in 1985.
10. Not only are photographs of the *Titanic* wreckage intriguing, but they also serve as a powerful reminder of man's vulnerability.

7-16 REVIEW THE SKILL

Circle the correlative conjunctions and underline the words, phrases, or clauses joined by the correlative conjunctions. Label the function of the compound part *S* (subject), *Pred* (predicate), *DO* (direct object), *PN* (predicate noun), *PA* (predicate adjective), *Adj* (adjective), *Adv* (adverb), *OP* (object of the preposition), or *Cl* (clause).

_____ 1. People have always been both curious and inquisitive about the ocean and its inhabitants.

_____ 2. Neither the bulky canvas suits nor the lead boots of standard equipment in the early 1900s were very conducive to underwater exploration.

_____ 3. Divers either could wear the heavy, bulky equipment or could invent something.

_____ 4. In the 1940s new scuba gear not only released air exclusively on the intake but also helped the diver's equilibrium.

_____ 5. This invention gave not only professional but also amateur divers an opportunity for longer dives.

_____ 6. Modern scuba equipment is neither bulky nor uncomfortable.

_____ 7. An efficient type of equipment is either the Jack Brown rig or the Hookah rig.

_____ 8. A diver can wear not only a wet suit but also a dry suit.

_____ 9. The name of the most serious physical danger is either decompression sickness or the bends.

_____ 10. Scuba divers avoid both underwater currents and hostile marine life.

7-17 USE THE SKILL

Combine a word or phrase from the first sentence with a word or phrase from the second sentence to make a compound sentence part joined by a correlative conjunction. In the blank write the new sentence. Try to use each type of correlative conjunction at least once.

1. Jim does not know anything about cleaning the decks of the ship. Dave does not know anything about cleaning the decks of the ship.

   _____

   _____

2. The captain asked Jim to swab the deck. The captain asked Dave to swab the deck.

   _____

   _____

3. Washing the dishes is one of Dave's hardest jobs. Peeling the potatoes is one of Dave's hardest jobs.

   _____

   _____

4. The cook works in a small kitchen. The cook's helpers work in a small kitchen.

   _____

   _____

5. Dave does not like to peel the potatoes. Dave does not want to peel the potatoes.

   _____

   _____

146   Chapter 7

6. The cook does not allow any dirty fish in his kitchen. The cook does not cook any dirty fish in his kitchen.

_____

7. The fish does not stay fresh for very long. The pork does not stay fresh for very long.

_____

8. Jim sweeps the galley after each meal. Dave sweeps the galley after each meal.

_____

9. The boys watch the whales playing on the surface of the ocean. The boys watch the dolphins playing on the surface of the ocean.

_____

10. Jim enjoyed his experiences on the ship. Dave enjoyed his experiences on the ship.

_____

7-18 REVIEW THE SKILL

Circle the conjunctions in each sentence and underline the words, phrases, or clauses joined by the conjunctions. Label the conjunction *A* (coordinating conjunction) or *B* (correlative conjunction).

_____ 1. Both sharks and rays belong to the class *Chondrichthyes*.

_____ 2. The unique skeletons of these fish are composed of strong yet flexible cartilage.

_____ 3. The skin of a shark is neither smooth nor soft.

_____ 4. Most sharks are timid and harmless.

_____ 5. Fewer people are killed by sharks than are killed by murderers or automobile accidents annually.

_____ 6. A shark has either large or powerful jaws, which contain several tows of teeth.

_____ 7. All sharks eat either large fish or microscopic plankton.

Prepositions, Conjunctions, and Interjections   **147**

_____ 8. Sharks use not only their eyes but also their nostrils to locate food.

_____ 9. A shark seizes its prey by biting and tearing the flesh.

_____ 10. They usually not only swallow but also digest their food whole.

Interjections

Interjections are words that can stand alone and be punctuated as a sentence or can appear as a part of a regular sentence. Interjections indicate emotion, agreement or disagreement, greeting, politeness, hesitation, or beginning. Many interjections show strong feeling.

Interjections can be single words or short phrases, such as "thank you" or "good-bye."

Emotion: *Whew!* I'm glad that test is over!
Agreement: *Yes,* I think I did well.
Greeting: *Hi,* Shawn, how did you do on the test?
Hesitation: Derek, *um,* didn't do very well.
Strong feeling: *Ouch!* Just thinking about that test hurts my head!

Because they do not have a real function in the sentence in which they appear, interjections are diagrammed apart from the rest of the sentence. Add the interjection on a separate line just above the left end of the diagram.

Ouch! That bee stung me.

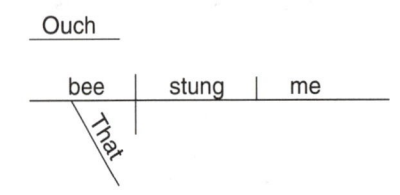

```
Ouch

bee  |  stung  |  me
  \That
```

From the Latin *interjicere*, meaning "to throw between," we get our English word *interjection*.

7-19 PRACTICE THE SKILL

Underline the interjections.

1. "Hey, have you ever heard about the USS *Maine?*"

2. "No, what happened?"

3. "Well, the ship was sunk on February 15, 1898, in Havana Harbor."

4. "An explosion ripped through the *Maine*'s hull. Bang!"

5. "Wow! Do you know the cause of the explosion?"

6. "No one is sure—sorry—but the fate of the *Maine* started the Spanish-American War."

Chapter 16: Commas to Separate
p. 328

7. "Did a mysterious explosion start a whole war? Incredible!"

8. "Yes, the cause was either a large mine beneath the ship or an accidental fire on the ship."

9. "I did not know that. Thanks."

10. "Sure, it was no problem."

7-20 REVIEW THE SKILL

Underline the interjections. Label the sentence patterns. Above each word of the sentence pattern, write its label.

1. "(You) Please tell me about the USS *Constitution*."

2. "Sure. Its nickname is Old Ironsides."

3. "Hey, it had an excellent battle record."

4. "Why, it challenged the mighty British navy and defeated several British ships in the War of 1812."

5. "Okay, why was its nickname Old Ironsides?"

6. "Well, cannonballs bounced off its thick wooden ironlike sides."

7. "Amazing! The *Constitution* must have been impressive."

8. "Yes, its design was revolutionary."

9. "Oh, it combined the best parts of different designs."

10. "That ship never lost a battle. Whew!"

7-21 PRACTICE THE SKILL

Label each underlined word *P* (preposition), *C* (conjunction), or *I* (interjection).

_____ 1. "Wretched! The voyage to America was absolutely wretched!" exclaimed a passenger.

_____ 2. In the late 1800s and early 1900s immigrants were coming to America by the thousands.

_____ 3. Most of these immigrants crossed the Atlantic in steerage, the cheapest and lowest of all of the classes.

_____ 4. Passengers from steerage were treated very differently from those in first and second class.

_____ 5. For example, Robert Louis Stevenson noted <u>on</u> his trip to New York aboard the Anchor Line's *Devonia* that people in steerage were referred to as males and females and people in first and second class as ladies and gentlemen.

_____ 6. Early conditions were so overcrowded <u>and</u> unsanitary that some years mortality rates reached as high as ten percent.

_____ 7. As time went on, some improvements were made, <u>but</u> still some liners had bunks that were only eighteen inches wide and that were stacked four beds high.

_____ 8. Passengers were huddled so closely together that they often felt <u>like</u> cattle.

_____ 9. The comfort <u>of</u> the liners slowly improved as the numbers of immigrants subsided.

_____ 10. Soon steerage became known as third class <u>or</u> tourist, and most of those passengers were vacationers from America's middle class.

7-22 REVIEW THE SKILL

Label each underlined word *P* (preposition), *C* (conjunction), or *I* (interjection).

_____ 1. Pearls develop inside oysters <u>and</u> other mollusks.

_____ 2. The mantle <u>of</u> the oyster puts out a substance, calcium carbonate, that lines the inside of its shell.

_____ 3. When something foreign (like a piece of sand) works its way into the shell, the calcium carbonate wraps <u>around</u> that substance.

_____ 4. <u>Wow</u>! The pearl that forms as a result of the process is beautiful.

_____ 5. Pearls may develop naturally in the sea, <u>or</u> they can be produced artificially in a hatchery.

_____ 6. Japan produces, <u>well</u>, almost all of the world's supply of pearls in hatcheries.

_____ 7. Of the few that are not produced in Japan, one beautiful variety of black pearls comes <u>from</u> French Polynesia.

_____ 8. Black pearls are larger <u>but</u> rarer than other types of pearls.

_____ 9. They may be black or silver or white. <u>Why</u>, some of them are even green.

_____ 10. Polynesian pearl farmers sell their products <u>to</u> many countries around the world.

7-23 USE THE SKILL

Rewrite the paragraph according to the directions below. Use what you have learned about the placement of prepositional phrases, conjunctions, and interjections.

¹It was a hot, humid day at camp, so Kristi and Abbie wanted to go tubing in the creek. ²Each girl selected an inner tube and carried it to the creek around her waist. ³"The water is freezing—brrr," said Kristi as they stepped into the creek. ⁴Kristi sat down carefully in the middle of her tube. ⁵Abbie leaped onto her tube. ⁶Kristi tried to stay in the middle of the current, but Abbie was all over the creek. ⁷When they were finished, Abbie was all wet, and Kristi was all wet. ⁸"Well," said Abbie, "at least we're not so hot anymore!"

- A. Move the adverbial prepositional phrase in sentence 2 to make the meaning clearer.
- B. Move the interjection in sentence 3 to a more appropriate place.
- C. Combine sentences 4 and 5 using a coordinating conjunction.
- D. Replace the phrase *all over the creek* in sentence 6 with several prepositional phrases showing specifically where Abbie was.
- E. Clarify the meaning of sentence 7 using a pair of correlative conjunctions.
- F. Re-read your paragraph. Make any other changes necessary to improve the clarity of the paragraph.

Prepositions, Conjunctions, and Interjections

7-24 Cumulative Review

In the blank write the appropriate word or words to replace the italicized word in parentheses.

Example: __the__   A submarine is able to travel above and under *(article)* water.

_____ 1. Attack submarines detect and *(verb, present tense)* enemy ships in times of war.

_____ 2. A United States Navy submarine, which may be 390 feet long, can move swiftly on the surface *(conjunction)* below the water.

_____ 3. Submarines can operate at a depth of 1,300 feet *(prepositional phrase)*.

_____ 4. An attack submarine *(auxiliary)* hold missiles and torpedoes.

_____ 5. Most modern submarines are nuclear powered, and *(pronoun, third person plural)* produce air and water for the crew.

_____ 6. These submarines *(conjunction)* their crews can remain underwater for months.

_____ 7. After a U.S. Navy submarine *(present perfect verb)* a few months, it will resurface.

_____ 8. A navy *(singular noun)* on a submarine may remain underwater for two or three months without surfacing.

_____ 9. *(Interjection)* That is exciting, but I wonder whether it becomes monotonous sometimes.

_____ 10. *(Indefinite pronoun)* of the submarines are equipped with libraries and game rooms for sailors to use in their leisure time.

_____ 11. Because submarines often maintain *(comparative adjective)* levels of oxygen than normal, sailors may be more tired than usual and require more sleep.

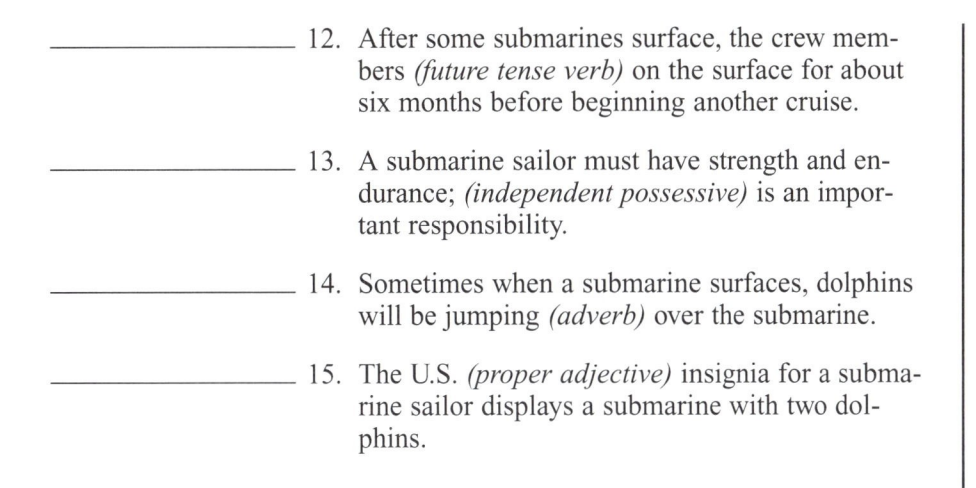

_____ 12. After some submarines surface, the crew members *(future tense verb)* on the surface for about six months before beginning another cruise.

_____ 13. A submarine sailor must have strength and endurance; *(independent possessive)* is an important responsibility.

_____ 14. Sometimes when a submarine surfaces, dolphins will be jumping *(adverb)* over the submarine.

_____ 15. The U.S. *(proper adjective)* insignia for a submarine sailor displays a submarine with two dolphins.

POLE VAULTING

Jules Verne's style in *Twenty Thousand Leagues Under the Sea* helps us form opinions about the characters and the author himself. Nemo and Aronnax seem to be very intelligent men, which leads us to believe Verne must be learned also. Verne wrote about airplanes, television, and space satellites before they were invented. He must have been extremely imaginative as well as knowledgeable.

- *Choose an interjection from the excerpt that not only characterizes the captain but also gives a hint of the time in which the story was written.*

Someone You Know: Writing a Character Profile

The profile, or side view, of someone's head often reveals his most prominent facial features. A long nose, a high forehead, or a jutting chin may not be so noticeable when you view someone face to face. But features like these will show up well in his profile. Nearly everyone's profile is unmistakable. You can recognize a person even if the profile is the only angle of his face you can see.

But there are some details that a profile does not reveal. A profile may not show the color of the eyes or the shape of the face. A dimple or a wrinkle or a freckle may be hidden on the other side of the nose. Discerning a person's feelings is difficult when looking only at his profile and not directly into his face. So a profile reveals prominent features—things nearly everyone would recognize—but not a great deal of personal detail.

The same is true of written profiles. A written profile of a character in a story describes him by his most prominent traits—the things by which anyone could recognize him—without going into much detail. In other words, it is a fairly short summary of what a character is like and what part he plays in the story.

Think about the many characters mentioned in the Bible. We are not often given details about a character's physical appearance, unless those details are important to the story. In most cases, we are kept at a distance from the character's deepest thoughts and feelings. But we are given events, decisions, and relationships to other characters that reveal the basics—the things that stand out most about that character's personality. We are given his achievements—the things in his life that make him noteworthy and exemplary. And many times, we are given his weaknesses—the things in his life that make him human and, in some cases, infamous.

Here is a character profile of Solomon.

> Solomon was king of Israel for forty years after the death of his father, David. Shortly after he came to the throne, the Lord told him to ask of Him anything he wanted. Solomon asked for an understanding heart to judge his people wisely. Because he had made an unselfish request, God blessed him with riches and honor. He became famous all over the world for his riches and wisdom. During his life, he wrote three thousand proverbs and over a thousand songs. We can read his writings in the books of Proverbs, Ecclesiastes, and Song of Solomon.
>
> Solomon kept peace in the kingdom during his reign. Rather than going to war, as David had done, he turned his energies to building projects. He built a beautiful temple for the Lord and palaces for himself and the pharaoh's daughter, his wife. The friendships that Solomon made with kings of other nations helped him get the materials he needed for building.
>
> The Bible tells us that Solomon had a great love for the Lord. But he also loved many women. He married foreign wives, and they eventually turned his heart away from the Lord. He even built altars and worshiped their false gods. Because he was unfaithful to the Lord, the Lord took ten tribes of the kingdom away from his family and gave them to Jeroboam.

Your Turn: Writing a Character Profile

Choose a Bible character whose life intrigues you. Write a profile of the character, giving a summary of the notable things Scripture mentions about that person. Remember to include character qualities that may not be specifically mentioned but are clearly revealed by the character's actions.

DASHING AHEAD! CRITICAL THINKING

The Case of the Poison Pen

Inspector Jameson's office was a mess. It had been a mess since three weeks ago when the department's maintenance crew had begun painting it. They had knocked holes in the cracked plaster, but they had not patched the holes. They had dragged a huge drop cloth in and had covered the window with it. They had even brought in brushes, rollers, and cans of paint, leaving them in a cluttered pile near the office door. But they had not returned. Jameson wanted to know why.

"Because they're painting the superintendent's office and conference room instead," Officer Bell said. "I wonder, sir, if I could finish the job for you?"

"Err, well, I don't know," Jameson said, pondering. "I don't guess it could do any harm. I'm sick and tired of having people come in here and see this mess. It doesn't seem to matter how many times I contact maintenance; the answer is always the same: 'Once we finish the superintendent's office, we'll get right back to yours, Inspector Jameson.'"

"Well," Bell said with a little cough, "we do know that the superintendent is, uh, very particular."

"Hard to please is what you mean—but you're too nice to say it." He paused and thought a moment.

"I painted my garage at home last summer," Bell added. "My wife says I did a fine job. She tends to be, uh, very particular too."

Jameson swung his feet off the desk and stood up. "Go ahead, Bell. I have to be out this afternoon anyway, and your tasks are rather light right now. If maintenance gets irritated at your initiative, perhaps it will give them incentive to get in here and do it themselves."

Right after lunch Bell started working on the project. He had just started on the wall nearest the door when Jameson burst back in. "Forgot my keys!" he said. Then he surveyed the little square of paint where Bell had begun. "Red? Red! I didn't requisition red paint! I'll feel like I'm trapped inside a . . . a—"

"Ventricle, sir?"

The buzzer on Jameson's intercom went off. He picked up the phone. "Yes?"

"Inspector, there's an Edith Crumb here to see you. She doesn't have an appointment."

"No, she doesn't, but I do! I've a dentist appointment, and I don't have time to see anyone right now."

"She's being rather insistent, I'm afraid. Wait a minute . . . where did she go?"

The receptionist's question was answered that very moment as the door once again burst open, hitting Bell as he bent over to dip the roller. Red paint spattered all over Bell—onto his stomach, chest, face, and even onto the place where hair would have been if he had had any. Miss Edith Crumb didn't seem to notice or care.

She was a small woman with white hair neatly pinned in a bun. She held out a stack of papers to the inspector.

"My name is Edith Crumb," she said. "These letters began appearing in the 'In' box on my desk two months ago. At first I didn't think anything of them. Just a disgruntled reader, I thought. I write, you know."

"I knew I'd heard your name before!" Bell blurted out. "You write for *What's News,* don't you?"

Miss Crumb turned and took a long, slow look at Officer Bell, from his paint-spattered tennis shoes to the top of his paint-spattered head. By the time she had finished her cold perusal, his face was as red as the paint on the dripping roller he held.

Prepositions, Conjunctions, and Interjections 155

"I'm here to talk to the detective, young man. Not to a painter." She turned back to Jameson.

Jameson stifled a smile. "Won't you sit down, Miss Crumb?"

Edith Crumb drew herself up to her full height of approximately four feet, eleven and three-quarters inches. "I will not! This won't take but a moment." She plopped the stack of papers on Jameson's desk. "As I said, I didn't think much of these letters at first. But they keep coming!"

"Who else in your office knows about these letters, Miss Crumb?"

"Well, there's Mr. Hector, who's in charge of Sales and Marketing. There's my editor, Ethel Stankhouse. Of course, various others know as well. But that really doesn't matter; I know who's writing them: Samantha Quincy. She left the magazine three months ago. She was head of Sales and Marketing prior to Mr. Hector's arrival. She never liked me, and I'm sure she's trying to scare me to stop my writing. After all, my articles are the reason most people buy the magazine."

"Let me look these over, Miss Crumb, and then we'll talk to people on your staff and also to Samantha Quincy."

"Well, see that you do! I'm tired of these threats, and, I don't mind telling you, they're starting to scare me a little. By the way," she added, "I've stacked the letters in the order in which I received them, with the most recent ones toward the bottom."

After Miss Crumb left, Jameson and Bell began looking over the threatening letters. "Your pen is mightier than a sword," one read, "but is it sharper?" Another read, "Thousands read your words, but you will eat them." The words were crudely cut from a magazine and carelessly applied to the paper.

Jameson flipped through the stack, reading various notes at random. He let out a low whistle when he read the most recent one. "Listen to this, Bell: 'You are highly respected in literary circles. What would you like on your tombstone?'"

Bell read it over Jameson's shoulder, wiping his hands on his white overalls. "Something like that would sure give me the creeps," he said. "Uh, I hate to bring it up, Inspector, but did you remember your dentist appointment?"

"I'll call and reschedule. This case intrigues me. Can you get me copies of some of Miss Crumb's *What's News* articles?"

"Yes, I, uh, happen to have a few issues at my desk." Bell scurried out and soon returned, arms overflowing with a jumbled stack of magazines.

Jameson picked up a copy and found Edith Crumb's article. "Hmmm," he said. He read several more. Bell, in the meantime, tried to wipe off paint that he had accidentally gotten on Jameson's door frame and glass. Jameson pretended not to notice.

"This Miss Crumb is quite opinionated. It seems to me, from what I've read, she just stirs up trouble. She seems to offend everyone. It will be difficult to find the one person who is mad enough to want to harm her. It may be that a whole group has gotten together to do her in."

"She seemed pretty sure this Samantha Quincy person is the guilty party," Bell noted.

"Samantha's dislike for Miss Crumb doesn't necessarily mean she's guilty, of course," Jameson said thoughtfully. "Here's the plan. You get changed and cleaned up. I'll call the magazine to see whether we can get in this afternoon to talk to some people. I'll also call Samantha Quincy to see whether she's available for an interview."

"I'll also fill out a requisition form for some paint remover, sir."

"Yes, yes, whatever. Meet me downstairs in fifteen minutes."

"And don't forget to call the dentist, Inspector."

Jameson sighed and picked up the phone.

Thirty minutes later Jameson and Bell were in the offices of *What's News,* waiting to see Hector Hector, Sales and Marketing Director. Several recent issues of the magazine lay on a little table in the lobby.

"Look at this," Jameson noted. "Their circulation has been steadily declining the last few months. Then it shot up dramatically last month. Wonder what's going on."

"Well, last month's issue was the one in which Miss Crumb revealed that she'd been receiving threatening notes. I guess—" Bell began, but he was interrupted as Hector Hector opened his office door.

"Come in, gentlemen, come in." Hector Hector, Sales and Marketing Director, was a small, dark-skinned man, balding, with a large, black mustache. The three men sat down, he behind his desk. "Miss Crumb told me you were coming. So terrible that someone as sweet and innocent as our little Miss Crumb could be the focus of such a disturbing campaign!"

"What can you tell us about the letters, Mr. Hector?"

Hector spread his hands wide. "I imagine you know as much as I do! She gets one every few days in the mail. I feel so sorry for her—she's such a wonderful woman."

"Do you know of anyone in the office who would have an interest in frightening or harming her?"

Hector shook his head dramatically. "Ridiculous! She's been with the magazine longer than anyone. She's like a grandmother to everyone around here. What possible reason could anyone here have for scaring her?"

"That's a good question, Mr. Hector. As soon as we have that answer, we'll have the answer to the case," said Jameson. "Could we talk to her editor, Ethel Stankhouse?"

"You are welcome to, Inspector. However, I must confess I don't know why you're interviewing people here. You should check the letters for fingerprints."

"That's a job for the boys down at the lab. They'll let us know what they find. But most criminals know enough nowadays to avoid leaving such obvious evidence."

"Hmph! I can tell you who the guilty person is, Inspector. It's Samantha Quincy, my predecessor."

"Why do you say that, Mr. Hector?"

"She and Miss Crumb never got along. Miss Crumb used her slight influence to get the magazine publisher to let Miss Quincy go several months back. Shortly after that the letters started arriving." Then he smiled. "I might add that circulation has increased since her departure . . . and, uh, since my arrival."

"Did you encourage Miss Crumb to go public in her column with the threats?" Jameson asked.

"Certainly not! I urged her to keep it a secret—wouldn't want anything to happen to the dear lady. But she insisted."

Jameson and Bell next interviewed Ethel Stankhouse, editor for *What's News.* The only thing of importance to come out of the interview was that Samantha Quincy had been of the opinion that Edith Crumb's columns were one reason that the magazine's circulation had dipped.

"Obviously she was wrong," said Miss Stankhouse, a tall, thin woman with mousy brown hair and eyes to match. "It was shortly after Samantha left that circulation began to increase."

Jameson and Bell's next stop was at Samantha Quincy's new office. She was now the Director of Sales and Marketing for *What's Mews,* a cat-lovers' magazine. Cats had the run of the offices, prowling everywhere.

After Mrs. Quincy and the detectives were seated in her office, she picked up a fat tabby that was circling her ankles and cuddled it under her chin. "How can I help you?"

Inspector Jameson told her of the afternoon's events. Mrs. Quincy rolled her eyes.

"I should have known!" she said. "I should have known Edith Crumb wouldn't be satisfied just to get me fired. She'd have to follow it up with slanderous attacks in an attempt to ruin this job for me as well!"

Samantha Quincy continued. "Edith Crumb, for all her grandmotherly appearance, is a very powerful woman. No one at *What's News* really likes her. They know that she shows poor judgment in her work and that she is part of the magazine's problems. But she's been there too long; besides that, she owns part of the magazine. Since my job was marketing, Edith blamed me for the drop in sales. When we disagreed on marketing strategies, she used her influence to get me fired."

She paused and put the cat back on the floor. "It's ironic, isn't it? She's part of the sales problem, and now her being in danger has increased circulation. People really enjoy reading about things like that. I'm so thankful, really, that I was fired from *What's News.* If I hadn't been, I wouldn't have this wonderful job here—I love cats!—and frankly, I'm making fifty percent more a year than I was at the other magazine."

Before you finish the story—

- *What would Samantha Quincy's motive be for writing the "poison pen" letters? What facts would imply that she is not guilty?*
- *Who are the other possible suspects besides Samantha Quincy? Can you think of what each one would gain from writing the letters?*
- *Who do you think is writing the letters? Why?*

The next day Jameson and Bell sat in Jameson's office discussing the case.

"I believe I know who the perpetrator of this crime is, Bell," Jameson said, leaning back in his chair with his feet on his desk.

"Really? Me too, sir."

"Tell me who you think it is and why. We'll see if we agree."

Bell sat down across from Jameson. His eyes were round with excitement behind his glasses. "Well, sir, I believe Miss Crumb is correct in her assumption that it's Samantha Quincy."

"Interesting! Why?"

"Well, it seems obvious to me that Mrs. Quincy and Miss Crumb didn't get along. This is Mrs. Quincy's way of getting revenge on Miss Crumb."

"So you think that Mrs. Quincy came up with a plan to hurt circulation, but it instead increased the sales for *What's News*?"

Bell sat back in his chair. "Well, the plan backfired. Miss Crumb hasn't received any letters in several days. I'll bet Samantha gave up since they were having the opposite effect from the one she wanted."

Jameson stood up and began pacing back and forth. "Your theory has merit, Bell, but I can see several holes in it. First of all, as I've said, Mrs. Quincy would not be interested in participating in a plot that would end up boosting sales for a magazine that had fired her."

"But—"

Jameson held up a finger to silence Bell. "As Director of Sales and Marketing, she would know a scandal of this type would increase, not decrease, sales. Also, remember that she's very happy in her present job and that she's making more money. Also, I don't see her as the personality type to seek revenge."

"So if she didn't do it, then who?"

"Someone who was interested in boosting the magazine's sales. Someone who had access to Miss Crumb's 'In' box—remember, that's where the letters appeared. Someone who would make statements in the letters such as 'Your pen is mightier than a sword,' 'Thousands read your words,' and 'You are highly respected in literary circles.' Those aren't the words of someone who dislikes Edith Crumb."

Bell's mouth dropped open. "Inspector! Are you implying that Edith Crumb wrote the letters herself?"

Just then the intercom on Jameson's desk buzzed. He picked up the receiver. "Yes? . . . Just a moment." Jameson hung up.

Now it was Bell's turn to stand and pace. "Miss Crumb owns part of the magazine, so she wants sales to stay high. She has access to her own 'In' box, of course. And she doesn't like Samantha Quincy, so she blames the crime on her. It all makes sense!"

"Except for one detail. Why would she come to the police for help if she knew we very well could discover that she was, uh, threatening herself, shall we say?"

Bell sat down again. "Maybe—maybe she thought we were too stupid to figure it out?"

"No, I think the guilty party is just outside my door. I've called the person down for questioning, but once we present all the facts, I think an admission of guilt will follow. The person's first mistake was in trying to trick us by saying that the letters had come in the mail to Miss Crumb. They had appeared on her desk, as she told us, and not in the mail. The second mistake was in saying that Miss Crumb was the one who wanted to go public with the letters. I spoke earlier today with Miss Crumb; she said she had not wanted to go public; she did it only at this other person's urging. Do you remember who said the letters had come in the mail? Do you remember who said Miss Crumb wanted to go public with the letters?" Jameson went to the door and dramatically flung it open just as Bell jumped to his feet and shouted, "Hector Hector, the Sales and Marketing Director, Inspector!"

- *Mr. Hector mentioned that the letters started arriving shortly after Mrs. Quincy's dismissal. This means that they coincided with what other event?*

- *Were you correct in your assumption earlier in the story about who was guilty? If you were wrong, why? What errors of judgment did you make?*

- *What else about Hector Hector's testimony might have led Jameson to believe he was being less than completely honest?*

Prepositions, Conjunctions, and Interjections

Chapter 8

Phrases and Clauses

A Will to Learn
by Charles Tindley

Grammar

> "My first plan was to buy every book I could which I thought contained anything that I should know. Then I entered by correspondence, all the schools which my limited means would afford, and sought to keep up the studies with any pupil who studied in the school room. I was able to attend the Brandywine Institute and to finish its Theological course. By correspondence, I took the Greek course through the Boston Theological School and the Hebrew . . . through the Hebrew synagogue on North Broad Street. . . . I took my studies in Science and Literature as a private student because I was unable to attend the Universities where these subjects were taught. Thus, while I was unable to go through the schools, I was able to let the schools go through me."

In the book *Free Indeed,* Mark Sidwell relates the story of Charles Albert Tindley (1851-1933), the author of several well-known hymns, including "Stand By Me" and "Leave It There." This excerpt is from the chapter entitled "Charles Tindley," in which Sidwell quotes from a book of Tindley's sermons.

- *What do you think of the speaker's character? Why do you think he was unable to attend the universities? What about his writing shows you he got a good education?*
- *Which sentence from this excerpt will you be most likely to remember?*

You probably chose the last sentence as the most memorable. It is unique not only in what it says but in how it says it. And even more remarkable is its tone: upbeat and forthright without being false or proud. Because Tindley lived when African Americans were denied entrance into universities solely because of the color of their skin, his academic achievements are admirable, and his spiritual triumphs are heroic.

Tindley sets up a play on words in the dependent clause ("while I was unable to go through the schools"); then he skillfully puts a twist on it in the independent clause. The result is a mixture of wisdom and humor, a reflection of the author himself. This chapter will teach you more about phrases and clauses such as Tindley used.

Phrases

A **phrase** is a group of related words that does not contain both a subject and a predicate. A phrase may contain a subject or a verb, but not both. Nearly every sentence contains phrases. A group of related phrases put together can become a sentence. You have already learned about possessive phrases and prepositional phrases. The following example contains five phrases:

Fanny Crosby's inspiration has given the world several hymns about God's love.

Fanny Crosby's inspiration is a phrase that functions as the complete subject of the sentence. The simple predicate of the sentence is the phrase *has given.* The phrase that acts as the direct object is *several hymns,* and *the world* is the phrase that makes up the indirect object. *About God's love* acts as an adjectival (prepositional) phrase that modifies the noun *hymns*. Notice that none of the phrases has both a subject and a verb.

Clauses

A **clause** is a group of related words that has both a subject and a predicate. If the clause expresses a complete thought, it can stand alone and is an **independent clause.** If the clause does not express a complete thought and cannot stand alone, it is a **dependent clause** (sometimes called a subordinate clause). A dependent clause depends on the independent clause for its complete meaning. When a dependent clause is written as if it were a sentence, it is called a fragment.

Subordinate means "lower in order."

In the examples below, notice the difference between an independent clause that can stand alone as a complete sentence and a dependent clause that does not express a complete thought:

Independent: Mr. Heidorn sang bass in the Easter cantata.
Dependent/Fragment: Because the music of the Easter cantata was important in the morning worship service.
Independent: Shannon Charles played the organ.
Dependent/Fragment: Since she had majored in organ at college.

Even though all of the example clauses have both a subject and a predicate, only the independent clauses express complete thoughts. The dependent clauses are fragments because of the subordinating words *because* and *since*. These fragments cannot stand alone as sentences. The chart below lists other common subordinating words.

after	although	as
as far as	as if	as long as
as soon as	as though	because
before	even though	if
in order that	provided	since

so	so that	than
until	what	whatever
when	whenever	where
whereas	wherever	while

In Summary

A **phrase** does not contain both a subject and a predicate.

A **clause** contains both a subject and a predicate.

An **independent clause** can stand alone as a sentence, but a dependent clause cannot stand alone as a sentence.

A **dependent clause** written as a sentence is a fragment.

8-1 Practice the Skill

Label each italicized group of words *P* (phrase), *IC* (independent clause), or *DC* (dependent clause).

_____ 1. *A piece of music contains five basic elements.*

_____ 2. These elements are *tone, rhythm, melody, harmony, and tone color.*

_____ 3. *Even though the tone is a sound of definite pitch*, many people refer to that sound as a note.

_____ 4. The rhythm adds character to a piece of music because a composer can vary *the time and accent of the notes* according to his preference.

_____ 5. The melody, or tune, of a song *is usually* what most people remember.

_____ 6. Whenever a composer repeats a melody throughout a piece of music, *he creates a theme.*

_____ 7. A composer develops harmony *if he sounds two or more notes simultaneously.*

_____ 8. The tone color is *the quality of the music,* which varies depending on the musical instrument used.

_____ 9. Because of this variety, *composers can manipulate the tone color* as they arrange music for a group.

_____ 10. *Although the sound of music differs around the world*, all music contains these five basic elements.

8-2 Practice the Skill

Underline the subject once and the verb twice in each clause. Place parentheses around each dependent clause. (HINT: The part of the sentence outside the parentheses should include a complete sentence.)

1. When air vibrates against an object a certain number of times per second, music occurs.

2. On stringed instruments the vibration comes from pressure on the strings, whereas on wind instruments vibration comes from the air moving through the mouthpiece.

3. Even though a bow across the strings causes pressure on some stringed instruments, fingers or a pick causes pressure on others.

4. Because a harp has forty-seven strings, it produces more tones than any other stringed instrument.

5. Since the modern harp stands about seventy inches tall, a harpist sits during a performance and rests the harp against his right shoulder.

6. A harpist uses the foot pedals on the pedestal so that he can control the pitch of the strings.

7. The pitch of the strings rises while the performer depresses the pedal.

8. Although the harp and harpsichord have similar names, they are completely different instruments.

9. A harpsichord resembles a harp since on both instruments the strings are plucked.

10. The harp is a national symbol in Ireland, where the instrument first appeared during the eighth century.

8-3 Review the Skill

Underline the subject once and the verb twice in each clause. Place parentheses around each dependent clause. Circle each subordinating word.

1. Even though many people own cassette tapes, compact discs are more popular.

2. Although CDs can break, they generally last longer than cassette tapes.

3. Storage is convenient because CDs are approximately twelve centimeters in diameter.

4. A CD allows the choice of any selection on the disc, whereas a cassette features only continuous play.

5. If a CD is a standard disc, it can hold at least seventy-four minutes of sound.

6. Audio sound waves are digitally coded while a CD is being recorded.

7. A laser light reads the digital code as the disc spins.

8. While audio CDs are the most popular type of CDs, other types are used for files and pictures.

9. Since MiniDiscs are only 6.4 centimeters in diameter, they must be played on a special compact disc player.

10. After compact discs were developed for audio, they became popular in CD-ROM for computers.

Simple Sentences

A **simple sentence** is made up of one independent clause. It must contain a verb and its subject. However, some sentences have compound parts. A simple sentence may have a compound subject, a compound verb, or both.

    Simple sentence: Many ancient *hymns ministered* to early believers.

Phrases and Clauses   165

Simple sentence with a compound subject: The *tunes* and *words* are still sung today.

Simple sentence with a compound verb: Composers *wrote* and *sang* the second-century hymns.

Simple sentence with a compound subject and compound verb: The *music* and the *words honored* and *glorified* our Lord.

Compound Sentences

A **compound sentence** consists of two or more independent clauses joined together, usually either by a semicolon or by a comma and a coordinating conjunction. The chart below lists commonly used coordinating conjunctions.

and	nor	but
yet	or	for

Compound comes from the Latin *companere,* meaning "to put together."

Simple: *Heather plays* the trumpet.
Simple: *She can*not *play* the piano.
Compound: *Heather plays* the trumpet, but *she can*not *play* the piano.

Simple: *Vernon Charlesworth penned* the words to "A Shelter in the Time of Storm."
Simple: *Ira Sankey wrote* the music.
Compound: *Vernon Charlesworth penned* the words to "A Shelter in the Time of Storm"; *Ira Sankey wrote* the music.

Just like simple sentences, compound sentences may also have compound parts.

Compound Sentence: Dannah baked a cake, but I frosted it.

Compound sentence with compound subject: Dannah and I ate some cake, and we drank a glass of milk.

Compound sentence with compound verb: Dannah washed and dried our cake plates; I put the remains in the refrigerator.

Compound sentence with compound subject and verb: Dannah and I sat and talked afterwards, for we were exhausted.

Diagram a compound sentence the same way you would diagram two simple sentences. Join the two diagrams with a vertical dotted line (with a platform in the middle for the conjunction) from the verb of the first sentence to the verb of the second sentence: **Dannah baked a cake, but I frosted it.**

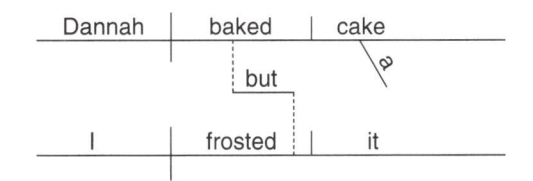

```
  Dannah  |  baked  |  cake
                    \ a
            : but
     I     |  frosted  |  it
```

IN SUMMARY

A **simple sentence** consists of one independent clause.

A **compound sentence** consists of two or more independent clauses.

8-4 PRACTICE THE SKILL

Underline the coordinating conjunctions. Label each sentence *S* (simple) or *Cd* (compound).

_____ 1. Francis Scott Key wrote the words to America's national anthem, "The Star-Spangled Banner."

_____ 2. The song was very popular shortly after 1812, but it did not become the official national anthem until 1931.

_____ 3. During the War of 1812, the American William Beanes was a prisoner on a British ship.

_____ 4. Aboard the ship, John Skinner and Francis Scott Key negotiated for his release.

_____ 5. The British agreed to Beanes's release, but they were preparing for an attack on Fort McHenry.

_____ 6. They held all three men aboard the ship until the end of the battle.

_____ 7. Scott, Skinner, and Beanes stayed up all night with great concern for their country.

_____ 8. At sunrise, the men detected the Americans' perseverance, for their flag still flew over the fort.

_____ 9. The turmoil of the night and the grand sight of the flag in the morning inspired Francis Scott Key's words to "The Star-Spangled Banner."

_____ 10. Francis Scott Key loved his country, and his beloved flag waves proudly over his grave today.

8-5 Review the Skill

In the blank, label each sentence *S* (simple) or *Cd* (compound). Label the sentence patterns. Above each word of the sentence pattern, write its label.

_____ 1. Godly women wrote many of our favorite hymns.

_____ 2. Charlotte Elliott lived with her brother, for she was very ill by the age of thirty.

_____ 3. In 1836 she wrote "Just As I Am" and later wrote over one hundred other hymns.

_____ 4. William B. Bradbury wrote the tune, but it originally accompanied words of a different song.

_____ 5. Thomas Hastings later put Bradbury's tune with the words of "Just as I Am."

_____ 6. Elliott wrote the words as a testimony of her relationship with the Lord, yet this song has blessed thousands around the world.

_____ 7. Another well-known song is "Nearer, My God, to Thee."

_____ 8. Sarah Flower Adams wrote the words, and her sister arranged the music to this popular song.

_____ 9. The band aboard the *Titanic* played this song; it comforted many passengers.

_____ 10. Contributions by other female hymn writers come from Fanny Crosby, A. Katherine Hankey, and many more.

Complex Sentences

A **complex sentence** also consists of at least two clauses. However, a complex sentence contains one independent clause and one or more dependent clauses:

$$\overset{S}{\text{John and Charles Wesley}} \overset{TrV}{\text{wrote}} \overset{DO}{\text{many powerful songs,}} \textit{although} \overset{S}{\textit{they}}$$
$$\overset{TrV}{\textit{did not arrange}} \overset{DO}{\textit{the music.}}$$

$$\overset{S}{\text{Charles Wesley,}} \textit{\overset{S}{who} \overset{LV}{was} also \overset{PN}{a preacher,}} \overset{TrV}{\text{wrote}} \overset{DO}{\text{"O for a Thousand Tongues."}}$$

Both sentences are complex sentences because each contains an independent clause *(John and Charles Wesley wrote many powerful songs; Charles Wesley wrote "O for a Thousand Tongues")* and a dependent clause *(although they did not arrange the music; who was a preacher)*. Notice that the independent and dependent clauses in both sentences contain subjects and predicates. Both dependent clauses contain subordinating words *(although, who)*.

The dependent clause may appear before the independent clause, within the independent clause, or after the independent clause.

Before: *Although many hymns were translated,* countless hymns have been written in English.

Within: The hymn writers, *because they had a firm faith,* wrote strong, inspiring hymns.

After: The composers wrote beautiful melodies, *whereas the authors wrote moving poetry.*

Compound or Complex?

Determining whether a sentence is compound or complex requires analyzing the clauses. If a clause contains subordinating words, it is dependent. If it does not, it is independent. Two independent clauses make a compound sentence; one independent clause and one or more dependent clauses make a complex sentence.

Compound: Our tour group visited London, and we saw Westminster Abbey.

Complex: Since most of the abbey's architecture is Gothic, it is generally considered a Gothic structure.

Compound: The abbey is a burial site for many famous persons, yet it is also a place of coronation for English monarchs.

Complex: Westminster Abbey, even though it is not the largest cathedral in London, has been the site of every English coronation since Norman times.

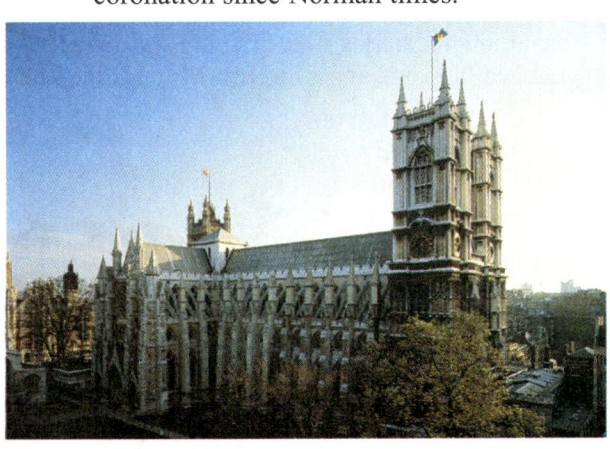

Chapter 16: Commas to Separate
pp. 326, 328

In Summary

A **complex sentence** consists of one independent clause and at least one dependent clause.

8-6 PRACTICE THE SKILL

Label each sentence in the following excerpt *S* **(simple),** *Cd* **(compound), or** *Cx* **(complex).**

¹ He found a pencil stub in a drawer and ripped up a grocery bag. ² He scribbled on the torn paper: Colverton—Eldridge warehouse. ³ Travis was whistling and calling for Skeeter. ⁴ Mark rushed to the front door, and [he] stuck the paper between the door and the doorjamb. ⁵ When he slammed the door shut, the paper fluttered in the breeze.

⁶ Travis came around the corner. ⁷ "Skeeter's not here!"

From *The Case of the Dognapped Cat* by Millie Howard ©1997 Bob Jones University Press.

1. _____
2. _____
3. _____
4. _____
5. _____
6. _____
7. _____

8-7 PRACTICE THE SKILL

Label each sentence *S* **(simple),** *Cd* **(compound), or** *Cx* **(complex).**

_____ 1. Because writers often consult different sources, they may produce contradictory accounts of a hymn's origin.

_____ 2. However, each account testifies of God's presence in the hymn writer's life.

_____ 3. Charles Wesley wrote many of his hymns so that others would manifest courage and faith in the Lord.

_____ 4. Wesley knew that God is great, powerful, and majestic; a Savior, Companion, and Friend; "an ever present help."

_____ 5. Although his brother John wanted no changes in Charles's songs, many of the songs were altered.

_____ 6. Even though Charles Wesley wrote six stanzas to "Rejoice, the Lord Is King," most modern hymnals include only four.

_____ 7. In 1747 Charles fell in love with Sarah Gwynne, yet he did not propose until two years later.

_____ 8. Charles Wesley died on March 29, 1788.

_____ 9. He was still writing hymns on his deathbed.

_____ 10. Wesley wrote his last hymn shortly before his death; the hymn was a poem of praise to the Lord.

8-8 Review the Skill

Label each sentence *S* (simple), *Cd* (compound), or *Cx* (complex).

_____ 1. "I, even I, will sing unto the Lord" (Judges 5:3).

_____ 2. "I will sing unto the Lord, for he hath triumphed gloriously" (Exodus 15:1).

_____ 3. "Therefore I will give thanks unto thee, O Lord, among the heathen, and I will sing praises unto thy name" (II Samuel 22:50).

_____ 4. "O Lord, open thou my lips; and my mouth shall shew forth thy praise" (Psalm 51:15).

_____ 5. "Because thy lovingkindness is better than life, my lips shall praise thee" (Psalms 63:3).

_____ 6. "With trumpets and sound of cornets make a joyful noise before the Lord, the King" (Psalm 98:6).

_____ 7. "I will sing praises unto my God while I have my being" (Psalm 146:2).

_____ 8. "Sing unto the Lord with the harp" (Psalm 98:5).

_____ 9. "But I will declare for ever; I will sing praises to the God of Jacob" (Psalm 75:9).

_____ 10. "When they had sung an hymn, they went out into the mount of Olives" (Matthew 26:30).

Adjective Clauses

An **adjective clause** is a dependent clause used like an adjective. Just as an adjective or an adjectival phrase modifies a noun or pronoun, an adjective clause modifies a noun or pronoun. Usually an adjective clause comes immediately after the noun or pronoun it modifies. An adjective clause answers the same question about the noun that a single adjective or an adjectival phrase answers *(which one?* and *what kind?)*. Remember that an adjective clause must have a subject and a verb.

Adjective: *Favorite* hymns at our church include "Jesus, the Very Thought of Thee" and "Nothing Between."

Adjectival Phrase: A favorite hymn *of my mother's* is "Amazing Grace."

Adjective Clause: Which hymns *that your church sings* do you enjoy most?

Adjective: He invested his *allowance* money in the bank.

Adjectival Phrase: He invested the money *from his allowance* in the bank.

Adjective Clause: He invested the money *that his father gave him for allowance* in the bank.

8-9 Practice the Skill

In the blank write the word modified by the italicized adjective clause.

_____ 1. Hymns, *which we can sing anytime,* have been written for various purposes.

_____ 2. Some hymns, such as "Holy, Holy, Holy! Lord God Almighty," are songs *that Christians sing as an act of worship.*

_____ 3. "Day by Day" is a hymn *whose words are sung as an encouragement to believers.*

_____ 4. Evangelistic hymns are sung as an appeal to sinners, *for whom Christ died.*

_____ 5. "Take My Life and Let It Be" was written as a prayer by Francis Ridley Havergal, *whose desire was to be more dedicated to Christ.*

_____ 6. "Amazing Grace" was written by a man *who desired to be Christ's humble servant.*

_____ 7. "How Great Thou Art" expresses the majesty of God, *who created the whole universe.*

_____ 8. "Away in a Manger" reminds us of the night *that Christ was born.*

_____ 9. "There Is a Fountain Filled with Blood" tells us of the one *who gave His life to save us.*

_____ 10. The words to "O Perfect Love, All Human Thought Transcending" by Dorothy Frances Gurney were composed for the author's sister, *who included the song at her wedding.*

8-10 Review the Skill

In the blank write the word modified by the italicized adjective clause.

_____ 1. One day a young actress *whose talent was well known* saw a young invalid girl through an opened door.

_____ 2. This young actress decided to encourage the young girl, *who appeared very weak.*

_____ 3. The actress was the type of person *for whom the young invalid prayed daily.*

_____ 4. The invalid, *who was a devout Christian,* led the actress to the Lord.

_____ 5. After this decision, the young actress gave up the only occupation *that she had ever known.*

_____ 6. Her father, *who was the head of the acting company,* convinced her to do one more show.

_____ 7. After the show, the young actress quoted to the audience the song *that spoke of her love for Christ.*

_____ 8. The song, *which means so much to many Christians,* was quoted for the first time after a theater performance.

_____ 9. The audience was touched, and the actress's father accepted the one *from whom he had been running for many years.*

_____ 10. "My Jesus, I love Thee, I know Thou art mine," is the first line of the song *that stirred the hearts of everyone in the audience.*

Relative Pronouns

Most adjective clauses contain **relative pronouns.** Relative pronouns are a type of pronoun because they take the place of a noun. They are called relative because they relate the adjective clause to a word in the independent clause. This word is the antecedent of the relative pronoun.

that	which	who
whom	whose	

      S   TrV   DO   S   TrV   DO
Rena was fertilizing the *rosebush.* Her mother planted the *rosebush* last week.
      S   TrV   DO DO   S   TrV
Rena was fertilizing the rosebush ***that** her mother planted last week.*

The relative pronoun *that* takes the place of the second *rosebush. That* also relates the adjective clause to the independent clause. The whole adjective clause, *that her mother planted last week,* modifies the antecedent *rosebush.*

Relative pronouns do more in the sentence than simply relate the dependent clause to the independent clause. A relative pronoun may also function as a subject, object, or possessive adjective within the dependent clause.

                          S   TrV   DO
Subject: The man ***who** conducts our school orchestra* also plays the cello.

                          DO S   TrV
Direct Object: His cello is one ***that** he received from his great-grandfather.*

                                 S   InV
Possessive adjective: The parents ***whose** students play in the orchestra* may attend a free concert next Thursday.

Object of The hand-carved instrument ***which*** *he is so fond of* is
preposition: quite valuable.

Look again at sentence two above.

$$\text{S LV PN DO S TrV}$$
His cello is one ***that*** *he received from his great-grandfather.*

First, notice that the sentence pattern of the adjective clause may be different from the sentence pattern of the independent clause. The sentence pattern of this independent clause is S-LV-PN; the sentence pattern of the adjective clause in the same sentence is S-TrV-DO. Second, notice that the word order within the adjective clause may be inverted. The clause *that he received from his great-grandfather* has the direct object *that* coming before the subject *he*.

When a relative pronoun acts as the object of a preposition, it is often the second word in the clause. The fourth sentence above is another example of inverted order in a dependent clause.

$$\text{S   S LV PA LV   PA}$$
The hand-carved instrument ***which*** *he is so fond of* is quite valuable.

This same sentence could be written this way:

$$\text{S   S LV PA LV   PA}$$
The hand-carved instrument *of **which*** *he is so fond* is quite valuable.

This version of the sentence puts the preposition and object of the preposition in their normal order. Usually either way of stating the sentence is grammatically correct.

Sometimes a relative pronoun is understood (omitted) when it is the direct object or the object of a preposition in the dependent clause.

This is a hymn *(that)* I will sing in church. *(understood DO)*
The hymn writer is one *(whom)* I'd never heard of. *(understood OP)*
The church *(that)* I attend is near our house. *(understood DO)*

In Summary

An **adjective clause** is a subordinate clause used like an adjective.

A **relative pronoun** introduces an adjective clause and relates the clause to a noun or pronoun in the main clause.

8-11 Practice the Skill

Place parentheses around each adjective clause. Underline each relative pronoun.

1. Many of the hymns that are a part of our church music today were written in the nineteenth century.

2. During the time after the Civil War, Ira Sankey was the best-known song leader who ministered in large revival meetings.

3. Ira Sankey was the congregational song leader for D. L. Moody, whose revival campaigns attracted thousands of people.

4. At the meetings, Sankey conducted choirs, which consisted of hundreds of people.

5. After a message about the Good Shepherd at a revival meeting, Moody requested a song that would reiterate the message.
6. Sankey pulled out of his pocket "The Ninety and Nine," which was written by Elizabeth Clephane.
7. Ira Sankey, whose musical talent was great, composed the music to this song during his solo.
8. The audience for whom it was sung loved the new song.
9. "There'll Be No Dark Valley" and "Faith Is the Victory" are other songs that were composed by Ira Sankey.
10. Many famous hymns that were composed by Ira Sankey are still sung today.

8-12 Review the Skill

Place parentheses around each adjective clause. Underline each relative pronoun. In the blank write the relative pronoun's function within the clause.

_____ 1. The history of classical composers, whose music is either instrumental or vocal, goes back to ancient Greece.

_____ 2. Soloists, for whom some composers wrote, may also have had instrumental accompaniment.

_____ 3. The conductor, who directs the orchestra, rehearses all pieces with the musicians repeatedly before an actual performance.

_____ 4. Churches that musicians composed for helped the growth of Western classical music.

_____ 5. Plainsong, which churches of the day used in their services, has one melody throughout the entire piece.

_____ 6. Churches sang the psalms, which were lyrical poems, to plainsong until around the ninth century.

_____ 7. Ludwig van Beethoven, who eventually went deaf, specialized in piano sonatas, string quartets, and symphonies.

_____ 8. Beethoven, whose works manifested great power and range, wrote mainly during the classical period.

_____ 9. The neoclassical movement, which began in the early 1900s, modeled its music after composers from earlier centuries.

_____ 10. Since the 1950s, nontraditional elements have appeared in the pieces that modern composers have produced.

8-13 USE THE SKILL

Using the relative pronoun in parentheses, combine each set of simple sentences to form a complex sentence. Be sure to place the adjective clause after the word it modifies.

Example: Joseph Henry Gilmore wrote a famous hymn. He was a preacher in the nineteenth century. *(who)*

Joseph Henry Gilmore, who was a preacher in the nineteenth century, wrote a famous hymn.

1. Joseph Henry Gilmore had his hymn published in a very unusual manner. Gilmore wrote "He Leadeth Me." *(who)*

2. While preaching a message on Psalm 23, Gilmore was impressed by the words "He leadeth me." The words are in verse 2. *(which)*

3. Gilmore wrote a poem about the verse. The Lord had blessed Gilmore with great writing ability. *(whom)*

4. He later forgot about the poem. He had written the poem and given it to his wife. *(that)*

5. Three years later Gilmore accepted the pastorate of a church in Rochester, New York. Gilmore's desire was to be a pastor. *(whose)*

6. Before he preached, he was looking through a hymnbook and found his own poem. The poem had been set to music. *(which)*

7. His wife had the poem published in a magazine. He had given it to his wife. *(whom)*

_____

_____

8. William Bradbury had set the words to music. William Bradbury was a popular composer. *(who)*

_____

_____

9. The new song gave Gilmore assurance that God was leading him to the right church. The title of the new song was "He Leadeth Me." *(whose)*

_____

_____

10. This well-known hymn has been a source of assurance and encouragement to many people. God had led Gilmore to write the hymn. *(which)*

_____

_____

8-14 USE THE SKILL

Add an adjective clause to each sentence by answering the question after the sentence.

Example: Charles Tindley bought many books. *(What kind of books did he buy?)*

Answer: Charles Tindley bought many books *that contained valuable information.*

1. Tindley taught himself to read from old newspapers. *(Where did he find the newspapers?)*

_____

_____

2. He traveled fourteen miles both ways to take lessons from a schoolteacher. *(What kind of teacher was she?)*

_____

_____

Phrases and Clauses   177

3. Tindley began his ministry as a church janitor. *(What did he do as a janitor?)*

   _____

   _____

4. About fifteen years after entering the ministry, Tindley became the pastor of the church. *(Which church did he pastor?)*

   _____

   _____

5. Charles Tindley led many lost souls to the Savior. *(What is Tindley famous for?)*

   _____

   _____

8-15 Cumulative Review

Above each italicized word, label it *N* (noun), *V* (verb), *Pro* (pronoun), *Adj* (adjective), *Adv* (adverb), *Prep* (preposition), *Conj* (conjunction), or *Inter* (interjection). Underline each compound sentence. Place parentheses around each complex sentence.

Because music is an important part of our worship, it should always honor and glorify the Lord in every aspect. David was an excellent *musician,* and his psalms are still sung as praise to the Lord. The Bible shows us that music has a powerful effect *on* us. David, *who* ministered to Saul's disturbed spirit, knew the influence of music. King Saul's spirit was soothed after David *played* on his harp. Music can be a *powerful* tool, and it needs to reflect the characteristics of our great God.

POLE VAULTING

Charles Tindley was born a slave and was the son of slaves living in Berlin, Maryland, around the time of the Civil War. Young Tindley learned to read by salvaging scraps of newspaper and poring over them by firelight. He was so determined to be educated that he walked fourteen miles at night going and coming to get to his schoolteacher's house. As an adult he accepted

Christ as his Savior and began studying for the ministry. Tindley later became pastor of one of the largest churches in Philadelphia. His best-known hymn is "Nothing Between."

> Nothing between my soul and the Saviour,
> Naught of this world's delusive dream;
> I have renounced all sinful pleasure,
> Jesus is mine; there's nothing between.
> Nothing between my soul and the Saviour,
> So that His blessed face may be seen;
> Nothing preventing the least of His favor,
> Keep the way clear! Let nothing between.

- *What is the dependent clause in the last four lines of "Nothing Between"?*

For Sale: Writing an Ad for a Table Game

What kinds of games do you enjoy? Do you like fast-paced games? Quiet games? Games that large groups can play? Word games? Math games? Games that test your memory skills?

Almost everyone enjoys some kind of game. Different games have different selling points, or qualities that make them appealing to a particular audience. Advertisers try to capitalize on these points when writing ads for a game.

What if a popular toy company commissioned you to invent a new table game? What kind of audience would your game appeal to—children or adults or both? Would it be a party game for large groups or a quiet board game for two? Would it have a board? A buzzer? A timer? What would be the object of the game, or in other words, what do you have to do to win?

Here's an example of an ad for a game called Hats Off.

> Baseball caps, cowboy hats, berets, and sunbonnets! If you've always wanted to be a wearer of many hats, then Hats Off is the game for you. For each hat card you're given, there's a matching card showing the wearer of the hat. Your job is to match up the hats and the hatless people by trading with other players—but you can tell others what you need only by doing a charade of the hat-wearer. Talking is not allowed, but laughter, of course, can't be helped. Remember, if you want to say something, keep it under your hat—because the one hat you don't want to wear is the dunce cap! This game makes lively entertainment for the whole family. It's simple enough for kids, but fun for people of all ages.

Notice how the selling points of this game were worked into the ad: it's simple, it's geared for all ages, it's funny, and it's unique. The ad also gives you an idea of how to play the game without going into a lot of detail (since that's what the instructions inside the box are for).

Your Turn: "Ad"ding Up

Use the questions below to help you come up with a list of selling points for your game.
- Is your game affordable?
- What type of audience does your game appeal to?

- In what setting would your game be appropriate? (at a party? in a math classroom? at a family fun night at home?)
- What makes your game challenging?
- What makes your game fun?
- What makes your game different from all other games?

Write an ad for your game, seeing how many of your top selling points you can include. Remember to give a brief description of how to play and what the object is, focusing on what makes this game different from any other. When you've finished, show your ad to a classmate or a family member and see whether you can sell him on the game.

Passing the Baton
Writing Across the Curriculum

Health

Think of an environmental or health problem that concerns you. Write a letter to a government official to express your ideas about the causes and effects of the problem. Government officials are usually interested in what younger people, who are also potential voters, have to say.

Several approaches are available to you for this assignment. One approach may be to research the causes of the problem. Who is responsible? What could be done to correct the problem? What might be the cost of correction? Do alternatives exist? What are the effects of the problem?

Another approach may be to conduct a public opinion survey with four or five neighbors. First, decide which problem most concerns your neighborhood. Then, compose four or five brief questions about the problem. Compile the results of the opinion poll.

A third approach would be to include your research in a letter to your local newspaper editor.

STRETCHING OUT

What's in a Name?

What is your full name? Most people will answer this question with at least two, and usually three, names. People who lived before the 1100s, however, would have answered with one. But after that time people's names began to reflect what they did for a living, where they were born, or who their parents were. John Cooper was the John who made barrels, William Fields was probably not living in the mountains, and Charles Harrison was the son of Harris.

Do you know anyone with the last name Baker? What do you think his ancestors did? Do you know a Weaver? A Carpenter? What names can you think of that might reflect a birthplace? Take a look at all the last names in your class. What history can you find there?

Chapter 9

Verbals and Verbal Phrases

Two Look at Two
by Robert Frost

Grammar

"Love and forgetting might have carried them
A little further up the mountainside
With night so near, but not much further up.
They must have halted soon in any case
With thoughts of the path back, how rough it was   5
With rock and washout, and unsafe in darkness;
When they were halted by a tumbled wall
With barbed-wire binding. They stood facing this,
Spending what onward impulse they still had
In one last look the way they must not go,   10
On up the failing path, where, if a stone
Or earthslide moved at night, it moved itself;
No footstep moved it. "This is all," they sighed,
"Good-night to woods." But not so; there was more.
A doe from round a spruce stood looking at them   15
Across the wall, as near the wall as they.
She saw them in their field, they her in hers.
The difficulty of seeing what stood still,
Like some up-ended boulder split in two,
Was in her clouded eyes: they saw no fear there.   20
She seemed to think that, two thus, they were safe.

Then, as if they were something that, though strange,
She could not trouble her mind with too long,
She sighed and passed unscared along the wall.
"This, then, is all. What more is there to ask?"   25
But no, not yet. A snort to bid them wait.
A buck from round the spruce stood looking at them
Across the wall, as near the wall as they.
This was an antlered buck of lusty nostril,
Not the same doe come back into her place.   30
He viewed them quizzically with jerks of head,
As if to ask, "Why don't you make some motion?
Or give some sign of life? Because you can't.
I doubt if you're as living as you look."
Thus till he had them almost feeling dared   35
To stretch a proffering hand—and a spell-breaking.
Then he too passed unscared along the wall.
Two had seen two, whichever side you spoke from.
"This must be all." It was all. Still they stood,
A great wave from it going over them,   40
As if the earth in one unlooked-for favor
Had made them certain earth returned their love."

- *To whom does the word "they" refer in line 4? What do you know about the two people? What do you think the couple are forgetting?*
- *Compare the lines when the doe appears and when the buck appears. Why do you think the writer chose to write the lines this way?*
- *Have you ever seen an animal in the wild close enough to touch?*

    Is the word *forgetting* used as a noun or a verb in the first line? We usually think of *forgetting* as a verb. But it can also be used as a noun. When it is used as a noun, we call it a verbal. In line 7, there is another verbal, but this time it is used as an adjective. What word is it? This chapter will show you how versatile verbs can be.

Verbals and Verbal Phrases

You have already learned the eight parts of speech and how they function in sentences. You have also learned that sometimes a word can function as several different parts of speech depending on how it is used in a given sentence. **Verbals** are special forms of verbs that are not used as verbs but rather function as other parts of speech. Because a verbal retains some of its verb qualities (it shows action, can be modified by an adverb, and may have objects), it is sometimes mistaken for a normal verb. However, verbals function in sentences just like nouns, adjectives, or adverbs. Therefore, the three types of verbals have their own names: participles, gerunds, and infinitives.

    The *playing* boy did not see the bumblebee.

In the sentence above, the word *playing* shows the action of a child at play and modifies the noun *boy*. *Playing* is a verbal; more specifically, it is a participle.

Participles

The **participle** is a verbal that acts as an adjective.

    Strips of *frying* bacon popped and crackled in the cast-iron skillet.
    The *smashed* pumpkin smelled sweetly rotten.

Frying is a verbal used to describe the bacon; it conveys the action of the verb *fry* and modifies a noun. *Smashed* also acts as part verb/part adjective because it shows the action of *smash* and describes the pumpkin. *Frying* and *smashed* both carry the action of verbs and describe nouns; therefore, both are participles. They are examples of two different types of participles: the present participle and the past participle.

Present Participle

The **present participle** consists of the first principal part plus *ing*. Like any adjective, a participle by itself usually comes before the noun it modifies. Sometimes another noun functioning as an adjective comes between the participle and the noun it modifies.

    A *running* man aroused curiosity in the neighborhood.

    The *tapping* sound eventually woke the household.

    The *idling* car engine sounded loud.

Remember, though, that the first principal part of a verb plus *ing* can also function as the main verb in a verb phrase. Consider carefully the function of an *ing* word in a sentence before identifying it as either verb or participle. A normal verb shows the action of the subject; a participle describes the subject or another noun in the sentence.

    Participal: *Hurrying,* Reba almost dropped her books.
    Progressive verb: Reba *was hurrying* to class when she almost dropped her books.

In the first sentence, the participle *hurrying* modifies *Reba;* in the second, *Reba* is the subject of *was hurrying,* which conveys Reba's action on her way to class.

In Summary

A **verbal** is a special verb form that acts as a noun, an adjective, or an adverb but retains some verb qualities.

A **participle** is a verbal that acts as an adjective.

The **present participle** consists of the first principal part plus *ing*.

9-1 Practice the Skill

Underline the present participles. Draw an arrow from each underlined participle to the noun it modifies. Some sentences may not contain a present participle.

1. The exciting life of a river otter is filled with fun and frolic.

2. Ironically, river otters are afraid of the water when they are very young.

3. Swimming parents sometimes carry their babies on their backs.

4. While the babies are learning, the parent will swim under the water and leave the little otters to keep themselves afloat.

5. After much practice with their parents, otters become amazing swimmers.

6. Because fishing otters find food quickly, they have much time for leisure and play.

7. Playing otters often catch fish just for fun.

8. During winter you may see a sliding otter on a snowy hillside.

9. River otters travel frequently while they are exploring.

10. Otters have close families, and a mourning otter will often grieve for days for a dead family member.

9-2 Review the Skill

Underline the present participles. Draw an arrow from each underlined participle to the noun it modifies. Some sentences may not contain a present participle. Label the parts of the sentence patterns. Above each word of the sentence pattern, write its label.

1. In addition to man, the earth is full of many interesting creatures.

2. One such animal is the amazing freshwater lungfish.

3. Today six species of lungfish inhabit the earth's waters.

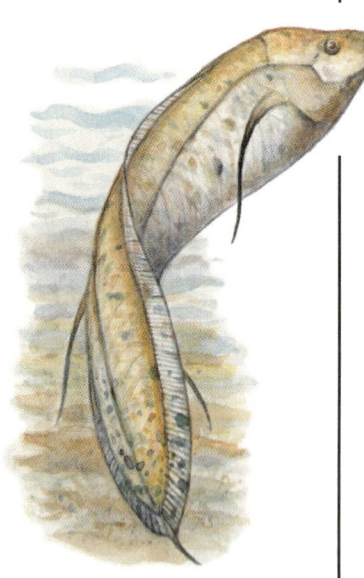

4. These differing species make their homes in South America, Africa, and Australia.

5. Most underwater creatures are surviving with the oxygen from their aquatic environments.

6. However, God has given African lungfish the surprising ability of oxygen intake from air.

7. The lungfish has a special lunglike breathing organ.

8. The burrowing African and South American lungfish can survive a drought.

9. The tunneling fish produces a cocoon from a slimy substance.

10. Estivating African lungfish breathe through a narrow passage to the surface until the drought's end.

Past Participle

The **past participle** is the same as the third principal part. (This is the form that uses *have* with the perfect tenses.) Like the present participle, the past participle expresses the action of a verb and describes a noun or pronoun. However, the past participle usually has a passive meaning.

The *chipped* tooth needed repair.
(The tooth *was chipped* by someone or something.)

The dental hygienist used a *filled* syringe to numb the area around the tooth.
(The syringe *was filled* by someone.)

Dimmed lights calm many patients.
(The lights *were dimmed* by someone.)

Because the past participle is also used as the main verb in some sentences, you must consider its use in the sentence. Before identifying the third principal part as a past participle or as a part of a complete verb, look at the sentence to see how it functions.

Past participle: The old *broken* tree would soon fall.
Passive verb: The oak *was broken* by the strong wind.

In Summary

The **past participle** is made up of the third principal part and has a passive meaning.

9-3 Practice the Skill

Underline the past participles. Draw an arrow from each underlined participle to the noun it modifies.

1. One of the most picturesque creatures is the *endangered* snow leopard.

2. The snow leopard's other *given* name is the ounce.

3. A *grown* snow leopard may reach a length of six or seven feet.

4. Snow leopards' beautiful tails account for roughly three feet of their total *recorded* length.

5. The snow leopard has *spotted* fur; its coat is gray with blackish leopard spots.

6. Sometimes the eyes of the snow leopard appear a soft, *muted* blue.

7. These cats dwell among the *snow-swept* steeps of the Himalayan and Altai Mountains as well as among other mountain ranges of central Asia.

8. Snow leopards also frequently reside below the mountain snowfall because of a lack of *needed* prey.

9. The snow leopard's *hunted* prey includes the markhor, a goat with spiral horns.

10. Photographs of the snow leopard have helped increase concern for the cat's protection in order that it not become another *lost* species.

9-4 Review the Skill

Underline the participles. Draw an arrow from each underlined participle to the noun it modifies.

1. The *spotted* skunk and the *striped* skunk are common types of skunks.

2. People normally know a skunk by its *striped* fur and offensive smell.

3. The *easily recognized* skunk is normally gentle and complacent.

4. A skunk's defense leaves an impression on *uninformed* enemies.

Verbals and Verbal Phrases 187

5. An alarmed skunk will warn its enemy.

6. The approached skunk will lift its tail high in the air.

7. The skunk will aim into the eyes of an undeterred enemy.

8. A sprayed victim endures burning eyes and smelly clothes.

9. Soiled clothes are often unusable; one must either bury or burn them.

10. A person must be extremely cautious around an offended skunk.

Participial Phrases

Because a participle is formed from a verb, it can also have modifiers. A participle and all of its modifiers make up a **participial phrase.** A participial phrase may follow or precede the noun it modifies. Notice that when the participial phrase comes first in the sentence, it is set off by a comma.

The man *running in the neighborhood* saw many people out in their yards.

Tapping at the window, Armand woke his family.

The past participle can also be part of a participial phrase, which can appear before or after the word being modified.

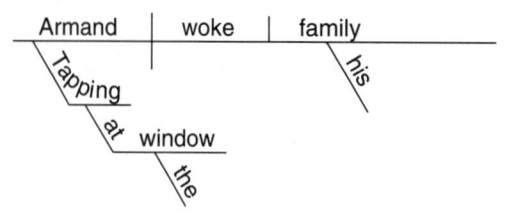

Ted's tooth, *chipped during a bad fall,* needed repair.

The dental hygienist used a syringe *filled with Novocain.*

Slightly dimmed lights relax the most anxious patients.

Participles and participial phrases are diagrammed as follows.

The tapping sound eventually woke the household.

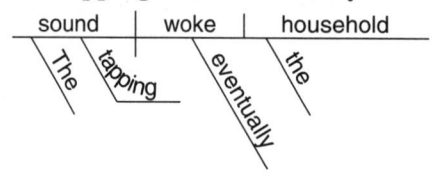

The chipped tooth needed repair.

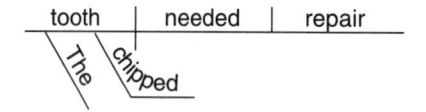

Tapping at the window, Armand woke his family.

The tooth, chipped during Ted's fall, needed repair.

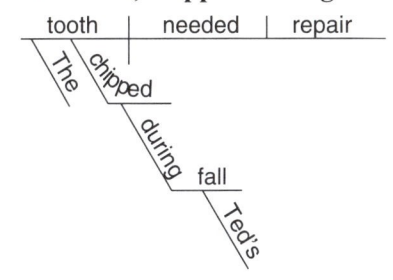

```
tooth    |   needed   |   repair
 \The  \chipped
          \during   fall
                    \Ted's
```

IN SUMMARY

A participle and all of its modifiers form a **participial phrase**.

9-5 PRACTICE THE SKILL

Underline the participles and participial phrases. Draw an arrow from each underlined participle or participial phrase to the noun it modifies. Label each underlined participle or participial phrase *present* (present participle) or *past* (past participle). Some sentences may not contain a participle.

_____ 1. Among the many creatures created by the Lord, certain birds have been extremely helpful to man.

_____ 2. Known for its gorgeous songs, the canary has enjoyed popularity as a domestic bird for years.

_____ 3. However, canaries also have served as indicators of threatening fumes and harmful gases in mines.

_____ 4. Because of its susceptibility to contaminated air, the canary has likewise saved lives in war because the bird's death alerts men to the presence of airborne poisons.

_____ 5. Another one of man's flying allies is the carrier pigeon.

_____ 6. Navigating carrier pigeons depend at least partly on the sun for their sense of direction.

_____ 7. These messengers aided long-distance communication before the invention of the telegraph and during the world wars.

Verbals and Verbal Phrases   189

_____ 8. The falcon has been hunting with man since before Christ's birth.

_____ 9. The peregrine falcon, diving as fast as 180 miles per hour, illustrates the swiftness of these birds.

_____ 10. Established as a popular activity among European nobility during and after medieval times, falconry became less popular when guns became available.

9-6 REVIEW THE SKILL

Combine the following pairs of sentences to make one sentence; insert a participle or participial phrase in the place indicated by the caret.

Example: There are many ^ dogs roaming the neighborhood. The dogs are constantly barking.
There are many barking dogs roaming the neighborhood.

1. The giraffe is the tallest animal ^. This animal is known to man.

   _____

   _____

2. The ^ male giraffe may be eighteen feet or taller. The male giraffe is towering.

   _____

   _____

3. Giraffes must live away from the ^ heat of the Sahara Desert. The heat is blistering.

   _____

   _____

4. They eat vegetation ^. This vegetation can be found on African grasslands.

   _____

   _____

5. The ∧ pattern of patches on a giraffe's coat disguises the animal from its predators. The pattern is interesting.

_____

_____

6. An adult giraffe need fear only a ∧ lion. The lion must be attacking.

_____

_____

7. A baby giraffe has more ∧ enemies, even though it may be up to six feet tall and 150 pounds at birth. Its enemies are threatening.

_____

_____

8. A ∧ giraffe can move at speeds of up to thirty-five miles per hour. The giraffe is galloping.

_____

_____

9. The giraffe's speed and powerful kick can sometimes keep away an ∧ enemy. The enemy has been discouraged.

_____

_____

10. The ∧ height of a full-grown giraffe scares many predators away. The height is intimidating.

_____

_____

Gerunds

The **gerund** is a verbal that functions as a noun.

      S   TrV   DO
Rappelling requires concentration.

S TrV   DO
I enjoy *skiing*.

Gerunds use the same form of the verb as the present participle: the first principal part plus *ing*. This may cause confusion since the two verbal types look similar. However, their functions are entirely different: the participle is an adjective; the gerund is a noun. As a noun, the gerund can function in any of the noun positions you have studied. A gerund may be a subject, direct object, indirect object, predicate noun, or object of the preposition.

Verbals and Verbal Phrases   191

Subject: *Staring* is impolite.
Direct object: Rajesh enjoys *reading*.
Indirect object: Sandra gave *studying* a momentary thought.
Predicate noun: His favorite activity is *singing*.
Object of preposition: We learn best by *doing*.

IN SUMMARY

A **gerund** is a verb form that functions as a noun in a sentence.

9-7 Practice the Skill

Underline the gerunds. Some sentences may not contain a gerund.

1. Some people are living without knowledge of certain African animals.
2. Finding information about Africa's bush baby may be difficult.
3. The animal's other name, the galago, might make researching tricky.
4. Wondering about the bush baby's peculiar name is common.
5. Perhaps crying gave the galago its other name, because the animal can sound like a child.
6. Because of its large ears and eyes, a galago's specialties are hearing and seeing.
7. This nocturnal creature spends much of its time in jumping.
8. This method of moving is the galago's way of travel in the tree limbs.
9. Of course, the galago also gives eating plenty of attention.
10. Insects, lizards, and fruit form part of the diet of the galago, which inhabits Africa's forests.

9-8 Review the Skill

Underline the gerunds. In the blank, label each underlined gerund *S* (subject), *DO* (direct object), *IO* (indirect object), *PN* (predicate noun), or *OP* (object of the preposition). Some sentences may not contain a gerund.

_____ 1. Constructing is a favorite activity of the inventive beaver.

_____ 2. The beaver cleans its fur by regular and careful grooming.

_____ 3. Beavers give cleaning an important role in their busy routine.

_____ 4. Beavers enjoy lying in anthills; the ants' feasting on parasites cleans the beaver.

_____ 5. These industrious animals chop down trees with their teeth. This process keeps their teeth from growing beyond a comfortable length.

_____ 6. Beavers in danger slap their tails on the water in warning to other beavers.

_____ 7. Before winter, the beaver will be storing bark for food.

_____ 8. Diving is the beaver's way of escape from predators.

_____ 9. Beavers can stay under the water for several minutes without breathing.

_____ 10. Beavers' best-known activity is building.

Gerund Phrases

Like a participle, a gerund can appear in a phrase. Because the gerund retains some of its verb qualities, it can be modified by adverbs.

>   PN
> Gayle's favorite hobby is *peacefully planting in her garden*.

>   OP
> Hope must pay more attention to *studying diligently for exams*.

The adverb *peacefully* in sentence one modifies the gerund *planting*. The adverb *diligently* in sentence two modifies *studying*. The other words in italics modify words within the two gerund phrases. In a sense, all of the words in each phrase work together as nouns: predicate noun and object of the preposition.

You have looked at the way a gerund functions as a noun and the way it is similar to a verb. Another way that a gerund is similar to a noun is that it can have adjective modifiers.

>   S
> *The recent housecleaning* involved the entire family.

>   OP
> Delores gave her coworkers a sample of *her delicious baking*.

>   S
> Sometimes *our best thinking* comes during relaxation.

In the last sentence, the gerund *thinking* is the subject, and the words *our* and *best* modify *thinking*. The other two sentences also contain adjectives modifying the gerund. All modifiers of the gerund are included in the gerund phrase.

Look at these examples of diagrams for gerunds and gerund phrases.

Rajesh enjoys reading.

Rajesh enjoys quietly reading in the park.

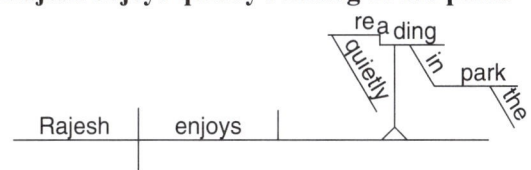

Chapter 6: Adverbs p. 116

IN SUMMARY

A **gerund phrase** consists of the gerund and all its modifiers. A gerund may be modified by adjectives or adverbs.

9-9 Practice the Skill

Place parentheses around the gerund phrases. Underline the gerunds.

1. (<u>Living</u> in Lapland's winter environment) is natural for reindeer.
2. By (the <u>wearing</u> of antlers), female reindeer resemble the males.
3. Man has succeeded in (reindeer <u>taming</u>).
4. (<u>Relying</u> on the reindeer) is a way of life for people in Lapland.
5. People in Lapland have given (the <u>domesticating</u> of the reindeer) much attention.
6. A domesticated reindeer's job is (<u>working</u> for his owner).
7. (<u>Pulling</u>) is relatively easy for reindeer.
8. Reindeer bring ease and speed to (the <u>transporting</u> of goods).
9. The male reindeer enjoys (<u>fighting</u> for control of a herd).
10. The Laplanders also practice (<u>cheesemaking</u> with reindeer milk).

9-10 Review the Skill

Place parentheses around each gerund or gerund phrase. Underline each gerund.

1. (<u>Sleeping</u> soundly in the winter months) is a characteristic of the grizzly bear.
2. Grizzly bears enjoy (the <u>eating</u> of berries and honey).
3. Another favorite pastime of the grizzly is (fish <u>catching</u>).
4. (<u>Teaching</u>) is an important job for the mother bear.
5. The winter season makes (<u>hunting</u> for food) more difficult.
6. They survive the cold months by (<u>resting</u> for long periods of time).
7. By (carefully <u>digging</u>), the mother makes a warm home for her new baby cubs.
8. A mother may spank her cub as a way of (<u>punishing</u>).
9. Young cubs are very curious, and their (inquisitive <u>wandering</u>) can sometimes get them into trouble.
10. One of the highest priorities for a mother grizzly bear is (the <u>protecting</u> of her young).

9-11 Practice the Skill

Label each italicized word G (gerund) or P (participle). Underline any adjective that modifies a gerund.

_____ 1. The raccoon likes the *making* of his home in a hollow tree.

_____ 2. Curious raccoons enjoy *exploring*.

_____ 3. *Rummaging* through garbage cans, raccoons acquire quick meals.

_____ 4. Raccoons have nimble fingers for the *opening* of containers and even doors.

_____ 5. A painful *pinching* by the raccoon's paw results in the catch of a crawfish.

_____ 6. The raccoon often dunks its food into water before a session of ravenous *indulging*.

_____ 7. In cold climates, *sleeping* raccoons spend most of the winter in their dens.

_____ 8. A raccoon's successful *hunting* is important for its survival.

_____ 9. Raccoons are sometimes identifiable at night by their *glowing* eyes.

_____ 10. These curious animals especially enjoy the surprise *finding* of shiny objects like coins or bits of metal.

9-12 REVIEW THE SKILL

Underline the gerunds and participles. In the blank, label each underlined word *G* (gerund) or *P* (participle). Draw an arrow from each participle to the word it modifies. Above each gerund, label its function *S* (subject), *DO* (direct object), *IO* (indirect object), *PN* (predicate noun), or *OP* (object of the preposition).

Example: __P__ The running dog will pass the school bus.

_____ 1. Seeing Eye® dogs are faithful and valuable assistants to their blind owners.

_____ 2. Dogs such as golden retrievers and Labrador retrievers serve by guiding.

_____ 3. Also, many of these highly trained animals are German shepherds.

_____ 4. Dogs preparing for positions with sightless owners undergo rigorous lessons for many months.

_____ 5. Dog guides must master the skill of accurately judging for distance and space.

_____ 6. For example, the dog must decide whether a hanging sign, much taller than his own head, is high enough for his owner's safe passage.

Verbals and Verbal Phrases

_____ 7. Disobeying is necessary if the owner gives dangerous instructions unknowingly.

_____ 8. Warning of things such as curbs and steps is also vital.

_____ 9. The intelligence seen in these dogs is truly remarkable.

_____ 10. In fact, one dog guide has received attention for bringing her owner's pajamas when the owner fell asleep on his couch.

Infinitives

Unlike participles and gerunds, which each have only one function—adjective or noun—the **infinitive** is a verbal that can function as three different parts of speech—noun, adjective, adverb—depending on the sentence in which it appears. The simple infinitive of a verb consists of the word *to* followed by the first principal part of the verb.

                    S   TrV   DO
Noun: Joanna loves *to paint*.

                 S LV   PN
Adjective: Dan is the person *to ask*.

                 S InV
Adverb: We go there *to eat*.

In the first example, *to paint* is the direct object of the verb *loves*. *To paint* tells what Joanna loves. In the second example, *to ask* is an adjective modifying the noun *person*. It tells which person Dan is: he is the person to ask. The infinitive in the last example is an adverb modifying the verb *go*; *to eat* tells why we go.

Remember, *to* plus a verb is an infinitive; *to* plus a noun or pronoun is a prepositional phrase.

After the speaker finished, we decided *to leave*. *(to + verb = infinitive)*

Arden went to *school*. *(to + noun = prepositional phrase)*

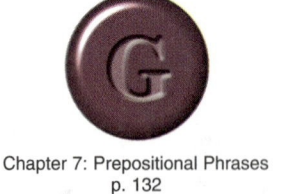

Chapter 7: Prepositional Phrases
p. 132

A gerund is the only verb form that can serve as an object of a preposition.
  Examples: He is interested in *going*.
                  She is occupied with *flying*.

Do not confuse the *to* of the infinitive with the preposition *to*.
  Incorrect: Singing is similar to speak slowly.
  Correct: Singing is similar to speaking slowly.

Some verbs are more likely to be followed by a gerund (*enjoy, give, avoid, admit, finish, risk, consider, appreciate, understand,* and so forth.)

Some verbs are more likely to be followed by an infinitive (*want, offer, hope, say, decide, ask, plan, wait,* and so forth).

In Summary

An **infinitive** is a verbal that can function as a noun, an adjective, or an adverb. An infinitive is identified by the word *to* plus a verb.

9-13 Practice the Skill

Underline the infinitives. Some sentences may not contain an infinitive.

1. Like all other animals, camels need water to survive.
2. Some camels like to bite; their owners put muzzles on them.
3. Camels make it easier for desert nomads to travel.
4. A camel can hear well, but it often pays no attention to commands.
5. Camels love to spit.
6. A calf can run when it is only a few hours old, and it calls to its mother with a soft voice like a lamb.
7. The tough, leathery skin pad on a camel's leg acts as a cushion when the camel kneels to rest.
8. A working camel cannot wear a bit and bridle because its mouth must be free to chew.
9. As a youngster, a calf will learn how to carry.
10. When a camel travels across the desert, food may be hard to find.

9-14 Review the Skill

Underline the infinitives. Label the function of each infinitive *N* (noun), *adj* (adjective), or *adv* (adverb). Some sentences may not contain an infinitive.

_____ 1. The hedgehog is an especially interesting animal to study.

_____ 2. To some people, hedgehogs are similar to porcupines.

_____ 3. To survive, the threatened hedgehog transforms itself into a spiky ball of spines.

_____ 4. As a result of this defense, hedgehogs have few foes to fear.

_____ 5. Hedgehogs like to eat.

_____ 6. One of the hedgehog's primary nighttime goals is to hunt.

_____ 7. It consumes worms, bugs, and more to live.

_____ 8. To navigate, the hedgehog uses its nose and ears.

_____ 9. Hedgehogs generally live alone; their usual reason for socializing is to mate.

_____ 10. For North Americans hedgehogs may be difficult to encounter; hedgehogs do not reside in North America.

Infinitive Phrases

Although infinitives act in ways different from verbs, they are still made from verbs and may be modified by adverbs or prepositional phrases. The infinitive and all of its modifiers make up the whole infinitive phrase.

    S   TrV   DO
We need *to walk quickly*.

    S   TrV   DO
We need *to walk across the bridge*.

Diagram infinitives and infinitive phrases as follows:

Joanna loves to paint.

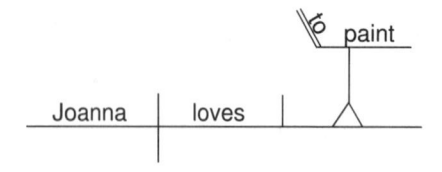

Joanna's ambition is to paint well.

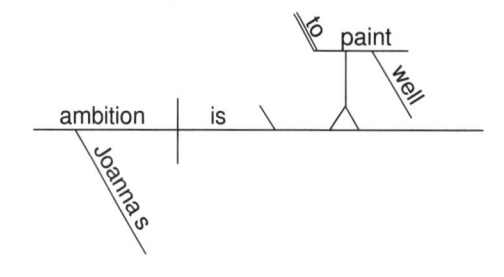

To paint with oils will be her next project.

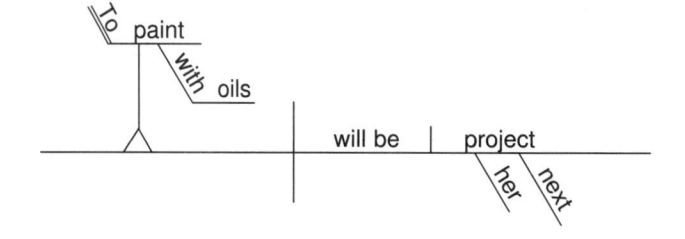

IN SUMMARY

The infinitive and all of its modifiers make up the **infinitive phrase**.

198   Chapter 9

9-15 Practice the Skill

Underline the infinitives and infinitive phrases. Some sentences may not have an infinitive phrase.

1. Canada geese are distinctive in their desire <u>to mate for life</u>.
2. Sometimes two ganders will decide <u>to fight for the affection of a female goose</u>.
3. During incubation, the goose's eggs need <u>to remain in the nest for twenty-five to thirty days</u>.
4. Both parents' instinct is <u>to protect carefully</u>.
5. After the eggs are hatched, the goslings are extremely susceptible to danger, and the parents must be alert constantly.
6. The male goose clears the water of potential dangers before the newly hatched goslings are allowed <u>to dive in</u>.
7. During the winter, geese travel together to a warm place <u>to survive</u>.
8. Canada geese are known for their intense loyalty to each other.
9. A Canada goose will not desert its partner, even if it must abandon its flight to warmer regions for the winter.
10. Geese have often sacrificed their own lives <u>to protect from predators</u>.

9-16 Review the Skill

Underline the infinitives and infinitive phrases. Some sentences may not have an infinitive phrase.

If looking for the creature with perhaps the thickest fur, man once had <u>to travel into the Andes Mountains</u>. There, the chinchilla is known <u>to live in its natural habitat</u>. Many people are undecided about which the chinchilla seems <u>to resemble</u>—a large gerbil or a small rabbit with shortened ears. Their fur is so dense that sixty hairs may be traced to one follicle. In fact, the fur is so fine that <u>to man's unaided sight</u> a single filament is nearly invisible. There is one fact you may be surprised <u>to learn</u>: one hair is finer than a strand of a spider's web! Such fur is important to the chinchilla because the animal may live at altitudes of fifteen thousand feet. Dwelling in these rocky places, chinchillas emerge at night <u>to feed</u>. They are vegetarians that eat seeds, plants, and berries.

9-17 Review the Skill

Underline the verbals (not the entire verbal phrases). Label each verbal *P* (participle), *G* (gerund), or *I* (infinitive). If the verbal is a modifier, draw an arrow from the verbal to the word it modifies.

_____ 1. Some people do not like barking dogs.

_____ 2. However, barking is not a problem with basenjis.

_____ 3. To find the unique basenji can be difficult.

_____ 4. Unlike other dogs, the basenji does not have the ability to bark.

_____ 5. Though usually silent, this dog can make a sound similar to yodeling.

_____ 6. Such noises and whines are the basenji's barking.

_____ 7. Ironically, the basenji likes to work as a herd dog, even without a true bark.

_____ 8. The basenji has a job to complete, so it wears a bell around its neck.

_____ 9. The ringing of the bell alerts everyone to the basenji's location.

_____ 10. Consequently, the mostly muted basenji still finishes the job.

9-18 Use the Skill

The following narrative tells of a young boy yearning for a pet. His mother has taken him to the local animal shelter, and there they survey their choices. Use an infinitive or infinitive phrase to complete each sentence.

Example: He determined __to find a pet__.

1. Jin-Su entered the pound _____
   _____.

2. After standing inside for a few moments, Jin-Su decided _____
   _____.

3. The man said the pound had many dogs and puppies _____
   _____.

4. _____

   made Jin-Su feel sad.

5. Jin-Su suddenly offered _____
   _____.

9-19 USE THE SKILL

Write a short paragraph about an animal you like. Then follow the remaining directions.

_____
_____
_____
_____
_____
_____
_____
_____
_____
_____
_____
_____
_____
_____
_____

Now label the sentence patterns of the sentences you have written. Can you observe a variety of patterns *(S-InV, S-TrV-DO, S-TrV-IO-DO, S-LV-PN, S-LV-PA)*? Can you find any participles, gerunds, or infinitives?

9-20 Cumulative Review

Combine the following pairs of sentences to make one sentence of the type indicated in parentheses. Underline any verbals in your new sentences.

1. A porcupine has stiff, prickly quills. A porcupine uses these quills to protect against attackers. *(complex)*

2. A porcupine quickly grows quills. The quills are fused hairs. *(complex)*

3. An experienced porcupine senses danger early. The porcupine releases its quills at the first sign of danger. *(compound)*

4. The projections on a porcupine's quills point backward. These projections are barbs. *(simple)*

5. Animals can easily kill a porcupine. A porcupine can be killed by flipping it over onto its back. *(simple)*

6. Porcupines are classified as rodents. They do not look as soft as other rodents. *(simple)*

7. Porcupines like to strip the bark off trees. They kill many trees this way. *(compound)*

8. Porcupines can cause pain with their sharp quills. Many animals avoid porcupines. *(complex)*

9. Each animal uses its own defense system in times of danger. Porcupines have their own unique defense system. *(compound)*

10. All animals are part of God's astounding Creation. We marvel at God's creative power. *(complex)*

POLE VAULTING

Robert Frost knew the advantages of verbals. Most verbals are formed from action verbs and keep a sense of action about them. They are also efficient. Compare "tumbled wall" to "a wall that had tumbled." Both phrases have the same meaning, but the first is tighter. All writers can make use of these advantages. Frost, however, found one more. Verbals help his poetry sound the way some New Englanders speak—sparingly and vividly.

- *Find an example of each kind of verbal in Frost's poem "Two Look at Two."*

Captions with Snap: Writing Photo Captions

If you're like most people, you like to get information in small bites. If you see a page with lots of text and a picture with a caption, you will look at the picture and read the caption first.

What general principles about captions for pictures can you draw from this observation? For one thing, they need to be short. For another, they need to sum up the meaning of the picture. And perhaps they should drum up some interest in the reader for the text on the page.

What is funny about the caption with this picture? Humor is not easy to write. What one person finds funny, another may not. For something to make many people laugh, it needs three things: a universal theme—a common experience or belief; a grain of truth; and a bit of a surprise, or twist, in meaning.

The caption with this picture has a common base—an activity that many people have engaged in at one time or another. It also has a little serious thread of truth: some teenagers often snack on foods that lack nutritional value. And it makes us laugh because at the end, the meaning takes a surprising turn.

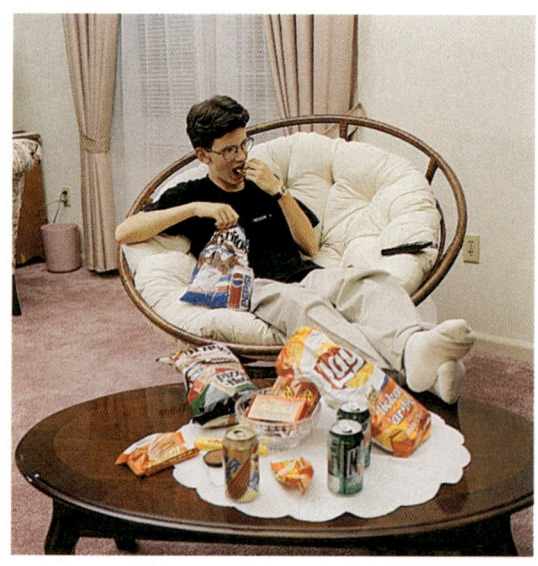

Ben always tries to balance his food groups: red, green, yellow, and blue bags.

Patty and her parents just after the big news.

Not all captions have to be humorous. Sometimes captions are better used to record information about people and events. Like all captions, informational ones need to be brief. They must be selective in how much and what is told. And ideally, they should be interesting; they should be more than a simple listing of names, for example.

Even if you know nothing about this family, what makes the caption interesting to you? Why? There is a universal theme even in this personal family photo.

Your Turn: Capping It Off

Get a few family photos or other informal photos and make humorous or informative captions for them. If you are permitted, make photocopies of your work and compile a class album.

DASHING AHEAD!
CRITICAL THINKING

The Case of the Missing Bell

"Officer Bell," said Inspector Jameson, "take possession of this evidence for me. I have just enough time to make my 9:30 meeting with the superintendent." Inspector Jameson glanced at the clock on the wall. "While I'm in the meeting, I'd like you to take care of the following jobs."

Officer Bell picked up a pencil and paper from his rather cluttered desk. "Yes sir. Go ahead, sir."

"This gun must be taken downstairs and checked in as evidence in the Musgrave case. Also, I'm expecting a reporter, a Carol Bridges, who wants information about the case. When she arrives, show her into my office, make her some coffee, and remember to close the door! We don't want her getting more information than we intend her to have."

Bell scribbled down Jameson's instructions, nodding his head, the tip of his tongue poking out one corner of his mouth. He caught up with the inspector and glanced at him over the top of his glasses. "Anything else, sir?"

"Get that Brinkerhoff report typed up as well." Jameson paused and pursed his lips. "That's all I can think of. I'm not looking forward to this quarterly budget meeting. But things must be accounted for. . . ."

Officer Bell dropped his head. "You can count on me, Inspector. I'll make sure it's all done right."

Don't make promises you can't keep, Jameson thought. But he said nothing as he crossed the room and entered the superintendent's newly painted office, joining the other solemn occupants gathered there. He chose a chair that allowed him to see through the glass partitions separating the office from the larger room. He began glancing through the handout given to him. A quick perusal revealed that "it" was not on the first page. The meeting began, and the inspector struggled to keep his thoughts focused on the rows and columns of figures printed on his handout.

His thoughts slipped into sorting out the facts of the Musgrave case. Remembering the gun, he glanced at Officer Bell's desk. The gun was missing, and so was Bell.

Good, Jameson thought. He's gone downstairs to check it in to the evidence room.

The time crawled by as the superintendent went through the budget, item by item, asking each one present to justify his department's expenses. Jameson couldn't stop worrying about that one item that he knew would catch the superintendent's attention. He hoped his explanation would be satisfactory. . . .

Thinking of the item naturally made him think of Officer Bell, who had just returned to his desk. Bell was shifting in his chair, shuffling papers. One sheet slid out of a folder and floated to the floor. Had Bell seen it?

Verbals and Verbal Phrases   205

Jameson's attention was jerked back into the room by the superintendent's gruff voice. "Inspector Jameson! Would you please explain expense 39?"

Jameson ran his eyes down the rows of numbers, even though he knew very well what the superintendent was referring to. "Expense 39 . . . expense 39 . . . " he muttered.

"Yes, you'll find it conveniently located between expense 38 and expense 40."

Jameson felt his ears getting red. "Oh, that. Paint remover. Well, sir, you see, that relates to a recent unfortunate incident in my office." He plunged into the long-dreaded explanation.

Before he could finish, however, the group's attention was drawn to a commotion on the other side of the glass. A large, unshaven man with scraggly hair had entered the room. He was dressed in blue jeans and a black leather jacket with fringe. He was standing next to Officer Bell's desk, waving his arms and talking loudly. Jameson couldn't make out the man's words, but he could hear his voice. He didn't sound happy.

The strangest thing about the man's behavior was that no one seemed to be at Bell's desk. The man was talking and gesturing to no one at all!

Then Bell reappeared, standing up from behind the desk. Had he been hiding behind his desk, afraid of the man? He should be ashamed of himself, an officer of the law cowering behind his desk, afraid of a potentially violent encounter! Jameson looked at the superintendent, concerned that he might have seen Bell's cowardly behavior.

The superintendent's eyes shifted from the scene outside the room to meet Jameson's. "Perhaps you'd better check on Officer Bell, Inspector. Then when you return, we can discuss expense 39 further."

"I'll be right back, sir." Jameson made a quick exit from the room, relieved to be escaping but concerned about the situation on the other side of the door.

As he entered the room, he saw that Bell had disappeared once again—and so had the mystery man! What had happened? Had Bell been taken hostage? Had the man left? Or was Bell hiding behind the desk again?

Before you finish the story—

- *What are some possible explanations for Bell's being behind the desk?*
- *Why do you think that Jameson's attitude toward Bell is so negative?*

As Jameson peered around Bell's desk, he saw Bell coming out of his—Jameson's—office with an empty coffee pot in his hand. "Just going to refill this like you said, sir. Then I'll get on that Brinkerhoff report." He started to walk to the office coffee maker.

"Just a minute, Bell," Jameson said. "Who was that man who was here a minute ago? Why were you hiding from him? Where did he go?"

Bell looked surprised at Jameson's questions. "I wasn't hiding from him, sir. I just bent down to get a paper I had dropped, and he didn't realize he was standing on it."

"Well, who was the man, and where is he now?"

"Oh, that was the reporter you told me was coming. Don't worry, I didn't say a word to him about the Musgrave case. And I closed your office door, just like you said to."

Jameson closed his eyes and clapped a hand to his forehead. He struggled to keep his voice under control. "Officer Bell, did I not distinctly tell you that the reporter would be a woman named Carol Bridges? That disreputable looking person is not a reporter! He looks like some kind of a . . . a nut! He might be in there destroying my office right now!" Jameson started for his office door.

"Uh, just a minute, sir—"

Jameson could tell Bell was following him, but he didn't want to stop. He burst into the office. "May I help you, sir?" he said in tones that sounded none too friendly.

The scruffy-looking man calmly rose to his feet from the seat near Jameson's desk. "Yes," he said, extending his hand. "My name is Carroll Bridges. I'm with the *Daily Record* newspaper, and I'm here to talk to you about the Musgrave case."

Jameson's jaw dropped open. "I was expecting a—I mean, the receptionist told me that Carol Bridges was coming, so I expected you to be . . ." He felt his face getting red. ". . . uh, much shorter. Won't you have a seat?"

Bridges sat down, and Jameson did as well. Officer Bell hovered by the door.

"Don't feel bad," the reporter said. "With a first name like Carroll, I have this trouble all the time. I apologize to you for my appearance. I'm on my way to an undercover assignment downtown, and I wanted to look the part."

"He was telling me all about it while you were in your meeting," Bell piped up. "Very exciting—he's doing a report on the way the public reacts to homeless people. He was just telling me how angry some people get at the homeless. Sometimes they get quite violent!" He paused. "Well, I'll go make the coffee and then get right on that Brinkerhoff report, just as you said, sir."

Jameson found himself smiling at Bell from across the desk. "Thank you, Officer Bell."

"You're welcome, sir." Bell left the office, whistling a little tune.

"He seems to be a fine officer. Very polite and competent," Bridges said.

"Yes, he's improving every day," Jameson said. "He makes an occasional mistake, but then we all do, don't we?"

- *Why did Inspector Jameson's mind jump to negative conclusions about Officer Bell?*
- *Did you realize that Officer Bell was involved with the expense report before "expense 39" came up in the meeting? What clues did you have?*
- *Did you suspect that the scruffy man was actually the reporter? Why didn't Jameson suspect that?*
- *What kinds of mistakes can we make when we judge things based on too little evidence? Can you think of a time when you made such a mistake?*
- *Give at least one other example of jumping to conclusions in the story.*

Verbals and Verbal Phrases   207

Chapter 10

Subject-Verb Agreement

Usage

In the competition pictured here, the men and their machines are working in agreement. Each athlete has a chair that suits his individual requirements better than any of his competitors' chairs would. In the race to write well, subjects are the drivers and verbs are their machines. Always put a noun with a verb that will make a winning combination.

Subject-Verb Agreement

Singular and **plural** are words that mean **number.** In every clause, the verb must agree with its subject in number. *Singular* means *one; plural* means *more than one.* A singular subject must have a singular verb; a plural subject must have a plural verb. When both the subject and the verb have the same number, then the subject and the verb **agree.**

Singular:	The girl *hikes* the trail daily.
	She *hikes* the trail daily.
Plural:	The girls *hike* the trail daily.
	They *hike* the trail daily.
Singular:	John-Paul *rides* his four-wheeler regularly.
	He *rides* his four-wheeler regularly.
Plural:	The friends *ride* their four-wheelers regularly.
	They *ride* their four-wheelers regularly.

Chapter 2: Plural Forms of Nouns
p. 23

ETYMOLOGY *Agreement* has its roots in Latin. The Latin prefix *ad,* meaning "to," was combined with a form of the Latin word *gratus,* meaning "pleasing." When two people agree, they are pleasing to one another. In subject-verb agreement, the subject and the verb are pleasing together.

Verbs form singulars and plurals differently from nouns. A noun forms a plural by adding *s* or *es* (one girl, two girl*s*). A verb generally does just the opposite to show number. A verb usually forms a singular by adding *s* or *es* (girls hike, girl hike*s*). This form change affects present-tense verbs with singular subjects in the third person (singular nouns and *it, he,* and *she*). Except for the past-tense form of the verb *be,* past-tense and future-tense verbs do not show number.

Chapter 3: Present Tense
p. 58

Chapter 3: Recognizing Verbs
p. 42

IN SUMMARY

In a sentence the subject and the verb must agree in number.
A singular subject must have a singular verb; a plural subject must have a plural verb.

10-1 PRACTICE THE SKILL

Underline the simple subject in each sentence. Then underline the correct verb from the choices in parentheses.

1. Grand Canyon National Park *(contains, contain)* one of the most beautiful canyons in the world.
2. The Grand Canyon's width *(varies, vary)* from less than one mile to eighteen miles.
3. The Colorado River *(flows, flow)* through the canyon.
4. Desert cacti *(grows, grow)* throughout the park.
5. Aspen, fir, and spruce trees *(lines, line)* the north rim.
6. Beavers, bighorn sheep, elk, lizards, mountain lions, mule deer, pronghorns, and snakes *(makes, make)* the park their home.
7. About four million tourists *(visits, visit)* the Grand Canyon every year.
8. Most visitors *(views, view)* the canyon from the south rim.
9. The north rim *(begins, begin)* ten miles away at the opposite side of the canyon.
10. The trail across the canyon *(takes, take)* visitors at least two days to hike.

10-2 REVIEW THE SKILL

Underline the simple subject in each sentence. Then underline the correct verb from the choices in parentheses.

1. William Randolph Hearst's San Simeon *(lies, lie)* about halfway between Los Angeles and San Francisco.
2. This magnificent house *(overlooks, overlook)* the Pacific Ocean.
3. Its furnishings *(comes, come)* from all over the world.
4. Greek statues *(surrounds, surround)* the outdoor swimming pool.
5. The indoor swimming pool *(re-creates, re-create)* a Roman bath.
6. The main dining room *(looks, look)* like the banquet hall of a medieval castle.
7. One *(imagines, imagine)* the shouts from one end of the table to the other.

8. Many famous people *(appears, appear)* on the list of guests that have stayed at the mansion.

9. Wild animals *(lives, live)* in a zoo on the property now but roamed the grounds freely when Hearst was alive and inviting his famous guests.

10. San Simeon *(demonstrates, demonstrate)* how far a man will go to get the best of everything.

Subject-Verb Agreement with Auxiliaries

If the verb in a sentence consists of an auxiliary or auxiliaries and a main verb working together, the first auxiliary must agree with the subject.

Forms of *Be, Have,* and *Do*

Be, have, and *do* are alike in two ways. First, as you learned in Chapter 3, these verbs can function as either main verbs or auxiliaries. Second, they are the only auxiliaries that change form to agree with a singular or a plural subject. Notice the change from *is* to *are, has* to *have,* and *does* to *do.*

	Present		Past	
	Singular	Plural	Singular	Plural
be	he is	they are	he was	they were
do	he does	they do	he did	they did
have	he has	they have	he had	they had

Do is often used in one of these three ways: to emphasize, to make a sentence negative, and to ask a question.

Singular: He *has helped* his father.
Plural: They *have helped* their father.
Singular: He *is helping* his father.
Plural: They *are helping* their father.
Singular: He *does help* his father.
Plural: They *do help* their father.

Remember that only the first auxiliary in the complete verb shows agreement. Even *be, have,* and *do* do not change form when they come later in the complete verb.

Singular: He *should have helped* his father.
Plural: They *should have helped* their father.
Singular: He *will be helping* his father.
Plural: They *will be helping* their father.

Notice that other auxiliaries do not change form between singular and plural.

Singular: He *can help* his father.
Plural: They *can help* their father.
Singular: He *might help* his father.
Plural: They *might help* their father.

Special Rules for *Be*

In form, the verb *be* is different from all other verbs. To make *be* agree in number with its subject, you must know each of its forms.

	Present		Past	
	Singular	Plural	Singular	Plural
First-person pronouns	I am	we are	I was	we were
Second-person pronouns	you are	you are	you were	you were
Third-person pronouns	he is	they are	he was	they were

All singular nouns and third-person singular pronouns *(it, he, she)* take *is* for the present tense and *was* for the past tense.

Present: The boy *is* a tour guide.
He *is* employed by the park.

Past: He *was* a Boy Scout in high school.
His brother *was* also a Boy Scout.

All plural nouns and pronouns and the second-person singular pronoun *(you)* take *are* for present tense and *were* for past tense.

Present: The neighbors *are* welcome.
They *are* our guests.
You *are* a guest also.

Past: Yesterday the girls *were* at camp.
We *were* aware of their absence.
They *were* on a mission—to earn badges.
You *were* glad about their success, *were*n't you?

The first-person singular pronoun *(I)* takes *am* for present tense and *was* for past tense.

Present: I *am* hungry.
Past: I *was* late for lunch.

In Summary

The verbs *be*, *do*, and *have* may be used as main verbs or auxiliaries.

When used as the first auxiliary in a complete verb, *be*, *have*, and *do* change form to agree in number with the subject.

The verb *be* has special singular and plural forms.

10-3 Practice the Skill

Underline the simple subject in each sentence. Then underline the correct verb from the choices in parentheses. In the blank label the verb you chose V (main verb) or Aux (auxiliary).

_____ 1. Big Ben *(is, are)* the famous bell in the clock tower in the Houses of Parliament in London.

_____ 2. It *(has, have)* a diameter of nine feet and a height of seven and one-half feet.

_____ 3. Big Ben *(was, were)* first rung in 1859.

_____ 4. It *(was, were)* installed during Sir Benjamin Hall's term as commissioner of works.

_____ 5. Sir Hall *(was, were)* nicknamed Big Ben, and the members of Parliament named the bell after him.

_____ 6. The bell *(does, do)* have a clock connected to it.

_____ 7. The clock *(is, are)* famous for its accuracy.

_____ 8. Before 1913 it *(was, were)* wound manually.

_____ 9. Since then, an electric motor *(has, have)* been its power.

_____ 10. Londoners *(does, do)* still hear Big Ben ring today.

10-4 Use the Skill

In the blank write the correct form of *be, have,* or *do* as indicated in parentheses to complete the sentence.

Example: ___is___ The Leaning Tower of Pisa _?_ a bell tower for that city's cathedral. *(be)*

_____ 1. The tower _?_ risen above the cathedral since 1173. *(have)*

_____ 2. _?_ the Leaning Tower of Pisa really lean? *(Do)*

_____ 3. The tower _?_ leaned several feet to the side. *(have)*

_____ 4. People _?_ wondered why the tower leans as it does. *(have)*

_____ 5. One suggestion _?_ that the architects built the tower to lean on purpose. *(be)*

_____ 6. _?_ most experts agree that the ground was simply not firm enough for a good foundation? *(do)*

_____ 7. They _?_ the idea that the builders did what they could to compensate. *(have)*

_____ 8. Tourists _?_ challenged by the climb to the top of the tower. *(be)*

Subject-Verb Agreement   213

_____ 9. A climber really _?_ feel as if he is leaning to the side as he makes his way up the 294 steps. *(do)*

_____ 10. _?_ the Italian citizens want to save their tower? *(do)*

Agreement with Indefinite Pronouns

Indefinite pronouns are called *indefinite* because they do not specify to whom or to what they are referring. Although indefinite pronouns do not have separate subjective and objective case forms, these pronouns do show number. Most indefinite pronouns are singular; some are plural; and some can be either singular or plural, depending upon the meaning of the sentence. An indefinite pronoun used as a subject must agree in number with the verb.

Singular: Everybody likes bananas.
Plural: Many like apples even more.

Chapter 4: Indefinite Pronouns p. 87

Always Singular				
another	each	everything	neither	one
anybody	either	less	nobody	somebody
anyone	everybody	little	no one	someone
anything	everyone	much	nothing	something

Always Plural				
both	few	fewer	many	several

Singular or Plural				
all	any	more	most	none	some

If you are unsure whether the indefinite pronoun in a sentence is singular or plural, examine the way it is used. Often a prepositional phrase will give a clue to the indefinite pronoun's meaning and number.

Singular: All of the library has been remodeled.
Plural: Some of the books are new.

In the first example, *all* is singular (and takes the singular verb *has*) because *all* refers to the singular *library*. In the second example, *some* is plural (and takes the plural verb *are*) because *some* refers to *books*, a plural noun.

IN SUMMARY

Some **indefinite pronouns** are singular; some are plural; some can be either singular or plural.

A verb must agree in number with an indefinite pronoun used as its subject.

10-5 Practice the Skill

Underline the simple subject in each sentence. Then underline the correct verb from the choices in parentheses.

1. Everyone in my family *(likes, like)* to go on vacation.
2. All of us *(has, have)* visited Niagara Falls.
3. Many of the tourists *(visits, visit)* the falls yearly.
4. Some *(likes, like)* to view the falls from the river on the *Maid of the Mist*.
5. However, most of the people *(observes, observe)* the churning water from the railings along the river's edge.
6. No one *(wants, want)* to go over the falls in a canoe.
7. Each of the falls *(has, have)* a name.
8. One *(is, are)* called the American Falls.
9. Another *(is, are)* known as the Horseshoe Falls.
10. Both *(is, are)* very beautiful.

10-6 Review the Skill

Underline the simple subject in each sentence. Then underline the correct verb from the choices in parentheses.

1. Few *(visits, visit)* Easter Island, to the far west of the country of Chile.
2. Of those who do, no one *(approaches, approach)* without realizing that there is something different about this place.
3. Everyone *(notices, notice)* immediately that huge statues cover the surface of the island.
4. All of the statues *(looks, look)* out over the Pacific Ocean.
5. Most of them *(is, are)* twelve to fifteen feet tall and weigh about 22.5 tons.
6. Some of the figures *(is, are)* as tall as thirty-two feet and weigh as much as 101 tons.
7. Each *(has, have)* a large head with a pointed chin and long ears.
8. Many *(questions, question)* how the early islanders could have moved the statues.
9. Several *(has, have)* proved by experiment that it is relatively easy for a group to carry a statue using ropes.
10. Nobody *(has, have)* yet explained why the statues are there, though, or why they are looking toward the ocean.

10-7 USE THE SKILL

In the blank write the correct present-tense form of the verb in parentheses.

Example: ____is____ All of the book *(be)* interesting to me.

_____ 1. Everybody *(have)* heard of the Eiffel Tower, no doubt.

_____ 2. Fewer *(know)* of the C. N. Tower in Toronto, Canada.

_____ 3. No one *(deny)* that at 1,815 feet and 5 inches, the C. N. Tower is truly colossal.

_____ 4. Some of the tower *(be)* devoted solely to the sending and receiving of communication signals.

_____ 5. However, most of the tower's visitors *(be)* just tourists, fascinated by the opportunity to travel so high.

_____ 6. Everyone *(like)* the Skypod, an enclosure at 1,150 feet that contains observation galleries and restaurants.

_____ 7. Some of the brave visitors *(dare)* to walk on the glass floor, which allows them to look straight down beneath their feet to the ground.

_____ 8. Several *(choose)* to go beyond the Skypod to the highest observation point, the Space Deck at 1,465 feet.

_____ 9. One sometimes *(feel)* the building moving a little at this height, a natural and safe occurrence for such a tall building.

_____ 10. Added together, all of the building *(weigh)* 145,600 U.S. tons.

Agreement with Compound Subjects

What type of verb should you use if the subject is compound? The rules for compound subjects are actually quite simple. When the compound subject is joined by *and* or *both-and,* the verb is plural.

> **Plural:** Bob *and* Bill *are* twins.
> **Plural:** Hiking *and* climbing *are* their favorite activities.

When the compound subject is joined by *or* or *nor* or *either-or* or *neither-nor,* the verb agrees with the subject that is closer to it.

> **Plural:** George *or* the boys *buy* milk at the store.
> **Singular:** The girls *or* Martin *bakes* delicious desserts.
> **Plural:** *Neither* punch *nor* the mints *are* on the table yet.
> **Singular:** *Either* cookies *or* cake *makes* an excellent party dessert.

IN SUMMARY

Compound subjects joined by *and* or *both-and* take a plural verb.

Compound subjects joined by *or, nor, either-or,* or *neither-nor* take a verb that agrees in number with the subject closer to the verb.

10-8 PRACTICE THE SKILL

Underline the simple subject in each sentence. Then underline the correct verb from the choices in parentheses.

1. Either the Painted Canyon of North Dakota or the Black Hills of South Dakota *(is, are)* good to visit on a trip west.
2. Both Mount Rushmore and Rushmore Cave *(is, are)* special points of interest in South Dakota.
3. Either Washington or Roosevelt *(is, are)* my favorite sculpture on Mount Rushmore.
4. Both Jefferson and Lincoln *(is, are)* also beautifully carved.
5. Neither John Quincy Adams nor Woodrow Wilson *(is, are)* one of the U.S. presidents on the face of Mount Rushmore.

6. Both Gutzon Borglum and his son *(was, were)* the supervisors of the sculpture of Mount Rushmore.
7. Neither my sister nor my brothers *(was, were)* familiar with Gutzon Borglum.
8. Neither Borglum nor his son *(was, were)* able to finish all of the sculptures.
9. Either Washington or Jefferson *(was, were)* designed and carved first.
10. Both government money and private donations *(was, were)* helpful in funding the million-dollar project.

10-9 Review the Skill

Underline the simple subject in each sentence. Then underline the correct verb from the choices in parentheses.

1. Determination and a little time *(is, are)* the main requirements for creating a city.
2. Either skeptics or a believer *(agrees, agree)* with this statement when faced with the example of Brasilia, the capital of Brazil.
3. Rio de Janeiro and São Paulo *(is, are)* cities on the coast of Brazil, but before 1960 not much activity took place in the country's interior.
4. Either the constitution of 1898 or Juscelino Kubitschek *(is, are)* primarily responsible for a new capital in the heart of the countryside. (Kubitschek was a politician.)
5. Three years and many workers *(was, were)* enough to turn an empty plot of land in the wilderness into a modern city.
6. Neither a decent road nor raw materials *(was, were)* close to the construction site, so airplanes had to fly in supplies.
7. Fans and critics *(argues, argue)* over the attractiveness of the city's modern architectural design.
8. The National Congress buildings and the cathedral especially *(attracts, attract)* attention.
9. Neither pedestrians nor cars *(has, have)* to share space with trucks because each group has its own roads.
10. The population of the city and its importance in the country *(grows, grow)* as time passes.

10-10 Use the Skill

In the blank write the correct present-tense form of the verb in parentheses.

Example: ____are____   His workers and his soldiers *(be)* important to a ruler.

_____ 1. Dirt or water *(be)* what one expects to find when digging a well.

_____ 2. Men and horses *(be)* what the peasants of Lintong found in 1974.

_____ 3. Neither life nor death *(separate)* an emperor from his army, or so the first emperor of China must have thought.

_____ 4. Life-sized soldiers and officers *(fill)* three underground chambers close to the spot where Qin Shihuangdi is believed to be buried.

_____ 5. Chariots and horses *(wait)* there also, as if ready to do the emperor's bidding.

_____ 6. Either facial expressions or posture *(distinguish)* the soldiers from each other.

_____ 7. Both weapons and horse bridles *(be)* made of metal.

_____ 8. Men and horses *(be)* ceramic.

_____ 9. Neither an archaeologist nor peasants *(have)* discovered the entrance to the emperor's tomb.

_____ 10. It is believed that court officials and servants *(rest)* permanently with the emperor, having been buried alive with him at the time of his death.

Intervening Phrases, Predicate Nouns, and Inverted Order

Intervening Phrases

Often words come between the subject and the verb in a sentence. These intervening, or interrupting, words can cause the reader to lose track of the subject. Always find the true subject of a sentence in order to make the verb agree with it.

One common interrupter is the **negative phrase.** The verb of the sentence must agree in number with the subject, not the words in the negative phrase.

> The *horses,* not the cow, *are* in the field.
> The *cow,* not the horses, *is* in the barn.

The subject of the first sentence is the plural noun *horses;* therefore, the verb must also be plural. In the second sentence, the subject *cow* is singular, so the verb must also be singular. The intervening negative phrases do not affect subject-verb agreement.

Prepositional phrases are other common interrupters. If a prepositional phrase comes between the subject and the verb, it does not affect the agreement of the subject and verb (though it may make the agreement clearer). The object of the preposition can never be the subject of the sentence. The verb must agree in number with the subject and not with the object of the preposition.

> The two *adventurers* in the photograph *climb* Mt. Abe regularly.
> The best *photograph* of the men *shows* them with the flag aloft.
> Both *climbers* in the picture *hail* from the same state.
> The *flag* in the pictures *represents* their home state of Washington.

Predicate Nouns of a Different Number

In sentences containing a linking verb, occasionally the subject and the predicate noun may not have the same number. One may be singular; the other may be plural. The verb must agree with the subject, not with the predicate noun.

> Randall's *contribution* to the hike *was* bottles of water.
> Sammy's *shoes are* a type of sandal.

Chapter 3: Linking Verbs and Predicate Nouns
p. 47

Chapter 1: Finding Subjects and Predicates in Inverted Order
pp. 6-7

Inverted Order

Sometimes the verb comes before the subject in a sentence. For example, this inverted order often happens when the words *there* or *here* introduce a sentence and come before the verb. *There* or *here* is almost never the subject of the sentence. In these sentences the subject follows the verb. The verb must agree with the delayed subject, not with the word *there* or *here*.

                       V   S
Singular: There *is* a *puzzle* on the table.

                 V   S
Plural: Here *are* several *pieces* of the puzzle.

The verb also comes before the subject in certain other declarative sentences and some interrogative sentences. In many interrogative sentences the subject comes after the first auxiliary (before the main verb). Always find the subject of the sentence so that you can make the subject and the verb agree.

                                V   S
Singular: On the closet floor *is* my storage *place* for shoes.

                  V   S
Plural: Where *are* your *shoes?*

               (Aux) S   V
Singular: *Has he found* my shoes yet?

IN SUMMARY

Negative phrases do not affect subject-verb agreement.
Prepositional phrases do not affect subject-verb agreement.
Predicate nouns do not affect subject-verb agreement.
Inverted sentence order does not affect subject-verb agreement.

10-11 PRACTICE THE SKILL

Underline the simple subject in each sentence. Then underline the correct verb from the choices in parentheses.

1. Why *(was, were)* the Eiffel Tower built?
2. It *(was, were)* built in celebration of the one hundredth anniversary of the French Revolution.
3. There *(is, are)* 12,000 metal parts and 2.5 million rivets in the Eiffel Tower.
4. At the top of the tower *(is, are)* the lantern and the radio antenna.
5. The most unpopular part for tourists *(is, are)* the steps; therefore, most tourists choose the elevator.
6. There *(is, are)* over 7,000 tons of iron that make up the tower.
7. All of the workers on the scaffolding *(was, were)* safe.
8. How long *(was, were)* they working on the project?
9. The tower, except for the elevators, *(was, were)* completed in twenty-six and one-half months.
10. The Eiffel Tower with all of its parts and rivets *(is, are)* very beautiful.

10-12 Review the Skill

Underline the simple subject in each sentence. Then underline the correct verb from the choices in parentheses.

1. Where *(is, are)* the Great Wall of China?
2. Across northern China from the Pacific coast to the Gobi Desert *(extends, extend)* the wall.
3. The Great Wall, not the Pyramids, *(is, are)* the longest structure ever built.
4. Estimates of the wall's length *(varies, vary),* but the figure is generally around 4,000 miles.
5. Why *(does, do)* the wall exist?

6. The original purpose of the wall *(was, were)* to join several smaller walls into one long defense against northern invaders.
7. The joined walls *(is, are)* a highway more than an obstruction, though.
8. The width of the wall *(allows, allow)* ten men or five horses to travel side by side across its top.
9. Tourists, not an army, *(walks, walk)* on the wall today.
10. Parts of the wall *(has, have)* crumbled due to age and exposure to the elements, yet the Great Wall is still an amazing architectural achievement.

Subject-Verb Agreement

10-13 USE THE SKILL

Some of the sentences below contain subject-verb agreement errors. Underline the incorrect verbs and write the correct verbs in the blanks. If the sentence is correct, write *C* in the blank.

_____ 1. The Statue of Liberty stands on Liberty Island in New York Harbor.

_____ 2. Chains representing slavery lies at her feet.

_____ 3. A torch and a lawbook are in her hands.

_____ 4. The statue stands 305 feet above sea level, and its weight are 225 tons.

_____ 5. The Statue of Liberty was a gift from France.

_____ 6. Its cost were eight hundred thousand dollars.

_____ 7. Everyone who sails into New York Harbor see the Statue of Liberty.

_____ 8. Neither hopeful immigrants nor a returning soldier have failed to gain encouragement from the statue's majestic form.

_____ 9. Many tourists come to see the Statue of Liberty each year.

_____ 10. The Statue of Liberty, along with many other American monuments, are there to remind us of the freedom and privileges in America.

10-14 USE THE SKILL

The paragraph below contains five subject-verb agreement errors. If the verb does not agree with its subject, underline the incorrect verb and write the correct verb in the blank below.

Are many of you able to swim? Sometimes people have trouble with this skill. Inability or fear keep them out of the water. Nobody sink in the Dead Sea, though. The salt content of the waters are so high that everything living floats. In fact, while most seas contain about five percent salt, the

Dead Sea has as much as twenty-five percent. How do the water become so salty? Although fresh water empties into the sea from nearby mountains and the Jordan River daily, much of it evaporates, leaving salt and other minerals behind. Saltiness and depth is the sea's claim to fame. At 1,286 feet below sea level, the Dead Sea is the lowest inland body of water on the earth.

A Photo Finish: Creating a Photo Essay

With the invention of the camera, and especially the later more convenient models, came a whole new way of telling a story. Now dramatic pictures could combine with crisp writing to capture a moment and powerfully document it.

Imagine for a moment how much greater the impact of reports from the Lewis and Clark expedition would have been had the explorers had some film. The drawings in their journals are remarkable and enlightening, and their written entries absorbing and brilliant—but a series of photos recording Sacajawea's meeting her family would be priceless.

But moments worthy of the photo essay do not have to be quite so monumental as an exploration of the Louisiana Territory. Small events can be intensely interesting if well photographed and well written.

Grandma said setting the table would be more helpful than asking when dinner would be ready.

Jonathan's stomach growled loudly during the Thanksgiving prayer.

Dad always gives Mom the first piece.

Subject-Verb Agreement

Choosing the Subject

The first step in making a photo essay depends on your approach. If you have a message that you want to express, start there. But be aware that some ideas make better essays than others. For example, it's easier to show a sequence—like someone making a jump shot and following through—than it is to create a mood.

Once you know your direction, you will have to get the photos that suit your purpose and tone. If you take pictures yourself, get out there and shoot. Or perhaps you know someone who is a good photographer you can call on. Or you can choose your subject another way: with existing photos.

If you have some photos that you want to use, start there. It's always good to have a number to choose from, to get the best set. Check through family albums or folders of travel photos for images with photo essay possibilities. You can also find great pictures in magazines and newspapers.

Choose good photos that can be combined to make a statement or tell a story. Use your creativity and your humor; perhaps the pictures can tell more than one story, depending on how you use them.

Choosing the Presentation

Once you have your goal in mind (to document a science experiment or to show changes in women's shoe fashions over the years, for example) and you have your pictures collected, it's time to decide how the photo essay should look. Will you put the whole thing on one page or board? Will you make a short book? Will you frame the essay?

Try to arrange the pictures so that even without captions, the audience will be able to understand the message or story. Remember, this is a visual essay that will be enhanced by text, not the other way around.

Supporting the Presentation

When you have the photos in the arrangement that best suits your goal, you can then write a title and captions. The words that fill out the essay must be as well chosen and carefully arranged as the visuals. Adequate captions give necessary information. Great captions expand the meaning of the pictures, giving details or facts that the pictures alone cannot.

For example, an adequate caption for this photo from an informational essay might be "This carpenter is hand sanding the frame he has made." A better caption adds interest and information: "In colonial times, cabinetmakers—or joiners—were the most skilled of carpenters, and much of the furniture they made is still in use today."

Captions must be brief—few people read long captions when there is a picture competing for attention. They must also be correct. Check the grammar, mechanics, and spelling of everything you write. Errors will show up especially clearly in text that is short and aimed at drawing attention.

A title is important too. Like the title of a book, it should get attention and cause the "reader" to look at the rest of the essay. A good title for a humorous pictorial essay on teaching someone to mount a horse might be "Getting a Leg Up—But Not Necessarily Over."

Finishing the Presentation

Secure your photos in the arrangement you have chosen. Add the captions neatly and artistically, checking one last time for correctness in grammar, mechanics, and spelling. Put in the title. Then view the whole essay as a single event. Does it transfer the emotion or tell the story or thrust home the message you wanted?

Your Turn: Getting the Picture

Put together a photo essay on a subject that is important to you.

HISTORY OF THE ENGLISH LANGUAGE

Later Modern English

Four hundred years ago, only one out of every hundred people in the world spoke English. Nearly all English speakers lived in Great Britain. Now one person out of every twelve around the world uses English. What caused the increase? England's colonization and trade throughout the world have been the greatest causes. English continues to be important in most of the countries of the former British Empire.

The most recent period in the history of English extends from 1800 to the present. Altogether, there may be more than 700,000 words in today's English, though of course no one could know them all. English is still growing. We constantly add new words, and sometimes we change the way we use old ones. English today is a flexible, expressive language—especially for those who learn to use it well.

Chapter 11

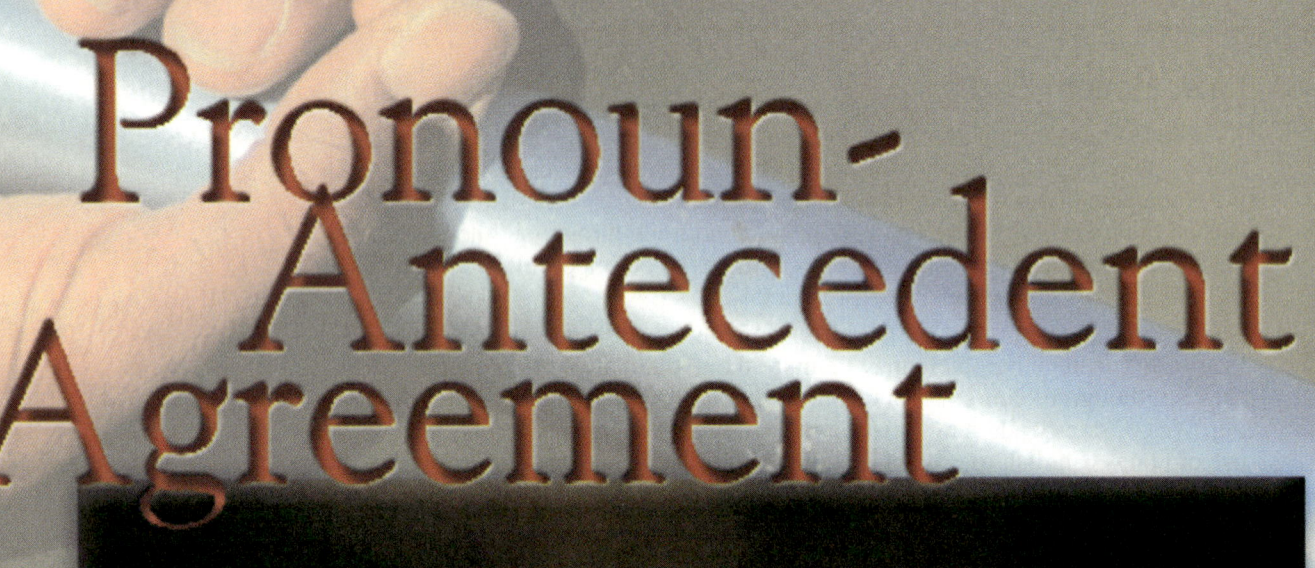

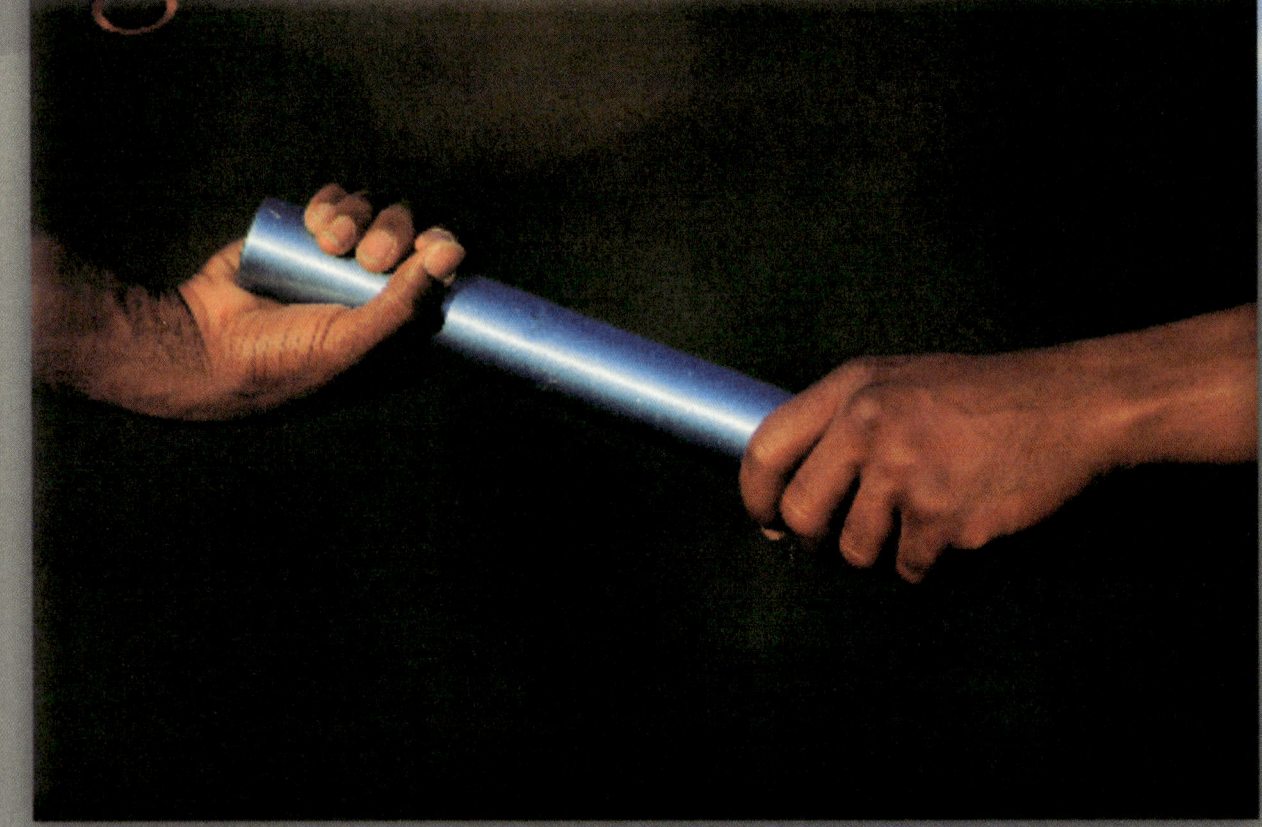

Pronoun-Antecedent Agreement

Usage

When a relay runner passes off a baton, he must look ahead and aim precisely at his teammate's hand. A careful writer must use the same care when handing off meaning from an antecedent to a pronoun. In both cases, a dropped baton can ruin an otherwise perfect race.

Agreement with Personal Pronouns

Number of Personal Pronouns

Pronouns and their antecedents must agree in number just as subjects and verbs must agree in number. If the antecedent is singular, the pronoun replacing it must also be singular.

> The *runners* began to filter toward the starting line. *They* were eager for the race to begin.

> The finish line was a yellow *tape*. *It* stretched from one side of the road to the other.

Gender of Personal Pronouns

Unlike verbs, pronouns often show gender as well as number. In other words, pronouns are masculine, feminine, or neuter. Pronouns and their antecedents must agree in gender as well as number.

> **Masculine:** *Mr. Ryerson* held one end of the tape tightly; *he* was prepared for the rush of runners.
> **Feminine:** *Mollie* leaned forward with *her* heart pounding.
> **Neuter:** The *race* was about to start. *It* would be an exciting competition.

In the first example, the masculine *Mr. Ryerson* is replaced by the masculine personal pronoun *he*. In the second example, *her* replaces *Mollie*. The antecedent is a singular feminine noun; therefore, the pronoun is also singular and feminine. The antecedent in the third example is neither masculine nor feminine. The neuter pronoun *it* replaces *race*.

If the antecedent clearly refers to a person but does not refer to a specific gender, use a singular masculine pronoun.

> Each *spectator* held *his* breath in anticipation.

Chapter 4: Pronouns and Antecedents
p. 78

Chapter 4: Personal Pronouns
p. 80

It can be difficult to assign a gender to certain nouns, especially those referring to animals. For example, is the noun *jaguar* masculine, feminine, or neuter? The answer depends on the context.

Neuter: The *jaguar* fished using *its* large paws.
Feminine: The *jaguar* fed *her* hungry cubs first.

The fishing feline in the first example could be male or female since the author gives no clue as to gender. However, in the second example the author reveals that the generous cat is the cubs' mother. Always consider the meaning of your sentence when choosing a pronoun to replace an antecedent.

ETYMOLOGY

The Latin prefix *ante* means "before," and the Latin verb *cedere* means "to go." The antecedent of a pronoun "goes before" it.

In Summary

Personal pronouns must always agree in number and, if appropriate, in gender with their antecedents.

11-1 Practice the Skill

Underline the correct pronoun from the choices in parentheses. Then underline the antecedent that the pronoun is replacing.

1. Numerous inventions testify to *(their, its)* creators' attentiveness to the details of everyday life.
2. Velcro is such an invention; *(they, it)* came from a man's attempt to copy part of God's handiwork.
3. Surprisingly, Velcro came about as a result of cockleburs that a Swiss man encountered while *(he, it)* was hunting.
4. George de Mestral became intrigued by the burs' adhering to *(its, his)* clothes and to *(their, his)* Irish Pointer.
5. Upon studying the cocklebur seeds under magnification, de Mestral found *(them, it)* to be surrounded by hooklike attachments.
6. De Mestral eventually duplicated nature's design, and nylon Velcro was introduced in the 1960s as a result of *(their, his)* efforts.
7. Nylon was choice material because people knew *(it, them)* to be strong.
8. Under the right conditions, Velcro is strong enough to support the weight of a person when *(it, he)* is suspended.
9. Velcro has been especially useful in children's products, and many sports products have been improved by *(them, it)* as well.
10. Today, baby products, shoes, certain toys, and blood-pressure cuffs display the ingenuity of George de Mestral as well as *(his, their)* determination to make Velcro a reality.

11-2 Review the Skill

In the blank write an appropriate pronoun that agrees with its antecedent.

_____ 1. Alexander Graham Bell knew that _?_ enjoyed working in the communication field.

_____ 2. _?_ most famous invention is the telephone.

_____ 3. Though _?_ was deaf herself, Mabel Hubbard, Bell's wife, founded the Aerial Experiment Association.

_____ 4. _?_ deafness inspired many of Bell's experiments.

_____ 5. Although people made fun of Bell's invention, _?_ soon realized the usefulness of the telephone.

_____ 6. _?_ ridicule did not stop Bell's work in both the communication and aeronautics fields.

_____ 7. _?_ persevered because he believed communication was the key to most problems.

_____ 8. Today you and I often forget the hard work that surrounded Bell's efforts; _?_ take much of modern technology for granted.

_____ 9. For instance, have you counted how many telephones are in _?_ home?

_____ 10. Because we have the telephone, _?_ lives are quite different from those of our ancestors.

Compound Antecedents

If the antecedent is compound, look at the conjunction joining the parts of the antecedent. If the nouns are joined by *and* or *both-and,* the pronoun must be plural. If the nouns are joined by *or, nor, either-or,* or *neither-nor,* the pronoun must agree with whichever noun is closer to it.

Plural: Tom *and* Coart are participating in *their* state fair.
Singular: The dogs *or* the cat will take *its* part in the fair.
Plural: *Neither* Jack *nor* the girls were in *their* booths at lunchtime.
Singular: *Either* the boys *or* the animal handler will appear on stage for *his* award.

Chapter 7: Conjunctions
pp. 139-40

In Summary

Use the conjunction with compound antecedents to determine the number of the pronoun. If the parts of the antecedent are joined by *and* or *both-and,* the pronoun must be plural. If the nouns are joined by *or, nor, either-or,* or *neither-nor,* the number of the pronoun is determined by the noun closer to it.

11-3 Practice the Skill

Underline the correct pronoun from the choices in parentheses.

1. The ancient Greeks and Romans used an abacus to solve *(his, their)* arithmetic problems.
2. Chinese students and their teacher would call *(his, their)* counting device a *suanpan*.
3. Neither Greek mathematicians nor a Roman schoolboy could complete work as quickly without an adding machine to help *(him, them)*.
4. Wooden disks or plastic beads are placed on rods on which *(it, they)* can slide.
5. The beads or disks are moved so that *(it, they)* indicate numerical values.
6. An adding machine or a calculator can help with accuracy, and *(it, they)* can solve a problem in a few minutes that would normally take days.
7. Some students and even possibly a business may still use types of adding machines to calculate *(its, their)* arithmetic.
8. Today a business or a student would use a calculator to make *(his, their)* work easier.
9. Neither businessmen nor scientists would find using an adding machine easier for *(him, them)* than pressing the buttons of a calculator.
10. Either graphing calculators or a computer software package can solve difficult problems, and *(it, they)* can save hours of work.

11-4 Review the Skill

If the italicized pronoun does not agree with its antecedent, write the correct pronoun in the blank. If the sentence does not contain an agreement error, write *C* in the blank.

_____ 1. Almost every child who has played with Legos will admit that *their* opinion of the toy is favorable.

_____ 2. Lego inventor Ole Kirk Christiansen busied himself with both carpentry and toy manufacture, but *they* were not equally enjoyable to him.

_____ 3. The Danish carpenter decided to choose between toys and carpentry because *its* dual demands on his time did not suit him.

_____ 4. When he made plastic Legos, Christiansen did not know whether his life or his finances would remain the same, and *it* certainly did not.

_____ 5. Not one person could claim that *they* would have guessed the family fortune to be several billion dollars.

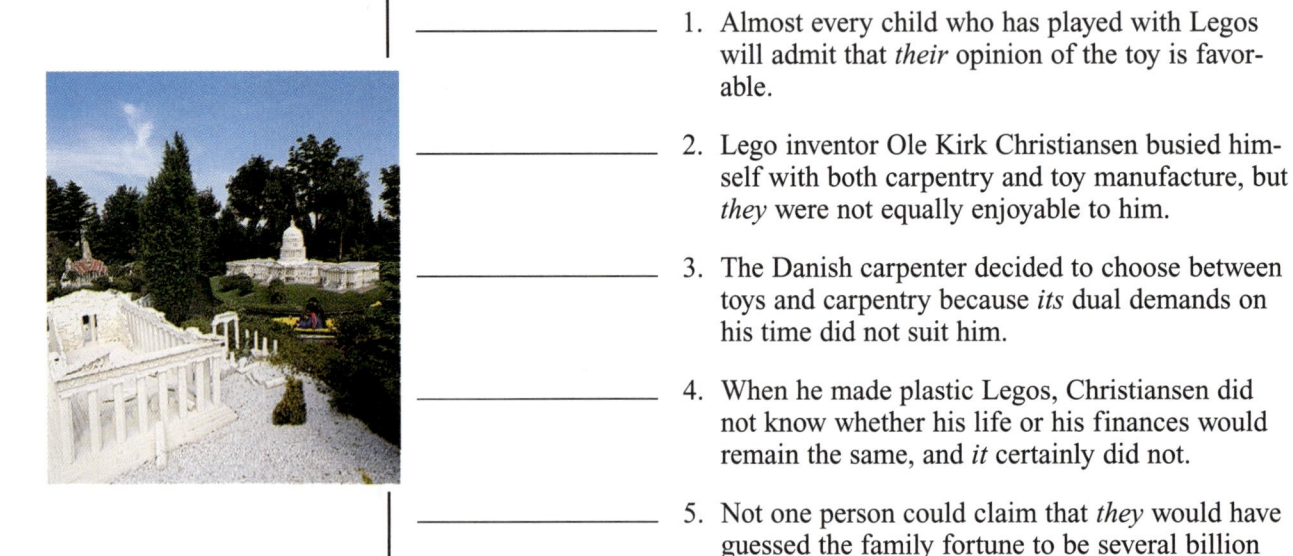

_____ 6. Many people wonder whether Lego has really sold more than one hundred billion blocks; *he* just cannot believe these statistics.

_____ 7. Neither one's creativity nor his enjoyment suffers when he plays with Legos; instead, *their* level usually increases.

_____ 8. In Billund, Denmark, Legoland is quite popular, and *it* thrills visitors.

_____ 9. Legoland's model of Chief Sitting Bull is a crowd favorite. *Their* structure of over one million blocks amazes visitors.

_____ 10. If you visit, you will find both the Statue of Liberty model and the Parthenon model memorable—*it* will not disappoint you!

Agreement with Indefinite Pronouns

Number of Indefinite Pronouns

The antecedent of a personal pronoun is usually a noun. Sometimes, though, the antecedent is an indefinite pronoun. The personal pronoun always has the same number (singular or plural) as its antecedent.

Singular: *Either* will submit *his* proposal.
Plural: *Several* believe *their* inventions to be the best.
Singular: *Everyone* has a different concept for *his* invention.
Plural: *Many* are prepared to present *their* designs.

For an indefinite pronoun that can be either singular or plural, consider the meaning of the sentence to determine the number of the pronoun. If the indefinite pronoun refers to only one thing, the personal pronoun should be singular. If the indefinite pronoun refers to more than one thing, the personal pronoun should be plural. Often a prepositional phrase gives a clue to the number of the indefinite pronoun.

Singular: *Most* of the floor was protected by *its* cover.
Plural: *Most* of the inventions were in *their* assigned spaces in the gymnasium.
Singular: *Some* of the spilled algae made *its* way onto the uncovered part of the gym floor.
Plural: *Some* of the students didn't realize that *their* projects could make a huge mess.

Refer to the chart of indefinite pronouns in Chapter 10 (p. 214) if you are unsure whether a certain indefinite pronoun is singular or plural.

Gender of Indefinite Pronouns

Indefinite pronouns themselves do not show gender. However, sometimes the context of a sentence may indicate gender for an indefinite pronoun. Choose a personal pronoun that will agree with its indefinite pronoun in both number and gender.

Neuter: *One* of the frogs remained in *its* tank.
Masculine: *Each* of the brothers brought *his* own rags to help clean up.
Feminine: *Another* of the girls ran to get *her* teacher's mop.

Chapter 4: Indefinite Pronouns
p. 87

Chapter 10: Indefinite Pronoun Chart
p. 214

What should you do if the context of the sentence does not indicate a specific gender but does clearly refer to people rather than animals or objects? If the indefinite pronoun is singular, use a singular masculine pronoun. Do not use a plural personal pronoun to refer to a singular indefinite pronoun.

Wrong: Someone thought to get their camera.
Right: Someone thought to get his camera.
Wrong: Everyone did their best to repair the damage to the invention.
Right: Everyone did his best to repair the damage to the invention.

IN SUMMARY

A personal pronoun that refers to an indefinite pronoun must agree in number with the indefinite pronoun.

A personal pronoun that refers to an indefinite pronoun must agree in gender with the context of the sentence.

Use a singular masculine pronoun to refer to a singular indefinite pronoun if the sentence does not indicate a specific gender.

11-5 PRACTICE THE SKILL

In the first blank write an object of the preposition. In the second blank write an appropriate pronoun that agrees with its antecedent.

Example: At first none of the ____boys____ showed ____their____ fear.

1. Each of the _____ began _____ science project.

2. One of the _____ demonstrated _____ volcano.

3. Many of her _____ stepped back for _____ safety.

4. Each of the _____ tried to hide _____ fear.

5. The volcano exploded! A few of the _____ who were standing nearby acquired wet, thick splotches on _____ clothing.

6. Something in the back of the _____ set off the fire alarm because of _____ smoke.

7. Everybody in the _____ walked outside to _____ class's meeting place.

8. After several minutes, most of the _____ were allowed back into _____ rooms.

9. Five of the _____ had been able to finish _____ presentations.

10. Some of the _____ would have to finish _____ on Friday.

11-6 PRACTICE THE SKILL

If the italicized pronoun does not agree with its antecedent, write the correct pronoun in the blank. If the sentence does not contain an agreement error, write *C* in the blank.

_____ 1. Each of the students really enjoyed *their* science experiments.

_____ 2. Everyone thought that the electricity experiment was *his* favorite one.

_____ 3. Most of the students experimented with combining *their* own chemicals.

_____ 4. Not many thought that *its* sulfur compound smelled very good.

_____ 5. Every one of the frogs looked shriveled in *their* formaldehyde.

_____ 6. One of the girls finished *their* project early.

_____ 7. All of the students gathered insects for *their* large science project.

_____ 8. Anyone who could not collect all *his* bugs did not receive a high grade.

_____ 9. No one handed *their* assignment in late.

_____ 10. Few considered science *his* most boring subject in school.

Pronoun-Antecedent Agreement

11-7 Review the Skill

Correct the sentences that contain an agreement error by underlining the incorrect pronoun and writing the correct pronoun in the blank. If the sentence does not contain an agreement error, write *C* in the blank.

_____ 1. Some of today's parents use Gerber baby food to feed his children.

_____ 2. Dan and Frank Gerber began to produce Gerber baby foods in 1928, and now his products appear in over sixty countries.

_____ 3. Neither Dan nor his father Frank lost his courage when it was suggested that they produce babies' soft-style food.

_____ 4. None of the Fremont Canning Company employees could predict whether its jobs would last long.

_____ 5. When Dan's wife Dorothy suggested the canned food, she had no idea that many around the world would someday buy such a product and even read the label in his own language.

_____ 6. Neither losses nor disaster resulted despite their potential to occur.

_____ 7. The improved choices and other advantages of the food were popular, and they created a demand for the item.

_____ 8. The Fremont Canning Company became successful making baby food. Now nearly everyone sees Gerber on the shelf of their local supermarket.

_____ 9. Either fruit or vegetables are available to those who would like to use it.

_____ 10. In some countries, you can find Gerber food made from seaweed, since some children like to eat them.

11-8 USE THE SKILL

Write an appropriate pronoun in the blank. Then underline the antecedent of each pronoun you supply.

_____ 1. According to Jim Winner, necessity is the mother of invention. _?_ turned a bad experience into a successful business venture.

_____ 2. After losing _?_ new Cadillac, Winner looked for a solution to car theft.

_____ 3. Winner invented the Club and helped popularize _?_ use.

_____ 4. Neither the ignition key nor door locks proved that _?_ could stop crooks.

_____ 5. Winner consulted law enforcement officers and a former robber while working on the device; _?_ input helped Winner develop the Club.

_____ 6. The steel Club makes a car or truck impossible to steer, thus lessening _?_ appeal for thieves.

_____ 7. The Club's features are designed so that even a busy mother can protect _?_ parked car.

_____ 8. Thanks to Winner's ingenuity, we now have another option for securing _?_ vehicles.

_____ 9. You can even purchase a Club for _?_ bike.

_____ 10. Everyone who buys the Club wants to protect _?_ vehicle.

11-9 CUMULATIVE REVIEW

Underline each pronoun. Rewrite the paragraph on the blanks provided, correcting the five errors in subject-verb agreement or pronoun-antecedent agreement.

Most of us uses pencils often. The earliest pencils were used by the Greeks and the Romans, but theirs was flat cakes of lead. The Greeks and the Romans wrote on papyrus, his early form of paper. Nicholas Jacques Conte developed a pencil made of graphite and clay, and her mixture proved to be as smooth and hard as pure graphite. In 1879 the Eagle Pencil Company patented the mechanical pencil, and many enjoys its efficiency.

Such Talk That Might Have Been: Writing Dialogue for a Painting

Great art inspires great art. Mostly this applies to paintings inspiring painters, poems inspiring poets, and so on.

But sometimes great paintings inspire poets and great stories inspire painters. Take, for example, this painting. What inspired this artist?

Giovanni Battista Carlone, *Joseph Sold into Bondage by His Brethren*, The Bob Jones University Collection.

And sometimes great art just inspires—humor, thoughtfulness, even joy. Here's another painting that inspired a group of students to write about it.

An Eavesdropper with a Woman, by Maes, 1655

    Rick: Hey, did you catch Mr. Barret's latest painting?

    Alan: What is it this time? More big Van Gogh stars?

    Rick: No. This one looks really old.

    Alan: I'll check it out after Earth Science.

(Later, in English class)

    Rick: Did you catch that painting in Mr. Barret's office?

    Alan: Yep.

    Rick: I actually think the starry Van Gogh thing was better.

    Alan: Where does the man get this stuff?

  Mrs. Lehman: Okay, class. I asked Mr. Barret if I could borrow this print for class today.

Rick *(whispering)*: Oh, this could be bad.

  Mrs. Lehman: What do you think when you look at this?

Alan *(whispering)*: That Mr. Barret needs to get out more.

  Mrs. Lehman: Would it help if I told you that the title is *An Eavesdropper*?

Pronoun-Antecedent Agreement

Sara:	The woman is listening to the lady upstairs, isn't she?
Mrs. Lehman:	Apparently. What is she supposed to be doing?
Kari:	Maybe polishing those vases?
Alan:	Who is the lady upstairs talking to?
Mrs. Lehman:	I don't know. Who might it be?
Rita:	A guy!
Kari:	Yes—her boyfriend!
Rick:	Maybe a bill collector.
Mrs. Lehman:	*(laughing)* How romantic, Rick!
Sara:	No, it's the servant of the man who wants to marry her. He is asking her whether his master can come to visit!
Mrs. Lehman:	Okay. So far you have talked about how the people in the picture might be related, what their stations in life might be, and what they might be saying or hearing. Now let's think about what happened right before this scene.
Andy:	Someone came to the door and the servant stopped working to listen in.
Mrs. Lehman:	Is the servant good or bad?
Sara:	Bad! Eavesdropping is wrong.
Rita:	Well, maybe it is. But the servant might just be very happy for her mistress! You know, like an old aunt or something! See, she is sort of smiling.
Rick:	I think she is nosy and she is worried that she won't have a job if the other lady gets married.
Mrs. Lehman:	There are lots of ways to look at this, I guess. So here's what I want each of you to do. Decide by looking at the details of the painting what you think the story is and then write some dialogue for the characters.

(After twenty minutes of working)

Mrs. Lehman:	So. How's it going? Everyone about ready to read his dialogue for *An Eavesdropper*?
Rick:	I've got mine.
Mrs. Lehman:	Let's hear it.

Rick: The rich lady says, "I have no more money, sir. Would you like to hire my maid instead?" And the maid is thinking, "Wow! A way better job!"

Rita: Let me read mine. The mistress says, "Please tell your lord that I would receive him kindly should he come to visit." And the servant says to herself, "At last the mistress will be happy!"

Alan: No—I've got it! The rich lady says, "Please keep your voice down—my maid might be listening!" And the maid says, "I have to listen in—or Mr. Barret will have a really boring painting to hang in his office someday!"

Your Turn: Putting Words into Their Mouths

Village School, by Steen, 1670

Take a good look at the painting called *Village School*. Try to decide what the characters are like, what their relationships to each other might be, what their different priorities are, what life is like for them every day, and what some of them might be saying or thinking. Then write lines of dialogue for the scene. Your dialogue should sound natural, logical, and interesting. It should relate directly to the scene depicted and establish some background for the characters. Present the lines according to your teacher's instructions.

Chapter 12

Pronoun Usage

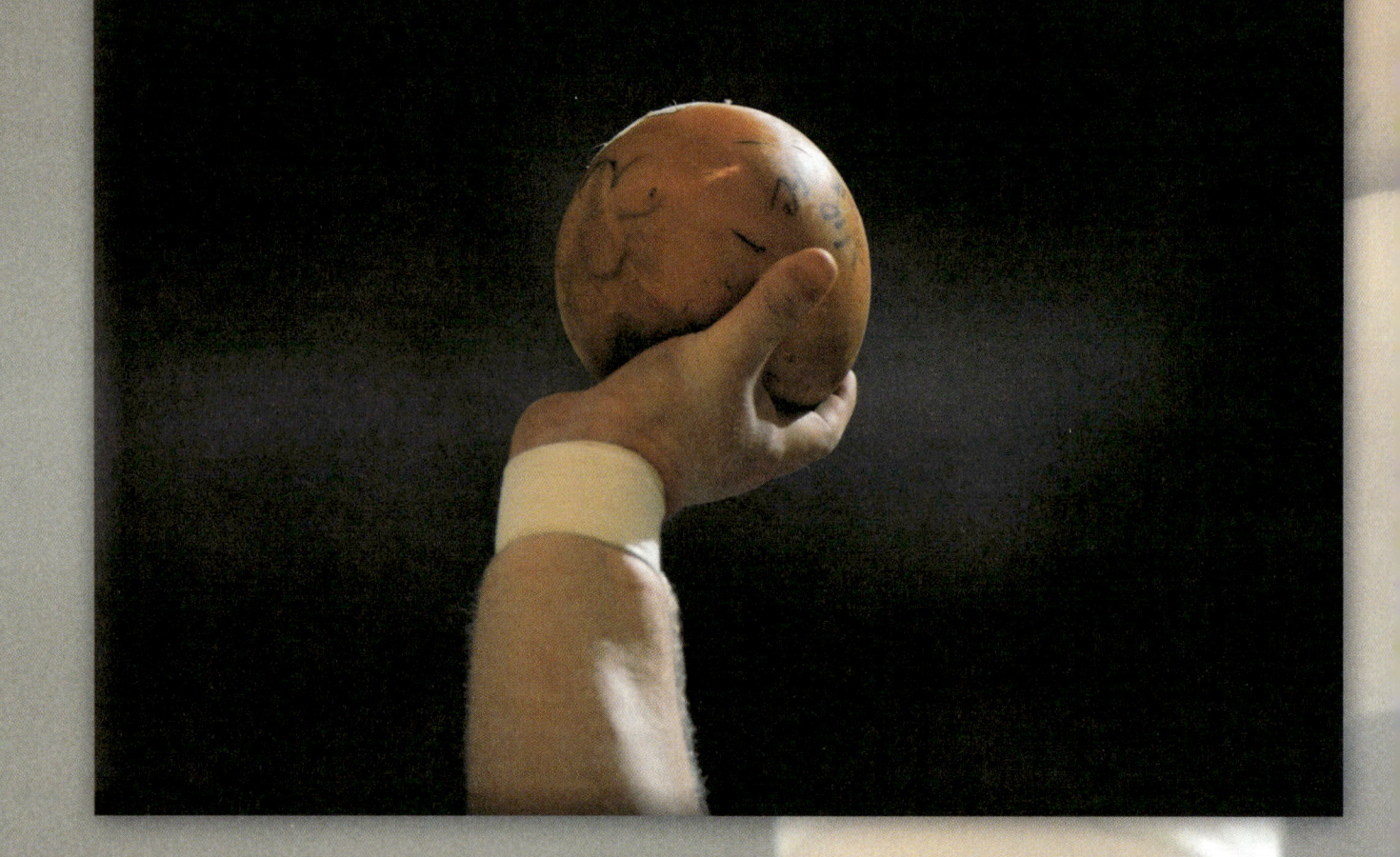

Usage

What event is represented in this photograph? Shot-putting. How can you be sure? You can see the athlete's strong arm and hand, you can sense the weight of the shot put in the hand, and you can recognize the throwing position just as surely as though you had seen a full-length photograph of a shot-putter.

Like the photograph, pronouns stand in for the larger pictures—nouns and noun phrases. The photographer chose to substitute one man's hand holding a shot put for a full portrait of a male athlete participating in this event. So writers can choose to use a pronoun without losing the basic qualities of the noun it represents.

Using Subjective and Objective Case Pronouns Correctly

All personal pronouns have four characteristics: **person, number, gender,** and **case.** The chart below shows personal pronouns in their various forms.

	Subjective Case	Objective Case	Possessive Case
Singular			
First Person	I	me	my, mine
Second Person	you	you	your, yours
Third Person			
neuter	it	it	its
masculine	he	him	his
feminine	she	her	her, hers
Plural			
First Person	we	us	our, ours
Second Person	you	you	your, yours
Third Person	they	them	their, theirs

Chapter 4: Personal Pronouns
p. 80

Using Subjective Case Correctly

Use the **subjective case** for pronouns functioning as subjects or predicate nouns.

Subject: *I* went to the awards ceremony.
We enjoyed the presentations.
They had good seats.

Predicate Noun: "May I speak with Judge Saunders?" "This is *she*."
The driver of that car is *he*.
The club members are *they*.

Informal speech does not insist on the latter part of the rule. Expressions such as "It's me" or "That's her" are now generally accepted in most conversations. However, formal written or spoken communication still requires "It is I." The problem often can easily be avoided. When a telephone caller asks to speak with Lewis, should Lewis answer, "This is he" or "This is him"? He could avoid the problem entirely by answering, "This is Lewis."

Compound Subjects and Compound Predicate Nouns

Use the same case rules for compound subjects and predicate nouns as you use for single subjects and predicate nouns.

Single: *I* brought a friend to the ceremony.
Compound: *Jolinda and I* brought a friend to the ceremony.
Single: The president of the class was *I*.
Compound: The co-presidents of the class were *Roger and I*.

If you are unsure which pronoun case to use in a compound, try dropping the other part of the compound. The correct choice will usually be clear.

Original: The youth pastor and *(I, me)* discussed Sunday's lesson.
Subjective: *I* discussed Sunday's lesson.
Objective: *Me* discussed Sunday's lesson.
Correct Choice: *The youth pastor and I discussed Sunday's lesson.*

Original: The winners of the soapbox derby were *(Leigh Ann and I, Leigh Ann and me)*.
Subjective: The winner of the soapbox derby was *I*.
Objective: The winner of the soapbox derby was *me*.
Correct Choice: *The winners of the soapbox derby were Leigh Ann and I.*

In Summary

Subjective case pronouns function as subjects and predicate nouns in sentences.

12-1 Practice the Skill

Underline the correct pronoun from the choices in parentheses.

1. Do *(you, he)* and *(they, them)* remember when the Czech Republic was formed?
2. *(Her, She)* and *(I, me)* remember hearing about it in the news.
3. Public dissatisfaction caused the communist leaders to lose power. *(They, Them)* resigned in 1989.
4. Because of tension between the Czechs and Slovaks, the leaders of the country had to make a decision. In 1992 *(them, they)* decided to split Czechoslovakia into two nations, the Czech Republic and Slovakia.
5. The Czech Republic became an independent country on January 1, 1993. *(They, It)* is a parliamentary democracy.
6. In the Czech Republic, the head of state is *(him, he)* whom the parliament elects as president.
7. The president appoints a prime minister. *(Him, He)* heads the government and oversees its daily operations.
8. The prime minister selects a cabinet. Together, *(him, he)* and *(them, they)* carry out the executive functions of government.
9. My grandmother is Czech. *(She, Her)* was born in Czechoslovakia in 1933.
10. *(Her, She)* and *(me, I)* hope to visit her birthplace this fall.

12-2 Review the Skill

In the blank write an appropriate pronoun to complete the sentence. Use a variety of pronouns; use *you* only once.

_____ 1. Have _?_ ever visited Washington, D.C.?

_____ 2. My family and _?_ went there on vacation last summer.

_____ 3. While there, _?_ toured the White House.

_____ 4. The residents of the White House are the president and _?_.

_____ 5. _?_ were not there when we visited, however.

_____ 6. Fans of the Red Room were my sister and _?_.

_____ 7. _?_ liked its red furniture and red walls.

_____ 8. _?_ and I also enjoyed the State Dining Room.

_____ 9. _?_ can accommodate one hundred and forty guests for a state dinner.

_____ 10. I would like to visit Washington again with _?_.

Using Objective Case Correctly

Use the **objective case** for pronouns used as direct objects, indirect objects, or objects of prepositions.

Direct Object: Great Britain governed the Australian colonies until the mid-1800s.
Great Britain governed *them* until the mid-1800s.

Indirect Object: The Parliament of the United Kingdom granted local governments self-legislation.
The Parliament of the United Kingdom granted *them* self-legislation.

Object of Preposition: Today Australians have a voluntary cooperation with the British.
Today Australians have a voluntary cooperation with *them*.

Compound Objects

Compound objects follow the same rules as single objects.

Single: I visited *her* in Australia last summer.
Compound: I visited *Sanna and her* in Australia last summer.

If you are unsure which pronoun case to use in a compound, try dropping the other part of the compound. The correct choice will usually be clear.

Original: I visited Sanna and *(she, her)* last summer.
Subjective: I visited *she* last summer.
Objective: I visited *her* last summer.
Correct Choice: I visited *Sanna and her* last summer.

Original: We traveled to the Gold Coast with Mick and *(he, him)*.
Subjective: We traveled to the Gold Coast with *he*.
Objective: We traveled to the Gold Coast with *him*.
Correct Choice: We traveled to the Gold Coast with *Mick and him*.

IN SUMMARY

Objective case pronouns are used in the object positions in a sentence: direct object, indirect object, and object of the preposition.

12-3 PRACTICE THE SKILL

Underline the correct pronoun from the choices in parentheses.

1. Peter Alexeevich was a powerful Russian czar, and his people gave *(he, him)* the nickname "Peter the Great."

2. Peter challenged the Turks with his newly superior navy and by defeating *(they, them)* gained a warm-water harbor.

3. His mother found Peter a wife, and the marriage was happy for *(he, him)* and *(she, her)*.

4. In England, he readily learned many new skills in shipbuilding and implemented *(they, them)* in his own country.

5. The story of Peter the Great inspires all of *(we, us)* to reach for our goals.

6. Ivan IV was also a czar of Russia, but most Russians were very intimidated by *(he, him)*.

7. My teacher told you and *(I, me)* that his name meant "awe-inspiring."

8. Ivan married Anastaysya Zakharima-Yureva on January 16, 1547, and he grieved for *(she, her)* after her death on August 7, 1560.

9. She left *(he, him)* six children.

10. One disastrous day, Ivan fought with his son and fatally wounded *(he, him)*.

12-4 Review the Skill

In the blank write an appropriate pronoun to complete the sentence. Use a variety of pronouns, but do not use *you* or *it*.

1. Yesterday, Mrs. Whitfield asked _?_ to go on a field trip with her eighth grade World Studies class.

2. Fortunately, I can help _?_.

3. I will be visiting our state's capital in Lansing, Michigan, with _?_.

4. Mrs. Whitfield gave _?_ a list of the names of the students in my group.

5. She wants _?_ to meet the governor.

6. Last month the students wrote letters to _?_.

7. Did you vote for _?_ in the last election?

8. In Michigan, the governor and lieutenant governor run on the same ballot, and voters elect both of _?_.

9. The state senators and representatives represent _?_ in our state government.

10. The governor, senators, and representatives make important decisions every day. We should pray for _?_.

12-5 REVIEW THE SKILL

Underline the correct pronoun from the choices in parentheses. In the blank label the underlined pronoun *S* (subject), *PN* (predicate noun), *DO* (direct object), *IO* (indirect object), or *OP* (object of the preposition).

_____ 1. The Dutch people have a constitutional monarchy. *(They, Them)* have a democratic form of government based on a constitution.

_____ 2. The monarch is the head of state. However, the constitution gives *(he, him)* or *(she, her)* very little real power.

_____ 3. Beatrix is the queen of the Netherlands. In 1980 her mother, Queen Juliana, retired and gave *(she, her)* the throne.

_____ 4. Unlike most monarchs of other countries, Dutch monarchs are not crowned. Instead, officials inaugurate *(they, them)*.

_____ 5. Queen Beatrix appoints all government officials. Also, all of the laws passed by Parliament are signed by *(she, her)*.

_____ 6. Beatrix's parents trained *(she, her)* from early childhood to be queen.

_____ 7. In 1961 *(she, her)* received a doctorate of law degree from the University of Leiden.

_____ 8. In 1966 Beatrix married Claus von Amsberg, a West German diplomat. *(He, Him)* became Prince Claus of the Netherlands after their marriage.

_____ 9. Prince Claus and Queen Beatrix have three sons. The eldest son is Prince Wilhelm-Alexander. The next king of the Netherlands should be *(he, him)*.

_____ 10. When Wilhelm-Alexander becomes king, the title and duties of head of state will transfer to *(he, him)*.

12-6 USE THE SKILL

In the blank write an appropriate personal pronoun to complete the sentence. Do not use *you* or *it*.

Example: _____*he*_____ Jeremy and _?_ are reading important books.

_____ 1. Jeremy and Zach enjoy reading important books as much as Sharon and _?_ do.

_____ 2. Have Jeremy and _?_ read *The Prince* by Machiavelli?

_____ 3. A friend lent the book to Sharon and _?_.

_____ 4. Sharon had never read about Machiavelli, but she had heard about _?_.

246   Chapter 12

_____ 5. In 1517 Machiavelli wrote about a new philosophy for political conduct that still influences you and _?_.

_____ 6. Sharon and _?_ learned that *The Prince* encourages a ruler to participate in wrong actions if the actions will have good results.

_____ 7. Jeremy and Zach, along with Sharon and _?_, do not agree with Machiavelli.

_____ 8. Sharon and I argued that one's wrong action can never have a good result, and Jeremy and Zach agreed with _?_.

_____ 9. Machiavelli worked hard for the rulers of Italy, but _?_ ultimately rejected him.

_____ 10. Jeremy, Zach, Sharon, and I read influential books because _?_ want to understand ideas.

12-7 USE THE SKILL

Answer the following questions in complete sentences using pronouns as compound subjects or compound objects or both.

Example: What would you discuss with a king?

He and I would discuss our countries.

_____

1. What would you do if you had an afternoon to spend with a king?

_____

_____

2. Would you want to invite your brother and sister (if you have them) to come too?

_____

_____

3. Why would all of you enjoy such an opportunity?

_____

_____

4. Why would the king like all of you?

_____

_____

Pronoun Usage   247

5. Which of you would like to visit the palace stables and ride horses?
   _____
   _____

6. Which of you would prefer a ride on a royal helicopter?
   _____
   _____

7. Which of you would like to eat in a banquet hall?
   _____
   _____

8. Would the king have a bodyguard and other servants?
   _____
   _____

9. What would those people do?
   _____
   _____

10. Whom would the king ask to come back for another visit?
    _____
    _____

Using *We* and *Us* Correctly

Occasionally, you may need to use the pronouns *we* and *us* in combination with nouns. Remember to use the subjective case pronoun *we* for subjects and the objective case pronoun *us* for objects. Dropping the noun from the sentence will help you choose the pronoun with the correct case.

Example: *(We, Us)* students earned good grades on the test.
Subjective: *We* earned good grades on the test.
Objective: *Us* earned good grades on the test.
Correct: *We* students earned good grades on the test.

Example: The teachers expected this result of *(we, us)* students.
Subjective: The teachers expected this result of *we*.
Objective: The teachers expected this result of *us*.
Correct: The teachers expected this result of *us* students.

IN SUMMARY

Use the subjective case pronoun *we* for subjects and the objective case pronoun *us* for objects.

12-8 PRACTICE THE SKILL

Underline the correct pronoun from the choices in parentheses.

1. *(We, Us)* Americans should be thankful for the free country in which we live.
2. God has blessed *(we, us)* citizens of the United States.
3. *(We, Us)* Christians should do what we can to give back to our country.
4. Many opportunities for service await *(we, us)* young people.
5. *(We, Us)* students should learn as much as we can about the government of our country and how it operates.
6. New leaders and new policies are often determined by *(we, us)* voters.
7. Knowledge of what we are voting on can lead *(we, us)* participants to better decisions.
8. In addition, *(we, us)* learners could one day become leaders ourselves.
9. Above all else, *(we, us)* believers have a responsibility to pray for our country.
10. God will do wonderful things for *(we, us)* people if we will ask to see Him work.

12-9 REVIEW THE SKILL

In the blank write the correct pronoun: *we* or *us*.

_____ 1. ? citizens need a leader who will promote righteousness and fair judgment in our country.

_____ 2. A good leader will further the cause of education for ? students.

_____ 3. His or her personal character will be a good example to ? young people.

_____ 4. For our children, ? parents would appreciate adequate health facilities and a healthful environment.

_____ 5. ? people cannot expect all these things from the government.

_____ 6. Creativity, hard work, and enthusiasm are required from ? citizens if we want to have a good country.

_____ 7. A good leader will inspire and cultivate moral character in ? people.

_____ 8. Any government authority, good or bad, must be respected by ? citizens.

_____ 9. A person in authority should not abuse power; ? followers need a servant-leader.

_____ 10. For ? citizens, a servant-leader works hard to make sure we have the best possible environment.

Pronoun Usage   249

Chapter 4: Interrogative Pronouns
p. 83

Using *Who* and *Whom* Correctly

The pronouns *who* and *whom* are often used to ask questions. *Who* is the subjective case form. *Whom* is the objective case form.

Subject: *Who* was on the phone?
Direct Object: *Whom* did the detective recognize?
Object of Preposition: She wanted to speak to *whom*?

Sometimes you may find it helpful to rearrange interrogative sentences into normal sentence order to see sentence patterns more clearly.

Original: *Whom* did the detective recognize?
Rearranged: The detective did recognize *whom*?

You may also want to rearrange some dependent clauses to see the sentence pattern.

Original: The suspect, *whom* the detective recognized, was ready to cooperate.
Rearranged: the detective recognized *whom*

IN SUMMARY

Who is the subjective case form; *whom* is the objective case form.

12-10 PRACTICE THE SKILL

Underline the correct pronoun from the choices in parentheses. In the blank label the case of the pronoun *subj* (subjective) or *obj* (objective).

Example: __subj__ (*Who*, Whom) planned our government?

_____ 1. (Who, Whom) is the head of government in the United States?

_____ 2. (Who, Whom) makes new laws?

_____ 3. By *(who, whom)* are the laws enforced?

_____ 4. *(Who, whom)* is in charge of all investigations?

_____ 5. By *(who, whom)* are the laws made and amended?

_____ 6. The president appoints the attorney general, *(who, whom)* is in charge of all investigations.

_____ 7. The surgeon general, *(who, whom)* is appointed by the president, is the chief medical officer.

_____ 8. The Supreme Court justices, *(who, whom)* are the final authorities, interpret the Constitution of the United States.

_____ 9. The vice president, *(who, whom)* the president chooses, is the second highest ranking official.

_____ 10. The Speaker of the House is a congressman *(who, whom)* is the head of congressional procedures.

12-11 Review the Skill

In the blank write the correct pronoun: *who* or *whom*.

_____ 1. ? ruled Spain after the Spanish Civil war until his death in 1975?

_____ 2. After Francisco Franco's death, partial control of the government was given to ? ?

_____ 3. The right to vote is given to ? ?

_____ 4. The people of Spain vote ? into office?

_____ 5. ? are the main government officials?

_____ 6. ? is the prime minister of Spain?

_____ 7. The role of advisor is delegated to ? ?

_____ 8. The king serves ? ?

_____ 9. ? is the head of state?

_____ 10. To ? is Juan Carlos married?

Juan Carlos

12-12 Review the Skill

In the blank write the correct pronoun: *we*, *us*, *who*, or *whom*.

_____ 1. ? students studied about Henry VIII in history class.

_____ 2. Our book tells ? that Henry VIII had six wives.

_____ 3. ? was Henry VIII's second wife?

_____ 4. ? learned yesterday that Anne Boleyn was his second wife.

_____ 5. Elizabeth was the daughter of Henry VIII and ? ?

_____ 6. ? was the most powerful political figure in England at this time?

_____ 7. The man ? challenged even the king was Cardinal Wolsey.

_____ 8. The teacher told ? that Cardinal Wolsey was replaced by Sir Thomas More.

_____ 9. Henry VIII was given a male heir by ? ?

_____ 10. Henry VIII was a man ? allowed his many different moods to lead him to despair and depression.

Pronoun Usage

Chapter 16: Apostrophe p. 340

Chapter 4: Interrogative Pronouns p. 83

Chapter 4: Personal Pronouns p. 80

Some Pronoun Problems

Possessive Pronouns and Contractions

Some possessive pronouns and contractions are homonym pairs. **Homonyms** are words that sound the same (and may or may not have the same spelling) but mean different things. Be careful to spell the possessive personal pronouns correctly—without apostrophes.

Your is a possessive pronoun.	The engraving in *your* textbook is of Julius Caesar.
You're is a contraction of *you are*.	*You're* probably aware that Caesar wore a leafy garland.
Its is a possessive pronoun.	*Its* laurel leaves signified military superiority.
It's is a contraction of *it is*.	*It's* a garland worn by Roman rulers.
Whose is a possessive pronoun.	*Whose* crown is kept in the National Museum of Wales at Cardiff?
Who's is a contraction of *who is*.	The Prince of Wales is the one *who's* wearing a demicrown.
Their is a possessive pronoun.	The crowns of Henry III and Eleanor of Castile are depicted on *their* tombs in Westminster Abbey.
They're is a contraction of *they are*.	*They're* presently unjeweled, although they appear to have had jewels in the past.
There is an adverb.	You can see many tombs *there*.
Theirs is a possessive pronoun.	Our class studied pictures of the crowns worn by Edward the Confessor and Casimir III. *Theirs* were very ornate.
There's is a contraction of *there is*.	*There's* even a picture of Peter the Great's crowns.

Courtesy Order

When you use personal pronouns in pairs that include first-person pronouns, put the one referring to yourself last.

> The teacher talked with *Joey and me*.
> The teacher talked with *him and me*.

> *John and I* will talk to the teacher.
> *He and I* will talk to the teacher.

Always mention the person you are addressing first.

> *You and he* had the correct answers.
> *You and they* will wait after class for further instruction.
> I will be going with *you and her*.

252   Chapter 12

IN SUMMARY

Do not confuse possessive pronouns with similar-sounding contractions; possessive pronouns do not contain apostrophes.

When using personal pronoun pairs, always mention the person spoken to first and yourself last.

12-13 PRACTICE THE SKILL

Underline the correct word from the choices in parentheses. If the word is a contraction, write the words that the contraction represents in the blank.

_____ 1. *(Whose, Who's)* asking *(her, me)* and *(her, me)* about the life of President Calvin Coolidge?

_____ 2. Oh, *(your, you're)* inquiring because *(your, you're)* younger brother is writing a report on his life.

_____ 3. *(I, She)* and *(I, She)* will tell the story to *(him, you)* and *(him, you)*.

_____ 4. *(Its, It's)* very interesting.

_____ 5. In 1905, Coolidge married Grace Anna Goodhue. *(Their, They're)* personalities were very different. She was fun and talkative; he was solemn and silent.

_____ 6. Vice President Coolidge and his family were taking *(their, they're)* vacation when President Harding died.

_____ 7. Calvin Coolidge was the only president *(whose, who's)* father, a notary public, administered the oath of office to him.

_____ 8. However, Attorney General Harry M. Daugherty questioned *(its, it's)* validity because Coolidge's father had authority to swear in only state officials from Vermont.

_____ 9. Coolidge is the president *(whose, who's)* known for the statement, "I do not choose to run for president in 1928."

_____ 10. Does that answer some of *(your, you're)* questions?

Pronoun Usage

12-14 REVIEW THE SKILL

Underline any incorrect pronoun and write its correction in the blank. If the sentence contains no pronoun errors, write *C* in the blank.

_____ 1. Are you on you're way to class?

_____ 2. Yes, its up on the next floor.

_____ 3. Who's class are you going to?

_____ 4. It's the one your mother teaches.

_____ 5. Me and you can walk to class together if you want.

_____ 6. How do you feel about being in your mother's class?

_____ 7. It's fine. No big deal.

_____ 8. Your mom wants to talk to you and Chip.

_____ 9. Their on their way!

_____ 10. Its fun to be a student in the school where your mother teaches.

Reflexive and Intensive Pronouns

Be careful to use **reflexive** and **intensive** pronouns correctly. Never use a reflexive or intensive pronoun in place of a regular personal pronoun.

Reflexive is from a Latin word meaning "to reflect." A reflexive pronoun "reflects" another noun in the sentence.

Intensive comes from a Latin root meaning "to stretch out," that is, "to extend." An intensive pronoun "extends," or gives emphasis to another word in the sentence.

Wrong: Vivian and *myself* studied the lineage of King David.
Right: Vivian and *I* studied the lineage of King David.
Right: *I* did not study the lineage of King David by *myself*.

Wrong: Jesus' heritage was interesting to Vivian and *myself*.
Right: Jesus' heritage was interesting to Vivian and *me*.
Right: *I myself* was interested in Jesus' heritage.

Never use nonstandard forms *hisself* or *theirselves*. Instead use *himself* or *themselves*.

Wrong: Josh found *hisself* a job to pay for a new bike.

Chapter 4: Reflexive and Intensive Pronouns p. 85

Right: Josh found *himself* a job to pay for a new bike.

Wrong: His parents *theirselves* had already bought it for him.
Right: His parents *themselves* had already bought it for him.

In Summary

Never use a **reflexive** or **intensive** pronoun in place of a personal pronoun.

Avoid the nonstandard forms *hisself* and *theirselves*.

12-15 Practice the Skill

In the blank write the correct reflexive or intensive pronoun to complete the sentence.

_____ 1. Just thirty minutes before the ceremony, Kirsten studied ? in the mirror.

_____ 2. Ted knew ? to be emotional in these types of situations.

_____ 3. Denise ? enjoyed the wedding song and violin solo.

_____ 4. The flower girl and ring bearer taught ? how to walk down the aisle properly.

_____ 5. The wedding cake ? was delicious.

_____ 6. Todd ? decorated the wedding car with bells and balloons.

_____ 7. The wedding party gathered ? together for a dinner after the rehearsal.

_____ 8. The entire day was in ? a miracle.

_____ 9. The bride and groom ? did not get any wedding cake on each other.

_____ 10. The father of the bride thought to ? that he had never seen a more beautiful bride.

Pronoun Usage

12-16 Review the Skill

Underline any incorrect pronoun and write its correction in the blank. If the sentence contains no pronoun errors, write *C* in the blank.

_____ 1. I myself read a biography on the lives of William and Mary of Orange.

_____ 2. We taught us about their lives.

_____ 3. You yourself stated that they were excellent rulers.

_____ 4. Mary devoted her to religious and charitable projects.

_____ 5. Mary's Catholic father, James II, became king of England in 1685. However, she herself was Protestant.

_____ 6. The Protestant religious and political leaders saved theirselves from problems with Catholic James II by asking Protestant William and Mary to take over the monarchy.

_____ 7. In 1688 William hisself landed in England and permitted James II to flee to France.

_____ 8. In 1689 William and Mary proclaimed them king and queen of England.

_____ 9. They limited theirselves and their power by adopting what became known as the Bill of Rights.

_____ 10. The College of William and Mary was founded in 1693 in Williamsburg, Virginia. William and Mary founded it themselves.

Clear Pronoun Reference

Unclear Antecedents

Every pronoun must have an antecedent. A pronoun's antecedent is the noun that comes before a pronoun and is replaced by the pronoun. A pronoun refers to its antecedent. When these references are clear, the resulting sentences can be meaningful. When the references are unclear, the resulting sentences will be either puzzling or misleading.

One kind of unclear antecedent reference problem is having two nouns nearby that are possible antecedents of the pronoun. You can correct this problem by rewriting the sentence to make the antecedent clear.

Unclear: When Nick whispered to Bruno, he looked confused.
Clear: Nick looked confused when he whispered to Bruno.
Clear: When Nick whispered to him, Bruno looked confused.

Unclear: LaDean told Jayna that her friends were planning a party.
Clear: LaDean told Jayna, "Your friends are planning a party."
Clear: LaDean told Jayna, "My friends are planning a party."

IN SUMMARY

Every pronoun must have a single, clear antecedent.

12-17 PRACTICE THE SKILL

In the blank write the letter of the sentence that has no problem with pronoun reference.

Example: __b__
a. Deana told Alia that she needed to work on her manners.
b. Deana told Alia, "I need to work on my manners."

1. _____
   a. The people of Hawaii elect a governor and a lieutenant governor, and they appoint the supreme court justices, circuit court justices, and members of the governor's cabinet.
   b. The people of Hawaii elect a governor and a lieutenant governor. Both then appoint the supreme court justices, circuit court justices, and members of the governor's cabinet.

2. _____
   a. In Hawaiian government, the governor appoints a judge; he must meet certain qualifications set down by the Hawaiian constitution.
   b. In Hawaiian government, the governor appoints a judge, who must meet certain qualifications set down by the Hawaiian constitution.

3. _____
   a. The government collects an income tax as well as a business volume tax that is returned to companies in capital for construction and grants.
   b. The government collects an income tax as well as a business volume tax, and it is returned to companies for construction and grants.

4. _____
   a. The county of Honolulu includes Oahu, which has a very unusual government.
   b. The county of Honolulu includes Oahu; it has a very unusual government.

Chapter 4: Pronouns and Antecedents
p. 78

5. _____ a. The Hawaiian constitutional convention wrote a very simple and clear governing document, and it instituted an organized government.
   b. The Hawaiian constitutional convention wrote a very simple and clear governing document that instituted an organized government.

6. _____ a. Pearl Harbor, which is an older military base, is located near Camp H. M. Smith.
   b. Pearl Harbor is located near Camp H. M. Smith, but it is an older military base.

7. _____ a. Rule by the upper class has been replaced by the labor movement, but they are still trying to retain some control in the government.
   b. Rule by the upper class, who are still trying to retain some control in government, has been replaced by the labor movement.

8. _____ a. The Democratic Party, which has grown bigger than the Republican Party, still struggles to win some elections.
   b. The Democratic Party has grown bigger than the Republican Party, but it still struggles to win some elections.

9. _____ a. To determine control of the schools, the cities and counties fight the federal bureaucracy, but they do not adjust quickly to change.
   b. To determine control of the schools, the cities and counties fight the federal bureaucracy, which does not adjust quickly to change.

10. _____ a. In order to gain control of Hawaii, Kamehameha and his troops defeated the local chiefs, and they became governors of the islands.
    b. In order to gain control of Hawaii, Kamehameha and his troops defeated the local chiefs, who later became governors of the islands.

12-18 REVIEW THE SKILL

Rewrite the following sentences to make the pronoun-antecedent relationship clear. If the sentence is correct, write *C* in the blank.

1. In Shakespeare's play *King Lear,* he decides to divide his kingdom among his three daughters.

   _____

   _____

   _____

2. King Lear and his courtier, Kent, meet with the daughters, and he has a foolish contest to determine which girl loves her father best.

   _____
   _____
   _____

3. Goneril declares that her love is inexpressible just before Regan claims single devotion toward their father. She says that her love cannot be put into words.

   _____
   _____
   _____

4. After her older sisters have spoken, Cordelia simply tells Lear that she loves him only as much as duty requires from a daughter.

   _____
   _____
   _____

5. After Kent tells the angry king that Cordelia's love is genuine, he banishes him from the kingdom.

   _____
   _____
   _____

6. Kent faithfully follows his king, but he has to disguise himself.

   _____
   _____
   _____

7. King Lear and the disguised Kent intend to live with Goneril and Regan, but they are extremely selfish and cruel.

   _____
   _____
   _____

Pronoun Usage

8. Realizing that Cordelia and Kent are honest and that Goneril and Regan are treacherous, Lear regrets his cruelty to them.

9. After Kent is recognized by Lear, he is overcome by grief.

10. While watching the king die, Kent sees from his tragic life that fulfilling duty and being honest are more important than empty flattery.

Indefinite Reference of Personal Pronouns: *They, It, You*

Occasionally in our speaking and writing we use a pronoun that has no definite antecedent. The antecedent for a pronoun like this is understood, much like the subject of an imperative sentence is understood. An indefinite pronoun like *someone* or *everybody* is intended to be indefinite and to refer to no definite individual or group. However, personal pronouns, such as *they, it,* or *you,* are normally expected to have clear antecedents and to refer to definite individuals or groups.

Indefinite *they*

In written English *they* should be used only with definite reference. Usually a specific noun or pronoun can be supplied in place of the indefinite *they.*

Indefinite *they*: In Alaska *they* are used to cold weather and snow.
    Corrected: In Alaska *people* are used to cold weather and snow.
More precise: *Alaskans* are used to cold weather and snow.

Indefinite *they*: During school *they* conduct fire drills.
    Corrected: During school *the administration* conducts fire drills.

Indefinite *it*

It should not be used as an indefinite in the phrase "it says." Use the specific name of the source of information instead.

Indefinite *it*: In our school newspaper *it* says that the walk-a-thon raised over one thousand dollars.
    Corrected: Our school *newspaper* says that the walk-a-thon raised over one thousand dollars.

It should not be used to refer to an implied idea. Pronouns should refer to nouns actually present in the passage.

Indefinite *it*: Joe won the contest, and *it* surprised me.
Corrected: I was surprised that Joe won the contest.
Corrected: Joe's victory in the contest surprised me.

Indefinite *you*

In informal speaking and writing, the personal pronoun *you* is often used as an indefinite pronoun to refer to people in general. *You* is also sometimes used to refer to the listener or reader when instructions are being given. Avoid using *you* as an indefinite pronoun in formal speaking or writing.

Informal: The chapel speaker said that *you* should memorize Scripture regularly.
Less informal: The chapel speaker said that a *person* should memorize Scripture regularly.
Most formal: The chapel speaker said that *one* should memorize Scripture regularly.

Informal: Be careful to handle all chemicals with *your* gloves.
Formal: *One* must be careful to handle all chemicals with *his* gloves.

IN SUMMARY

The personal pronouns *they*, *it*, and *you* should have definite antecedents.

Avoid using *you* as an indefinite pronoun except in informal speaking or writing.

12-19 PRACTICE THE SKILL

In the blank write the letter of the sentence that has no problem with pronoun reference.

1. _____
   a. The legend of King Arthur says that he became the king of Britain by pulling a sword from a stone.
   b. In the legend of King Arthur, it says that he became the king of England by pulling a sword from a stone.

2. _____
   a. In Britain, the people were joyful when Arthur married Princess Guinevere.
   b. In Britain, they were joyful when Arthur married Princess Guinevere.

3. _____
   a. When Guinevere and Arthur were married, it was an important event for the country.
   b. Guinevere and Arthur's wedding was an important event for the country.

4. _____
   a. Camelot is the most famous city of the legend.
   b. They say that Camelot is the most famous city of the legend.

Pronoun Usage

5. _____ a. In Camelot, you could see the famous Knights of the Round Table.
       b. In Camelot, one could see the famous Knights of the Round Table.

6. _____ a. The men were the strongest and best in Britain, and it was a symbol of justice and bravery.
       b. The men were the strongest and best in Britain, and the Round Table was a symbol of justice and bravery.

7. _____ a. The people of Britain all considered Sir Lancelot to be the greatest knight of them all.
       b. They all considered Sir Lancelot to be the greatest knight of them all.

8. _____ a. If you read the story, you will read of Lancelot's promise to be loyal to Arthur.
       b. If one reads the story, one will read of Lancelot's promise to be loyal to Arthur.

9. _____ a. Arthur may have been a real person, but most of it is just fascinating legend.
       b. Arthur may have been a real person, but most of the story is just fascinating legend.

10. _____ a. The legend of Arthur forms the basis for innumerable stories; everyone should read some of them.
        b. The legend of Arthur forms the basis for innumerable stories; they should read some of them.

12-20 REVIEW THE SKILL

Rewrite the following sentences to make the pronoun-antecedent relationship clear. If the sentence is correct, write *correct* on the line.

1. Our British literature teacher believes that you should be familiar with the history of England.

   _____

   _____

2. In our literature book it says that the first Tudor ruler was Henry VII.

   _____

   _____

3. Henry VIII influenced the history of England by separating the Church of England and the Roman Catholic Church. He made the monarch the head of it.

   _____

   _____

   _____

4. Henry VIII is remembered for his pleasure-seeking lifestyle, his cruelty, and his six wives.

5. The first three of Henry's six wives were Catherine of Aragon, Anne Boleyn, and Jane Seymour. She gave birth to Edward VI.

6. Henry VIII also had two daughters, Mary and Elizabeth. When Edward VI died, she became queen.

7. They did not want Catholic Mary to become queen.

8. Mary distrusted Elizabeth, so she avoided her.

9. Mary Queen of Scots was Elizabeth's cousin. She had her tried and executed for high treason.

10. Elizabeth never married but used her single status to her advantage.

Pronoun Usage

12-21 Cumulative Review

Rewrite the paragraph on the blank lines provided, correcting the ten errors in subject-verb agreement, pronoun-antecedent agreement, and pronoun usage.

    Sir Winston Leonard Spencer Churchill were a great statesman whose known for his great leadership as prime minister of Great Britain during World War II. In England they praise him for his many contributions to his country. He was a noted speaker, author, painter, soldier, and war reporter. In 1953 he won the Nobel Prize for literature. Surprisingly, he had not performed well in school as a child; in fact, he stuttered and spoke with a lisp when he was young. In addition, his parents did not has much time for him. They're roles as Lord Randolph and Lady Churchill kept they very busy. However, Winston did not let it discourage him. He attended the Royal Military College at Sandhurst and graduated eighth in a class of 150. Its hard to believe that such a great orator once stuttered and did poorly in school. Clearly, anything are possible with determination and hard work. Americans and Englishmen alike admires Churchill for his accomplishments.

Think Clearly—Write Clearly: Writing Explanations

Writing clearly requires thinking ahead. Clear writing is always the goal, but it is especially crucial in explanations.

Perhaps you have been the victim of unclear directions. Have you tried to put a set of metal shelves together or to read about photosynthesis and gotten completely confused? If you were not paying attention, then the problem might have been with you.

But if the writing was unorganized, wordy, or riddled with irrelevant details, it stands to reason that you were confused. As a writer, you want to treat your readers with more respect.

Writing with Direction

If someone asked you how to use a stapler, what would you say? You might not need to say anything but could rather just show the person how it worked.

Suppose, however, that you could not demonstrate but had to explain over the telephone. That circumstance would make the explaining more difficult, wouldn't it?

Giving good explanations of how to do something or of how something works requires much of the writer. One of the most important demands is organization.

What better order for directions on using a stapler would you suggest for this paragraph?

> (1) Press down on the stapler firmly and evenly until it clicks and folds the points of the staple under. (2) Evenly line up the papers to be stapled. (3) Remove the stapled papers. (4) The papers may be held either straight in the stapler or at an angle so that the staple will be crosswise in the corner. (5) Hold the upper left-hand corner of the papers under the head of the stapler. (6) Place your other hand on the head of the stapler, the heel of your hand directly over the staple. (7) The papers should be under the stapler no more than half an inch from the top and half an inch from the left side.

What other improvements can you suggest for this explanation? Can you see how good organization is the cornerstone of clear expository writing?

Writing with Clarity

Some explanations may have perfectly good organization but remain cloudy because the style is wordy or imprecise. How would you rate this paragraph on readability?

> Experts in the process of reading use the term *metacognition* to refer to a reader's being able to express or at least recognize those things he knows and those things he does not know. They try to observe the reader in the process of deciding to correct a misreading or to take advantage of reading cues from his background knowledge.

Rather rough going, isn't it? Such writing is sometimes regarded as exceptionally learned. But it is only exceptionally lazy. Notice in this rewritten paragraph that what seemed difficult to understand becomes quite easy to follow.

> Reading experts call the ability of a reader to think about his own reading skills *metacognition*. They can judge a reader's metacognition by how he corrects his own reading mistakes and how he uses what he already knows about reading and life to read a new text.

Signs of wordiness are too many prepositional phrases (especially phrases starting with *of*), too-long sentences, and repetition of ideas. Can you find examples of all these signs in the first version? And can you see how they were eliminated in the second?

Writing with Focus

Besides organization and clarity, focus is a skill writers of explanations cannot do without. Maybe you have a friend who gives every detail when he tells you about something that happened to him. He starts with information from three days before the event occurred, gives an account of the weather even when it has nothing to do with what happened, spends much time deciding exactly when everything took place, and adds details that may be interesting but have no bearing on his point.

While such tactics may make amusing conversations when you have time for them, they make frustrating reading material. And when you are trying to grasp a procedure, extra details can be like gnats swarming around your head.

How would you streamline this explanation?

> Buttoning a button seems like a simple task, but there are actually several steps in the process. First, you make sure that the top button and the top buttonhole are evenly aligned. Then take the button in one hand between the thumb and first two fingers. Some people hold the button with a thumb and three fingers, but this hold is awkward.
>
> Next, open the buttonhole with your other thumb and first two fingers. Pull the button and buttonhole toward each other. On a well-made garment there will probably be extra material under the buttonhole panel for support. On earlier clothes, loops of fabric served as buttonholes.
>
> Now push the button through the buttonhole with your thumb. Draw the material around the button with your fingers. Voilà!

Is there more here than you really need to be able to understand the process? How would deleting the extra material affect the form of the writing?

Your Turn: Making It Plain

Try writing an explanation in five to seven sentences. Perhaps you could tell how to hang up a coat, open a soft drink can, or find a word in a dictionary. Or if you prefer, explain how something works—a hinge or a zipper, for example. (Choose a simple subject; explaining how to program a computer will take far more than seven sentences, no matter how organized and concise you try to be.)

Go over the process you are planning to explain. Try to think of all the details, of any step that may be confusing to someone who is trying to follow and is unfamiliar with the topic.

Do not include unnecessary information or get the steps out of order. There is no need, for example, to tell about taking the coat off or getting the soft drink out of the vending machine.

Then after you have written the explanation, read it over. Think through the process as you read, even trying to follow the directions yourself. Have you left out any steps? Do you expect the reader to fill in too much for himself? Could he complete the action by following your lead? Do you have any distracting details?

STRETCHING OUT

The Sky's the Limit

The stars and the moon brighten not only the heavens but also our language. Have you ever heard anyone call August "the dog days of summer"? That's because Sirius, the dog star, rises above the horizon at that time of year. And the tradition of calling a farewell or last appearance a "swan song" goes back to an ancient myth about the constellation Cygnus (the swan) and a musician who mourned the death of his friend in song.

A "honeymoon" comes from the long-ago custom of married couples' drinking a beverage sweetened with honey for the first month (or "moon") to sweeten their marriages. And when we say things happen "once in a blue moon," we are referring to the rare phenomenon of the moon's appearing slightly blue after a large volcanic eruption. Can you think of any other familiar sayings with origins in the skies? Given time, you're certain to have a few ideas dawn on you.

Chapter 13

Using Adjectives and Adverbs Correctly

Usage

Javelin throwing combines strength, grace, and precision. A good throw requires a firm grip on the javelin and a powerful thrust, a smooth arc through the air, and a clear sticking point within boundaries to mark the end of the flight. When a writer uses adjectives and adverbs, he must be something of a javelin thrower. He must have a firm grasp of the meaning of his words and use them with confidence. He must often choose from among several synonyms the one that will give his sentence the most graceful flow. And he must know how to make his meaning land within the boundaries of his reader's understanding and how to make it stick.

Adjective or Adverb?

Because both adjectives and adverbs are modifiers, the two sometimes confuse people. Speakers and writers sometimes incorrectly use an adverb where an adjective is necessary or an adjective in the place where an adverb should go. To choose the correct modifier, you need to know the function of the word being modified. Use an adjective to modify a noun or pronoun. Choose an adverb to modify a verb, an adjective, or another adverb. Careful analysis of your sentences will help you to make the right choices.

Adjective: The three-year-old appears *slight* for his age.

Adverb: The toddler seems *slightly* thin.

Both sentences above follow the sentence pattern S-LV-PA. *Slight* in the first sentence describes the subject and completes the sentence pattern following the linking verb. The adverb *slightly* would be incorrect because an adverb cannot modify a noun nor can it complete the sentence pattern. In the second sentence *slightly* is correct because it modifies the predicate adjective *thin* and answers the question *to what extent?* about the predicate adjective. *Slight* would not fit in this sentence because an adjective cannot modify another adjective.

Chapter 5: Adjectives
p. 96

Chapter 6: Adverbs
p. 116

IN SUMMARY

Use adjectives to modify nouns or pronouns.
Use adverbs to modify verbs, adjectives, or other adverbs.

13-1 PRACTICE THE SKILL

Label each underlined word *(adj)* adjective or *(adv)* adverb.

_____ 1. Giant sequoias are <u>huge</u> trees of the redwood family.

_____ 2. They are <u>largely</u> uncommon.

_____ 3. They grow <u>only</u> in part of California's Sierra Nevadas.

_____ 4. The <u>giant</u> sequoia is also called the Sierra redwood.

_____ 5. The giant sequoia boasts a <u>large</u> trunk and great height.

_____ 6. <u>Sometimes</u> giant sequoias are over three hundred feet tall and about a hundred feet around.

_____ 7. Moreover, the big tree's bark becomes <u>quite</u> thick.

_____ 8. In fact, records of bark over a foot thick <u>currently</u> exist.

_____ 9. Have you <u>ever</u> seen a giant sequoia?

_____ 10. Many giant sequoias grow in Sequoia National Park, which was established in 1890. <u>Only</u> Yellowstone National Park is older.

13-2 REVIEW THE SKILL

Label the sentence patterns. Underline each adjective once and each adverb twice. Draw an arrow from each adjective or adverb to the word it modifies.

1. Botany introduces us to wondrously diverse plants.

2. The parasitic mistletoe grows naturally on host trees.

3. Mistletoe becomes easily visible on leafless trees.

4. Mistletoe looks noticeably strange as a clump of green in the bare branches.

5. Mistletoe actually pierces the tree's bark and gets nourishment without being in soil itself.

6. Mistletoe can be seriously destructive to trees.

7. Apple trees are frequently unfortunate victims of mistletoe.

8. Sometimes mistletoe will grow on oak trees.

9. Mistletoe berries are harmful to people.

10. Birds are the usual cause of the spread of mistletoe seeds.

13-3 USE THE SKILL

Underline each incorrect adjective or adverb. Write the correct modifier in the blank. If the sentence is correct, write *C* in the blank.

_____ 1. Cacti might seem strangely to some people, but these plants are wonderful creations.

_____ 2. Old man and fishhook cacti are especial interesting species.

_____ 3. The old man cactus looks elderly and odd with its blanket of white hairlike growth.

_____ 4. The fishhook cactus has spines that are bent at the tips and that close resemble a fishhook.

_____ 5. In fact, some pioneers and Indians used the spines as hooks, so perhaps they work real well for fishing.

_____ 6. Of course, cacti remain famous for water storage ability.

_____ 7. Some cacti perform marvelous at water storage.

_____ 8. They can grow twenty percent in girth when rain makes water easy available.

_____ 9. Cacti also produce fruit, and some is healthful to eat and tastes good.

_____ 10. In fact, the stems of prickly pear cacti become edibly as a fried food once their spines are removed.

Good or *Well*? *Bad* or *Badly*?

The words *good* and *well* can be especially confusing. Remember that *good* is an adjective and that *well* is an adverb.

Adjective: The steak tasted *good*.

Adverb: The chef seasoned the meat *well*.

Because *good* follows the linking verb *tasted* in this example, *good* is a predicate adjective describing the subject steak. *Well* would be incorrect because it is an adverb, and adverbs cannot be predicate adjectives. The adverb *well* is correct in the second sentence because it modifies the verb *seasoned* and answers the question *how?* about the verb. *Good* would be incorrect because adjectives do not modify verbs.

Bad and *badly* are two other words that give students trouble. *Bad* is an adjective, and *badly* is an adverb.

Adjective: The two-year-old boy's behavior was *bad* during the recital.
Adverb: After the disturbance, the musician performed *badly*.

In the first sentence, *bad* is correct because it is a predicate adjective describing the child's behavior. *Badly* is the correct choice for the second sentence because it modifies the verb *performed* and answers the question *how?* about the verb.

In Summary

Use *good* and *bad* as adjectives.
Use *well* and *badly* as adverbs.

13-4 Practice the Skill

Underline the incorrect adjective or adverb. In the blank write the correct modifier. If the sentence is correct, write C in the blank.

_____ 1. Pitcher plants are carnivorous plants that catch insects good.

_____ 2. These plants are probably not so well known as Venus's-flytrap.

_____ 3. Special leaves on the plant look like small pitchers and collect rainwater good.

_____ 4. The top edge of this pitcher is a red, nectar-rich rim that does not function bad at drawing insects.

_____ 5. The insect's experience becomes badly after landing on the rim.

_____ 6. The bug's chance of escape does not look well once it has fallen off the nectar-covered, waxy edge into the pitcher's depths.

_____ 7. The insect has no good chance of escape since furry hairs pointing downward line the pitcher's inside walls.

_____ 8. Such devices for trapping victims mean bad things for insects caught by pitcher plants.

_____ 9. Like the flytrap, pitcher plants must seem badly in the eyes of a snared bug.

_____ 10. The plant secretes special enzymes to help it digest the insect good.

13-5 USE THE SKILL

In the blank write the correct modifier to complete the sentence: *good, well, bad,* or *badly.*

Example: __well__ I can ski _?_ like my brother.

_____ 1. One _?_ example of an interesting plant is Venus's-flytrap.

_____ 2. Venus's-flytrap is a carnivorous plant that can survive _?_ in nitrogen-low soil.

_____ 3. The flytrap apparently uses nutrients from insects to compensate for _?_ soil conditions.

_____ 4. Insects caught in a Venus's-flytrap perform _?_ at escaping.

_____ 5. Six trigger hairs work _?_ at springing the leaf's two halves shut when a large insect is inside.

_____ 6. Spiny hairs that work like bars on the leaf's edges make the closed leaf a _?_ snare.

_____ 7. Small bugs that would make a _?_ meal escape through the closed leaves.

_____ 8. Before the leaf reopens in one to two weeks, juices from the plant digest the insect _?_.

_____ 9. Insects landing on the flytrap's leaves usually suffer a _?_ fate.

_____ 10. Maybe to the plant, an insect lunch tastes _?_.

Double Negatives

In standard English we use only one negative word to make a sentence convey negative meaning. Using another negative word along with the adverb *not* is called a **double negative** and should be avoided in both speaking and writing. To correct a double negative, eliminate one of the negative words.

Wrong: I did*n't* eat *nothing* for breakfast.
Right: I did*n't* eat *anything* for breakfast.
I did *not* eat *anything* for breakfast.
I ate *nothing* for breakfast.

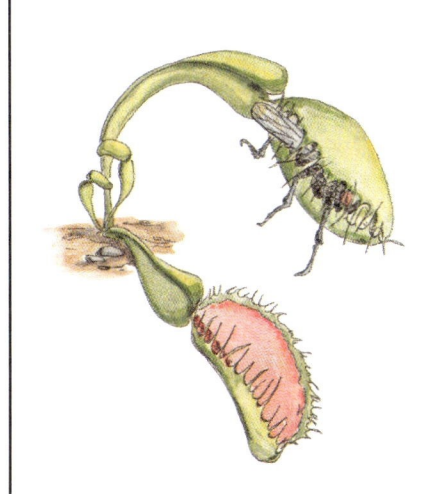

Wrong: Joan had*n't* gone *nowhere* for vacation.
Right: Joan had*n't* gone *anywhere* for vacation.
Joan had *not* gone *anywhere* for vacation.
Joan went *nowhere* for vacation.

Wrong: Lori can*not* eat *no* peanuts.
Right: Lori can*not* eat peanuts.
Lori eats *no* peanuts.

ETYMOLOGY

Negative comes from a Latin root that means "to say no."

ESL

When a sentence with the word *some* is made negative, *some* is replaced by *any*.

Examples:
1. Kai drank *some* coffee.
   Kai did*n't* drink *any* coffee.
2. They have *some* nice decorations.
   They do*n't* have *any* nice decorations.

IN SUMMARY

Use only one negative word to make a sentence convey negative meaning.

13-6 PRACTICE THE SKILL

Underline the double negatives. Write the correction in the blank. If the sentence is correct, write *C* in the blank.

_____ 1. Most vegetation does not normally make any light.

_____ 2. Some people may think there aren't no glowing plants.

_____ 3. Some scientists, however, don't find nothing strange about plants that emit light.

_____ 4. A few fungi are bioluminescent, but you might not never know that by seeing them in daylight.

_____ 5. The glowing Japanese moonlight mushroom isn't safe for anyone to eat.

_____ 6. America's poisonous jack-o'-lantern mushroom produces light, so you do not need to go nowhere exotic to see a luminous mushroom.

_____ 7. Fungi cannot emit no flickering like fireflies.

_____ 8. Luminous fungi don't produce flashing lights either—only steady blue, green, or yellow glows.

_____ 9. Someone not knowing no better may say such fungi don't make enough light to be photographed at night, but they do.

_____ 10. No one will find anything useful about bioluminescence if scientists don't study it more.

13-7 REVIEW THE SKILL

Underline the double negatives. Write the correction in the blank. If the sentence is correct, write *C* in the blank.

_____ 1. Lilies aren't never purchased as often as roses, but lilies are just as beautiful.

_____ 2. Lilies should not ever be grown in dark soil but in light soil with excellent drainage.

_____ 3. Most lilies do not grow nowhere but in the Northern Hemisphere.

_____ 4. If you never study lilies, then you will not never know some of a lily's characteristics.

_____ 5. Some kinds don't produce no flowers.

_____ 6. Some cannot grow nowhere but in a woody area.

_____ 7. We eat some lilies.

_____ 8. Many people do not never know that garlic and asparagus are part of the lily family.

_____ 9. Some species, such as the madonna lily and regal lily, don't like no shade, but other species don't like sun.

_____ 10. Lilies have no fewer than two thousand different species.

Using Adjectives and Adverbs Correctly

Adjectives and Adverbs in Comparisons

As you have already learned, many adjectives and adverbs have comparative and superlative forms that show degrees of comparison. Be careful to use these forms correctly. The comparative form compares two things. The superlative form compares three or more things.

Comparative: The Australian stamp is *newer* to my collection than the Swiss one.
Superlative: The Italian stamp is the *newest* one of all.

Comparative: I often play the cello, but I play the viola *more often*.
Superlative: I play the piano *most often*.

Comparative: I sew well, but Laura sews *better* than I do.
Superlative: Doug sews *best*.

In Summary

Use the **comparative form** of adjectives and adverbs to compare two things or two groups of things.

Use the **superlative form** of adjectives and adverbs to compare three or more things.

13-8 Practice the Skill

Underline the correct adjective or adverb from the choices in parentheses.

1. Among all the early botanists, Gregor Mendel is perhaps *(more, most)* famous.

2. Mendel was a nineteenth-century monk whose scientific work receives recognition *(more, most)* often than his religious endeavors.

3. Mendel experimented with peas, hawkweeds, and beans. He found the hawkweeds the *(harder, hardest)* plants to study.

4. Mendel's experiments with pea plants are *(better, best)* known than his other experiments.

5. Mendel carefully bred peas to test whether certain plants would produce *(taller, tallest)* offspring than others.

6. He also tested to see why some pods were *(fuller, fullest)* than other pods.

7. Of all research in genetics up to that time, Mendel's contributions were the *(more significant, most significant)*.

Chapter 5: Comparing with Adjectives
pp. 99-100

Chapter 6: Comparing with Adverbs
p. 122

Chapter 5: Adjectives that cannot be made comparative or superlative
p. 100

Chapter 6: Adverbs that cannot be made comparative or superlative
p. 122

8. Since all of Mendel's laws are important, it is hard to say which ranks *(higher, highest)*.

9. People overlook Mendel's work with meteorology and bees *(more, most)* often than they do his work with plants.

10. Though not fully recognized for his work while alive, Mendel provides a *(good, best)* example of the lasting results that hard work can bring.

13-9 REVIEW THE SKILL

In the blank write an appropriate adjective or adverb to complete the sentence. Use your imagination, but be sure to write the correct type of modifier for each situation.

_____ 1. My _?_ cousin Akeen is the most dedicated marine botanist I know.

_____ 2. He works for a _?_ research laboratory in Florida.

_____ 3. Akeen works on Saturdays more _?_ than other researchers.

_____ 4. He can make _?_ sea trips on Saturdays than he can on weekdays.

_____ 5. Once, while collecting red algae, Akeen lived _?_ on the ocean for three days.

_____ 6. He usually submits his reports _?_ than other workers too.

_____ 7. I think kelp was the most _?_ plant he studied last year.

_____ 8. His kelp project was completed more _?_ than usual because of the weather.

_____ 9. The lab employees are more _?_ than I thought they would be.

_____ 10. I think those people work the most _?_ of any I have met.

Double comparisons also should be avoided. To correct a double comparison, eliminate one of the comparative or superlative words.

Wrong: Solomon was the *most wisest* man who ever lived.
Right: Solomon was the *wisest* man who ever lived.

Wrong: The deep red rose is *more beautifuler* than the yellow one.
Right: The deep red rose is *more beautiful* than the yellow one.

IN SUMMARY

Avoid double comparisons.

13-10 PRACTICE THE SKILL

In the blank write the correct comparative or superlative form of the adjective or adverb in parentheses. Avoid double comparisons.

_____ 1. Compared to other edible fungi, truffles are generally much ?. *(expensive)*

_____ 2. People do not raise truffles on farms because compared to all other environments, these fungi do ? in the wild. *(well)*

_____ 3. Despite their other locations, truffles seem to appear ? among the roots of beech and oak trees. *(frequently)*

_____ 4. France, Italy, Spain, and North Africa are the ? truffle-producing areas in the world. *(great)*

_____ 5. Of all countries, France is cited ? for its large truffle harvest. *(often)*

_____ 6. Truffles can be brown, black, pink, or white; but some truffles will be ? than others. *(dark)*

_____ 7. Of the many truffle varieties, the Périgord truffle is perhaps ?. *(desirable)*

_____ 8. Truffles vary in size and may become as large as six inches across; the ? truffles are only one-quarter of an inch in diameter. *(small)*

_____ 9. Pigs and dogs can find truffles ? than humans can because truffles grow about twelve inches underground. *(easily)*

_____ 10. Dogs and pigs locate truffles ? than humans do because the animals can detect the truffles' scent. *(well)*

13-11 USE THE SKILL

Underline the errors in adjective or adverb usage and write the correction in the blank. If the sentence is correct, write *C* in the blank.

_____ 1. The *Victoria amazonica* water lily is likely the most biggest of all water lilies.

_____ 2. This Amazonian lily, named for England's Queen Victoria, seems unbelievably with its five-to-six-foot-wide leaves.

_____ 3. Most observers have probably not seen nothing like the lily's bloom.

_____ 4. Its flower smells sweet like pineapple and can be over one foot wide.

_____ 5. Perhaps the unusual fact about these lilies is that a person can stand on them.

_____ 6. Some people think it looks well to stand on the floating leaves for pictures.

_____ 7. Compared to the person taking the picture, the one posing must stand most cautiously.

_____ 8. If someone fell into the water, the unfortunate victim would feel badly.

_____ 9. Individuals who are heavier than 250 pounds should not attempt any daring pictures.

_____ 10. One leaf that held such weight was from an exceptional lily located in Missouri, but not every plant is as strong.

13-12 Cumulative Review

Rewrite the paragraph on the blanks provided, correcting the ten errors in subject-verb agreement, pronoun-antecedent agreement, pronoun usage, or adjective and adverb usage.

Plants is a wonderful part of God's creation. Every type of plant have its own special design by God. Everything that Him creates is perfectly. Plants make we think of God's beauty and creative power. It reflect His character. From the smaller of all seeds to the most gigantic trees, God exquisite designs every pattern. Each design is unique in their own way. Plants have not never flourished as good as they did in the Garden of Eden before Adam and Eve sinned.

_____

_____

_____

_____

_____

_____

From Both Sides: Scripting a Debate

People debate every day—they just don't often call what they are doing a debate. They are more likely to call it an argument or a discussion or a friendly disagreement. Have you debated with someone today? Perhaps your friends think that the team you like is going to lose the big game and you defended your choice. Or perhaps your family "debated" where to eat out for a birthday celebration.

Some debates are formal. Presidential candidates often face off on television, answering questions and challenging the opponent's ideas. Colleges and universities and some high schools have debate teams that present two sides of an issue in a strictly formatted order.

Informal or formal, debates have this in common: they present opposing views, and one side usually is more convincing. Good debaters can argue both sides equally well. Why do you think it is important to know both sides of an argument? You are better equipped to answer an opponent's challenges if you have thought of the arguments he might throw at you.

Here is a script of an informal debate on the importance of manners. Which side of the debate do you think makes the stronger case?

Vicky: Even though manners take more time, they actually save time in the long run.

Karen: I think manners are overemphasized. Why take time to say, "Hello, Macon residence. May I help you?" when you can just say "Hello"?

Vicky: It takes longer if you don't say that. You say, "Hello," and then the other person has to say "Is this the Macon residence?" and then you say, "Yes, it is." See—takes longer.

Karen: It seems about the same to me.

Vicky: Even if it is the same, it is more kind not to make the caller ask. And then you can just get on to why he called.

Karen: I think it seems more unfriendly—sort of stiff, like at a business. Just a "hello" seems much kinder to me.

Vicky: So you are saying that telephone manners are too time-consuming and too unfriendly?

Karen: For the home, yes.

Vicky: But not a business?

Karen: Right.

Vicky: Then we agree on one point—that telephone manners are important at work?

Karen: Yes.

Vicky: How can I convince you that they are just as important at home?

Karen: You can't.

Vicky: Would it matter to you that every etiquette book I have looked at says they are?

Karen: No.

Vicky: Or that our teacher says so?

Karen: I like Mrs. Franklin. But it's her job to know all sorts of rules that do not always help in the real world. Manners are supposed to make life run more smoothly and keep us from hurting others, right?

Vicky: Agreed.

Karen: Well, if answering the phone according to the rules makes the caller feel put off, then manners in that case have not done what they are supposed to do.

Vicky: More people will be offended if you don't follow good manners than will be pleased if you don't.

Karen: Well, don't call me, then!

If you were the judge of this debate, which side would you choose as the "winner"? On what did you base your decision? Do you make choices on emotional preferences or logic or both?

What logical elements were employed in this discussion? Vicky referred to etiquette books and to an expert in the field, a teacher. Karen defined the purpose of manners and applied the definition to a situation. These are logical tactics.

What emotional tactics were used? Vicky appealed to the need for being kind to others. Karen defended her perceived distinction between business calls and calls to a home.

Good debates have room for both logical and emotional appeals. It is usually the speaker who uses both well who will get more people to agree with his point of view.

Your Turn: Seeing Both Sides

Choose a topic that you have strong feelings about. Write down all the logical reasons that support your point of view. Then look at the issue from the other side and just as carefully record logical support for that view.

Then write a script for an informal debate in which both sides argue well for opposing positions.

Using Adjectives and Adverbs Correctly

Chapter 14

Using Troublesome Words Correctly

Usage

All athletes have personal hurdles to clear. For some there are mental obstacles: fear of failure, fear of success, fear of falling. Some athletes have physical challenges. Still other problems—such as rain, loose stones on the track, or a spill the runner beside him takes—have nothing to do with the athlete. But a trained and disciplined athlete who overcomes hurdles, personal and otherwise, can count himself a winner whether he takes a prize or not.

Some hurdles in writing are common to all writers. This chapter will help you take a look at the track ahead. No need to let a loose stone throw your race.

Often words that have similar spellings or pronunciations are confused with each other. We have all heard the small child who sings confidently, "I may never ride in the *Calvary*"; he has mistaken *Calvary* for *cavalry*. Words that have similar meanings are sometimes even more difficult to use correctly than those with similar sounds. This chapter lists definitions and examples of some of the most commonly confused words.

Troublesome Verbs

Three verb pairs give many people trouble. The confusion in using these verbs often comes from not understanding the meaning of each word in the pair or from mistaking a transitive verb for an intransitive one. Knowing the verbs' meanings and principal parts will help you to use them correctly.

Lie/lay

The verb *lie* means "to recline." When *lie* in any of its forms is used, the verb never has a direct object. It is intransitive and used only in the S-InV sentence pattern.

lie:	Every afternoon I **lie** on the plush new carpet to rest.
lying:	My dog often joins me when I **am lying** there.
lay:	Yesterday I **lay** on the couch instead.
lain:	I **had lain** there for only ten minutes before I fell asleep.

Chapter 3: Transitive & Intransitive Verbs
pp. 43-45

Chapter 3: Principal Parts
pp. 55-57

The verb *lay* means "to put or place." *Lay* is a transitive verb and must have a direct object.

lay: Every afternoon I **lay** my backpack on my bed.
laying: I **have been laying** it on my bed all year.
laid: Yesterday I **laid** my backpack on the table.
laid: Mom was surprised that I **had laid** my backpack down neatly.

The confusion between *lie* and *lay* is probably due to the fact that the past tense of *lie* sounds the same and is spelled the same as the present tense of *lay*. Always think carefully about your meaning ("to recline" or "to put") and the principal parts (*lie, lay, lain* or *lay, laid, laid*) before choosing which verb to use.

Rise/raise

Rise means "to go up." The verb *rise* is intransitive.

rise: The muffins **rise** quickly.
rising: They **are rising** right now.
rose: The bread **rose** slowly yesterday.
risen: By now both loaves **have risen** to twice their size.

The verb *raise* means "to make something go up." It is a transitive verb, which needs a direct object.

raise: A student **raises** his hand in class when he has a question.
raising: I **was raising** my hand when the teacher called on me today.
raised: Sheilah **raised** the trophy after her victory in the race.
raised: She **has raised** a trophy in the last three races she has run!

As with *lie* and *lay,* be sure of your meaning and of the principal parts before you decide which form of *rise* or *raise* to use in speaking or writing.

Sit/set

The verb *sit* means "to be in a seated position." *Sit* is an intransitive verb.

sit: I **sit** at a keyboard to answer my e-mail.
sitting: I **had been sitting** at my dad's desk.
sat: Last week I **sat** at a new desk to use the computer.
sat: Because I **had sat** at the same desk for so long, the new one seemed strange.

The verb *set* means "to put or place." It is transitive and requires a direct object.

set: Jordan **sets** his books on the shelf.
setting: He **will be setting** them there tomorrow.
set: He **set** them there yesterday.
set: However, his sister **has set** the books on the floor so that she can dust.

14-1 PRACTICE THE SKILL

Underline the correct verb from the choices in parentheses.

1. Development in printing technology *(rose, raised)* competition between newspaper publishers.
2. People had to *(sit, set)* the newspaper type in proper position and prepare the type with the proper ink.
3. This type, which consisted of raised characters carved on separate wood or metal blocks, *(sat, set)* on a wooden shelf waiting to be used.
4. Newspaper men *(rose, raised)* very early in the morning.
5. These men had to be sure they *(sit, set)* everything in order and had the type arranged and ready to use.
6. If these men *(lay, laid)* down, they would probably fall asleep.
7. The men had to *(sat, set)* each letter down carefully next to the others.
8. When they *(rose, raised)* the letter board, every letter had to remain in place.
9. To protect their backs from hurting, some printers *(sat, set)* in high-back chairs while they arranged the letters.
10. After everything was finished, the men would *(lie, lay)* down in complete exhaustion.

14-2 REVIEW THE SKILL

In the blank write the correct form of *lie/lay*, *sit/set*, or *rise/raise*.

Example: _____sit_____ I usually study while I _?_ at my desk.

_____ 1. Dad _?_ from his chair to get the newspaper.

_____ 2. He _?_ it on the end table in the living room.

_____ 3. He often _?_ in his chair when he reads the newspaper.

_____ 4. I usually _?_ on the sofa while I read the newspaper.

_____ 5. When I'm finished, I usually _?_ it on Dad's chair.

_____ 6. It _?_ there until Dad has time to read it.

_____ 7. Dad _?_ the money for the paper on the shelf near the door.

_____ 8. The delivery person _?_ on his bicycle and waits to be paid.

_____ 9. Recently, the publishers have _?_ the price of our local newspaper.

_____ 10. However, the newspaper's quality has not _?_.

Using Troublesome Words Correctly

More Troublesome Verbs

May/can

The auxiliaries *may* and *can* are often used interchangeably; however, *may* usually means "to be allowed or permitted to," and *can* generally means "to have the capacity to do something."

    may: You may go to the ball game after supper.

    can: You don't need a ride—you can walk to the park.

Shall/will

Shall and *will* are two more auxiliary verbs that sometimes give students trouble. In older styles of English, such as the English of the King James Bible and of Shakespeare, *shall* and *will* often had different meanings. Today *will* usually indicates the future. *Shall* has two main uses, both with the first-person pronouns *I* and *we*: in a question of preference or in a formal statement.

    shall: **Shall** we go now?
           Shall I find you a seat?
           We **shall** make every effort to serve you in the future.
           I **shall** strive to make your stay a pleasant one.

    will: I **will** attend the concert tonight.
          Jordan **will** accompany me.
          You **will** meet us afterwards, won't you?

14-3 PRACTICE THE SKILL

Underline the correct verb from the choices in parentheses.

1. *(May, Can)* we attend the performance of *Two Gentlemen of Verona* tonight, Mom?
2. Deborah *(may, can)* give us a ride.
3. Mr. Pierce *(will, shall)* direct the play.
4. Where did you *(lay, lie)* our tickets?
5. *(Will, Shall)* we find our seats now?
6. We *(set, sat)* on the main floor in the fifth row.
7. Soon the curtain *(raised, rose)*.
8. The actors *(may, can)* play their parts well.
9. *(Will, Shall)* we go home now?
10. *(May, Can)* we go to see another play sometime soon?

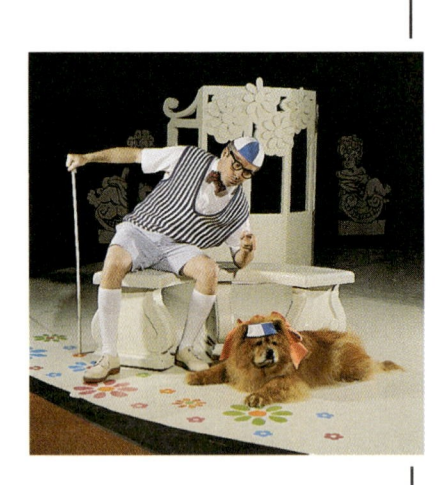

14-4 REVIEW THE SKILL

Underline the correct verb from the choices in parentheses.

1. Before the Spanish-American War, two publishers *(lay, laid)* other matters aside in order to focus on the rivalry between Spain and America concerning Cuba.
2. *(Shall, Will)* we look at the lives of these two men?
3. Joseph Pulitzer built up two major newspapers, the *St. Louis Post-Dispatch* and then the *New York World*, by refusing to *(sit, set)* still.
4. He had an amazing ability to *(sit, set)* facts down in such a way that any event could seem exciting.
5. Unlike Pulitzer, William Randolph Hearst *(rose, raised)* quickly through the ranks of the newspaper business because of his father's influence.
6. *(May, Can)* you see how these men could have helped to create a war?
7. Revolutionary forces in Cuba tried to *(rise, raise)* support by feeding information about Spanish atrocities to major American newspapers.
8. Pulitzer and Hearst took this sometimes misleading information and used it to *(rise, raise)* above the competition by being the most sensational.
9. However, this episode wasn't the end of the story for Joseph Pulitzer. *(May, Can)* I tell you the conclusion?
10. Pulitzer donated money for a school of journalism to teach honest reporting. He *(shall, will)* be remembered for the Pulitzer Prizes he established for outstanding journalism, literature, and music.

Other Troublesome Words

Some words cause confusion because they are similar to other words in pronunciation, spelling, or meaning. Other troublesome words are not really words at all but nonstandard forms or spellings of other words. Be sure to use the correct word.

a/an: *A* is used only before words that begin with a consonant sound. *An* is used before words beginning with a vowel sound.

Bonnie brought **a** tray of brownies.
She also brought **an** apple pie.

accept/except: *Accept* is a verb that means "to receive"; it is never a preposition. *Except* is a preposition that means "not including."

I guess I must **accept** someone else's help.
Every tent **except** mine had been raised.

ain't: *Ain't* is a nonstandard contraction for *am not*. Replace *ain't* with *is not, am not, are not, isn't,* or *aren't*.

Wrong: We **ain't** late for the meeting.
Right: We **aren't** late for the meeting.

Chapter 5: Articles
p. 102

alot/a lot: *Alot* is not a word; it is a misspelling of *a lot*.

Wrong: Rorie has **alot** of time on his hands now that he's broken his leg.
Right: Rorie has **a lot** of time on his hands now that he's broken his leg.

alright/all right: *Alright* is not a word; it is a misspelling of *all right*.

Wrong: His leg is broken, but his arm is **alright**.
Right: His leg is broken, but his arm is **all right**.

between/among: *Between* is a preposition generally used to compare just two items or people. *Among* is a preposition used to compare three or more items or people.

The peach was divided **between** the two sisters.
Gardening tasks were divided **among** the garden club members.

bring/take: *Bring* implies movement toward the speaker or listener whereas *take* refers to movement away from the speaker or listener.

Please **bring** your books to class with you.
When you are finished cleaning, **take** the garbage to the curb.

14-5 PRACTICE THE SKILL

Underline the correct word from the choices in parentheses.

1. Laura Ingalls Wilder is *(a, an)* favorite author of mine.
2. She wrote *(a lot, alot)* of books based on her experiences growing up in the Midwest in the 1870s and 1880s.
3. All of the "Little House" books *(accept, except)* *Farmer Boy* are about the life of Mrs. Wilder; *Farmer Boy* is based on the childhood of her husband, Almanzo Wilder.
4. These books are generally *(accepted, excepted)* as a vivid literary saga of the settling of the American frontier.
5. Although the frontier presented many dangers, Laura and her family were *(alright, all right)*.
6. *(Ain't, Aren't)* the "Little House" books interesting?
7. *(Among, Between)* all of Mrs. Wilder's books, I like *Little Town on the Prairie* the best.
8. When you come to my house, please *(bring, take)* *On the Banks of Plum Creek*.
9. I need to *(bring, take)* *Little House in the Big Woods* back to the library.
10. Laura Ingalls Wilder was *(a, an)* exceptional writer.

14-6 Review the Skill

Underline the correct word from the choices in parentheses.

1. *(Between, Among)* all of the detective characters in fiction, Sherlock Holmes is perhaps the best known.
2. Arthur Conan Doyle, *(a, an)* medical doctor, created the character of Holmes in 1885.
3. The story might have been *(alot, a lot)* different if Conan Doyle had stayed with the first name he chose for his character, "Sherringford Holmes."
4. Holmes amazes everybody with his ability to observe facts and to *(sit, set)* down conclusions based on his observations.
5. Holmes *(ain't, isn't)* a completely fictional character, for Conan Doyle based him loosely on a medical professor who had the same uncanny powers of observation.
6. Holmes, often together with his friend Watson, *(accepts, excepts)* clients at his residence at 221B Baker Street.
7. Dr. Watson makes an excellent narrator for the stories since Holmes often *(brings, takes)* him along on his cases. However, Watson doesn't always know what is going on until the end.
8. *(Between, Among)* the novel and the short story, Doyle more frequently chose the short story to relate Holmes's adventures.
9. Conan Doyle tried to kill Holmes off after nine stories, but fans protested and were not satisfied until a new story demonstrated that the detective was *(alright, all right)*.
10. Plays and film versions of his cases *(will, shall)* help Sherlock Holmes stay fresh in the imagination of the mystery-loving public.

More Troublesome Words

Calvary/cavalry: *Calvary* is the hill outside Jerusalem where Jesus was crucified. *Cavalry* means "troops trained to fight on horseback."

One of my favorite hymns recounts Jesus' painful journey to **Calvary**.
Tennyson's poem "The Charge of the Light Brigade" is about a famous **cavalry** battle.

fewer/less: *Fewer* is used with plural count nouns (items that can be counted), such as *fewer coins*. *Less* is properly used with noncount nouns, such as *less water*.

Margo had **fewer** papers to take home than William. William had **less** time for soccer practice because of his additional homework.

hear/here: *Hear* is a verb meaning "to receive sound by the ear." *Here* is an adverb meaning "at or in this place."

From our apartment we can **hear** the bubbling brook.
Wait **here** while I get my fishing rod.

how come/why: *How come* is an informal expression for *why* and does not belong in academic writing. *Why* is an adverb meaning "for what purpose, reason, or cause."

Informal: **How come** we're wearing our blue jerseys for the game?
Standard: **Why** the hummingbird can fly is one of the great scientific mysteries.

learn/teach: The verb *learn* means "to get knowledge by study or experience." *Teach* means "to give knowledge or skill to another person or an animal."

We **learn** by listening.
Darla is **teaching** her pupils to paint.

led (v)/lead (n): People often confuse *led* and *lead* because they sound alike. *Led* is the past tense of the verb *lead,* meaning "to show the way by going in advance." The noun *lead* is a type of metal.

Joe **led** the way down the steep path.
Current EPA regulations require that paint cannot include **lead.**

loose/lose: The adjective *loose* means "unfastened." The verb *lose* means "to misplace or not to win."

Her **loose** shoelace caused a problem during the 5K race.
Did you **lose** your jacket?
Maureen was relieved that she did not **lose** the race.

14-7 Practice the Skill

Underline the correct word from the choices in parentheses.

1. In history class, our teacher *(learned, taught)* us that President Theodore Roosevelt was a writer, rancher, hunter, and explorer.

2. After graduation from Harvard in 1880, Roosevelt was *(accepted, excepted)* into Columbia University Law School.

3. Roosevelt did not often *(loose, lose)* elections in his political campaigns. In 1881 at the age of twenty-three, Roosevelt won his first election to the New York State Assembly.

4. After the death of both his wife and his mother in 1884, Roosevelt had *(fewer, less)* political responsibilities.

5. He moved to the Dakota territory and owned two cattle ranches on the Little Missouri River. *(Hear, Here)* the hard life and endless activity helped to ease the sorrow of his loss.

6. Wearing the clothes of a cowboy, Roosevelt often spent *(fewer, less)* time out of the saddle than in it.

7. His experience with horses helped him form the First Volunteer *(Calvary, Cavalry)* Regiment during the Spanish-American War.

8. Roosevelt *(lead, led)* the regiment in a charge up Kettle Hill. The regiment, also known as the Rough Riders, became nationally famous because of this battle.

9. *(How come, Why do)* few people know that Theodore Roosevelt wrote *The Naval War of 1812* and a four-volume series called *The Winning of the West*?

10. After contracting a fever in Brazil, Roosevelt lost his ability to *(hear, here)* out of his left ear.

14-8 Review the Skill

In the blank write the letter of the correct sentence.

1. _____
   A. How come we have dictionaries?
   B. Dictionaries teach us how to use words.

2. _____
   A. The Greeks and Romans led the way with lists of unusual words.
   B. Medieval scholars used books that taught the meanings of a few hard Latin words by using alot of easier ones.

3. _____
   A. By the end of the Middle Ages, Latin was loosing popularity to national languages like German and French.
   B. German and French had their own difficult words and raised a need for new dictionaries.

4. _____
   A. The first English dictionary was published in 1604 and consisted of about three thousand words originally from other languages.
   B. Over a century later Nathan Bailey published a English dictionary that included for the first time almost all the words in the language, not just the difficult ones.

5. _____
   A. You may hear of the Englishman Samuel Johnson and his famous dictionary.
   B. He wanted his dictionary to show people how to speak and write English correctly so that there would be less errors.

6. _____
   A. Hear in America Noah Webster is better known.
   B. He planned to be a lawyer originally but later decided to accept a teaching job.

7. _____ A. Webster made a major contribution to American education, but he ain't so well known for his teaching as for his textbook writing.
   B. One of the books he wrote helped many students learn to spell.

8. _____ A. His reputation lays primarily in the work he started in 1800.
   B. In that year he began work on three dictionaries, the final of which contained no fewer than seventy thousand entries.

9. _____ A. Even today a lot of people use revisions of Webster's dictionary.
   B. However, those who like very detailed information and have time to set down for a while would enjoy looking at the *Oxford English Dictionary*.

10. _____ A. The *O.E.D.* is all right if you don't have to carry it too far. The first edition fills up twelve volumes; the second edition has twenty volumes.
    B. Would you like to have someone learn you how to be a lexicographer (a person who writes dictionaries)?

Still More Troublesome Words

passed/past: The past tense of *pass* is *passed,* meaning "moved ahead." *Past* can be used as an adjective that means "no longer current" or as a noun that means "before the present."

We **passed** several restaurants before we selected one.
Past vacations have required us to eat at various restaurants.
In the **past** Dad has not enjoyed Mexican food.

peace/piece: *Peace* means "harmonious relations." A *piece* is a part of a whole.

The two countries signed a treaty and were finally at **peace**.
Now both nations have a **piece** of the disputed territory.

plane/plain: The noun *plane* can refer to an airplane or a flat surface. The adjective *plain* usually means "ordinary" or "obvious."

Dora's uncle flies a **plane** in an airshow.
The wings of his aircraft are long **planes** designed to lift the craft off the ground as air passes around them.
He usually wears a **plain** blue uniform when he flies.
Although he would not brag, the **plain** facts about his flying record show him to be a careful pilot.

quiet/quite: *Quiet* is an adjective meaning "silent." *Quite* is an adverb meaning "completely" or "really."

Jack stayed **quiet** for the whole sermon.
The grandparents were **quite** impressed by his maturity.

than/then: *Than* is a conjunction used to introduce the second part of a comparison. *Then* means "at that time" or "next in order."

David is a better writer **than** I.
He rises early in the morning and likes to write **then**.
First, he wrote a short story; **then** he wrote a poem.

to/too/two: The preposition *to* means "toward." *Too* is an adverb meaning "in addition to," "excessively," or "very." *Two* is a number word often used as an adjective.

We ran **to** the stop sign.
Mary ran **too**.
We don't run **too** fast.
We run at least **two** miles every morning.

wear/where: *Wear* is a verb that means "to have on" or "to damage." *Where* is an adverb indicating place or position.

Did you **wear** your new shoes?
Be careful not to **wear** them out.
Where are your old ones?

14-9 PRACTICE THE SKILL

Underline the correct word from the choices in parentheses.

1. Elizabeth Barrett was a *(plain, plane)* girl who from an early age suffered chronic weakness in her lungs.
2. Her brother's drowning while both were living by the sea at Torquay *(quiet, quite)* shocked her and weakened her already frail health.
3. After her family moved to London, she seemed to become a permanent invalid. Barrett spent most of her time in a *(quiet, quite),* darkened room writing letters and poetry.
4. Robert Browning admired Barrett's *Poems* and wrote a letter *(to, too, two)* her.
5. The *(to, too, two)* of them met, fell in love, and were married secretly in 1846.
6. Soon afterward, the Brownings moved to Italy, *(wear, where)* Elizabeth's health improved remarkably.

7. The birth of a son in 1849 added to the Brownings' *(peace, piece)* and happiness.
8. During her lifetime Elizabeth Barrett Browning's poetry was more admired *(than, then)* her husband's poetry.
9. However, her husband's fame soon *(passed, past)* hers.
10. Today Robert Browning's poetry is read much more widely *(than, then)* his wife's poetry.

14-10 REVIEW THE SKILL

In the blank write the letter of the correct sentence.

1. _____
   A. Have you ever kept a diary?
   B. If you haven't, how come?

2. _____
   A. A diary can be quiet a worthwhile item.
   B. It can help you keep your memories of the past.

3. _____
   A. A diary can remind you of your feelings than so that you can see how you have changed.
   B. Eventually, your diary could then be valuable to other people.

4. _____
   A. Diaries are great resources for those who want to learn about other times.
   B. Your children might like to here about their parents' daily lives.

5. _____
   A. Other readers might enjoy learning about your life two.
   B. A diary can provide a window for a person to see what the past was like.

6. _____
   A. A diary can take its reader to another time by showing the little details of everyday life.
   B. The reader can see what foods the people ate alot of.

7. _____
   A. He can also discover wear people went in their free time.
   B. The Englishman Samuel Pepys wrote a famous diary.

8. _____
   A. He was a politician and a government official too.
   B. In his lifetime he came out alright through the Great Plague of 1665, the Great Fire of 1666, and an invasion of England by the Dutch.

9. _____
   A. His personal account of these events is more interesting than an official report.
   B. Through descriptions of his own and others' lives, his diaries also show the lack of piece for people who aren't following God.

10. _____
    A. Samuel Pepys would likely have received less attention if he had never written about his times.
    B. Isn't it plane to see that it's a good idea to keep a diary?

14-11 USE THE SKILL

Underline each incorrect word and write the correction in the blank. If a sentence is correct, write *C* in the blank.

_____ 1. Alot of good writers consistently keep journals.

_____ 2. Those who write every day are usually better writers then those who write only sporadically.

_____ 3. Not only does a journal hold a record of passed events, but it also teaches you how to organize your ideas.

_____ 4. Those who keep journals learn how to put their thoughts into words, and they learn how to describe detail too.

_____ 5. When writing in your journal, you can transform a plane event into an exciting narrative.

_____ 6. Mom says that I may have enough money to buy a journal.

_____ 7. I need to find a quite time when I can write in my journal every day.

_____ 8. Some days I have less incidents to write about than other days.

_____ 9. I will be able to think more clearly after I have layed down for a few minutes.

_____ 10. I sat my journal down by the fireplace and left it lying there during my nap.

14-12 CUMULATIVE REVIEW

Rewrite the paragraphs on the blanks below, correcting the fifteen errors in subject-verb agreement, pronoun-antecedent agreement, pronoun usage, adjective or adverb usage, or with troublesome words.

    During the summer I often raise early and sit at the kitchen table to eat breakfast. My dog, Waggles, bring the newspaper to me as I eat. Hurriedly I turn to the comics. The comics page is my favorite section of the paper. Between all of the different comic strips, I like Charles Schulz's "Peanuts" the best. The fact that it appears in no fewer than two thousand different newspapers proves it's popularity with other readers too.

    This year in school I learned that "Hogan's Alley" is generally excepted as the first widely popular comic strip. They lead the way in the development of modern-day comic strips. It first appeared in 1895 in the Sunday edition of the *New York World*. This first comic strip was quiet simple. The strip told about the adventures of a mischievous little boy named Mickey Dugan. R. F. Outcault, the strip's creator, had Mickey where a yellow outfit, and the nickname "The Yellow Kid" was born. The comic strip known in passed issues as "Hogan's Alley" soon became known as "The Yellow Kid."

Using Troublesome Words Correctly

In the 1930s, plane and simple cartoons gave way to more fully developed and detailed ones. During this time adventure strips raised in popularity. "Prince Valiant" and "Superman" were two strips that began in 1937 and 1938 respectively. Both were written very good. However, comics began to loose their popularity in the 1940s when television became widespread. By the 1960s comics had regained some of their popularity. Today comics appeal not just to children; alot of adults read them as well.

When Friends Meet Friends: Writing a Book Report

Have you ever read a book that made you want to share it with someone else? You liked the characters so much that you felt they were your friends, and you wanted all of your other friends to meet them. You wanted to present the book to others in the most inviting way possible so that everyone else would want to read it.

One way to present a book report invitingly is to make it into an actual invitation. Who should do the inviting? We usually receive invitations from our friends. Why not have the invitation come from a friend—one of the characters you have met in the story?

Book reports usually include four things:
- a description of the setting (the place and time of the story),
- an introduction to the characters,
- a summary of the story's plot up to a point of crisis (the high point of the action), and
- your opinion of the book.

Here's an example of how one student included each of these elements in his book report using the invitation format.

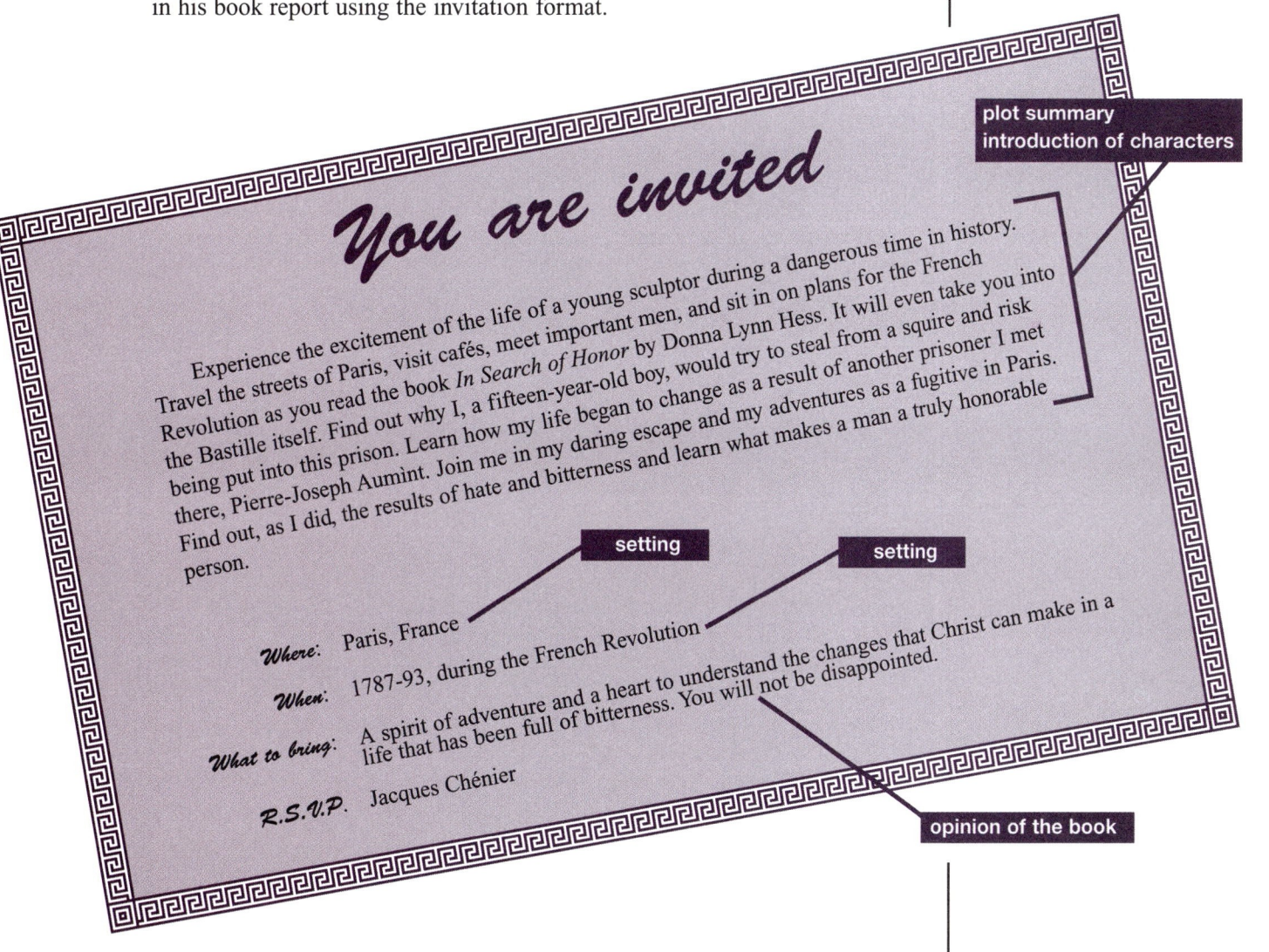

You are invited

Experience the excitement of the life of a young sculptor during a dangerous time in history. Travel the streets of Paris, visit cafés, meet important men, and sit in on plans for the French Revolution as you read the book *In Search of Honor* by Donna Lynn Hess. It will even take you into the Bastille itself. Find out why I, a fifteen-year-old boy, would try to steal from a squire and risk being put into this prison. Learn how my life began to change as a result of another prisoner I met there, Pierre-Joseph Aumìnt. Join me in my daring escape and my adventures as a fugitive in Paris. Find out, as I did, the results of hate and bitterness and learn what makes a man a truly honorable person.

Where: Paris, France
When: 1787–93, during the French Revolution
What to bring: A spirit of adventure and a heart to understand the changes that Christ can make in a life that has been full of bitterness. You will not be disappointed.
R.S.V.P. Jacques Chénier

Using Troublesome Words Correctly

ESL

R.S.V.P. is an acronym for the French phrase *répondez s'il vous plait,* which literally means "respond if you please." A person who receives an invitation with R.S.V.P. on it is expected to reply to the sender with an answer of "Yes, I will attend" or "No, I am sorry I cannot come."

Your Turn: Inviting Friends In

Now write your own invitation to a favorite book. Try to think of the book as not just a story to be read but an experience to be lived. Think of the characters as real people. Choose the character that you liked most to be the one to send the invitation. It could be the main character, but it doesn't have to be. Include specific details to keep the level of interest high. And remember—don't give the whole story; give just enough to whet your reader's appetite. If the invitation is written well, he will have no choice but to come.

Use this outline to keep your ideas focused:

You are invited

- **To:** (introduction to characters and plot summary—include title and author)
- **Where:** (setting—place)
- **When:** (setting—time)
- **What to bring:** (your opinion—how you want the reader to feel about the book)
- **R.S.V.P.** (name of the character issuing the invitation)

Passing the Baton
Writing Across the Curriculum

Lists

Does making a list count as a writing activity? Making a list is usually a personal writing activity—you may be the only one who will see it. Using the following ideas, make lists of twelve to fifteen items.

- Foods that you like or dislike

- Activities you enjoy or do not enjoy

- Things you would buy for the beginning of the school year

- Things you would need at the beach or in the mountains

- Things you would like to know more about

- Places you would like to visit or avoid

Chapter 15
Capitalization

Usage

Every runner knows how crucial a good start is. And every writer should know too. A capital letter is a start—sometimes of a long run like a sentence and sometimes of a sprint like a proper noun. Any writer not comfortable with his starting blocks might find himself out of the running.

As you learned in Chapter 2, we capitalize proper nouns and their abbreviations, but we do not capitalize common nouns. The problem comes when we must decide which nouns are common and which are proper. We also capitalize some other words, such as the first word in a sentence. The rules of capitalization in this chapter can help you decide which words to capitalize in your own writings.

Chapter 2: Identifying Common and Proper Nouns
p. 29

Proper Nouns: People and Places

Names and initials	**W**arren **B**axter **I**nga **M. L**indstrom
Titles used with a name	**P**resident **W**ilson **G**rand **D**uchess **O**lga **D**r. **J**oanne **J**anos **J**oanne **J**anos, **M.D.**
• Do not capitalize titles used in place of a person's name.	The **s**enator issued a statement today.
Family words used as proper nouns	Did you remember to send **G**randmother a birthday card?
• If a word for a family relationship is modified by an adjective, it is not being used as a proper noun.	My **g**randmother coached a basketball team when she was young.

Countries Continents	**A**rgentina **S**outh **A**merica
Cities States	**B**ismarck **N**orth **D**akota
Sections of a country or the world • Do not capitalize compass words when they indicate direction.	**U**pper **P**eninsula **M**iddle **E**ast a **n**orthbound flight
Geographic features	**G**rand **C**anyon **G**reat **P**lains (*But:* The **m**ountains are beautiful in winter.)
Recreational Areas	**S**uperior **N**ational **F**orest **C**entral **P**ark (*But:* My cousin played in the **p**ark all afternoon.)
Streets and Roads	**C**edar **B**oulevard **P**oinsett **H**ighway (*But:* I live on the **s**treet next to the school.)
Bodies of Water	**R**ice **C**reek **A**tlantic **O**cean (*But:* Dad and I like to fish in that **r**iver.)
Planets Stars Satellites Other heavenly bodies	**M**ercury **A**lpha **C**entauri **I**o **U**rsa **M**ajor
• Capitalize the words *earth, sun,* and *moon* only when they are listed with another specific heavenly body.	The two *Viking* spacecraft launched from **E**arth orbited **M**ars. (*But:* The **m**oon and **s**tars are hidden by clouds tonight.)
• Never capitalize *earth* when it is preceded by *the.*	What is the **e**arth's circumference?

15-1 PRACTICE THE SKILL

Underline each capitalization error.

1. Looking into the night sky, we can see the Moon and the stars.
2. The Earth does not orbit the Sun alone; there are eight other planets.
3. Planets that have a size and density similar to the Earth's are known as terrestrial Planets.
4. The terrestrial planets are Mercury, Venus, earth, Mars, and pluto.
5. Jovian planets, jupiter, saturn, uranus, and neptune, are larger than the earth and have low densities.

6. The reddish planet in the sky is Mars; it has two moons, phobos and deimos.
7. The first planet to be observed by a space probe was venus.
8. Because of its unusual pattern of orbit, the planet pluto is sometimes closer to the Sun than Neptune.
9. The large size of the Sun is hard to comprehend, but a Star in the constellation orion, betelgeuse, is even five hundred times larger.
10. Our sun is just one Star among an innumerable group of stars called the milky way.

15-2 REVIEW THE SKILL

Underline each capitalization error and write the correction in the blank. If the sentence is correct, write C in the blank.

_____ 1. Did you know that my uncle Jim lives in colorado?

_____ 2. Jim d. Bowen lives in the western part of the state near the Colorado River.

_____ 3. Uncle Jim and aunt Lily have always lived in the West.

_____ 4. Jim and Lily enjoy the beautiful Mountains in Colorado.

_____ 5. Their Doctor, Jonathan Carr, M.D., lives in an apartment on Crystal Street in the city of Grand Junction.

_____ 6. The Great Sand Dunes National Monument is one of the most unusual sights in north America.

_____ 7. Impressive peaks of the Rockies can be found in the Rocky mountain National Park.

_____ 8. Cherry Creek Lake is near Denver, Colorado.

_____ 9. Many farmers work in the eastern area of Colorado, part of the Great plains.

_____ 10. My aunt and uncle will take me to visit the Parks in Colorado.

Proper Nouns: More People and Places (and related terms)

Names of religions	Christianity Hinduism
All nouns and personal pronouns referring to the one true God	Jesus taught **H**is disciples.
• Do not capitalize common nouns or pronouns referring to mythological gods.	According to Greek mythology, the driver of the sun chariot was the god Apollo.
The words *Holy Bible* or *Bible* and the parts of the Bible as well as the names of sacred writings of other religions	Old Testament Genesis Talmud
Buildings Structures Monuments	Chrysler Building Golden Gate Bridge Jefferson Memorial
Aircraft Spacecraft Ships Trains	*Spirit of St. Louis* *Voyager 2* *Andrea Doria* *Orient Express* (*But:* We traveled by plane on our vacation this year.)
Businesses	Summit Gifts American Broadcasting Company (ABC) (*But:* a gift shop)
Brand names of business products	Band-Aid Rollerblade Ford Mustang (*But:* in-line skates, a Ford car)
Government departments Programs Political parties	Central Intelligence Agency (CIA) Head Start Federalist Party
Schools	Riverside High School University of Virginia USC (*But:* a high school)
Organizations	Riverside Lions Future Farmers of America (*But:* the team, the club)
Members of most organizations	a Republican a Boy Scout

15-3 PRACTICE THE SKILL

In the blank write the letter of the choice that follows capitalization rules correctly.

1. _____
   A. toyota Camry
   B. new Testament
   C. the team of basketball players

2. _____
   A. the university of Oklahoma
   B. NASA
   C. a College in Massachusetts

3. _____
   A. the Confederates
   B. a Soldier
   C. the book of revelation

4. _____
   A. Pizza hut
   B. Oceanspray juice
   C. Orange Juice

5. _____
   A. the new Chevrolet Truck in the garage
   B. the Washington Monument
   C. the tallest Building in Washington, D.C.

6. _____
   A. traveling on Northwest airlines
   B. the space shuttle *Columbia*
   C. Princeton university

7. _____
   A. Aphrodite, the Greek Goddess of love
   B. the third book of the bible, Leviticus
   C. Wetterland Music Company

8. _____
   A. Robson academy
   B. the democratic convention
   C. the Modern Language Association

9. _____
   A. the Baseball team in Atlanta
   B. the Toronto Bluejays
   C. the atlanta Braves

10. _____
    A. the statue of Liberty
    B. Brownville Technical school
    C. a band member

15-4 REVIEW THE SKILL

Underline each capitalization error and write the correction in the blank. If the sentence is correct, write *C* in the blank.

_____ 1. One of the most nourishing foods that god provides for mankind is milk.

_____ 2. In the old testament, the richness of Canaan is emphasized when it is described in Exodus 33:3 as "a land flowing with milk and honey."

_____ 3. Milk has always been a significant source of nutrition, and people in africa and Asia have raised cattle specifically for milk for thousands of years.

Capitalization

_____ 4. In 1856, Gail Borden developed a procedure for milk condensation, and the company borden still processes milk today.

_____ 5. Most states process milk according to conditions prescribed by the fda. Milk that meets these conditions is known as grade A milk.

_____ 6. The students of Brookview High school in Indiana have formed a health club to encourage nutritious eating habits.

_____ 7. The club, Healthy start, teaches students about nutrition and proper eating habits.

_____ 8. The club meets in the johnson Building every Tuesday after school.

_____ 9. The Members of the club are encouraged to drink at least two glasses of milk per day.

_____ 10. The students of Brookview High in Healthy Start realize how important milk is for mind and body.

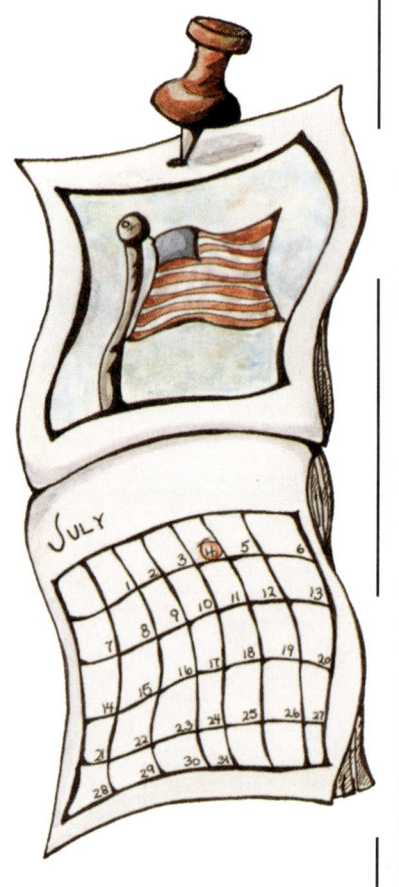

Proper Nouns: Cultural and Historical Terms

Nationalities	**M**exican, **C**anadian
Races	**H**ispanic, **A**sian
Languages	**S**panish, **M**andarin
Flags	**U**nion **J**ack, **O**ld **G**lory
Months	**J**anuary, **F**ebruary
Days	**F**riday, **S**aturday
• Do not capitalize the names of the seasons.	autumn, winter
Holidays	**E**aster, **R**osh **H**ashanah
The abbreviations B.C. and A.D. • Notice that B.C. ("before Christ") is correctly placed after the year and that A.D. (*anno Domini*, "in the year of the Lord") is correctly placed before the year.	Julius Caesar first explored England in 55 B.C. William of Normandy conquered England in A.D. 1066.
The abbreviations A.M. and P.M. may be either capitalized or not. (Whichever you choose, be consistent in your writing.)	8:00 A.M., 5:00 P.M. 8:00 **a.m.**, 5:00 **p.m.**
Historical events and periods	**B**oston **T**ea **P**arty **R**enaissance **R**oaring **T**wenties

Historical documents	**M**ayflower **C**ompact
	Treaty of **V**ersailles
Special events	**A**utumn **L**eaves **F**estival
	New **Y**ork **W**orld's **F**air

15-5 PRACTICE THE SKILL

Find each capitalization error. In the blank write the letter of the correction.

_____ 1. During the Middle Ages, New Year's day was celebrated in the month of March.

    A. ages
    B. Day
    C. march

_____ 2. The new year at that time began on March 25, which was a Christian Holiday known as Annunciation Day.

    A. march
    B. holiday
    C. annunciation day

_____ 3. Several holiday customs, including giving gifts to the emperor, were established by the ancient romans.

    A. Holiday
    B. Ancient
    C. Romans

_____ 4. In a.d. 567, the Church outlawed several Roman customs for many Europeans.

    A. A.D. 567
    B. roman
    C. europeans

_____ 5. After 1600, January 1 once again became the first day of the year. In 1752 the date became the official date for New Year's Day for americans.

    A. january
    B. Official
    C. Americans

_____ 6. New Year's Day, a Winter holiday, occurs one week after Christmas.

    A. new year's day
    B. winter
    C. christmas

_____ 7. A four-day celebration for the Chinese People involves colorful dragon costumes and begins in January or February.

    A. chinese
    B. people
    C. Dragon

_____ 8. Jews celebrate New Year's in the Fall on a day they call Rosh Hashanah.

    A. jews
    B. fall
    C. rosh hashanah

Capitalization

_____ 9. Many Americans observe New Year's eve by staying up until 12:00 a.m. to bring in the new year.
   A. Eve
   B. 12:00 A.M.
   C. Year

_____ 10. Many special celebrations occur on New Year's Day, including the Tournament of roses Parade in California.
   A. day
   B. tournament
   C. Roses

15-6 REVIEW THE SKILL

Underline each capitalization error and write the correction in the blank. If the sentence is correct, write *C* in the blank.

_____ 1. Various tribal people roamed into what is now Germany about 1000 B.C., and some settled just north of the Roman Empire around 100 b.c.

_____ 2. Because several Germanic tribes settled there, including the Franks and Goths, the romans called the land Germania.

_____ 3. The unification of Germany did not take place until january 18, 1871, when Wilhelm I became the first emperor of the German Empire.

_____ 4. The reformation in Germany began in 1517 after Martin Luther challenged the teachings of the Roman Catholic Church.

_____ 5. Beginning in 1934, Hitler ruled Nazi Germany and had millions of European Jews killed. He wanted only those of the aryan race to live in Germany.

_____ 6. Several Nazi officials were tried for their war crimes in the famous nuremberg trials.

_____ 7. After defeating Germany in World war II, world leaders met at the Potsdam Conference and took away much of Germany's land.

_____ 8. German is the official language of Germany. It is, along with French and Italian, also one of the official languages of Switzerland.

_____ 9. In the Winter, skiing is a popular sport in the mountains of Germany.

_____ 10. Many tourists visit Germany for oktoberfest.

Proper Nouns: Titles

Capitalize the first and last words in a title as well as all other important words. Do not capitalize an article, a coordinating conjunction, the *to* of the infinitive, or a preposition of fewer than five letters unless it is the first or last word in the title.

Newspapers and magazines	*Chicago Tribune, New York Times* *Time, Reader's Digest*
Literary compositions	*The Pilgrim's Progress* "Jabberwocky" *Hamlet*
Musical compositions	the *Emperor* Concerto "Silent Night"
Works of art	Rodin's *The Thinker* Monet's *Water Lilies*
Television and radio programs	*Wide World of Sports* *Morning Edition*
Specific courses of study	Advanced Algebra History of Civilization Physics 112 (*But:* Did you remember to bring your textbook to history class?)

15-7 PRACTICE THE SKILL

In the blank write the letter of the choice that is capitalized correctly. (Items 1-8 are titles, and items 9-10 are course names.)

1. _____
   A. "What a friend we have in Jesus"
   B. "What a Friend we Have in Jesus"
   C. "What a Friend We Have in Jesus"

2. _____
   A. *A Tale of Two Cities*
   B. *A tale of two cities*
   C. *a Tale of Two Cities*

3. _____
   A. "the necklace"
   B. "The necklace"
   C. "The Necklace"

4. _____
   A. "The Meaning of the look"
   B. "The Meaning of the Look"
   C. "The meaning of The Look"

5. _____
   A. "Weep No More, My Lady"
   B. "Weep no more, my Lady"
   C. "Weep no More, my Lady"

6. _____ A. *Chicago tribune*
B. *Chicago Tribune*
C. *chicago tribune*

7. _____ A. *American History*
B. *american history*
C. *American history*

8. _____ A. *sixty minutes*
B. *Sixty Minutes*
C. *Sixty minutes*

9. _____ A. world history II
B. World History II
C. world History II

10. _____ A. Introduction to Art
B. Introduction to art
C. introduction to art

15-8 Review the Skill

Underline each capitalization error and write the correction in the blank. If the sentence is correct, write *C* in the blank.

_____ 1. *Reader's digest* claims to sell more magazines than any other.

_____ 2. My favorite Shakespearean play is *macbeth*.

_____ 3. I really enjoyed calculus 101.

_____ 4. Handel's *messiah* is performed every year on certain holidays.

_____ 5. Michelangelo's *Moses* is a famous sculpture.

_____ 6. One of my favorite poems is "The Road Not Taken" by Robert Frost.

_____ 7. Norman Rockwell used to supply illustrations for the *Saturday evening post*.

_____ 8. Every day *good morning, America* broadcasts the weather.

_____ 9. Mr. Rochester is one of the main characters in the novel *Jane Eyre*.

_____ 10. One very exciting short story is "the most dangerous game."

First Words and Parts of a Letter

The first word in a sentence	**D**o you like to participate in sports?
The first word in a line of dialogue	Mark said, "**M**y favorite sport is soccer."
Do not capitalize the second part of a divided quotation unless the second part is the beginning of a new sentence.	"**I** do enjoy watching football games," said Carlos. "**D**oes that count as participation?" "**M**aybe it does," replied Ethan, "**i**f you mentally make the plays along with the players."
The first word in a line of poetry	**O**h for a closer walk with God, **A** calm and heavenly frame; **A** light to shine upon the road **T**hat leads me to the Lamb!

Only the first word (and any proper nouns or proper adjectives) in each item of a formal outline	I. **H**ounds
	  A. **N**orwegian elkhound
	  B. **D**achshund
	  C. **B**eagle
	II. **R**etrievers
	  A. **L**abrador retriever
	  B. **G**olden retriever
	  C. **C**hesapeake Bay retriever

The first word and all nouns in the greeting of a letter	**D**ear **M**ina, **D**ear **F**riends,
The first word in the closing of a letter	**S**incerely, **R**espectfully yours,

Chapter 16: Quotation Marks p. 335

15-9 Practice the Skill

In the blank write the letter of the choice that is capitalized correctly.

1. _____
   - A. Dear mother,
   - B. Dear sir,
   - C. Dear Jenny,

2. _____
   - A. The car is in the garage.
   - B. the car is in the garage.
   - C. the Car is in the garage.

3. _____
   - A. I. Winter Games
       - A. Cross-country Skiing
       - B. Tobogganing
   - B. I. Winter games
       - A. Cross-country skiing
       - B. Tobogganing
   - C. I. Winter Games
       - A. cross-country skiing
       - B. tobogganing

4. _____
   - A. Samuel said, "Denise, it is snowing."
   - B. Samuel said, "denise, it is snowing."
   - C. Samuel said, "Denise, It is snowing."

Capitalization

5. _____ A. Sincerely yours,
   B. Sincerely Yours,
   C. sincerely yours,

6. _____ A. What a friend we have in Jesus,
      all our sins and griefs to bear.
   B. what a friend we have in Jesus,
      all our sins and griefs to bear.
   C. What a friend we have in Jesus,
      All our sins and griefs to bear.

7. _____ A. "The game is canceled," Said Caleb, "because of the snow."
   B. "The game is canceled," said Caleb, "Because of the snow."
   C. "The game is canceled," said Caleb, "because of the snow."

8. _____ A. "We are playing volleyball on Thursday," said Alicia. "would you like to come?"
   B. "We are playing volleyball on Thursday," said Alicia. "Would you like to come?"
   C. "We are playing volleyball on Thursday," Said Alicia. "Would you like to come?"

9. _____ A. Spirit of God, descend upon my heart;
      Wean it from earth, through all its pulses move;
   B. Spirit of God, descend upon my heart;
      wean it from earth, through all its pulses move;
   C. spirit of God, descend upon my heart;
      Wean it from earth, through all its pulses move;

10. _____ A. Dear Sarah and family,
    B. Dear Sarah and Family,
    C. Dear Sarah And Family,

15-10 Review the Skill

Underline the five capitalization errors.

Dear Mom and dad,

I am really enjoying my week at camp. there are seven other campers in my cabin. We're trying to win points for our team by winning as many games and contests as possible. My counselor, Steve, often asks, "Are you doing your best?"

Last night the speaker said, "joseph was successful because he was faithful in the little things even as a teenager." I've never thought about Joseph as a teenager before. "When he did not understand his difficult situation," the speaker continued, "He had confidence that God was working out everything for his good."

Tomorrow we will be hiking and swimming. This week has been full of great activities, but I'm still looking forward to seeing you on Saturday.

Your Son,
Brendon

Proper Adjectives and Single Letters as Words

Proper adjectives	**T**hanksgiving dinner **I**rish linen **J**oe's neighbor
Do not capitalize a word modified by a proper adjective unless the two together form a proper name.	The **B**ritish **I**sles are home to many people who are not **B**ritish citizens.
The personal pronoun *I*	Josey and **I** were partners in biology class.
The interjection *O*	Hear our prayer, **O** Lord.
Single letters used as words	Marcus earned a **B** on the physics test. Sara's mom wants her to eat an orange every day for vitamin **C**. The first note that Jeremy learned to play on the piano was middle **C**.

15-11 PRACTICE THE SKILL

In the blank write the letter of the choice that is capitalized correctly.

1. _____
   A. American transportation by waterways remains a fascinating part of american history.
   B. American Transportation by waterways remains a fascinating part of American History.
   C. American transportation by waterways remains a fascinating part of American history.

2. _____
   A. My classmates and i wonder what it would have been like to travel on an English ship like the *Mayflower*.
   B. My classmates and I wonder what it would have been like to travel on an English ship like the *Mayflower*.
   C. My classmates and I wonder what it would have been like to travel on an english ship like the *Mayflower*.

3. _____
   A. I would have enjoyed riding one of the fast American clipper ships.
   B. I would have enjoyed riding one of the fast American Clipper ships.
   C. I would have enjoyed riding one of the fast American Clipper Ships.

4. _____
   A. Many American cities are built on Natural harbors.
   B. Many American Cities are built on natural harbors.
   C. Many American cities are built on natural harbors.

5. _____
   A. The first steamboat to cross the atlantic Ocean was the American *Savannah*.
   B. The first steamboat to cross the Atlantic Ocean was the American *Savannah*.
   C. The first steamboat to cross the Atlantic ocean was the American *Savannah*.

Capitalization

6. _____ A. The *Servia* was the first passenger ship made completely from steel to cross the Atlantic Ocean.
   B. The *Servia* was the first Passenger ship made completely from steel to cross the Atlantic Ocean.
   C. The *Servia* was the first passenger ship made completely from steel to cross the atlantic Ocean.

7. _____ A. The Chesapeake Bay Bridge-Tunnel in Virginia is 17.5 miles long.
   B. The Chesapeake bay bridge-tunnel in Virginia is 17.5 miles long.
   C. The Chesapeake bay Bridge-tunnel in Virginia is 17.5 miles long.

8. _____ A. Engineers still build Drawbridges to allow ships to pass.
   B. Engineers still build drawbridges to allow ships to pass.
   C. Engineers still build Drawbridges to allow Ships to pass.

9. _____ A. Lighthouses, which help ships navigate along a rocky Shore, are operated by the Coast Guard.
   B. Lighthouses, which help ships navigate along a Rocky Shore, are operated by the Coast Guard.
   C. Lighthouses, which help ships navigate along a rocky shore, are operated by the Coast Guard.

10. _____ A. Boston Light, the country's oldest lighthouse, has been flashing since 1716.
    B. Boston Light, the Country's Oldest Lighthouse, has been flashing since 1716.
    C. Boston Light, The Country's Oldest lighthouse, has been flashing since 1716.

314   Chapter 15

15-12 REVIEW THE SKILL

Underline each capitalization error and write the correction in the blank. If the sentence is correct, write *C* in the blank.

_____ 1. Sheep are valuable for clothing and food. The largest sheep, living in the Altai mountains of Siberia and Mongolia, are about four feet tall.

_____ 2. A notable sheep with a wide spread of horns lives in Asia and is known as the Marco polo sheep.

_____ 3. There are many different kinds of North American wild sheep.

_____ 4. Sheep with fine wool are mostly descendants from the Spanish Merino Sheep.

_____ 5. A few sheep are raised for milk, such as the East Friesian Dairy sheep that live in Germany.

_____ 6. Anna earned an a on her poetry test.

_____ 7. "Since then, my God, thou hast
So brave a palace built; o dwell in it,
That it may dwell with thee at last!"
From "Man" by George Herbert

_____ 8. She enjoys reading poetry, but i prefer novels and short stories.

_____ 9. In *The Scarlet Letter,* Hester was condemned to wear the letter *a* on all her clothing.

_____ 10. Anna and I agree that Frost is one of our favorite American Poets.

15-13 CUMULATIVE REVIEW

Rewrite the paragraph on the blanks below, correcting the fifteen errors in subject-verb agreement, pronoun-antecedent agreement, pronoun usage, adjective or adverb usage, troublesome words, or capitalization.

Railroads are an important means of trade and transportation, and they are another interesting part of american history. The first railroad cars were pulled along the tracks by horses. In 1831 the first steam-powered railroad in America was built in South Carolina. Railroads played an important part in the Civil war, so much so that an "rush" to complete the first transcontinental railroad line began in 1869. By 1916 automobiles began to surpass railroads as a best means of transportation, and the railroads were making fewer profit on passenger transportation. By 1971 the United States government had formed amtrak, a national railroad passenger corporation, in order to keep passenger service in operation. Each of the Amtrak railroad lines generate their own prophet and also receives subsidies from the federal government. Today many large American cities operates subways, which are really underground railroads. In 1897 Boston became the first north American city to build it's own subway. Today two of the most famous subway systems in America is the systems in New York City and Washington, D.C. Railroads and subways continue to be real useful for their contribution to trade and they're transportation for passengers.

Aesop Revisited: Writing a Short Fable

Perhaps when you were small, someone read you stories that ended with the line "And the moral of the story is. . . ." Such stories are called fables. You may consider reading fables to be appropriate only for the very young. But the writing of fables is for people who have lived long enough to be able to teach something about life.

Aesop is probably the most famous fable writer. He was a Greek slave around 600 B.C. who had a gift for telling animal tales with sharp messages. The French writer Jean de La Fontaine used fables in the 1600s to criticize his society. Although the fables were not meant for children, many children still read and enjoy them. The American writer James Thurber took the fable form and used it to satirize life in the "fast lane." Some of his fables have become part of American lore.

The Conventions of the Genre

Fables have several traits that make them fables. First, they are usually about animals acting in human ways. Part of the reason for this device is that it makes seeing the truth easier on the reader. If the silly or stubborn character does not look quite so much like him, the reader can more readily reject his silliness or stubbornness.

Second, they teach a lesson. All writing has some message in it, even when it claims not to. Every writer has a point from which he views his world—and when he writes anything, his philosophy comes through. Fables exist to teach. Fable writers frame a story so that some truth about life will be clear and memorable for the reader.

Third, fables are short. They present their characters and situations only to make the moral stand out. They tell only as much story as they need to get the meaning to the reader.

Here's a modern fable. Can you state its moral?

> A cat and a dog sat together on a wide wooden porch on a summer afternoon. The dog, rather old and lame in one leg, was snoozing with his eyes half shut. The cat was sitting up, calmly swinging his tail from side to side.
>
> "You know," said the cat, "I believe they're growing a little tired of you." "They" were, of course, the humans of the house.
>
> "Why do you say that?" asked the dog, opening his eyes fully.
>
> "Because," said the cat, "they don't play chase with you nearly as often as they once did. And have you noticed they don't take you for walks every day? Sometimes they let two or three days pass between your strolls through the park. It's easy to see. They've wearied of you. And after all, it must be rather tiresome to be licked by a great, sloppy tongue and to find shaggy brown hairs all over their rugs." The cat cocked his head and smiled slowly. "If I were you," he said, "I wouldn't try so hard."
>
> The dog was sitting up now, leaning forward. "Try hard to do what? What do you mean?"

The cat blinked. "Why, try so hard to please them, that's what. I wouldn't go out there in the soaking dew to bring in their newspaper. I wouldn't come running when they call me. I wouldn't set up such a howl when a prowler comes around the yard. Not if they treated me the way they treat you."

The dog put his head on his paws and said no more for a very long time.

At last a horn honked, and a car pulled into the drive. The dog, not quite as spry as he once was, scrambled up and stood wagging his tail. The cat watched him. "Don't go running to meet them again like a fool," he said. "Remember what I told you."

The human man got out of the car and gave the familiar whistle. The dog barked and sprang down the steps. He ran toward the man, limping a little. The cat only shook his head. "Fool," he muttered. He leaped gracefully into the porch swing and curled up in a ball.

In a moment, the dog trotted past, carrying one of the man's parcels between his teeth. The man followed with his arms full of grocery bags. They disappeared into the house.

The dog returned alone. He lay down on the porch again. When the paper boy rode by and dropped the newspaper on the drive, the dog scrambled up again. He hobbled off the porch, grabbed the paper, and brought it to the door, where he laid it down.

The human woman opened the door, patted the dog on the head, picked up the paper, and went inside.

"You see?" the cat mocked. "She hardly even spoke to you. What kind of thanks is that?"

The dog put his head on his paws and was silent.

Night came. The cat left the porch for his nightly rounds of the neighborhood. When the human woman came to the door and called the cat's name, he did not appear. The woman sighed. Then she looked down at the dog. "Come on in," she said gently. "Why don't you sleep inside tonight where it's cool?"

When the cat returned, the front door was shut fast. He leaped up on the windowsill and saw the dog resting inside on a soft rug. The remains of a juicy steak lay in his bowl nearby. "I suppose you're happy now," the cat hissed.

The dog looked up at the cat in the window, a little puzzled. "Yes, I'm happy," he said with a slight wag of his tail. "But not just now. I always have been."

For once, the cat had nothing to say.

Your Turn: Telling "Tails"

Think of something you want to make a reader understand. Write the message in one short statement. Then think of a story that would bring that message to life. Create an animal character or characters and choose a setting.

Write your rough draft. Remember, the story does not need to be very long. Read it to someone and ask him to state the moral of the story without your telling him what it is. If he guesses correctly, you can write the final draft.

If his answer differs from your original intent, ask yourself whether the story does indeed make the other point. Then ask yourself whether you want to keep that idea or adjust your story so that your original message is clearer.

Passing the Baton
Writing Across the Curriculum

Math

Choose one of the following lists of ingredients for a recipe. Only the ingredients are listed, not the amounts. Create a recipe by supplying the proportions and then give it an unusual name. Include procedures, times, and temperatures as well. If you wish, you may add an ingredient of your choice.

- eggs, flour, sugar, salt, milk, baking powder
- hamburger, salt, pepper, tomatoes, beans, onions, peppers

Chapter 16

Punctuation

Usage

Athletes use stopwatches to mark the ends of races, to help them control the pace of their practices, and to track their progress. All writers have stopwatches too—punctuation marks that end sentences, control the pace of thoughts, and keep the reader on track.

End Marks

Periods

Use a period at the end of a declarative sentence.

> I will need a coat this morning.

Use a period at the end of an indirect question.

> I asked her whether she wore her coat.

Use a period at the end of an imperative sentence that does not express strong emotion.

> Get your coat, please.

Chapter 1: Sentence Types
pp. 2-3

Question Marks

Use a question mark at the end of an interrogative sentence.

> Has it gotten colder outside since last night?

Exclamation Points

Use an exclamation point (sometimes called an exclamation mark) at the end of an exclamatory sentence.

> Oh, it has started snowing outside!

Use an exclamation point at the end of an imperative sentence that expresses strong emotion.

> Close that door now!

Use an exclamation point after an interjection that expresses strong emotion.

> Ouch! I shut the door on my foot.

Chapter 7: Interjections
p. 148

16-1 PRACTICE THE SKILL

Insert the correct end mark for each sentence.

1. Think about your favorite athletic competition
2. The Olympic games are very exciting
3. When were the games first held
4. Remember this important date
5. In 776 B.C. the first recorded games were held
6. How did the Olympic games get its name
7. The early games were held in Olympia, Greece
8. Wow! The first Olympics had only one event—a footrace
9. In A.D. 394 the last of the original Olympic games occurred
10. The tradition was revived in 1896 with an emphasis on both education and athletics

16-2 REVIEW THE SKILL

Insert the correct end mark for each sentence.

1. The first ice skaters tied animal bones to the bottoms of their shoes
2. I can't imagine skating on bones
3. When were metal blades first used
4. In A.D. 1250 the first iron blades replaced the polished bones
5. Find out when steel blades were first used
6. Steel skates were introduced in the last half of the nineteenth century
7. Do you like to skate outdoors
8. Watch out for the thin ice
9. Some speed skaters can skate up to thirty-five miles per hour
10. Can you skate that fast

Other Uses for Periods

Initials and Abbreviations

Use a period after most initials or abbreviations.

Names and titles	Mr. H. K. Barker Jr. Rosa Santiago, M.D.
• Do not use a period after most abbreviations of the names of government agencies and international organizations, including well-known businesses.	USAF (United States Air Force) UN (United Nations) IBM (International Business Machines)
Terms in Addresses	Rosewood Ave. P.O. Box 50235 Calif.
• Do not use a period after state or province postal abbreviations.	MA (Massachusetts) NB (New Brunswick)
Times and Dates	9:00 P.M. A.D. 1500
Measurements	2,000 lbs. 50 ft.
• Do not use a period after abbreviations of metric measurements.	52 m 7 kg

Outlines and Lists

Use a period after each number or letter that shows a division of an outline.

> I. First main idea
> A. Supporting idea
> B. Supporting idea
>   1. Supporting detail
>   2. Supporting detail
> II. Second main idea

Use a period after each number or letter that precedes an item in a list.

> 1. walk dog
> 2. wash car
> 3. dry dishes

Decimals

Use a period as a decimal point.

> $6.34
>
> 36.78°F
>
> 25.9%

Chapter 15: Outline Capitalization
p. 311

16-3 PRACTICE THE SKILL

Insert any missing periods or decimal points in the following sentences. If the sentence is correct, write *C* in the blank.

_____ 1. The Stadium of Olympia was destroyed in the sixth century but was uncovered by archaeologists in the late 1800s

_____ 2. This discovery caused Baron Pierre de Coubertin to suggest a renewal of the Olympic games, and the IOC (International Olympic Committee) was born.

_____ 3. The Olympic flag represents the continents that participate in the games by five interlocking rings in these colors:
1 black,   4 red, and
2 blue,   5 yellow.
3 green,

_____ 4. St. Louis, Missouri, was the first city in the United States to host the modern Olympic games.

_____ 5. Two cities in the United States have hosted the Olympics twice: Los Angeles, CA, and Lake Placid, NY

_____ 6. The Olympics have been held at high altitudes, such as the 7,349 ft of Mexico City.

_____ 7. They have sometimes ended in tragedy, as the 1972 Olympics in Munich, West Germany, did when terrorists entered the Israeli athletes' compound in the early morning of Sept 5, killing some athletes and taking others hostage.

_____ 8. Some events are judged on a point system. A 10.0 is the highest possible score for diving and gymnastics, and a 6.0 is a perfect score in figure skating.

_____ 9. In 1996 Donovan Bailey of Canada won the shortest footrace, the 100 m run, in less than 10 seconds—984 seconds exactly.

_____ 10. Carlos Lopes of Portugal won the longest footrace, the 26 mi marathon, in just over 2 hrs in 1984.

16-4 Review the Skill

Insert any missing periods or decimal points in the following sentences. If the sentence is correct, write *C* in the blank.

_____ 1. The USCF (United States Cycling Federation) establishes rules for road racing.

_____ 2. Mountain bikes, which are built for biking in rugged places, have 26 in wheels.

_____ 3. A popular children's bike, the BMX, is built for racing.

_____ 4. These are three main types of bike racing:

   1 track racing,

   2 road racing, and

   3 motocross racing.

_____ 5. A bicycle introduced in 1870 was called the high-wheeler because its front wheel was 1.5 m high.

_____ 6. The first safety bicycle with equal-sized wheels was produced by J K Starley.

_____ 7. Three men biked 700 mi across Alaska.

_____ 8. They traveled past Mt McKinley, which is 20,320 ft high.

_____ 9. They carried less than 20 lbs. to make their load light as they crossed dangerous ice and turbulent rivers.

_____ 10. During their seven-week adventure, they once had to travel for 25 hrs without rest to escape a dangerous storm on the ice.

Commas

Commas in a Series

Use a comma to separate three or more items in a series.

>Harry, David, Matt, and Bryce all passed the biology test.
>(*But:* Nick and Frank did not pass the test.)
>
>The best students listen to the teacher, read the textbook, and study their notes.

Punctuation

Chapter 5: Adjectives
p. 96

Chapter 1: Comma Splices;
Fused Sentences
pp. 10-11

Chapter 7: Conjunctions
pp. 139-40

Chapter 8: Compound Sentences
p. 166

Sometimes use a comma to separate two or more adjectives that modify the same noun. Usually use a comma if you can reverse the order of the adjectives or replace the comma with the word *and* without changing the meaning.

> That tall, thin plant needs direct sunlight.
> That thin, tall plant needs direct sunlight.
> That tall and thin plant needs direct sunlight.
> (*But:* Who broke the new clay flower pot?)

Use a comma to separate the first independent clause from the conjunction in a compound sentence. (Do not use a comma before a conjunction that joins the parts of a compound predicate.)

> Joe likes Mexican dishes, but Mark prefers Greek cuisine.
> (*But:* She walked down the street to the doctor's office but rode the bus to the mall.)

16-5 PRACTICE THE SKILL

Insert any missing commas in the following sentences. If a sentence is correct, write *C* in the blank.

_____ 1. Football, basketball, and baseball have fascinated Americans for many years.

_____ 2. Elementary high school college and professional teams play football.

_____ 3. American football teams have eleven players but Canadian teams have twelve.

_____ 4. Strength speed and physical contact are basic elements of the rough tough football game.

_____ 5. Two peach baskets a soccer ball and an indoor gymnasium were the equipment for the first game of basketball.

_____ 6. Basketball was originally played to keep a team in shape and to provide intense well-rounded competition between the football and baseball seasons.

_____ 7. Basketball is a fast exciting and challenging sport between two five-player teams.

_____ 8. The most popular American sport must be baseball.

_____ 9. Many believe that baseball was invented in America in 1839, but some historians mention the sport in England before that time.

_____ 10. The first catcher's mask was worn in 1875 and the first chest protector was worn in 1885.

16-6 REVIEW THE SKILL

Insert any missing commas in the following sentences. If a sentence is correct, write *C* in the blank.

_____ 1. Walking rafting and riding animals are three of the oldest forms of transportation.

_____ 2. Cars were invented later and riding the rapids became unnecessary.

_____ 3. Rafting was revived and became a recreational sport in the 1960s.

_____ 4. Small adventurous groups travel together in one raft down the river.

_____ 5. Brave rafters enjoy rivers that contain white-water rapids.

_____ 6. Some rivers have steep waterfalls and some can be very dangerous.

_____ 7. The cold clear water is exhilarating but it can also cause hypothermia.

_____ 8. Several rafting companies rent rafts and offer guided trips down white-water rivers.

_____ 9. Groups of rafters usually enjoy spending time outdoors together and they also sometimes engage in water battles on the river.

_____ 10. Rafting is a challenging sport and it is a good way to enjoy the beautiful mountain rivers.

Commas to Separate

Use a comma to separate some introductory words from the rest of the sentence.

> First, I set all the ingredients on the counter.
> Finally, the cake was ready after two long hours.

Use a comma or a pair of commas to separate a noun of direct address from the rest of the sentence. A noun of direct address names the person being spoken to.

> Patricia, will you close the door when you leave?
> Will you close the door, Patricia, when you leave?
> Will you close the door when you leave, Patricia?

Use a comma to separate a mild interjection from the rest of the sentence.

> Oh, Holly forgot her car keys.
> Take them to her, please.
> Yes, I can do that for her.

Use a comma or a pair of commas to separate an interrupting phrase that could be left out of the sentence.

> By the way, Renee and Billy are all-star basketball players.
> Marcus and Denise, on the other hand, do not like sports at all.

Use a comma to separate an introductory dependent clause from the independent clause in a complex sentence.

> Because her mother coaches a volleyball team, Kris learned the game well.

Use a comma to separate a long introductory prepositional phrase from the rest of the sentence; also use a comma to separate two or more introductory prepositional phrases from the rest of the sentence. Do not use a comma if the phrase is immediately followed by a verb.

> During the very stormy day, huge puddles formed in the roads.
> By the side of the road, a disabled car was waiting for help.
> (*But:* On top of the car next to the road was a stray kitten.)

16-7 PRACTICE THE SKILL

Insert any missing commas in the following sentences. If the sentence is correct, write *C* in the blank.

_____ 1. As soon as school begins in the fall many Americans look forward to the beginning of football season.

_____ 2. In very early times before the development of modern sports, there existed ball-kicking games similar to football.

_____ 3. One of these games for example was played by the ancient Greeks.

Chapter 7: Interjections p. 148

Chapter 8: Independent/Dependent Clauses p. 162

Chapter 7: Prepositional Phrases p. 132

_____ 4. During the first century B.C. the Romans introduced the game to England.

_____ 5. When football was first played in the United States it was similar to soccer.

_____ 6. In the early days of the development of football in America, teams could have up to twenty-five players.

_____ 7. Finally a convention in 1880 decided the issue.

_____ 8. Walter Camp of Yale persuaded the delegates to establish a standard of eleven players on each team.

_____ 9. Oh did you know that the first professional game was played in 1895?

_____ 10. Although football is a very popular sport a 1991 attempt to begin a spring season failed.

16-8 REVIEW THE SKILL

Insert any missing commas in the following sentences. If a sentence is correct, write *C* in the blank.

_____ 1. Ashley how was volleyball practice?

_____ 2. It was a good practice Mom.

_____ 3. Well why don't you tell me about it?

_____ 4. Before we practiced volleyball Coach Green assigned some warm-ups.

_____ 5. Next, we practiced setting and spiking.

_____ 6. Coach Green in fact wants me to become the setter for the team in a few weeks.

_____ 7. Do you think you're ready Ashley for that responsibility?

_____ 9. I have to practice an extra hour on Friday.

_____ 10. Because I like setting and working hard I think I'm really going to enjoy this new position Mom.

Punctuation 329

Commas with Quotations, Dates, and Addresses; and Commas in Letters

Use a comma to separate a direct quotation from the rest of the sentence in written dialogue.

> "Josey is going to school," said Mom.
> "Maybe," she said, "she'll bring that book to you."
> Marta replied, "Well, it is in my locker."

Use a comma to separate the month and day from the year. Do not use a comma between only the month and day or month and year.

> Jane Austen was born on December 16, 1775.
> Ludwig van Beethoven also was born on December 16.
> Was he born in December 1775 too?

Use a comma to separate a full date (month, day, and year) from the rest of the sentence.

> December 16, 1770, is Beethoven's birthday.

At the end of a sentence, use a comma to separate the city from a state or a country.

> Robert Louis Stevenson was born in Edinburgh, Scotland.
> He later lived near St. Helena, California.

Before the end of a sentence, use a pair of commas to set off a state or country in an address.

> My sister moved to Athens, Georgia, after graduating from college.
> Athens, Greece, is an interesting place to visit.
> (*But:* The Carson family went to Rome for their vacation.)

Do not use a comma to separate the ZIP code from the state in an address.

> Matt Schultz
> 187 Alma Blvd.
> Sterling, WI 24078
>
> Write to me at this address: Matt Schultz, 187 Alma Blvd., Sterling, WI 24078.

Use a comma after the greeting of a friendly letter and after the closing of all letters.

> Dear Matt,
> Sincerely yours,

Chapter 15: Capitalization of Letter Parts
p. 311

16-9 PRACTICE THE SKILL

Insert any missing commas. If an item is correct, write *C* in the blank.

_____ 1. Imagine an exchange of letters that took place in March 2000 between Joe and his friend Adam, who enjoys professional golf.

_____ 2. Dear Adam

_____ 3. I have recently developed an interest in golf and wondered whether you would send some information on the history of the game to the following address: Joe Vaughan 101 Main St. Suntown TN 01234.

_____ 4. Dear Joe

_____ 5. I myself have loved golf since my first game in June 1965, and I am glad that you have taken an interest in it.

_____ 6. Most people believe that the modern game of golf originated in Edinburgh Scotland.

_____ 7. The city of Edinburgh proclaimed the establishment of an annual golf competition on March 17, 1744.

_____ 8. An article I once read said "The winner of the competition became the official judge for the next game."

_____ 9. On May 14 1754 the town of St. Andrews organized its own competition with established rules similar to those we have today.

_____ 10. Sincerely yours

Adam

16-10 REVIEW THE SKILL

In the blank write the letter of the sentence that has the correct punctuation.

1. _____ A. Jesse Owens was born in Danville, Alabama.
   B. Jesse Owens was born in Danville Alabama.
2. _____ A. He was born in September 1913.
   B. He was born in September, 1913.
3. _____ A. In Ann Arbor, Michigan he broke three track-and-field world records.
   B. In Ann Arbor, Michigan, he broke three track-and-field world records.
4. _____ A. He broke the records on May 25, 1935 at a college competition.
   B. He broke the records on May 25, 1935, at a college competition.

Punctuation 331

5. _____ A. He qualified for the 1936, summer Olympics.
   B. He qualified for the 1936 summer Olympics.
6. _____ A. In Berlin, Germany, he competed in the Olympic games.
   B. In Berlin, Germany he competed in the Olympic games.
7. _____ A. "Owens greatly disappointed Adolf Hitler," my teacher explained "because Owens beat the Germans in several track-and-field events."
   B. "Owens greatly disappointed Adolf Hitler," my teacher explained, "because Owens beat the Germans in several track-and-field events."
8. _____ A. After the games, Owens said "I've never felt like that before."
   B. After the games, Owens said, "I've never felt like that before."
9. _____ A. He returned to the United States as a famous man.
   B. He returned to the United States, as a famous man.
10. _____ A. Jesse Owens died on March 31, 1980.
    B. Jesse Owens died on March 31 1980.

Semicolons and Colons

Semicolons

Use a semicolon to separate two independent clauses in a compound sentence with no coordinating conjunction.

> Mandy saw her dad at the dentist's office; she met her mom at the library.

Colons

Use a colon to separate the chapter and verse in a Bible reference.

> Psalm 118:24

Use a colon to separate the hour from the minutes in an expression of time.

> 6:15 P.M.

Use a colon after the greeting of a business letter.

> Dear Sir:
> Dear Dr. Russell:

Use a colon to introduce a list of items at the end of an independent clause.

> You will need these ingredients for a cake: flour, sugar, eggs, and butter.

Chapter 8: Compound Sentences p. 166

Chapter 15: Capitalization of a Greeting p. 311

16-11 PRACTICE THE SKILL

Insert any missing semicolons or colons in the following sentences. If a sentence is correct, write *C* in the blank.

_____ 1. For many centuries skis were a means of transportation over the snow skiing was not considered a sport.

_____ 2. It was these people who used skis to help them in their travel the Norwegians, the Swedes, and the Lapps.

_____ 3. The first recorded skier in the United States was "Snowshoe" Thompson; he was born and reared in Norway.

_____ 4. Beginning in 1850 Thompson used his skis to deliver the mail he delivered the mail for twenty years between northern California and Carson Valley, Idaho.

_____ 5. Many skiers enjoy the high-speed thrill down the mountain slopes others enjoy the competition.

_____ 6. Three types of skiing provide competition for skiers: Alpine skiing, Nordic skiing, and freestyle skiing.

_____ 7. The first ski clubs appeared among Norwegian and Swedish settlers these clubs appeared in Wisconsin and Minnesota over one hundred years ago.

_____ 8. I would like to learn to ski meet me on the northern slopes at 8:30 tomorrow morning.

_____ 9. I will need to take these things warm clothes, a pair of thick gloves, and a good dose of courage.

_____ 10. I often remind myself of my favorite verse: "I can do all things through Christ which strengtheneth me" (Phil. 413).

16-12 REVIEW THE SKILL

Insert any missing semicolons or colons in the following sentences. If a sentence is correct, write *C* in the blank.

_____ 1. Swimming is one of the world's oldest sports we know that people as far back as Bible times were swimmers.

_____ 2. Isaiah speaks of swimming when he writes in Isaiah 2511, "And he shall spread forth his hands in the midst of them, as he that swimmeth spreadeth forth his hands to swim."

_____ 3. In Acts 2742-44, we see from Paul's shipwreck that there were swimmers and nonswimmers in the New Testament.

_____ 4. Because swimming is an enjoyable sport and good exercise, most people like it.

_____ 5. Some people get up before 600 A.M. to enjoy a few laps before the day begins; sometimes this is called Polar Bear Swimming.

_____ 6. Because swimming builds both muscle tone and endurance, a regular swimming workout is one of the best ways to stay in shape.

_____ 7. The following are three common types of swim strokes the crawl, the breaststroke, and the butterfly.

_____ 8. Swimming was a common activity in England by the mid-1800s today's modern pools keep swimming popular.

_____ 9. Several people have swum the English Channel it is twenty-one miles wide at its narrowest point.

_____ 10. In 1940 John Sigmund swam 292 miles down the Mississippi River he swam for almost ninety hours.

Quotation Marks

Use quotation marks to show words taken from another source.

> William Shakespeare wrote these words: "A rose by any other name would smell as sweet."

Use quotation marks to show the words of the speakers in a dialogue. (Do not use quotation marks with indirect quotations.)

> Quotation: "May I borrow your book?" Sam asked.
> Indirect quotation: Sam asked to borrow the book.

Follow these rules for using other punctuation with quotation marks.

- Use a comma to separate the quotation from the rest of the sentence.

  > Luci said, "Let's go to Hamburger Haven. I want a milkshake."
  > "I would like a cheeseburger," said Lorena.

- Always place periods and commas before the quotation marks.

  > Luigi remarked, "I prefer hot dogs with slaw."
  > Yuri considered the choices. "I will eat almost anything," he decided.

- Place question marks and exclamation points either before or after the quotation marks, depending upon the meaning of the sentence. If the entire sentence is a question or an exclamation, place the question mark or exclamation point after the quotation marks.

  > Did Luci mention a flavor when she said, "I want a milk shake"?
  > Only Yuri would say, "I will eat almost anything"!

  If only the quotation is a question or an exclamation, place the question mark or exclamation point before the quotation marks.

  > Yuri asked, "Are you hungry?"
  > Lorena replied, "Yes, I am starved!"

  No period or comma follows a question mark or exclamation point.

- Always place semicolons and colons outside the quotation marks.

  > Washington Irving is remembered for stories such as "The Legend of Sleepy Hollow"; several of his stories were collected in *The Sketch Book* in 1820.

  > These are the main characters in Irving's "The Legend of Sleepy Hollow": Ichabod Crane, Katrina Van Tassel, Brom Van Brunt, and the mysterious Galloping Hessian.

  Use quotation marks around these kinds of titles:

Short stories	"Rip Van Winkle"
Chapters	"Discoveries"
Poems	"Opportunity"
Essays	"The Art of Seeing Things"
Periodical articles	"Doing Things Right!"
Songs	"Beneath the Cross of Jesus"
Television and radio episodes	"To Walk on the Bright Side"

Chapter 15: Capitalization of Quotations
p. 311

16-13 PRACTICE THE SKILL

Insert any missing quotation marks in the following sentences. If a sentence is correct, write *C* in the blank.

_____ 1. Mrs. Helbert asked the class, Did you enjoy our unit on sports?

_____ 2. Susan responded, I have learned about many different kinds of sports.

_____ 3. I wanted to learn more about skiing, she said, since Dad enjoys it so much.

_____ 4. Well, said Mrs. Helbert, what about the rest of you?

_____ 5. Harrison said that he enjoyed the lesson about the Olympic games.

_____ 6. John, what do you think? asked Mrs. Helbert.

_____ 7. I really liked all the history that we learned about different sports, especially baseball, said John.

_____ 8. Brad added that he liked reading about football.

_____ 9. I'm glad all of you have enjoyed something about the sports unit, said Mrs. Helbert.

_____ 10. Now just study it well for the test tomorrow, she added as the bell rang to dismiss the class.

16-14 REVIEW THE SKILL

In the blank write the letter of the sentence that shows correct usage of quotation marks.

1. _____ A. "Swimming is fun, said Todd, I especially like to dive."
   B. "Swimming is fun," said Todd. "I especially like to dive."
2. _____ A. "Swimming is good exercise too," said Sarah.
   B. "Swimming is good exercise too, said Sarah."

3. _____ A. Sarah says that she swims one hour three times each week.
   B. Sarah says "that she swims one hour three times each week."

4. _____ A. "I don't think I could ever swim as well as Sarah," said Rebecca, "because she's been swimming a long time."
   B. "I don't think I could ever swim as well as Sarah", said Rebecca, "because she's been swimming a long time."

5. _____ A. Sarah answered, "Oh, don't worry about that; with practice, you'll be a great swimmer!"
   B. Sarah answered, "Oh, don't worry about that; with practice, you'll be a great swimmer"!

6. _____ A. A discussion of the health benefits of swimming appears in the article Swimming for Exercise.
   B. A discussion of the health benefits of swimming appears in the article "Swimming for Exercise."

7. _____ A. The article says, "Swimming provides an excellent workout for both the upper and lower body."
   B. The article says, "Swimming provides an excellent workout for both the upper and lower body".

8. _____ A. Have you read the section that says, "Swimming builds endurance?"
   B. Have you read the section that says, "Swimming builds endurance"?

9. _____ A. Many people ask, "What if I cannot swim well?".
   B. Many people ask, "What if I cannot swim well?"

10. _____ A. The article states, "It may be profitable for some to consider taking lessons"; others may need only to practice.
    B. The article states, "It may be profitable for some to consider taking lessons;" others may need only to practice.

Underlining for Italics

Underline or italicize words and letters being discussed. (Use underlining in handwritten papers. Italic print, the equivalent, is used in printed books or papers.)

> Did you know that the word <u>music</u> used to be spelled with a <u>k</u> at the end?
> Did you know that the word *music* used to be spelled with a *k* at the end?

Underline or italicize the names of large vehicles.

Ships	*Titanic*
Planes	*Spirit of St. Louis*
Trains	*Orient Express*
Spacecraft	*Columbia*

Punctuation 337

Underline or italicize the titles of long works.

Books	*The Cay*
Magazines	*National Geographic*
Newspapers	the *Portland Oregonian* (The word *the* is not part of a newspaper's title.)
Musical compositions	Brahms's *A German Requiem*
Television and radio series	*Masterpiece Theatre*
Epic poems	*Beowulf*
Plays	*Oklahoma!*

Underline or italicize the names of works of art.

| Paintings | *The Ascension* |
| Sculptures | *Spoonbridge and Cherry* |

16-15 PRACTICE THE SKILL

Insert any missing underlining for italics. If a sentence is correct, write *C* in the blank.

_____ 1. The word sports could bring many different images to mind.

_____ 2. One might think about reading the Soccer Journal.

_____ 3. Another might picture himself watching a game on Monday Night Football.

_____ 4. Some probably read the sports page in USA Today to get a general overview of everything going on in the world of sports.

_____ 5. Others may prefer to read a book like the Official Encyclopedia of Baseball for detailed information about one sport.

_____ 6. Some people would like to learn about the U.S. yacht America, the first vessel to win the America's Cup.

_____ 7. Young people may enjoy reading Stuart's Run to Faith, which tells of Stuart Baltz's experience on the varsity track team at his school.

_____ 8. Christians would appreciate the information about sports in Billy Sunday, a play about the preacher who started out as a baseball player.

_____ 9. A band director might even associate sports with John Philip Sousa's Washington Post March or another march that is played at halftime of a sporting event.

_____ 10. Sports provide interest and education no matter what we think of when we hear the word mentioned.

16-16 REVIEW THE SKILL

Insert any missing quotation marks or underlining for italics. If the sentence is correct, write *C* in the blank.

_____ 1. A Midsummer Night's Dream is one of Shakespeare's most popular plays.

_____ 2. Have you read The Early Years yet? It is the first chapter in our textbook.

_____ 3. Nathaniel Hawthorne wrote a short story called Young Goodman Brown about the life of a Puritan man.

_____ 4. "Holy Sonnet 10," a poem showing the ultimate weakness of death, was written by John Donne.

_____ 5. In 1819 the Savannah became the first steam engine to cross the Atlantic Ocean.

_____ 6. The Gingham Dog and the Calico Cat is a humorous poem by Eugene Field.

_____ 7. The beautiful Canon in D is Pachelbel's most famous musical work.

_____ 8. Benjamin West created many beautiful paintings including The Ascension of Christ.

_____ 9. Oh, Susanna! is a well-known American folk song.

_____ 10. If you like stories about adventure, danger, and heroes, you should read the epic poem Beowulf.

Apostrophes

Use an apostrophe to show an omission of letters or numbers.

> Did you know that *o'clock* is a contraction for the phrase *of the clock?*
> Many people name the stock market crash of '29 as one cause of the Great Depression.

Use an apostrophe to form the plurals of letters, signs, and words.

> How many *b*'s are in the word *bubble?*
> Do not use *&*'s to replace *and*'s in formal writing.

Do not use an apostrophe to form the plural of numbers.

> Queen Victoria ruled Great Britain for most of the 1800s.

Use an apostrophe to form the possessive of nouns.

- To form the singular possessive, add *'s* to the singular form of the noun.

cat	cat's	The cat's collar is new.
puppy	puppy's	The puppy's leash is tangled.
James	James's	James's pets are playful animals.

- Traditionally, only an apostrophe is added to the proper names Jesus and Moses.

Jesus	Jesus'	Call upon Jesus' name.
Moses	Moses'	Miriam was Moses' sister.

- If a plural ends with an *s,* add only an apostrophe to make it possessive.

boys	boys'	Who is those boys' mother?

- If a plural does not end with an *s,* add *'s* to make it possessive.

men	men's	The ties are in the men's department.

Chapter 12: Possessive Pronouns and Contractions p. 252

Chapter 6: Adverbs p. 116

Chapter 2: Possessive Forms of Nouns p. 26

16-17 PRACTICE THE SKILL

Insert any missing apostrophes in the following sentences. If a sentence is correct, write *C* in the blank.

_____ 1. *Skydiving* does have a *y* but no *z*s or any of the other letters needed to spell *crazy,* which is what some consider the sport to be.

_____ 2. Skydiving began in the 1930s, when air shows were popular.

_____ 3. World War II increased skydivers' prestige by making practical use of their parachuting skills.

_____ 4. With the end of the war, skydivers chose to continue the activity for sport.

_____ 5. The first American sport-parachuting center opened in Massachusetts in '59.

_____ 6. Judges at parachuting competitions rate a diver's body position in the air, his work with other divers, and his landing.

_____ 7. By the early 1970s, several divers had mastered the landing and could touch down directly on a target.

_____ 8. A diver in free fall (before he has opened his parachute) shouldn't do turns or loops unless he has had much diving experience.

_____ 9. In group competitions, several divers can join hands or pass a baton when they're correctly controlling their speed and rate of descent.

_____ 10. A skydiver's equipment will include two parachutes on a harness, boots, helmet, goggles, and gloves.

16-18 REVIEW THE SKILL

Insert any missing apostrophes in the following sentences. If a sentence is correct, write *C* in the blank.

_____ 1. Bowling is one of many peoples favorite sports.

_____ 2. Bowlers roll a heavy ball down a wooden lane and try to knock down pins in groups of ten.

_____ 3. In the United States, bowling was popular in the early 1900s, but professional bowling did not begin until the '50s.

_____ 4. If a bowler doesnt knock down all the pins during his first try, he is allowed to bowl again.

_____ 5. Knocking over all the pins on the first try is called a *strike*.

_____ 6. Hitting all of the pins by the end of the bowlers second try is called a *spare*.

_____ 7. Making three strikes in a row is a difficult feat; it's called a *turkey*.

_____ 8. A bowler wears special shoes because bowling shoes soft soles will not scratch the floor.

_____ 9. Bowlings popularity is largely due to the fact that the sport is quite easy to learn.

_____ 10. A perfect score of three hundred isnt easy to achieve; a bowler must bowl twelve strikes in a row.

Hyphens

Use a hyphen between the words of multiword numbers from twenty-one to ninety-nine.

> Eleven of the twenty-six students have younger siblings.

Use a hyphen between the two parts of a written-out fraction.

> Only one-half of the students have older siblings.

Use a hyphen to show the omission of a connecting word.

> The play will be presented October 12-15.

Use a hyphen to divide words at the end of a line. (Divide words only between syllables; never divide a one-syllable word.)

- Leave at least two letters and a hyphen on the first line.

    Wrong: We have a new puppy. Are pets allowed in your a-
    partment building?

    Right: We have a new puppy. Are pets allowed in your apart-
    ment building?

- Put at least three letters on the next line.

    Wrong: A soldier must never behave in a coward-
    ly way.

    Right: A soldier must never behave in a cow-
    ardly way.

- Leave the hyphen on the first line; do not carry it to the second line.

    Wrong: Although chemistry is interesting, I prefer geol
    -ogy and botany.

    Right: Although chemistry is interesting, I prefer geol-
    ogy and botany.

16-19 PRACTICE THE SKILL

Insert any missing hyphens in the following sentences.

1. Rugby is a popular sport in Great Britain, New Zealand, France, Aus tralia, and South Africa.

2. It might be described as one third soccer, one third American football, and one third something entirely its own.

3. Athletes had been using their feet in ball games since the Middle Ages, but twenty three years into the nineteenth century, something new came along.

4. Tradition at England's Rugby School says that William Ellis, a foot ball player, apparently got tired of kicking the ball. He picked it up and ran with it instead.

5. The game that eventually resulted uses a ball that is 24 25.5 inches in circumference and 11 11.5 inches in length, making it bigger than an American football.

6. The field is bigger than an American football field, which may cover only one half the space of the Rugby playing area.

7. Both Rugby and football have goal areas, but the Rugby goal is usually twenty five yards long, while football's end zone is only ten.

8. Rugby players can score 2 3 points, depending on whether they have made a try (similar to a touchdown) or a kick of some sort.

9. The person carrying the ball may pass it off, but only sideways or back wards, since none of his teammates are allowed to be in front of him.

10. If the player carrying the ball is tackled, he drops it so that each indi vidual team can try to retrieve it.

16-20 REVIEW THE SKILL

Insert any missing hyphens in the following sentences. If a sentence is correct, write *C* in the blank.

_____ 1. A popular and exciting sport around the world is horseman ship, which involves training and riding horses.

_____ 2. The attractive and handsome Clydesdale is much taller than the average man, while the Shetland pony's height is usually under forty six inches.

_____ 3. Young horses tend to be more spirited; therefore, it is wise for a beginner to start on a trained horse that is about fourteen years old.

_____ 4. Jumping competitions are usually short events, but horses and their riders also compete in cross-country events that can be over ten and one half miles long.

_____ 5. The movement of a horse is called its *gait*. A faster gait is called the canter, in which the horse moves about 10 12 mph.

If a word can be divided at the end of a line, rewrite the word in the blank with a hyphen at each place the word could be divided. If the word cannot be divided with a hyphen, write *C* in the blank.

Example: gallop gal-lop

_____ 6. saddle

_____ 7. thoroughbred

_____ 8. pony

_____ 9. competition

_____ 10. Traveller

Parentheses

Use parentheses to enclose words, phrases, or clauses that give additional information. Keep your meaning clear by limiting the number of parenthetical expressions you use.

> Charles Lindbergh (1902-74) was a pioneer in aviation.
> The president of the club (Cooper Smith) was presented with an award.
> One of the most popular pets is the house cat *(felis cattus)*.

Punctuation marks usually go outside the parentheses. However, when an entire sentence is enclosed in parentheses, a question mark or an exclamation point goes before the final parenthesis.

> "Let every soul be subject unto the higher powers" (Rom. 13:1).
> Terry, I hear that our meeting (can you come?) will be on March 16.

16-21 PRACTICE THE SKILL

Insert any missing parentheses in the following sentences. If the sentence is correct, write *C* in the blank.

_____ 1. Gymnastics is a sport based on acrobatic exercise skillful and coordinated; each performance is called a *routine*.

_____ 2. In the early 1800s, Friedrich Jahn a German schoolteacher built the first modern gymnastic equipment.

_____ 3. Although gymnastics in various forms has always been a part of the modern Olympic games, the popularity of the sport grew dramatically in the 1970s, mostly because of television coverage.

Punctuation   345

_____ 4. Gymnastics helps to develop important physical qualities in an athlete balance, flexibility, and strength.

_____ 5. Male gymnasts can compete in six events: the floor exercise, the pommel horse a side horse, the rings, the horse vault, the parallel bars, and the horizontal bar.

_____ 6. Female gymnasts compete in just four events: the side horse vault, the uneven parallel bars, the balance beam only four inches wide, and the floor exercise.

_____ 7. Those who take part in all the events are called all-around gymnasts; others those in only one or two events are called specialists.

_____ 8. Both men and women perform vaults across the horse, but men vault across the length of it and women across the width.

_____ 9. Both also participate in the floor exercise a routine performed on a square mat.

_____ 10. The men's floor exercise 50-70 seconds has a shorter time limit than the women's floor exercise 70-90 seconds.

16-22 PRACTICE THE SKILL

Insert any missing parentheses in the following sentences. If the sentence is correct, write *C* in the blank.

_____ 1. An inventor from Belgium in the late eighteenth century Joseph Merlin made the first roller skate.

_____ 2. Before the 1970s, roller skate wheels (now made of strong plastic) were sometimes made out of wood.

_____ 3. J. L. Plimpton significantly improved the roller skate when he designed a process cramping that allowed the wheels to continue moving along curves.

_____ 4. Skates that connect to one's own shoes are called clamp-on skates.

_____ 5. Most people roller skate for recreation. However, many skate in one of the two basic types of competitions artistic skating and speed skating.

_____ 6. Indoor speed skaters compete on an oval track 100 meters 328 feet in length.

_____ 7. Specialized skates speed skates are built with wheels that allow the skate to move faster than regular skates.

_____ 8. At a skating rink where people pay to rent skates, speed skates are usually more expensive than regular skates.

_____ 9. A newer type of skate the in-line skate has wheels in a straight line in the middle of the skate.

_____ 10. Many people exercise outdoors using in-line skates also known by the brand name Rollerblades.

16-23 USE THE SKILL

Add punctuation marks to the following sentences: periods, question marks, exclamation points, commas, semicolons, colons, quotation marks, underlining for italics, apostrophes, hyphens, and parentheses.

1. A physical fitness program is an important part of a persons education

2. Many kinds of physical activities contribute to a persons agility endurance flexibility and strength

3. Although each one influences the other physical fitness and good health are not the same

4. A person who is physically fit generally a person who exercises regularly will have more energy and feel better than someone who does not exercise

5. Is a persons physical fitness determined by such factors as age heredity, and behavior

6. These are the health habits that contribute to physical fitness

    1 regular sleep,

    2 proper nutrition,

    3 regular medical and dental care, and

    4 personal cleanliness.

7. Your body is the temple of the Holy Ghost I Cor 619 therefore you have a responsibility to care for it properly

8. Participating in sports is fun and it also contributes to your emotional, mental and physical health

9. Several books such as Physical Fitness: A Wellness Approach are available to help a person plan a good physical fitness program

10. If you plan to participate in a sport check your health habits first to determine whether you are physically fit

16-24 Cumulative Review

Rewrite the paragraph on the lines below, correcting the ten errors in subject-verb agreement, pronoun-antecedent agreement, pronoun usage, adjective and adverb usage, troublesome words, capitalization, or punctuation.

 Have you ever run in a race Running can be challenging and invigorating! God's command for we is to run in the race of life We should strive to finish good, to obtain the prize and to hear Christ say, "Well done, thou good and faithful servant". Paul write, "I press toward the mark for the prize of the high calling of God in Christ Jesus" (phil. 3:14. Run the Christian race faithfully; don't just set on the sidelines.

_____

_____

_____

_____

_____

_____

348 Chapter 16

Beginning, Middle, End: Writing an Essay Answer

Explain the two different attitudes toward walls in Robert Frost's poem "Mending Wall."

Michele stared at the question, chewing on the end of her pencil. She remembered the day they had discussed that poem in class. A scene flashed through her mind of two farmers walking along a stone wall, one on each side, picking up fallen stones and setting them back in place. Mrs. Schmidt had even brought in pictures of stone walls and passed them around. And she remembered that one of the farmers had liked the wall and one hadn't. But how was she supposed to write about the poem? Where should she begin? The room was so quiet that she could hear the ticking of the clock, and it made her nervous. Time was running out. She grasped her pencil more tightly. "Think," she told herself. "And whatever you do, don't panic."

Essay questions are different from any other kind of question on a test. They are the questions that really test your understanding. Anyone can repeat facts and figures he has memorized or make a logical guess at a multiple choice question. But an essay shows how much and how well you have thought about the things you have learned.

What do you do first when you see an essay question on a test? Start writing furiously, hoping somehow to atone in length for what you lack in knowledge? Sit and stare out the window until the teacher announces there are only five minutes left? What is the first thing you *should* do?

Believe it or not, sitting and staring is the better way to begin. You can't answer a question well until you have thought about it. Just make sure you keep an eye on the clock while you're thinking so that you don't get caught with a blank page when the bell rings.

It often helps to have a scrap of paper on hand to jot some notes as you think. Give yourself about five minutes to write down ideas on your scrap paper—before you write a word on the test itself.

The next step is to organize your ideas. What logical progression can you find in your thoughts? What is your most important idea? How can you arrange your ideas so that they will be most effective? Put little numbers in the margins or scribble a simple outline to jog your memory as you write.

Perhaps you're thinking, "But all this would take too long! I won't have time to answer the question." You'll be surprised how much faster your writing will flow if you've taken time to organize your ideas first.

The final step is to write your answer. A paragraph is usually sufficient to answer an essay question. Think of your paragraph as a kind of sandwich. The top piece of bread is your thesis, or the main point of your answer. It should be stated clearly in one sentence. The meat of your paragraph is the development of this thesis. Included in the development are the ideas you have organized on your scrap paper: reasons the thesis is true, examples that prove the thesis, comparisons and contrasts that support the thesis, or other support. The bottom piece of bread, the last sentence, is a restatement of the

Punctuation   349

thesis. Following the sandwich structure will keep your essay focused, and you will end up with an answer your teacher can really sink his teeth into.

Here's how Michele's essay turned out when she applied the sandwich method.

> In the poem "Mending Wall," the speaker does not seem to like the wall, but his neighbor, another farmer, does. The neighbor thinks that walls make good neighbors. His father has told him that, and he continues to believe it. But he has no good reason for keeping a wall between the two farms. The speaker, on the other hand, does not seem to like having the wall, even though he goes along with his neighbor's idea. He has noticed that even nature doesn't seem to like walls, since walls crumble and fall apart if left alone. He sees no reason for having the wall since neither farmer has cows to keep penned in. The speaker seems to feel that the wall is a barrier to friendship. At the end of the poem, the neighboring farmer sticks to his opinion that walls are good, but the speaker does not agree and seems to feel a little sorry for his neighbor.

Your Turn: Making Your Own Sandwich

Use the sandwich method to answer one of the following essay questions.

- Contrast the attitudes of the two brothers in the parable of the prodigal son (Luke 15:11-32).
- Discuss the importance of extracurricular activities for junior high students.
- Explain why Christians should or should not take an active role in the government of their nation.

Chapter 20: Essays
p. 419

Chapter 17

Spelling

Conditioning, although sometimes boring and difficult, increases a runner's energy, tones his muscles, and improves his breathing; it gives him an advantage in the last leg of the race. Learning to spell is one way a writer conditions for his event. A writer who tends to his spelling can leave less conditioned competitors behind in the stretch.

Spelling Hints

Spell by syllables.

Dividing a word into its individual syllables will help you to spell it correctly. Think about *prefixes, suffixes,* and other word parts as you are spelling words by syllables.

mis + spell =	misspell
dis + courage =	discourage
thankful + ly =	thankfully

ETYMOLOGY *Suffix* comes from two Latin words that mean "to fasten under." Today *suffix* means a syllable(s) added at the end of a word.

Use a dictionary.

Use your dictionary to look up words when you are unsure of the correct spelling. Though you may be unsure of a word's spelling, you probably know enough of the word to find it in the dictionary.

Keep a list of words that are problems for you.

When you realize that you have misspelled a particular word, add the word to your list.

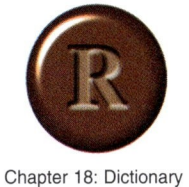

Chapter 18: Dictionary
p. 374

Look for possible groupings among your problem words.

If you notice that your list of problem words includes several similar words, try to figure out or find a rule for that group. For example, if you have problems with *ie* and *ei,* study that rule and write those words correctly.

Study your list of problem words systematically.

Begin by writing a word several times, concentrating on its appearance and its sound. Repeat this procedure on three or four different days within the next week. Then ask someone to quiz you on that word. If you can write the word correctly without hesitation, transfer it to your "learned" list. If a problem remains, keep working on the word.

Spelling Singular Present-tense Verbs and Plural Nouns

If the word ends in *ch, sh, s, x,* or *z,* add *es.*

bunch	bunches
marsh	marshes
mass	masses
ax	axes
buzz	buzzes

If the word ends in *y* preceded by a consonant, change final *y* to *i* and add *es.*

try	tries
lily	lilies
folly	follies

If the word ends in *y* preceded by a vowel, add *s.*

buy	buys
pray	prays
chimney	chimneys

If the word ends in *f* or *fe,* consult your dictionary. For most, add *s;* for others, change the *f* to *v* and add *es.*

chief	chiefs
fife	fifes
elf	elves
life	lives

If the word ends in *o*, consult your dictionary. For most, add *es*; for others add *s*.

go	goes
potato	potatoes
trio	trios
portfolio	portfolios

Add *s* to most other words.

bug	bugs
plate	plates
jar	jars
board	boards

Some nouns have irregular plural forms. Consult your dictionary for nouns with irregular plurals.

alumnus	alumni
goose	geese
deer	deer

17-1 PRACTICE THE SKILL

In the blank write the correct singular present-tense form or plural form of each italicized word.

_____ 1. The crocodile is an intriguing and dangerous *reptile*.

_____ 2. It is different from an alligator with its narrower snout and its fourth *tooth* visible on each side of its closed jaws.

_____ 3. Possibly the largest and most dangerous *type* of crocodile is the saltwater crocodile.

_____ 4. This type eats a variety of animals and sometimes can even *attack* humans.

_____ 5. It has the *ability* to stay underwater for more than an hour.

_____ 6. In the winter, however, it likes to come up onto the *beach* to lie in the warm sun.

_____ 7. Although the crocodile is not the fastest reptile, it can *carry* itself rather quickly when attacking.

_____ 8. Saltwater crocodiles were hunted almost to extinction in Australia before being protected by *law* in the late 1960s and early 1970s.

_____ 9. Saltwater crocodiles in Australia *rely* partly on the existence of crocodile farms for survival.

_____ 10. Farms help fulfill a lady's *wish* for a crocodile-skin purse while still allowing the crocodile population of Australia to flourish.

17-2 Review the Skill

Underline the misspelled word and write the correction in the blank. If the sentence is correct, write *C* in the blank.

_____ 1. A rancher in Texas has several varietys of animals living on his land.

_____ 2. Among them are foxes, sheep, mice, cows, and horses.

_____ 3. Small animals live in the bushs and scrub weeds.

_____ 4. The rancher tries to keep his animals safe from harmful insects and snakes.

_____ 5. Mosquitoes breed in the wet areas near the eastern cities in Texas.

_____ 6. The rancher raises champion palominos that win many trophys.

_____ 7. The rancher may determine the age and health of his horses by looking at their tooths.

_____ 8. Cattle thieves sometimes steal livestock from the ranches.

_____ 9. The sheriffs are concerned about unlawful activitys in their counties.

_____ 10. A ranch owner either buys and sells land and animals or earns money by raising crops.

17-3 USE THE SKILL
Underline the five misspelled words. Write the corrections in the blank.

Ducks live in wetlands. A duck has webbed feet for swimming, and it waterprooves its feathers with oil from a special oil gland. Under the oiled feathers lies a soft layer of feathers called *down*. A female duck hatchs between five and twelve ducklings each year in the spring. A duckling usually enjoys swimming just a few hours after it is born. A male duck, called a drake, usually displaies a variety of colorful feathers. A duck loses its old feathers and grows new ones each year in a process called molting. After the yearly molting process and after the ducklings have learned to fly, ducks gather in the lakes and marshes before migrating. A group of ducks usually flyes to the same place each year to avoid harsh winters. While one group of ducks travels only a short distance, another gos thousands of miles to secure a warm home for the winter.

Spelling with *ie* or *ei*

When the sound is "long e," put *i* before *e* except after *c*.

i before *e*	except after *c*
believe	ceiling
yield	perceive
grief	receipt
Exceptions:	caffeine, either, leisure, neither, protein, seize, sheik, weird.

When the sound is "long a," put *e* before *i*.

e before *i*		
vein	beige	sleigh

17-4 PRACTICE THE SKILL
Complete the word correctly. Write either *ie* or *ei* in the blank.

1. gr_____ve
2. n_____ther
3. perc_____ve
4. sh_____ld
5. br_____f
6. dec_____t
7. fr_____ght
8. rel_____ve
9. r_____gn
10. conc_____t

Spelling 357

17-5 Review the Skill

In the blank write the letter that corresponds to the correctly spelled word.

1. _____ A. leisurely
   B. liesurely
2. _____ A. weird
   B. wierd
3. _____ A. theif
   B. thief
4. _____ A. chief
   B. cheif
5. _____ A. deceiver
   B. deciever
6. _____ A. caffiene
   B. caffeine
7. _____ A. sliegh
   B. sleigh
8. _____ A. receipt
   B. reciept
9. _____ A. concievable
   B. conceivable
10. _____ A. lightweight
    B. lightwieght

17-6 Use the Skill

Underline the five misspelled words. Write the corrections in the blank.

My neice is sewing her wedding dress. What an acheivement it will be for her to complete the project! The piece of cloth to make the dress is twelve yards long. She also needs eight yards of netting. Her veil is made of lace, just as her mother's veil was. We beleive that the bride's dress will be beautiful. My niece's nieghbor, Rachelle, is in the wedding. Rachelle's sister will bring the cake, which will weigh over twenty pounds! At the reception, white decorations will hang from the ceiling. The bride and her family will be releived when the wedding day arrives.

_____

Adding Suffixes

Doubling a final consonant

If a one-syllable word ends with a single consonant preceded by a single vowel, double the final consonant before adding a suffix.

hop	hopped
run	running
spin	spinner

If a multisyllable word with its main accent on the final syllable ends with a single consonant preceded by a single vowel, double the final consonant before adding a suffix.

begin	beginning
admit	admitted
confer	conferring

If a word ends with a single consonant preceded by two vowels, do not double the final consonant before adding a suffix.

droop	drooping
pair	paired
fool	foolish

Changing final *y* to *i*

If a word ends with a consonant and *y*, change the final *y* to *i* before adding a suffix.

fry	fried
cleanly	cleanliness
mercy	merciful

However, if the suffix itself begins with *i*, do not change final *y* to *i*.

fry	frying
apply	applying
fortify	fortifying

Dropping final silent *e*

Drop the final silent *e* that is preceded by a consonant before adding a suffix beginning with a vowel.

live	living
achieve	achievable
tune	tuning
Exceptions: noticeable, courageous	

Keep the final silent *e* before adding a suffix beginning with a consonant.

live	lively
achieve	achievement
tune	tuneful
Exceptions: truly, argument, judgment	

Spelling

17-7 Practice the Skill

Add the suffix to the word. Write the new word in the blank.

_____ 1. delay + ing

_____ 2. admire + able

_____ 3. cry + ed

_____ 4. sixty + eth

_____ 5. pave + ment

_____ 6. use + ing

_____ 7. swim + er

_____ 8. forbid + en

_____ 9. fear + ful

_____ 10. spot + er

17-8 Review the Skill

In the blank write the letter that corresponds to the correctly spelled word.

1. _____ A. stoping
           B. stopping
2. _____ A. coatted
           B. coated
3. _____ A. tiring
           B. tireing
4. _____ A. lovly
           B. lovely
5. _____ A. modifying
           B. modifiing
6. _____ A. happyness
           B. happiness
7. _____ A. snapped
           B. snaped
8. _____ A. sluggish
           B. slugish
9. _____ A. grinned
           B. grined
10. _____ A. gainned
           B. gained

17-9 USE THE SKILL

In the blank write the correct form of the word in parentheses.

_____ 1. The polar bear is the largest flesh-eating animal on land. A male's ? can be more than 1,600 pounds. *(wieght or weight)*

_____ 2. Polar bears are amazing ?, with white fur for blending into the snow and ice, black skin for absorbing the sun, and membranes in the nose for warming and moisturizing the arctic air. *(creation, plural)*

_____ 3. Scientists are very interested in the ? of this huge beast and have tried to attach radio collars or ear transmitters to track its movements. *(activity, plural)*

_____ 4. Recently, researchers have considered ? a collar with a video camera around the bear's neck that would film his adventures. *(fit + ing)*

_____ 5. Most polar bears spend their winters and springs out on the ice ? for food. *(look + ing)*

_____ 6. Seals are the main menu item, and bears often wait in ambush just outside seals' ? holes. *(breathe + ing)*

_____ 7. In the summer the ice melts and the bears return to land, ? themselves with sleeping and roaming for the summer and fall months. *(occupy + ing)*

_____ 8. Since the bears do not eat during this time, they must have built up large layers of fat to keep ? from starving. *(them + self, plural)*

_____ 9. Sometimes ? of bears will come too close to people and get into trouble. *(batch, plural)*

_____ 10. The town of Churchill has a special jail that can ? up to twenty-three bears for temporary imprisonment. *(receive or recieve)*

17-10 Cumulative Review

Rewrite the paragraph on the blanks below, correcting the ten errors in subject-verb agreement, pronoun-antecedent agreement, pronoun usage, adjective and adverb usage, troublesome words, capitalization, punctuation, or spelling.

Going to the zoo and feedding the animals has always been favorite activitys for young children; Some classes go to the zoo every year for a field trip. Some of the animals recieve special attention from its observers. Most children love to look at the elephants, giraffes, deer, chimpanzees, rhinoceroses, and other animals. The children have to move quick if they want to see all the animals. They should bring there lunchs if they want to spend the whole day at the zoo?

_____

_____

_____

_____

_____

_____

_____

_____

_____

_____

Minding Your Own Business: Writing a Business Letter

Perhaps you have never had an occasion to write a business letter. And perhaps you think that all business letters are boring and long. Although most business letters are more formal in tone and somewhat more careful about precision and format than personal letters, many are anything but dull.

One author, writing to his publisher to ask how his book was selling, sent only this: "?" His publisher replied: "!" (And so ended the shortest business correspondence on record.)

A business letter is not so different from a personal letter, but it does have more parts and usually a more reserved tone. The tone of a business letter should be polite, and the style should be concise. A business letter should always be typed; if typing is impossible for some reason, the letter must be neatly written.

Here is an example of a business letter that makes a request:

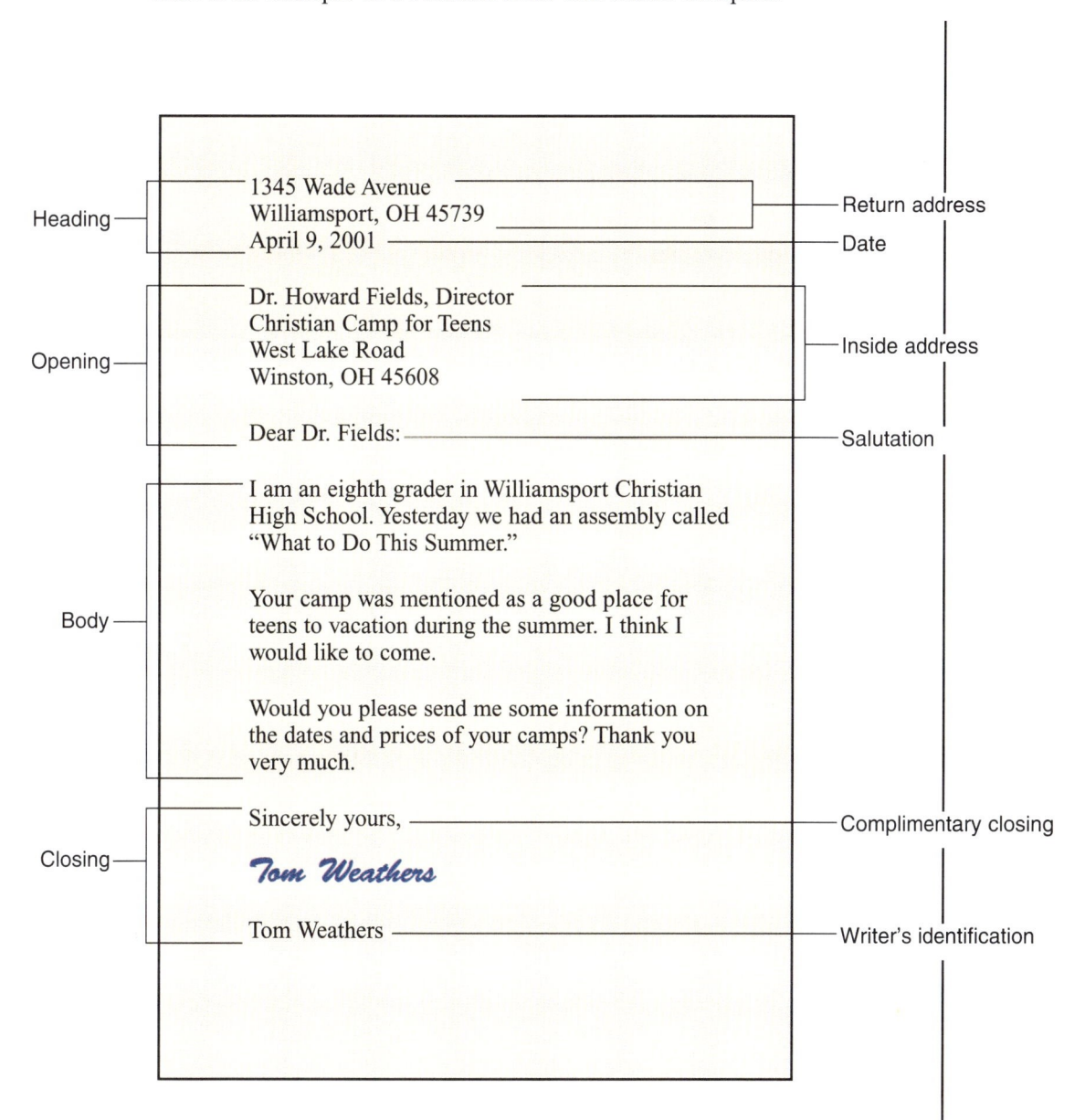

Heading
- 1345 Wade Avenue — Return address
- Williamsport, OH 45739
- April 9, 2001 — Date

Opening
- Dr. Howard Fields, Director — Inside address
- Christian Camp for Teens
- West Lake Road
- Winston, OH 45608

- Dear Dr. Fields: — Salutation

Body

I am an eighth grader in Williamsport Christian High School. Yesterday we had an assembly called "What to Do This Summer."

Your camp was mentioned as a good place for teens to vacation during the summer. I think I would like to come.

Would you please send me some information on the dates and prices of your camps? Thank you very much.

Closing

Sincerely yours, — Complimentary closing

Tom Weathers

Tom Weathers — Writer's identification

Notice the different parts of the business letter. There is a heading, which includes the writer's address and the date. The opening includes the address of the person receiving the letter and the salutation, or greeting. The body is the main part of the letter—the message. The closing is a complimentary closing and the writer's name and signature.

Notice also how the letter is punctuated and set up on the page. Whether typed or handwritten, the spacing and form are the same. All lines begin at the left margin. The paragraphs of the body are single-spaced, but there is a double space between paragraphs, between heading and body, and between body and closing. The writer has both signed his name and typed it below his signature.

Does the letter have a polite and appropriately serious tone? Does it make a request clearly and briefly? Do you think the person who received the letter would be favorably impressed by the character of the writer?

Spelling 363

Writing a Good Request Letter

Here is a short list of techniques that will make your business letter represent you well.

1. Decide exactly what you want the letter to accomplish.
2. Write out the request in one sentence.
3. Write a rough draft of your letter.
    a. Introduce yourself briefly.
    b. Explain why you are writing.
    c. State your request.
    d. Express thanks.
4. Read over the rough draft carefully.
    a. Have you been brief, clear, and polite?
    b. Is your request simply stated?
    c. Are form and punctuation correct?
    d. Would you like to receive this letter yourself?
5. Produce the letter on clean white paper—use only one side!
6. Proofread for spelling, grammar, punctuation, and form.
7. Sign the letter.

Your Turn: Asking Like a Pro

Choose one of the following situations (or come up with one yourself) and write an appropriate request letter. Feel free to make up names and addresses if you are not writing a real letter.

- You want to raise money for a mission trip to Kenya.
- You want to get information about a book from its author.
- You want to know whether someone would make a trade.

Chapter 18

Library Skills

Reference

What Can I Find in the Library?

Libraries today contain much more than books. You can often find magazines, newspapers, audio cassettes, videocassettes, and puppets. You can attend classes, listen to lectures, or view displays on interesting topics. Some libraries even offer free computer access. Today's libraries provide a broad selection of information and tools for you to use. Before you can use these tools, however, you need to know where to find them.

Libraries usually are organized into several sections. Sometimes these sections may be separate rooms in the library building. Sometimes the sections may be areas of shelves set apart from the other shelves. Each section contains a different type of library material.

Books, of course, are still the main feature of most libraries. Librarians arrange books on shelves called stacks. These stacks usually take up the most space in any library.

The **periodical** section contains materials published at regular intervals, such as monthly magazines or daily newspapers. Because they are published regularly, periodicals are an excellent source for current information about a wide variety of topics.

The **reference** section contains nonfiction books and other materials that are noncirculating. In other words, they cannot be checked out of the library. Some libraries reserve an entire room for reference materials. A capital letter *R* or the abbreviation *REF* on a book's spine indicates that the book belongs in the reference section.

Many libraries now have a separate section for **audio-visual** materials. These materials may include audio cassettes, compact discs, videocassettes, works of art such as paintings and sculptures, or even puppets and games for children. The letters *AV* usually refer to the audio-visual collection.

Most libraries place the books written for **children** and **young adults** in a separate area of the library. This area usually contains both circulating and reference books and may even have its own periodical section and audio-visual materials. The capital letters *J* (for juvenile) or *YA* (for young adult) on a book's spine indicate that the book belongs to this section.

How Are the Books Arranged?

All books fall into one of two categories: fiction or nonfiction. **Fiction** books, although sometimes based on facts, tell about events from an author's imagination. Regardless of their topics, fiction books are arranged on the shelf alphabetically by the authors' last names. If two authors share the same last name, their books are arranged alphabetically by the authors' first names. If a library has more than one book by the same author, the author's books are arranged alphabetically according to the first words of the titles (not including *A, An,* or *The*). The list below shows the order in which these books would appear on a library shelf.

>Lois Lenski, *Strawberry Girl*
>Delos Lovelace, *That Dodger Horse*
>Maud Hart Lovelace, *Emily of Deep Valley*
>Maud Hart Lovelace, *What Cabrillo Found*
>Stephen W. Meader, *Whaler 'Round the Horn*

Some libraries separate the **mystery fiction** and **science fiction** books from the other fiction books. These libraries have shelves marked *mystery fiction* or *science fiction.* In addition, the book spines are usually marked with the letters *MYS* for mystery fiction or *SCI* for science fiction.

Nonfiction books present facts on almost every subject. Tractors, animals, inventions, famous writers, and countries are examples of subjects covered by nonfiction books. Most libraries use the **Dewey Decimal System** of classification to arrange nonfiction books. The classification numbers are found on the spine of each book.

Melvil Dewey developed this system to bring together all the different books on a particular subject rather than having them scattered throughout the library. He divided knowledge into ten subject categories. To these categories he assigned numbers.

000–099	Generalities (including encyclopedias and general reference works)
100–199	Philosophy and Psychology
200–299	Religion (including mythology)
300–399	Social Sciences (including government, education, and etiquette)
400–499	Language
500–599	Natural Sciences and Mathematics (including physics, chemistry, and biology)
600–699	Technology (including occupations and professions)
700–799	The Arts (including sports)
800–899	Literature and Rhetoric (including short stories and plays)
900–999	Geography and History (including travel and biography)

A **biography** is a book written by one person about another person's life; an **autobiography** is a book about the author's own life. Many libraries separate the biographies and autobiographies from the other nonfiction books and shelve them in a separate area of the stacks. A capital *B* or the Dewey Decimal number 920 or 921 on the spine of a book indicates that the book is a biography or an autobiography. Biographies and autobiographies are arranged alphabetically by the last name of the subject, not the author. For example, a biography about George Washington would be shelved with other biographies under *W* for Washington.

Some large libraries use the **Library of Congress System** instead of the Dewey Decimal System. The Library of Congress System uses letters and numbers instead of numbers only and has twenty-one subject categories instead of ten. For example, the book *Birds' Eggs* has the Dewey Decimal number 598.233 and the Library of Congress call number QL 675.W32. Be sure you understand the system that your library uses.

18-1 PRACTICE THE SKILL

Number the titles and authors of the following fiction books in the order in which they would appear on the fiction shelves of a library.

_____ Elizabeth Yates, *Sound Friendships*

_____ Kate Seredy, *The Good Master*

_____ Howard Pyle, *Men of Iron*

_____ Geoffrey Trease, *Cue for Treason*

_____ Ian Serraillier, *The Silver Sword*

_____ L. M. Montgomery, *The Story Girl*

_____ John R. Tunis, *Duke Decides*

_____ Rutherford Montgomery, *Kildee House*

_____ Marjorie Kinnan Rawlings, *The Yearling*

_____ L. M. Montgomery, *Anne of Avonlea*

18-2 REVIEW THE SKILL

Using the Dewey Decimal chart on page 368, write the number of the correct category for each of the following books.

_____ 1. *Baseball's Wacky Plays*

_____ 2. *Far-Out Facts*

_____ 3. *Religions Around the World*

Library Skills

_____ 4. *How Math Works*

_____ 5. *The Land and People of Korea*

_____ 6. *Social Smarts: Manners for Today's Kids*

_____ 7. *Adolescent Psychology*

_____ 8. *Winds and Weather*

_____ 9. *The Young Jane Austen*

_____ 10. *101 Words and How They Began*

_____ 11. *The Oxford Treasury of Classic Poems*

_____ 12. *Living with Learning Disabilities*

_____ 13. *How to Paint in Oil*

_____ 14. *Fun with German*

_____ 15. *Inventions of the Twentieth Century*

How Are the Books Labeled?

Every book in the library has a label on its spine. For a nonfiction book, this label contains the book's **call number.** The call number is the Dewey Decimal number and the first letter of the author's last name. Sometimes the label will also contain a **section letter** (such as *R*) if the book belongs in a separate section of the library (such as reference). Fiction books usually do not have call numbers. A fiction book is labeled with the first few letters of the author's last name and the capital letter *F.* The label may also include a section letter if the book belongs in a special section, such as *MYS* (mystery) or *YA* (young adult).

The call number that appears on a book's spine will also appear in its **catalog entry.** Traditionally, libraries used **card catalogs** as tools to help people find the books they wanted. Today, many libraries have converted their card catalogs to on-line **computer catalogs.** Both types of catalogs contain the same information in approximately the same format. Computer catalogs, however, offer the user more ways to search for information.

How Do I Use the Card Catalog?

A card catalog is a cabinet with small drawers, usually located near the library entrance. Here are cards containing information on each book in the library. The three types of cards in the card catalog are the **author card,** the **title card,** and the **subject card.** These cards are alphabetized together (not separated into three groups) in the drawers. Each kind of card has a different top line: the author card starts with the author; the title card starts with the book's title; and the subject card starts with the subject of the book. Each card includes the title, the author, the place of publication, the date of publication, the publisher, the number of pages, and the call number (for a nonfiction book).

To use the card catalog, you need to know the author, the title, or the subject of the book you want. Perhaps you want a book by a particular author, but you are not sure of the title. Find the author card, which is filed alphabetically according to the author's last name. If there is more than one author by that same last name, the cards under that last name will be arranged alphabetically by the first names. For example, under *Browning,* the name *Browning, Elizabeth Barrett,* would come before *Browning, Robert.* Both fiction and nonfiction books have author cards.

Title cards are placed alphabetically in the drawers according to the first word in the title (again, not including *A, An,* and *The*). There are title cards for both fiction and nonfiction books.

If you do not know the titles or authors of nonfiction books on a subject that interests you, look for subject cards in the card catalog. There may be more than one subject card for some books. Subjects include noteworthy people, geographic locations, languages, countries, and other topics of interest.

When you find the card for the book you want, first write down the call number from the upper left-hand corner of the card (for a nonfiction book); then copy the name of the author and the title of the book. With this information you can ask for the book or go to the shelf and get it yourself.

How Do I Use the Computer Catalog?

Instead of individual filing cards, a computer catalog contains electronic records for each book. Each record includes the same information you would find on an author, title, or subject card in the card catalog. In fact, a computer catalog may contain more information than a card catalog. For instance, some computer catalog records include a summary of the book. The summary can help you decide whether the book will be helpful to you. In addition, most computer catalogs also contain information about each book's status. In other words, the computer catalog can tell you whether a book is available or already checked out. If the book is already checked out, the catalog may tell you when it is due to be returned.

Using the computer catalog is similar to using the card catalog. First, you need to know the author, the title, or the subject of the book you want to find. Next, type the information you know into the computer, according to the instructions on the screen. The computer will begin to search for the book you need by comparing the words you typed to the information in its database. When it finds a match, the computer screen will display the record for that book. If the information you typed was not specific enough, the computer screen will display a list for you to choose from. For instance, if you type the subject rather than the title, the screen will list several books about that subject. To see the record for an individual book, simply type the number displayed next to that title on the list.

If you want more information about the book, you may need to type an additional command, such as *F* for full title record. Look at this example of the full title record for a book about holidays in Sweden.

Library Skills

	MATERIAL:	Book
date of publication	CALL NUMBER:	394.26 Sw12
publisher	AUTHOR:	Swahn, Jan Ojvind
city of publication	TITLE:	Maypoles, crayfish and Lucia: Swedish holidays and traditions / Jan-Ojvind Swahn; [translation by Roger Tanner].
	PUBLICATION:	Stockholm: The Swedish Institute, 1994.
	DESCRIPTION:	47 p.: ill. (some col.), music: 24 cm.
number of pages	NOTES:	Lyrics of songs in Swedish.
contains illustrations	NOTES:	Bibliography: p. 47.
	SUBJECT:	Holidays—Sweden.
special contents	SUBJECT:	Sweden, Social life and customs.
height of book's spine		

The computer catalog at one library might be somewhat different from the computer catalog at another library. Be sure to ask the librarian for help if you do not know how to use your library's computer catalog.

18-3 Practice the Skill

Using the catalog entry below, answer the following questions.

MATERIAL: Book

CALL NUMBER: J 516 VanCleav

AUTHOR: VanCleave, Janice Pratt

TITLE: Janice VanCleave's geometry for every kid: easy activities that make learning geometry fun.

PUBLICATION: New York: Wiley & Sons, c1994.

DESCRIPTION: ix, 221 p.: ill.: 23 cm.

NOTES: Glossary: p. 213.

SUBJECT: Geometry—Juvenile literature.

SUBJECT: Geometry.

SUBJECT: Mathematical recreations.

1. What is the complete title of the book?

2. What company published the book?

3. Where was the book published?

4. In what year was the book published?

5. What is the book's call number?

6. Does the book contain illustrations? How do you know?

7. Under what subject headings would you find other books on the same topic?

8. How would you find other books by the same author?

9. How would you type the author's name in the computer?

10. What extra information is given about the book?

18-4 Review the Skill

Choose five topics from the list below. Use your library's card catalog or computer catalog to find one book on each topic. List the title, author, and call number for each book you choose.

1. Native American folklore

   _____

   _____

2. logic

   _____

   _____

3. professional sporting events

   _____

   _____

4. poetry

   _____

   _____

5. Parliamentary procedure

   _____

   _____

6. fossils

   _____

   _____

7. Latin grammar

   _____

   _____

8. farm machinery

_____

_____

9. Andes Mountains

_____

_____

10. church history

_____

_____

How Do I Use the Specific Reference Works?

Dictionaries

Dictionaries are the most common tool used for learning about words and languages. An **unabridged dictionary** gives the most complete list of words and definitions. Although an abridged dictionary, or **desk dictionary,** is not as complete as the unabridged dictionary, it contains most of the words that you will need for your own reading and writing.

A dictionary gives a word's spelling, syllabification, pronunciation, definitions, different forms, parts of speech, synonyms or antonyms, and capitalization. The information in a good dictionary is reliable because it comes from the speech and writing most often accepted by educated people. Many dictionaries also list abbreviations, geographic names, and biographical names; they may even include a brief history of the English language or a handbook of style and usage. Notes and guides in your dictionary can help you understand the content of the dictionary. To use your dictionary in the right way, you will want to become familiar with all its features.

Finding the Word

At the top of each dictionary page you will find two words in large dark print. These **guide word**s tell you the first and last word defined on that page. Words that alphabetically come between those two words will also appear on that page.

The **entry** is the word being defined (usually printed in bold type) and all the information about that particular word. Look here for the proper spelling of a word. Most dictionaries will also list other forms of the word. For example, an entry for a verb will list the verb's principal parts. Remember that the entry word itself is always the base form of the word.

various similar or related trees. [ME < OE *oser* and OFr. *osier*, both < Med.Lat. *osera, osiera*.]

O·si·jek (ō′sē-ĕk, -yĕk′). A city of E Croatia on the Drava R. ESE of Zagreb; under Turkish rule from 1526 to 1687. Pop. 103,600.

O·si·ris (ō-sī′rĭs) *n. Myth.* The ancient Egyptian god whose annual death and resurrection personified the self-renewing vitality and fertility of nature.

-osis *suff.* **1.** Condition; process; action: *osmosis*. **2.** Diseased or abnormal condition: *neurosis*. **3.** Increase; formation: *leukocytosis*. [Lat. *-ōsis* < Gk., n. suff.]

Os·kar II (ŏs′kär, ôs′-). See **Oscar II**.

Os·lo (ŏz′lō, ŏs′-). Formerly (1624–1925) **Chris·ti·a·ni·a** (krĭs′tē-än′ē-ə, -än′-, krĭs′chē-). The cap. of Norway, in the SE part at the head of the **Oslo Fjord**, a deep inlet of the Skagerrak; founded c. 1050 and rebuilt and renamed in 1624 by Christian IV (1577–1648). Pop. 448,747.

Os·man I (ŏz′mən, ŏs′-, ŏs-män′) also **Oth·man I** (ŏth′mən, ōth-män′). 1258–1326? Founder of the Ottoman dynasty that controlled most of NW Asia Minor.

Os·man·li (ŏz-män′lē, ŏs-) *n., pl.* **-lis. 1.** An Ottoman Turk. **2.** Ottoman Turkish. — *adj.* Ottoman. [Turk. *osmānli* = Os-MAN (I) + *-li*, adj. suff.]

os·mat·ic (ŏz-măt′ĭk) *adj.* Having or characterized by a well-developed sense of smell. [< Gk. *osmē*, smell.]

os·mic[1] (ŏz′mĭk) *adj.* Of, relating to, or containing osmium, esp. in a compound with valence 4 or a valence higher than that in a comparable osmous compound. [OSM(IUM) + -IC.]

os·mic[2] (ŏz′mĭk) *adj.* Of or relating to odors or the sense of smell. [Gk. *osmē*, smell.] — **os′mi·cal·ly** *adv.*

osmic acid *n.* See **osmium tetroxide**.

os·mics (ŏz′mĭks) *n. (used with a sing. v.)* The science that deals with smells and the olfactory sense.

os·mi·rid·i·um (ŏz′mə-rĭd′ē-əm) *n.* A mineral that is a natural alloy of osmium and iridium with small inclusions of platinum, rhodium, and other metals. [OSM(IUM) + IRIDIUM.]

os·mi·um (ŏz′mē-əm) *n. Symbol* **Os** A hard metallic element, found in small amounts in osmiridium and platinum ores and used as a platinum hardener and in making pen points and instrument pivots. Atomic number 76; atomic weight 190.2; melting point 3,000°C; boiling point 5,000°C; specific gravity 22.57; valence 2, 3, 4, 8. See table at **element**. [< Gk. *osmē*, smell (< the odor of osmium tetroxide).]

osmium tetroxide *n.* A poisonous compound, OsO₄, with a pungent smell, used as a stain and a tissue fixative.

os·mom·e·ter (ŏz-mŏm′ĭ-tər, ŏs-) *n.* A device for measuring osmotic pressure. [OSMO(SIS) + -METER.] — **os′mo·met′ric** (ŏz′mə-mĕt′rĭk, ŏs′-) *adj.* — **os·mom′e·try** *n.*

os·mo·reg·u·la·tion (ŏz′mə-rĕg′yə-lā′shən, ŏs′-) *n. Physiol.* Maintenance of an optimal constant osmotic pressure in the body of a living organism. [OSMO(SIS) + REGULATION.]

os·mose (ŏz′mōs, ŏs′-) *intr. & tr.v.* **-mosed, -mos·ing, -mos·es.** To diffuse or cause to diffuse by osmosis.

os·mo·sis (ŏz-mō′sĭs, ŏs-) *n., pl.* **-ses** (-sēz). **1.a.** Diffusion of fluid through a semipermeable membrane until there is an equal concentration of fluid on both sides of the membrane. **b.** The tendency of fluids to diffuse in such a manner. **2.** A gradual, often unconscious process of absorption or learning. [< *osmose* < earlier *endosmose* < Fr. : Gk. *endo-*, endo- + Gk. *ōsmos*, thrust, push (< *ōthein*, to push).] — **os·mot′ic** (-mŏt′ĭk) *adj.* — **os·mot′i·cal·ly** *adv.*

osmotic pressure *n.* The pressure exerted by the flow of water through a semipermeable membrane separating two solutions with different concentrations of solute.

osmotic shock *n.* The rupture of bacterial or other cells in a solution following a sudden reduction in osmotic pressure.

os·mous (ŏz′məs) also **os·mi·ous** (-mē-əs) *adj.* Of, relating to, or containing osmium in a compound with a valence lower than that in a comparable osmic compound.

os·mun·da (ŏz-mŭn′də) also **os·mund** (ŏz′mənd) *n.* Any of several ferns of the genus *Osmunda*, having bipinnately compound fronds and edible crosiers. [NLat. *Osmunda*, genus name < ME *osmunde*, a fern < OFr. *osmonde*.]

Os·na·brück (ŏz′nə-brŏŏk′, ŏs′nä-brük′). A city of NW Germany NE of Münster. Pop. 153,587.

os·na·burg (ŏz′nə-bûrg′) *n.* A heavy coarse cotton fabric, used for grain sacks, upholstery, and draperies. [After *Osnaburg* (Osnabrück).]

os·prey (ŏs′prē, -prā) *n., pl.* **-preys. 1.** A fish-eating hawk (*Pandion haliaetus*) having plumage that is dark on the back and white below. **2.** A plume formerly used to trim women's hats. [ME *osprai* < AN *ospreit* < Med.Lat. *avis prede*, bird of prey : Lat. *avis*, bird; see **awi-*** + Lat. *praedae*, genitive of *praeda*, booty, prey; see **ghend-***.]

OSS *abbr.* Office of Strategic Services.

os·sa (ŏs′ə) *n.* Pl. of **os**².

Os·sa (ŏs′ə), **Mount.** A peak, 1,979.1 m (6,489 ft), of the Olympus Mts. in N Greece.

os·sa·ture (ŏs′ə-chŏŏr′, -chər) *n.* A framework or skeleton, as for a building. [Fr. < Lat. *os, oss-*, bone. See **os²**.]

os·se·in (ŏs′ē-ĭn) *n.* The collagen component of bone. [OSSE(OUS) + -IN.]

os·se·ous (ŏs′ē-əs) *adj.* Composed of, containing, or resembling bone; bony. [< Lat. *osseus* < *os, oss-*, bone. See **ost-***.] — **os′se·ous·ly** *adv.*

Os·set (ŏs′ĭt, ô-sĕt′) also **Os·sete** (ŏs′ēt′, ô-sĕt′) *n.* A member of a people of mixed Iranian and Caucasian origin inhabiting Ossetia.

Os·se·tia (ŏ-sē′shə, ə-syĕ′tē-yə). A region of the central Caucasus in Georgia and SW Russia; annexed by Russia between 1801 and 1806. — **Os·se′tian** *adj. & n.*

Os·set·ic (ŏ-sĕt′ĭk) *adj.* Of or relating to Ossetia, the Ossets, or their language or culture. — *n.* Their Iranian language.

os·si·a (ô-sē′ə) *conj. Mus.* Or else. Used to designate an alternate section or passage. [Ital. < *o sia*, or let it be : *o*, or (< Lat. *aut*) + *sia*, third pers. sing. pr. subjunctive of *essere*, to be (< Lat. *esse*; see **es-***).]

Os·sian (ŏsh′ən, ŏs′ē-ən) *n.* A legendary Gaelic hero and bard of the third century A.D.

os·si·cle (ŏs′ĭ-kəl) *n.* A small bone, esp. of the middle ear. [Lat. *ossiculum*, dim. of *os*, bone. See **ost-***.] — **os·sic′u·lar** (ŏ-sĭk′yə-lər), **os·sic′u·late** (-lĭt) *adj.*

Os·si·etz·ky (ŏs′ē-ĕt′skē ô′sē-), **Carl von.** 1889–1938. German journalist who won the 1935 Nobel Peace Prize.

os·si·fi·ca·tion (ŏs′ə-fĭ-kā′shən) *n.* **1.** The natural process of bone formation. **2.a.** The hardening or calcification of soft tissue into a bonelike material. **b.** A mass or deposit of such material. **3.a.** The process of becoming set in a rigid conventionalism, as of behavior. **b.** Rigid unimaginative convention.

os·si·frage (ŏs′ə-frĭj, -frāj) *n.* **1.** See **lammergeier**. **2.** *Archaic.* An osprey. [Lat. *ossifraga* < *ossifragus*, bone-breaking : *os, oss-*, bone; see **ost-*** + *frangere*, to break; see **bhreg-***.]

os·si·fy (ŏs′ə-fī′) *v.* **-fied, -fy·ing, -fies.** — *intr.* **1.** To change into bone; become bony. **2.** To become set in a rigid conventionalism. — *tr.* **1.** To convert (a membrane or cartilage, for example) into bone. **2.** To mold into a rigidly conventional pattern. [Lat. *os, oss-*, bone; see **ost-*** + -FY.] — **os·sif′ic** (ŏ-sĭf′ĭk) *adj.*

Os·si·ning (ŏs′ə-nĭng′). A village of SE NY on the Hudson R. N of White Plains; site of Sing Sing state prison (estab. 1824). Pop. 22,582.

os·so bu·co (ô′sō bōō′kō, ŏs′sō) *n., pl.* **osso bu·cos.** An Italian dish consisting of braised veal shanks in white wine. [Ital. *ossobuco*, marrowbone : *osso*, bone + *buco*, hole.]

os·su·ar·y (ŏsh′ōō-ĕr′ē, ŏs′yōō-) *n., pl.* **-ies.** A container or receptacle for the bones of the dead. [LLat. *ossuārium* < neut. of Lat. *ossuārius*, of bones < *os, oss-*, bone. See **ost-***.]

os·te·al (ŏs′tē-əl) *adj.* **1.** Bony; osseous. **2.** Relating to bone or to the skeleton.

os·te·i·tis (ŏs′tē-ī′tĭs) *n.* Inflammation of bone or bony tissue.

Ost·end (ŏs-tĕnd′, ŏs′tĕnd′) also **Oost·en·de** (ō-stĕn′də). A city of NW Belgium WSW of Bruges. Pop. 69,129.

os·ten·si·ble (ŏ-stĕn′sə-bəl) *adj.* Represented or appearing as such; professed. [Fr. < Med.Lat. *ostēnsibilis* < Lat. *ostēnsus*, p.part. of *ostendere*, to show : *ob-*, ob- + *tendere*, to stretch; see **ten-***.] — **os·ten′si·bly** *adv.*

os·ten·sive (ŏ-stĕn′sĭv) *adj.* Seeming or professed; ostensible. — **os·ten′sive·ly** *adv.*

os·ten·so·ri·um (ŏs′tən-sôr′ē-əm, -sōr′-) also **os·ten·so·ry** (ŏ-stĕn′sə-rē) *n., pl.* **-so·ri·a** (-sôr′ē-ə, -sōr′-) also **-so·ries.** *Rom. Cath. Ch.* See **monstrance**. [Med.Lat. *ostēnsōrium* < Lat. *ostēnsus*, p.part. of *ostendere*, to show. See OSTENSIBLE.]

os·ten·ta·tion (ŏs′tĕn-tā′shən, -tən-) *n.* **1.** Pretentious display meant to impress others; boastful showiness. **2.** *Archaic.* The act or an instance of showing; an exhibition. [ME *ostentacioun* < OFr. *ostentacion* < Lat. *ostentātiō, ostentātiōn-* < *ostentāre*, freq. of *ostendere*, to show. See OSTENSIBLE.]

os·ten·ta·tious (ŏs′tĕn-tā′shəs, -tən-) *adj.* Characterized by or given to ostentation; pretentious. See Syns at **showy**. — **os·ten·ta′tious·ly** *adv.*

osteo- or **oste-** *pref.* Bone: *osteoarthritis*. [Gk. < *osteon*, bone. See **ost-***.]

os·te·o·ar·thri·tis (ŏs′tē-ō-är-thrī′tĭs) *n.* A form of arthritis, occurring mainly in older persons, that is characterized by chronic degeneration of the cartilage of the joints. — **os′te·o·ar·thrit′ic** (-thrĭt′ĭk) *adj.*

os·te·o·blast (ŏs′tē-ə-blăst′) *n.* A cell from which bone develops; a bone-forming cell. — **os′te·o·blas′tic** *adj.*

os·te·oc·la·sis (ŏs′tē-ŏk′lə-sĭs) *n., pl.* **-ses** (-sēz′). **1.** The process of dissolution and resorption of bony tissue. **2.** Surgical fracture of a bone, performed to correct a deformity. [OSTEO- + Gk. *klasis*, breakage (< *klan*, to break).]

os·te·o·clast (ŏs′tē-ə-klăst′) *n.* **1.** A large multinucleate cell found in growing bone that resorbs bony tissue, as in the formation of cavities. **2.** An instrument used in surgical osteoclasis. [OSTEO- + Med.Lat. *-clastēs*, breaker < LGk. *-klastēs* < Gk. *klastos*, broken < *klan*, to break).]

os·te·o·cyte (ŏs′tē-ə-sīt′) *n.* A branched cell embedded in the matrix of bone tissue.

os·te·o·gen·e·sis (ŏs′tē-ə-jĕn′ĭ-sĭs) *n., pl.* **-ses** (-sēz′). The formation and development of bony tissue. — **os′te·o·ge·net′ic** (-ō-jə-nĕt′ĭk), **os′te·og′e·nous** (-ŏj′ə-nəs) *adj.*

os·te·o·gen·ic (ŏs′tē-ə-jĕn′ĭk) *adj.* **1.** Derived from or com-

18-5 PRACTICE THE SKILL

Underline the entry words that would appear on a dictionary page with the guide words *garnet* and *gash*.

1. garnish
2. Gascony
3. gasp
4. garret
5. gasket
6. gas chamber
7. gasoline
8. garment
9. garner
10. garter snake

18-6 PRACTICE THE SKILL

Using the sample guide words, write the number of the page on which you would find each entry word.

852 mercantile/Mercury
853 mercy/merit
854 meritocracy/mesosphere

_____ 1. mercer
_____ 2. meritorious
_____ 3. mere
_____ 4. meringue
_____ 5. mercurial
_____ 6. Merovingian
_____ 7. mesh
_____ 8. merry
_____ 9. merchant
_____ 10. merino

18-7 PRACTICE THE SKILL

Using the sample dictionary page, answer each question.

_____ 1. What is the alternate spelling of *osmous?*

_____ 2. What is the plural form of *osmosis?*

_____ 3. *Ossa* is the plural form of what word?

_____ 4. What is the correct spelling of the adjective form of the noun *osteoarthritis?*

_____ 5. What is the correct spelling of the past tense form of the verb *ossify?*

_____ 6. What is the definition of *osteitis?*

_____ 7. How many definitions are listed for the word *osteoclast?*

Library Skills 377

_____ 8. The word *osteal* is what part of speech?

_____ 9. Part of the word *ossature* comes from a Latin word meaning what?

_____ 10. How many pronunciations are acceptable for the word *Ossian*?

Pronouncing the Word

Most dictionaries show the entry word's **syllabification** by placing dots or hyphens between syllables. Recognizing syllable divisions will help you learn to pronounce words that appear difficult at first glance; a syllable of few letters is much easier to pronounce than a word of fifteen letters. Syllable divisions will also help your spelling. When you can hear the sound of the individual syllables, you will be less likely to leave out letters or even entire syllables when you spell the word.

Immediately after the entry word will be its **pronunciation,** a respelling that shows you how to pronounce the word correctly. Some of the symbols used in the respelling may be unfamiliar to you. Near the front of the dictionary and at the bottom of each page, a **pronunciation guide** lists the symbols used in that dictionary to represent sounds. The respelling also shows syllable divisions and stress. An accent mark indicates which syllables are emphasized, or stressed, when pronounced. Some words may have more than one accent mark if more than one syllable is pronounced with stress. The largest accent mark indicates the strongest stress in a word.

18-8 PRACTICE THE SKILL

Using the sample dictionary page, draw vertical lines between the syllables of each word. Underline the syllable that is stressed most strongly.

1. osmoregulation
2. ossifrage
3. osmatic
4. Oslo
5. ostensible
6. ossicle
7. osteogenesis
8. osteoclasis
9. osmometer
10. Ostend

18-9 REVIEW THE SKILL

Using the sample dictionary page, answer the following questions.

_____ 1. How do the two pronunciations of *osmometer* differ?
   a. The *s* is pronounced differently.
   b. The *t* is pronounced differently.
   c. Both of the above.

_____ 2. How do the two pronunciations of *Osnabrück* differ?
   a. The *o* and the *s* are pronounced differently.
   b. The *a* and the *ü* are pronounced differently.
   c. Both of the above.

_____ 3. How do the two pronunciations of *osprey* differ?
   a. The *o* and the *s* are pronounced differently.
   b. The *ey* is pronounced differently.
   c. Neither of the above.

_____ 4. How do the two pronunciations of *ossature* differ?
   a. The *o* is pronounced differently.
   b. The *t* is pronounced differently.
   c. Neither of the above.

_____ 5. How do the two pronunciations of *Ossetia* differ?
   a. The first syllable is pronounced differently.
   b. The last syllable is pronounced differently.
   c. Each syllable is pronounced differently.

_____ 6. The *o* in *osnaburg* sounds most like the *o* in which of the following words?
   a. toy
   b. hot
   c. bow

_____ 7. The *o* in the first pronunciation of *Ossetia* sounds most like the *o* in which of the following words?
   a. blow
   b. spot
   c. son

_____ 8. In which of the following words is the o͞o sound found?
   a. ossature
   b. osteoclast
   c. ossicle

_____ 9. In which of the following words is the ô sound found?
   a. osmous
   b. osprey
   c. ostensorium

_____ 10. The sound of the third syllable in *osteoclasis* can be found in which of the following words?
   a. awoke
   b. clock
   c. book

Using the Word

Most dictionaries also include a **function label** to indicate the entry word's part of speech. Many words can function as more than one part of speech. For example, the word *walk* would have function labels for noun and verb.

Next you will find the **definition** or meaning of the word; some words may have several definitions. Be sure that you choose the one that best fits the meaning of what you are reading or writing. Some dictionaries also list synonyms (words with the same or similar meaning) of the entry word.

Some entry words are not suitable in every situation. A **usage label** indicates special areas of meaning. Usage labels can limit a word or one of its definitions by field (*mus.* for music or *phys.* for physics) or by style. For example, a word labeled *informal* is unacceptable in formal writing although it may be used in informal speaking.

Most dictionaries also include the **etymology,** or the word's history. Knowing the history of a word can sometimes help you to understand why that word is spelled a certain way or how the word came to have several different meanings.

18-10 PRACTICE THE SKILL

Using the sample definitions, write the number of the definition that corresponds to the italicized word.

> **balance** (băl'əns) *n.* 1. A weighing device. 2. A state of equilibrium. 3. A harmonious arrangement of parts or elements, as in a design. 4. Something that is left over, a remainder.

_____ 1. Please put those vegetables in the *balance;* I want to buy one pound.

_____ 2. The *balance* of colors in that wallpaper sample is especially pleasing.

_____ 3. After he pays his share of the bill, I will pay the *balance.*

_____ 4. "Let me be weighed in an even *balance* that God may know mine integrity" (Job 31:6).

_____ 5. Do you maintain a *balance* between your school responsibilities and your other interests?

_____ 6. Before writing another check, he called the bank to find out the amount of the *balance* in his account.

_____ 7. Because she has good *balance,* Sharon does well in gymnastics.

_____ 8. The new choir arrangement has a pleasant *balance* in melody and harmony.

_____ 9. After leaving a certain amount of money for the injured man's upkeep, the Good Samaritan promised to pay the *balance* when he returned.

_____ 10. John arranged his food to keep a good *balance* on his lunch tray so he would not drop it.

18-11 REVIEW THE SKILL

Using the sample dictionary page, answer the following questions.

_____ 1. From what language does the word *ostensible* originally come?

_____ 2. *OSS* is the abbreviation for the name of what organization?

_____ 3. What is the meaning of the Greek word from which we get the prefix *osteo-*?

_____ 4. What is the original name of *Oslo*?

_____ 5. The second definition of *ossifrage* is prefaced with what usage label?

_____ 6. The word *osmium* can be used as what part(s) of speech?

_____ 7. Under what word would you find synonyms for *ostentatious?*

_____ 8. The word *ossia* is associated with what special field?

_____ 9. Does the word *osmose* function as a transitive verb or an intransitive verb?

_____ 10. Where is *Ostend?*

Special Types of Dictionaries

Not all dictionaries are alike. In fact, there are many different types of specialized dictionaries. A **foreign language dictionary,** like an English dictionary, lists and defines words. Many foreign language dictionaries have two sections, one listing English words with their translations in a foreign language and the other listing words from a foreign language with their translations in English.

Other dictionaries define special terms or provide information not found in a regular dictionary. A **biographical dictionary** gives information on important people from the past and the present. A **geographic dictionary,** or **gazetteer,** lists places and their locations. It provides not only a correct pronunciation of the name of a place but also a description of its geographic features (such as rivers or mountains) and other helpful information (such as population).

Thesaurus

A **thesaurus** is a treasury of synonyms, words with similar meanings. Some also give antonyms, words with opposite meanings. Some thesauruses list the main words alphabetically with synonyms listed after each main word. Others group words by meaning with a detailed alphabetical index in the back. A thesaurus can help you find just the right word to add variety and precision to your writing.

Encyclopedias

Encyclopedias contain articles on almost every imaginable subject. These articles are arranged alphabetically. The volumes of an encyclopedia are usually labeled with one or more letters as well as with a numeral.

Find the article you need with the help of guide words at the top of each page. These words tell you the topic of the first article on each page, somewhat like the guide words that help you find words in a dictionary.

Check also in the index to find the pages where articles on your topic appear. Some sets of encyclopedias have an index in each separate volume, while others have a special volume (usually the last volume) that is the index for the entire set.

Investigate other references on the same topic when the encyclopedia gives them. They help you find articles with important additional information. These additional references, called cross-references, are often listed at the end of the article under a heading such as "See also."

Almanacs

An **almanac** supplements the encyclopedia by giving current information. An almanac includes tables of weights and measures, lists of sports statistics, names of award winners, information about government agencies and programs, summaries of recent events, and other miscellaneous facts. Most almanacs are published every year. You can find the information you need by looking in the almanac's index, which may appear at the front, like a table of contents, instead of at the back, where most indexes appear.

Atlases

An **atlas** is a collection of maps. It can provide some of the same information as a geographic dictionary. Some atlases may contain only political maps, which show political divisions such as countries, states, or cities. Another atlas may include topographical maps, which show geographic features such as mountain ranges and bodies of water. The most commonly used atlas contains road maps, which show the roads connecting various cities. Some atlases also include information about populations, crops, weather, and similar facts. Every atlas has an index that lists the page number where you can find the map you need.

Books of Quotations

A **book of quotations,** such as Bartlett's *Familiar Quotations,* allows you to find a quotation by looking up its author, first line, or subject. Most books of quotations also list each quotation's original source and date.

Concordances

A **Bible concordance** lists key words from the Bible with a number of references to verses where the key words appear. When you can remember only part of a verse, look up an important word from the verse, a key word, in the concordance's alphabetical list.

For example, if you remember reading a verse that says something about nurture and admonition, you could look up *admonition* and find Ephesians 6:4 as well as other verses listed there. If the particular passage you want is not listed, try another key word. Not all key words or passages will appear in every concordance.

Many concordances are available in software form for use on computers. These products make searching the Scriptures even easier. For example, finding all the occurrences of the phrase "kingdom of God" in a paper concordance would be time consuming and prone to error. But in a software version it takes less than a second.

Readers' Guide to Periodical Literature

The ***Readers' Guide to Periodical Literature*** is the most commonly used periodical index. In the same way that the card catalog or computer catalog can help you find a specific book, the *Readers' Guide* can help you find a specific periodical article. It lists articles from approximately two hundred fifty magazines by subject and by author. Each entry will tell you the article's subject, its title, its author, the magazine in which it appears, the issue number or date of the magazine, and the page numbers where you can find that particular article.

subject heading

article title GARDENS AND GARDENING

Container gardening: a movable feast for the eyes. Marya Ramirez.
il. *Home Gardener* 3:21-23+ My '97

includes illustrations

author

date

magazine title

issue number

indicates article continues on other pages

beginning page number

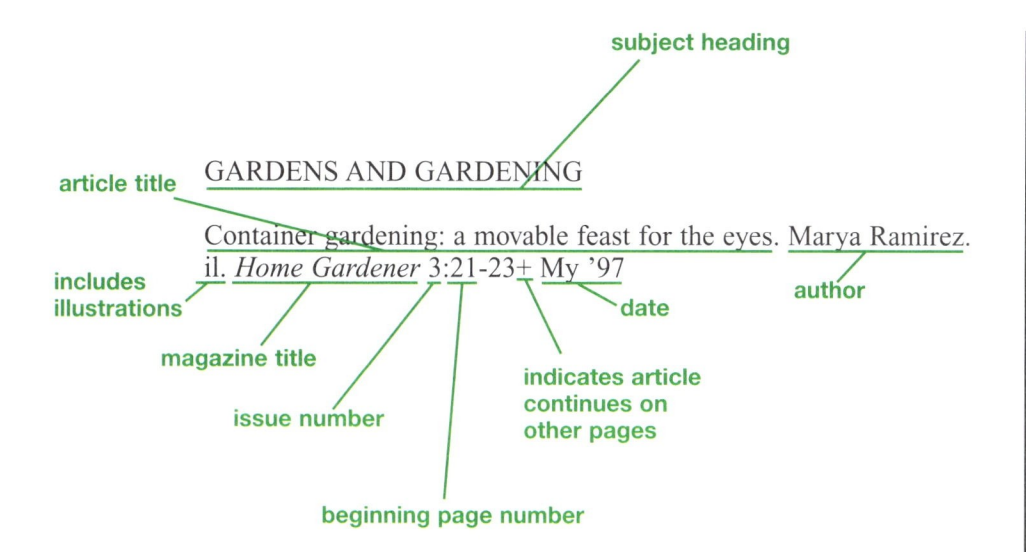

18-12 PRACTICE THE SKILL

In the blank write the letter of the reference tool you would use to find the answer to each question.

- a. desk dictionary
- b. foreign language dictionary
- c. thesaurus
- d. biographical dictionary
- e. geographic dictionary
- f. encyclopedia
- g. almanac
- h. atlas
- i. book of quotations
- j. concordance
- k. *Readers' Guide to Periodical Literature*

_____ 1. When was the city of Brandon, Manitoba, founded?

_____ 2. What is the Swedish word for *house*?

_____ 3. Were any magazine articles about Agatha Christie published in February 1976?

_____ 4. In what parts of the world do elm trees grow?

_____ 5. Who won the marathon in the 1972 summer Olympic games?

_____ 6. Who was Philip Henslowe, and when did he live?

_____ 7. Which road connects Missoula, Montana, and Spokane, Washington?

_____ 8. What is a synonym for the word *adventure*?

_____ 9. The letters *HMS* stand for what phrase?

_____ 10. What verse in Philippians contains the phrase "the glory of God"?

18-13 Practice the Skill

Use the entry from the *Readers' Guide to Periodical Literature* to answer each question.

> OCEANOGRAPHY
>
> Treasures of the Deep. Semaj Patterson. il *Ocean Exploration* 52:8-11 D '99

1. What is the title of the article?

   _____

2. When was the article published?

   _____

3. What is the subject heading under which the article is listed?

   _____

4. On what page of the magazine does the article begin?

   _____

5. What is the title of the magazine in which the article appears?

   _____

6. Who is the author of the article?

   _____

7. What is the issue number of the magazine?

   _____

8. An article can be located by what two ways in the *Readers' Guide*?

   _____

9. How could one find other articles by the same author?

   _____

10. What is another subject heading that could be searched for related topics?

    _____

Chapter 19
Study Skills

Developing an Interest

Most of us have several areas of interest. Suppose you know of no one who enjoys the same things as you. You would have no one with whom you could talk and share your ideas. God has gifted each of us with a unique curiosity about specific areas. Sometimes we may not think that we like a subject at first. Then the teacher does a class demonstration or states a fact that we find particularly exciting, and we start to learn more about that subject. Most of us have had the experience of not liking something at first and then learning to like it after additional time and experience with it. Interests can be developed and information can be learned by using several methods.

1. Sit in your chair correctly; do not slouch. Acting interested can help a person become interested.
2. Concentrate on the teacher or the reading. When you find yourself mentally wandering away, immediately bring yourself back to conscious concentration on the teacher and what is taking place in the classroom.
3. Practice guessing. What will the teacher or book say next?
4. Listen (or read) to learn. Try to learn while you are listening to the teacher or doing your homework. The more you learn and do in class, the less time you will need to spend studying out of class.
5. Write down (or mark) important points. If the teacher or textbook emphasizes a point, write it down.
6. Connect the information that you are learning. How does what you are learning now connect to what you learned yesterday or even to what you learned in another class?
7. Ask (or write down) questions, especially about information that you do not understand. Try to find the answers in your textbook. If you do not find them, request to see the teacher at a convenient time.

Using the Parts of a Book

When you understand the parts of a book, you can find the information in it more quickly. Finding information quickly will help you to stay interested in the subject. Not all books contain all of these parts, nor are the parts arranged in the same order in all books.

Every book, though, begins with a **title page,** which gives the title of the book, the name of the author or editor, the name of the publisher, and the place of publication. On the back of this page is the **copyright page,** which lists, among other things, the year that the book was copyrighted. *Copyright* means that the author or publisher has the legal right to that book; no one else can reprint any part of it without permission.

A **table of contents** gives the chapter or unit divisions with page numbers in numerical order. A **list of illustrations** is similar to a table of contents; it lists where the pictures are in the text.

CONTENTS

Ready Reference to Maps ... vi

UNIT I
THE WORLD AS GOD MADE IT
- Chapter 1 Geography: Finding Our Place in the World ... 2
- Chapter 2 The Earth's Surface ... 17
- Chapter 3 Climate ... 37

UNIT II
THE WORLD AS MAN SUBDUES IT
- Chapter 4 Industry ... 60
- Chapter 5 Society ... 86

UNIT III
NORTHERN AMERICA
- Chapter 6 The Northeastern United States ... 116
- Chapter 7 The Southern United States ... 142
- Chapter 8 The Midwestern United States ... 168
- Chapter 9 The Western United States ... 189
- Chapter 10 Canada ... 223

UNIT IV
LATIN AMERICA
- Chapter 11 Middle America ... 246
- Chapter 12 South America ... 271

UNIT V
WESTERN EUROPE
- Chapter 13 British Isles and Scandinavia ... 300
- Chapter 14 Continental Europe ... 324
- Chapter 15 Mediterranean Europe ... 348

UNIT VI
CENTRAL EURASIA
- Chapter 16 Eastern Europe ... 370
- Chapter 17 Russia ... 393
- Chapter 18 Caucasus and Central Asia ... 414

UNIT VII
ASIA
- Chapter 19 South Asia ... 428
- Chapter 20 Southeast Asia ... 447
- Chapter 21 East Asia ... 463

UNIT VIII
THE MIDDLE EAST
- Chapter 22 The Persian Gulf ... 490
- Chapter 23 The Eastern Mediterranean ... 508

UNIT IX
AFRICA
- Chapter 24 North Africa ... 538
- Chapter 25 West and Central Africa ... 551
- Chapter 26 East and South Africa ... 569

UNIT X
OCEANIA
- Chapter 27 Australia and New Zealand ... 596
- Chapter 28 Pacific Islands ... 615
- Chapter 29 The Last Frontiers ... 630

Glossary ... 642
Index ... 649
Photo Credits ... 660

Some books also include **acknowledgments,** the names of people the author or editor wants to thank. Some books also have an **introduction** or **preface,** which states the purpose of the book.

The largest part of every book is the **text.** In both fiction and nonfiction books, the text is usually divided into units, sections, or chapters.

Many nonfiction books also contain additional sections of information that are placed after the text. One of these is the **bibliography;** it lists either the books that the author used in writing the text or the titles of some additional books about the same subject.

Extra helps, such as charts, diagrams, long lists, and notes of explanation, are included in the **appendix.** One kind of appendix is a **glossary,** which gives the definitions of special vocabulary used in the text. Many textbooks have glossaries and other appendixes.

An **index** is an alphabetical listing of key words and phrases with all the page numbers where they appear in the text. Sometimes the index also lists the page numbers of the illustrations.

Index

Afghanistan, 414, 422-24
Africa. *See* Central Africa; East Africa; North Africa; South Africa; West Africa
agriculture, 61-63, 143-44, 146, 153, 156, 160, 170, 173, 176-83, 210-11, 228, 294, 352, 364, 447, 451, 465, 496-98, 525, 583, 602
Ahaggar Mountains, 544
air masses, 40-43
Alabama, 157-58
Alabama River, 158
Alamo, 165
Alaska, 193, 217, 219-20
Alaska Highway, 241
Alaska Range, 219
Albania, 83, 384-85
Alberta, 238-39
Aleutian Islands, 219
Alexander the Great, 3, 92, 110
Alexandria, 532
Algeria, 543-44
Algiers, 543
Allegheny Mountains, 145
Allegheny Plateau, 132, 133, 147, 148
Allegheny River, 133
alloy, 67
alluvial plain, 23
alluvium, 23
Almaty, 419
alpine zone, 122
Alps, 32, 47, 329, 342-46, 359, 377, 380-81
Alsace-Lorraine, 328

Anglican Church, 305, 310
Angola, 587-88
animal husbandry, 62-63
animism, 552, 574, 587
An Nafud, 494
Annamese Mountains, 451
Antarctica, 49, 630-33, 634
Antarctic Circle, 39, 630
Antarctic Peninsula, 632
Antigua, 268-69
Anti-Lebanon Mountains, 521
Apennine Mountains, 357-58
Appalachian Mountains, 119-20, 125, 130, 133, 135, 145, 147-48, 152, 154, 157, 158, 225, 227, 231
Appalachian Plateau, 147, 171
Appalachian Trail, 157
Apulia, 358-59
aquaculture, 468
aqueduct, 209
aquifers, 605
Aquitainia, 331
Arabah, 525
Arabian Peninsula, 492
arable land, 105
Aral Sea, 419-20
arches, 148, 191-92
Arches National Park, 191-92
archipelagos, 242, 285
Arctic Circle, 39, 219-20
Ardennes, 335
Argentina, 286-88
Arizona, 191, 206
Arkansas, 162, 164
Arkansas River, 164

Auschwitz, 375
Austin, TX, 165
Australia, 596-609
Australian Alps, 600-601
Austria, 345-46
authoritarian government, 108-9
autonomous republics, 404, 408-9
axis, tilted, 38-39
Axum, 575
Ayers Rock, 608
Azerbaijan, 417-18
azimuthal projection, 11
Aztec Empire, 248-49

Babel, Tower of, 96
Babylon, 3, 66, 83, 501
Badlands, 185
Baffin Island, 242
Baghdad, 502
Baha'i, 506
Bahamas, 265
Bahrain, 499
Baja California, 255
Bali, 460
Balkan Mountains, 383, 386
Balkan Peninsula, 380
Baltic Rim, 370-77
Baltic States, 376-77
Baltimore, MD, 137
Baluchistan, 440
Bangkok, 454
Bangladesh, 440
bar, 24
Barbados, 269
Barbary Coast, 538-40

You may notice that fiction books usually have only a title page, a copyright page, a table of contents, and text. This is true because the main purpose of fictional writing is usually to entertain, not to inform.

Study Skills 389

ETYMOLOGY *Book* grew out of an Old English word for *beech,* a kind of wood. *Book,* then, refers to the old practice of carving letters into wood.

19-1 Practice the Skill

In the blank write the letter of the book section that would give you the information requested. Letters may be used more than once.

A. title page
B. copyright page
C. table of contents
D. acknowledgments
E. preface
F. text
G. bibliography
H. appendix
I. glossary
J. index

_____ 1. the main part of the book
_____ 2. the title of the book
_____ 3. names of people whom the author wants to thank
_____ 4. listing of other books about the same subject
_____ 5. listing of the page numbers on which a certain word is used
_____ 6. the definition of a science word in a science book
_____ 7. the purpose of the book
_____ 8. the chapter or unit divisions with page numbers
_____ 9. the name of the publisher
_____ 10. maps or charts

19-2 Practice the Skill

Use the sample table of contents (page 388) and index (page 389) to find the answer to each question. In the blank write the letter of the correct answer.

_____ 1. Which chapter would tell you about Alexander the Great?
    A. 3
    B. 5
    C. 16
    D. 23

_____ 2. Which page would give you information on aqueducts?
    A. 468
    B. 358
    C. 331
    D. 209

_____ 3. The Alps are mentioned in all of the following chapters except
    A. 3.
    B. 5.
    C. 14.
    D. 16.

_____ 4. You could read about the Balkan Peninsula in the same chapter that you would find information on

   A. Apulia.
   B. the Aral Sea.
   C. Auschwitz.
   D. Antigua.

_____ 5. In which chapter would you find references to agriculture?

   A. 11
   B. 13
   C. 15
   D. 18

_____ 6. On what page would you search for information about An Nafud?

   A. 494
   B. 552
   C. 587
   D. 605

_____ 7. Animal husbandry is discussed in the same unit as

   A. aquifers.
   B. arable land.
   C. archipelagos.
   D. azimuthal projection.

_____ 8. Chapter 18 tells about

   A. Angola.
   B. Alsace-Lorraine.
   C. Almaty.
   D. Arabah.

_____ 9. On what page are both the Appalachian Mountains and the Appalachian Plateau discussed?

   A. 125
   B. 147
   C. 171
   D. 227

_____ 10. Chapter 7 covers all of the following geographic features except

   A. the Allegheny Mountains.
   B. the Appalachian Trail.
   C. the Arkansas River.
   D. the Apennine Mountains.

Reading Textbooks

Getting something new is always exciting. Whenever you receive a new textbook, take a few minutes to look through the book. Look at the pictures and read the captions, much as you would a family photo album. Stop to read interesting parts that catch your interest as you leaf through the book for the first time. Look over the table of contents. The table of contents will tell you two important things: the major topics in the textbook and the logical organization that the author uses to discuss those topics.

Organization is very important to textbook authors. Look again at the table of contents to see how the author has logically organized the chapters and units of the textbook. The sequence in which the author has chosen to

Study Skills 391

give the information also has significance. He may have started from the simplest to the most difficult concept, or he may have decided to state the information in chronological order. Look to see whether you can determine from the table of contents how the book has been organized.

Turn to the text and look at a chapter in the book. Chapters are organized in a particular way as well. The chapter may have bold headings that introduce main topics and smaller bold headings to introduce smaller parts of the main subject. Each heading tells you which part of the topic will be discussed. The rest of the information in most textbooks is in regular paragraphs. When the teacher makes a reading assignment, read each paragraph looking for the one topic in that paragraph. If you have trouble understanding the information, write the topic sentence in your notebook. Then look into the paragraph for details that you can list under the topic sentence. By reading the chapter this way, you are also making study notes that will help you to study more efficiently for the test. Read the information under the pictures and study the pictures and illustrations as well. These are ways that help you to understand better the information that the author has placed in the chapter.

Improving Your Study Time

The purpose of studying is to learn information. Sometimes intelligence has nothing to do with good grades. Usually the students who make the best grades are the ones who have learned the best methods for studying. The following ideas will help you to prepare better for study time.

1. Be prepared for each class period.
   - Come to class with your textbook.
   - Bring paper, pen, and notebook.
   - Bring any assignment that is due for that day.
   - Be in class on time.

2. Take time every day to prepare for each class.
   - Write down all homework assignments in an assignment booklet.
   - Have a definite place to keep papers and returned assignments.
   - Take home every book that is needed for that day's assignments.
   - Have a definite place at home where you always study.
   - Keep all needed materials in that place at all times.
   - Study in a quiet place, not near a television or while talking to a friend on the telephone.

Put these study skills to practice and organize your study time. When you sincerely and consistently do your homework and prepare for tests, the Lord will help you conquer many difficulties.

Scheduling Your Study Time

First, establish a priority schedule. Although you probably keep a busy schedule, you generally have time to do what has to be done. To create priorities means that you decide what is the most important and do that first. Then decide what is next and so forth. Establish a monthly and a weekly calendar for yourself. Place in it all the activities in which you are involved, such as church, sports practice, family obligations, and after-school jobs. Then schedule in study time for each evening.

Second, a detailed homework schedule is a must. Place all assignments and test dates in an assignment book or calendar on a daily basis. If you have no assignment for a particular class for that day, write *none* in the assignment booklet so that you will know that you did not simply forget to write down the assignment.

When a teacher assigns a long-term project, write the assignment down on the day that it is due as well as on several days well before the due date. Schedule time to work on one part of the assignment each week and continue to work until the project is completed by or before the due date.

Third, have a plan for your daily study schedule. This plan must include the *when, where,* and *how* of the study time.

When: You have choices. Your choices are to study right after school or between supper and bedtime. Stick to your schedule and do not stay up late to complete an assignment or put off until morning an assignment that is due that day. Be consistent once your study schedule has been established, and you will not have to stay up late or rise early on a regular basis in order to complete assignments.

Where: Establish one place to study. Choose a well-lighted and comfortable place. If you are very tired on a particular day, ask your mom or another family member to check in on you occasionally in case you fall asleep. By choosing one study place, you condition your mind to study when you are in that place.

How: Which subject do you study first and for how long? Look at your assignment book. Decide which subject is your hardest or which of that day's assignments will require the most time. You probably will discover that working from hardest to easiest is the better plan. Then if you complete all the assignments and have any additional time to do so, return to the hardest for a brief review session.

Once you have determined the order of your study, decide approximately how long the homework for each class usually takes. Of course, on some evenings the times will vary. You should always set aside some time to review. These review sessions will save study time later by allowing the information to become firmly rooted in your long-term memory.

Using Profitable Memory Techniques

After you complete your daily reading and written homework assignments, you will need to study for your tests and quizzes. Here are some techniques to improve your memory.

1. Read through the class notes for each class on a daily basis.

2. Pay attention as you study. Determine to remember, and remind yourself not to be mentally lazy.

3. Ask yourself questions about your notes and answer them aloud. Write down questions regarding material that is unclear to you; then ask the teacher those questions when you return to class.

4. Make flash cards from your study notes. Write a question on one side and the answer on the other side.

5. Create your own written quizzes as you study. Put the quiz away for a day or two and then try to answer the questions. Those that you cannot answer correctly are the ones that need extra study time.

6. Ask a friend or family member to quiz you occasionally.

Study Skills 393

7. Cluster information that you are learning. When you are given much information at one time to study, such as for a final exam, try to organize the material into related groups or clusters. Learn the information by category groups: the industrial products from New England, the industrial products from the Middle Atlantic states, the industrial products from the Southwest, and so forth.

8. Use mnemonic [nĭ-mŏn´ĭk] or other memory devices to help you remember. Create rhymes, acronyms, acrostics, or other word games during your study times to help you remember detailed information. An acronym is a word in which each letter stands for another word. An acrostic is a word in which each letter stands for a word or phrase. Here is an example of an acronym:

> To remember the names of the Great Lakes (Superior, Huron, Michigan, Erie, Ontario), rearrange the first letters (S, H, M, E, O) into a single word: HOMES.

Improving Your Reading Comprehension

School work requires much reading. You probably do not understand the meaning of every word that you read, and you do not always have time to look up every word. How can you discover the meanings of these words while you continue to read your assignments?

Context Clues

One method is defining a word from context clues. You discover enough clues from other words in the sentence to give you at least an understanding of its meaning in the sentence. Look around the italicized word below to understand by context what the word *disheveled* means.

> His clothes were *disheveled* because he had slept in them for days.

Disheveled means to be in disarray or disorder.

Definitions

Sometimes the writer may write the definition of an unfamiliar word into the sentence. Keep reading because the definition may be the sentence.

> As always, Charles was accompanied by his *goombah,* an older boy who was on hand should trouble arise.

Restatements

If the text does not give a definition of the word, look for a restatement. Extra information may be included after the word that may explain it.

> The *foofaraw* surrounding the arrival of the spelling bee champion—the parades, banners, flowers, crowds, and ear-splitting applause—made one think that the queen had arrived.

What does *foofaraw* mean? The sentence mentions five things that happened as the winner of the spelling bee arrived. You probably guessed that foofaraw means "a fuss over a trifling matter."

Examples

Sometimes the meaning of a word may be revealed by examples. The examples used may give enough information to enable you to guess the meaning of the unknown word.

> The most-anticipated *soiree* of the year is the junior-senior banquet.

What does *soiree* mean? The sentence above gives an example of what is so looked forward to. From this example, you can determine that *soiree* means "a party or reception." A dictionary then would further inform you that a *soiree* is an evening party or reception.

19-3 PRACTICE THE SKILL

In the blank write a definition of the word in italics. Use context clues to determine the definition.

1. The general was truly a *redoubtable* man. Everyone was a little afraid of him.

   _____

   _____

2. His reading of the newspaper was only *cursory* because he had so many other things that he needed to do.

   _____

   _____

3. Our teacher said that pencils were *indispensable* for the test, so we could not get along without them.

   _____

   _____

4. We hope that Mrs. Johnson will *recuperate* from surgery before she comes back so that she can work with the same energy that she once did.

   _____

   _____

5. We clapped for the cellist because we thought her performance was *laudable*.

   _____

   _____

6. Because he was not concerned about his grades, the student was *nonchalant* about his homework.

   _____

   _____

7. The detectives verified in court that the signatures on the document were *legitimate*.

   _____

   _____

8. Olivia had a fear of heights, and she allowed her *inhibition* to keep her from riding the roller coaster at the park.

   _____

   _____

9. The infamous Blackbeard was a *freebooter* who robbed and destroyed other ships on the sea.

   _____

   _____

10. Wesley was silent and dejected, and no one knew the reason for his strange, *melancholy* mood.

    _____

    _____

19-4 Review the Skill

In the blank write a definition of the word in italics. Use context clues to determine the definition.

1. Audrey is extremely excited about the new books she received for her birthday because she is an *avid* reader.

   _____

   _____

2. Even though he was persistently questioned, Grandpa did not *divulge* the secret about the surprise party.

   _____

   _____

3. While hiking back from the waterfall, the campers found it especially difficult to climb up the *precipitous* mountainside.

   _____

   _____

4. In order to construct an exact square, Erica made sure that the opposite lines were *parallel* and would not cross.

   _____

   _____

5. Brian's enthusiasm and friendliness made him very popular at school. Everyone enjoyed his *vibrant* personality.

   _____

   _____

6. From the ominous sky and strong winds, Mr. Holt could *deduce* that there would be a storm that night.

   _____

   _____

7. Because the baby was due in a few weeks, it was *imperative* that the new room be completed quickly.

   _____

   _____

8. During Christmas vacation, Ronnie did not hang up his clothes or make his bed. He became ashamed of the *slovenly* appearance of his room.

   _____

   _____

9. The dress had a *gaudy* appearance. The bright red satin would have looked better without the glittering sequins.

   _____

   _____

10. At the extravagant dinner party, Dawn had a difficult time choosing from the *plethora* of appetizers.

    _____

    _____

Word Parts

All words come from a root word; in fact, some root words are words themselves. Many words also have prefixes and suffixes. Sometimes knowing the meanings of parts of a word will give you enough clues about the meaning of the complete word.

Prefixes

A **prefix** is added to the beginning of a word.

Prefix	Meaning	Example
circum-	around, about	circumnavigate
intro-	in, inward	introspection
re-	again, backwards	reversible
sub-	under	submarine

Suffixes

A **suffix** is added to the end of the word.

Suffix	Meaning	Example
-ion	action, process	exception
-ate	act upon in a particular manner	accelerate

Roots

A **root** is the main part of the word or one of the main parts of the word. Many roots can stand alone as words without any prefixes attached.

Root	Meaning	Example
act	do	react
bene	well, good	benevolent
fact	make, do	benefactor
spect	look at, watch	inspection
vert	verse, turn	introvert

19-5 PRACTICE THE SKILL

Using the definitions of the prefixes, suffixes, and roots given above, guess the definitions of the words given below. Write your answer in the blank.

1. circumspect _____

2. revert _____

3. benediction _____

4. subvert _____

5. circumscribe _____

6. subsolar _____

7. return _____

8. spectator

9. activity

10. satisfaction

19-6 Review the Skill

In the blanks write a sentence using the word as you defined it in 19-5 Practice the Skill.

1. circumspect

2. revert

3. benediction

4. subvert

5. circumscribe

6. subsolar

7. return

8. spectator

9. activity

10. satisfaction

Taking Tests

Studying and doing homework is part of learning, but it is also part of an organized plan to help you do well on tests and quizzes. You have no doubt learned that waiting to prepare an assignment until the night before it is due is not a good way to earn good grades for a class. The more often you review material and the longer the period of time, the more information your memory will retain.

How to Take Classroom Tests

1. Before you begin, look over the test to see how many and what type of questions there are.
2. Read all directions carefully.
3. Work through the entire test in one of two ways:
    - Start at the beginning of the test and keep going. Answer those questions about which you are confident and those about which you are 50 to 75 percent certain of the answers. In some way mark those questions that you do not know or need to spend more time thinking about. Come back to them later.
    - Start at the most difficult section of the test and do it first. (Be careful, however, not to spend too much time on that one section!) Again, mark questions with which you are having problems and come back to them later.
4. Try to answer all questions, even if you have to guess at some.
5. Think carefully and be selective about what you write. It is better to write a little about what you do know than to write a lot about what you do not know.
6. Write neatly. Correct answers will not count if the teacher cannot read what you have written.

How to Answer Objective Test Questions

Multiple Choice

1. Read each question carefully. Formulate an answer before you look at the choices.
2. Read all of the choices carefully. Eliminate those that you know are wrong.
3. Choose the best answer from the choices that are left.

Example: __C__   Which of the following animals is *not* a marsupial?
   A. kangaroo
   B. wombat
   C. giraffe
   D. opossum

Matching

1. Read each question carefully. Formulate an answer before you look at the choices.
2. Match the questions and answers that you know are correct.
3. From the choices remaining, choose the best answer for each question.

Example: A. William Bradford
          B. Anne Bradstreet
          C. Cotton Mather
          D Jonathan Edwards

__D__ 1. "Sinners in the Hands of an Angry God"

__B__ 2. "To My Dear and Loving Husband"

__A__ 3. *Of Plymouth Plantation*

__C__ 4. *An Essay for the Recording of Illustrious Providences*

True/False

1. Read each item carefully. If any word in the item is false, the entire item is false.
2. Look for words like *always* or *never;* these words often signal a false item.

Example: __false__ A word ending in *ing* always functions as a predicate.

Short Answer

1. Accurately and completely answer the questions that you know.
2. If you do not know the answer, make the best guess you can. You may receive partial credit for your answer.

Example: __Esther__ What Bible queen saved her people from destruction?

How to Take Standardized Tests

Periodically you will be required to take standardized tests. You will have a better chance of doing well if you are familiar with the types of questions usually included on standardized tests.

Reading Comprehension

The reading comprehension section tests your ability to analyze a written passage. The questions may ask about the main ideas, details, or meaning of the passage. You may have to evaluate information or draw conclusions. The following strategies will help you on this part of the test:

1. Look at the questions briefly.
2. Read the paragraph and answer the questions you definitely know.
3. Read the other questions carefully as time allows, eliminating answers that you know are incorrect.
4. Choose the most logical answer from those remaining.

Example: The Young Voters Group canvassed the entire area, passing out leaflets for their candidate. Many had the opportunity to enlist the help of others in distributing yard signs and getting community members registered to vote. The group's political effort was a success.

__B__ In this paragraph the word *canvassed* means
   A. to cover an area with fabric
   B. to solicit voters
   C. to construct a tent
   D. to obstruct justice

Study Skills   401

The paragraph has no information leading the reader to think that *to cover an area with fabric* or *to construct a tent* would be the correct choice. Some might humorously say that *to obstruct justice* comes close to the truth, but *to solicit voters* is clearly the intended answer.

Vocabulary

Standardized tests also contain a vocabulary section that tests your knowledge of common English words. This section may include two types of questions. One type gives a sentence (or part of a sentence) with a word in bold print. You must then choose the word that best matches the meaning of the word in bold print. Context clues will help you choose your answer.

__B__   The forlorn lady retreated to her **chamber** to consider the king's advice.

   A. castle
   B. room
   C. thoughts
   D. court

Another type of question may list several sentences, each including the same underlined word. You must choose the sentence in which the word has the same meaning as in the original sentence.

__D__   The senator was accused of being part of the right wing.

   A. The ball player had to wing the ball to home plate.
   B. The injured bird could not use its left wing at all.
   C. One wing of the house contained five bedrooms.
   D. One wing of the state's house of representatives proposed a bill.

In the original sentence, *wing* means "either of two groups with opposing views." *Wing* in the first choice means "to throw." In the second choice, *wing* means "a movable organ for flying." In the third choice, *wing* means "a structure attached to a building." *Wing* in the fourth choice means "either of two groups with opposing views."

Grammar, Usage, and Mechanics

Standardized tests often combine questions about grammar, usage, and mechanics in one section. Other tests include several separate sections of questions. Depending on the test, the questions may appear in different formats. For example, the test may show a sentence with several words underlined and labeled, requiring you to choose the word that contains the error. If the sentence is correct, you choose the "no error" option.

Example: __C__   Ginger, the cat, runs through bushs regularly. No error
                      A   B   C   D

The correct choice is C because the correct spelling should be *bushes*.

402   Chapter 19

Another type of question may show you a sentence with part of the sentence underlined. You must choose one of the possible replacements for the underlined part. If the underlined part is correct, choose the answer that indicates that no change is necessary.

___A___   One of the packages <u>have lost its</u> bow.

         A. has lost its
         B. has lost their
         C. have lost their
         D. correct as is

Choice A is correct because the verb *has* agrees with the singular subject *One,* and the pronoun *its* agrees with the singular antecedent *One.*

Other standardized tests have separate sections for mechanics (capitalization and punctuation). The question may divide one sentence into several parts. Each part is listed separately. You choose the part that contains an error. If the sentence is correct, choose the answer that indicates that no change is necessary.

___B___   A. Hattie ran to the window
           B. and looked outside;
           C. but she saw nothing.
           D. no mistakes

Choice B contains an error. A semicolon usually joins independent clauses without a coordinating conjunction. A comma is the proper punctuation to separate two independent clauses joined by a conjunction.

19-7 PRACTICE THE SKILL

Reading Comprehension: **Read the paragraph and answer the following questions. In the blank write the letter of the correct answer.**

French engineer Alexandre Gustave Eiffel started his career building railway bridges. The success of his early projects landed him the job of creating the ironwork for the Statue of Liberty. His best-known work is the Eiffel Tower, built in 1889 to celebrate the centennial of the French Revolution. He designed the tower to top out at a height of 300 meters, or well over 900 feet. He spent his later days studying the new field of aerodynamics.

_____ 1. The topic of the above paragraph is

         A. the French Revolution.
         B. French engineering.
         C. Alexandre Gustave Eiffel.
         D. the Eiffel Tower.

_____ 2. Alexandre Eiffel worked on all of the following except

         A. highway overpasses.
         B. the Eiffel Tower.
         C. the Statue of Liberty.
         D. railway bridges.

Study Skills

_____ 3. The Eiffel Tower was built mainly to
   A. set a record for the highest building.
   B. put France ahead of America in engineering.
   C. make Alexandre Eiffel a famous engineer.
   D. commemorate the anniversary of the French Revolution.

Vocabulary: In the blank write the letter of the definition that most closely matches the word in bold print.

_____ 4. John's grades **fluctuate** a good deal without seeming to settle in one range.
   A. to vary irregularly
   B. to maintain consistently
   C. to increase dramatically
   D. to run efficiently

In the blank write the letter of the sentence in which the definition of the word in bold print most closely matches that of the first sentence.

_____ 5. I will have to **fly** once I get home if I'm going to be ready to leave by 6:00.
   A. A **fly** in my room kept me up last night.
   B. I don't like to **fly** on days when the airport is very busy.
   C. The kids **fly** through their supper when it's light enough to go back outside to play.
   D. Tori hit a **fly** ball over the left fielder's head.

_____ 6. Amanda tripped on her long dress, and the **color** of her face turned a bright shade of pink.
   A. Because she has dark hair and fair skin, black is a good **color** for her to wear.
   B. The children like to **color** with bright crayons.
   C. Uncle Jim likes to **color** his stories by adding fantastical details.

Grammar, Usage, and Mechanics: In the blank write the letter that corresponds to the error in the sentence.

_____ 7. The <u>Harrises</u> <u>has</u> decided where they will take <u>their</u> next trip.
           A   B   C

_____ 8. A. Adam will visit the drug store
         B. on Main street for a
         C. cool, refreshing glass of lemonade.
         D. correct as is

_____ 9. A. Ted's mother asked him to
         B. go to the grocery store,
         C. and to pick up his sister at school.
         D. correct as is

In the blank write the letter of the correct replacement for the underlined section of the sentence. If the sentence is correct, choose D.

_____ 10. Some of the children <u>brought their books</u> to class.
         A. brought their book
         B. brought his book
         C. brought her book
         D. correct as is

404   Chapter 19

19-8 REVIEW THE SKILL

Reading Comprehension: Read the paragraph and answer the following questions. In the blank write the letter of the correct answer.

The Hawaiian Islands were discovered by Captain James Cook in 1778. In the 1800s, many Americans went to Hawaii for business, and some went as missionaries. Friendship with the United States grew, and the Pearl Harbor naval base was established in 1887. Many Americans and Hawaiians hoped for the annexation of the islands by the United States. When Queen Liliuokalani came to power in 1891, she strongly opposed the movement, and U.S. President Cleveland decided not to annex Hawaii at that time. The islands finally became a territory of the U.S. in 1900, and Hawaii became the fiftieth state in 1959.

_____ 1. The paragraph is mainly about
   A. American exploration of Hawaii.
   B. hostility between native Hawaiians and America.
   C. how Hawaii became a part of the United States.
   D. rulers of the United States and Hawaii.

_____ 2. In this paragraph *annex* most likely means
   A. to add or attach.
   B. to prevent a political decision.
   C. to develop a friendship.
   D. a business treaty.

_____ 3. According to the paragraph, the annexation process was delayed mainly because
   A. the business competition between Hawaii and the United States had increased.
   B. the establishment of a naval base at Pearl Harbor angered the Hawaiians.
   C. the friendship between Hawaii and the United States had increased, and there was no need for annexation.
   D. Queen Liliuokalani had power and opposed annexation.

Vocabulary: In the blank write the letter of the definition that most closely matches the word in bold print.

_____ 4. Josh's **frugal** mother loves bargains and buys only when there is a sale.
   A. possessing a shrewd sense of business
   B. extravagant
   C. thrifty
   D. unrestrained

_____ 5. Arching its back after a long nap, the **lethargic** cat yawned and settled back down on the coach.
   A. unable to sleep
   B. stiff
   C. energetic
   D. lazy and sluggish

In the blank write the letter of the sentence in which the definition of the word in bold print most closely matches the meaning in the first sentence.

_____ 6. Karen **framed** her question so that Brad could not ignore the issue.

    A. Before going to see the principle, Mike thought about how he would **frame** his apology.
    B. Kim bought some new **frames** for her reading glasses.
    C. Although his fingerprints were found at the crime scene, the defendent claimed that he had been **framed**.
    D. The bride's picture **frame** complemented her wedding portrait.

Grammar, Usage, and Mechanics: **In the blank write the letter that corresponds to the error in the sentence.**

_____ 7. The <u>actress'</u> final scene <u>was</u> her best <u>performance</u>. <u>No error</u>
           A   B   C   D

_____ 8. Some of the children <u>were lying</u> on the floor.

    A. was lying
    B. were laying
    C. was laying
    D. correct as is

_____ 9. A. Neither the cows
    B. nor the horse
    C. are in the barn.
    D. correct as is

In the blank write the letter of the correct replacement for the underlined section of the sentence. If the sentence is correct, choose *D*.

_____ 10. One of the students <u>take all of their books</u> home every night.

    A. takes all of their books
    B. take all of his books
    C. takes all of his books
    D. correct as is

Chapter 20

Composition Skills

The Writer's Toolbox

Reference

The Writing Process

What happens when someone wants to build a house? First, the person decides what kind of house he needs. Then he draws up blueprints and plans the details of the house. He must collect all the necessary materials—concrete, wood, nails, glass—and tools. Eventually he uses the materials and tools to construct the house according to the blueprints. But the house is still unfinished. Before anyone can live in the house, someone must lay the carpet, paint the walls, and install the light fixtures. Building a house is a process that takes time.

Writing a paper is also a process that takes time. What is the writing process? It is a series of steps that results in a composition of some kind. In other words, good writing never "just happens." No one, not even a professional writer, can produce a perfect paper without completing the entire process. Following the steps of the writing process will help you produce a good paper.

Planning

Choosing a Topic

Before you begin to write, you must choose a **topic.** Some people have trouble thinking of anything to write about; other people have so many ideas that they have trouble choosing just one. Choose a topic that you enjoy. If you like your topic, you will be excited to write about it, and you will keep your reader interested in what you have to say. If you need help thinking of a topic, try these methods.

Making a List

Examine your own life for topic ideas. Make a list of people, places, events, and objects in your experience. To help you remember your past, examine photograph albums, scrapbooks, journals, and diaries. To help you examine your present, make a map of your house, your school, or your neighborhood. Think about your daily routines. Observe the people around you. Your list will be full of possible topic ideas. Here is an example:

1. 10th birthday party
2. school trip to Washington, D.C.
3. family vacation to England
4. summer camp when I broke my leg
5. my brother's high school graduation
6. the basketball championship
7. my dog
8. my brother's goldfish
9. our tree fort in the back yard
10. feeding ducks on the lake in the park

Asking Questions

Use the journalist's questions to help you identify details about something that interests you. Ask yourself *who? what? where? when? why?* and *how?* The answers to these questions may lead to more questions. Eventually you will have several ideas to explore. Look at this example:

> Who? Mom, Dad, Dan, and me
> What? family vacation
> Where? England, especially London
> When? last summer
> Why? Dad's business trip
> How? airplane, bus, rented car

Brainstorming

Brainstorming is a technique you can use by yourself or with a group of students. Start by listing one topic. Then write down everything about that topic that you can remember. When you have finished, you will have many topic possibilities, both general and specific. For example, here is the result of someone's brainstorming session about a family vacation in England.

- vacation in England
- rain
- double-decker buses
- driving on the left side of the road
- London
- Buckingham Palace
- changing of the guard
- the Tower of London
- crown jewels at the Tower
- prisoners in the Tower
- dungeons
- moats
- castles
- knights
- armor

410   Chapter 20

Clustering

Clustering is similar to brainstorming but goes one step further. Instead of brainstorming's simple list, clustering yields a diagram that shows relationships between ideas. Clustering will help you generate topic ideas and suggest ways of organizing your information. Write down one general topic and circle it. Then write down any related ideas and circle them. Next, draw lines connecting ideas to one another and to the main topic. Look at this example:

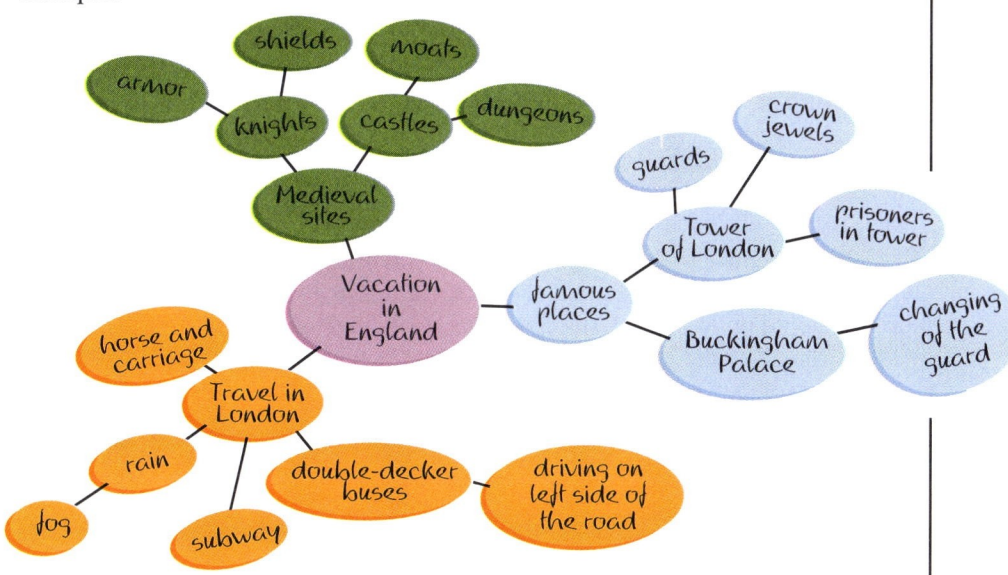

Freewriting

Freewriting can help spark your creativity. Choose a general topic. Then set yourself a time limit (five minutes, for example) and determine to write about that topic for the entire time without stopping. Do not stop to change a word or to correct your punctuation. When you finish, read what you have just written and look for ideas to explore further.

> I guess I'll write about our trip to England last summer. But what about England? I mean, we saw so much stuff. London was probably the most interesting. The Tower of London was cool. All those prisoners who were kept there years ago. I definitely wouldn't want to be one of them! It seems like most of the prisoners ended up without their heads. Being a guard might not be so bad. Except for the weird uniforms, I mean. Maybe I'd rather be a knight. Then I could wear armor. Were there really any dragons to fight? And did King Arthur and his knights of the round table ever exist? If the teacher tells us to look stuff up, maybe I'll try to do some research about knights in England centuries ago.

Narrowing Your Topic

After you choose your topic, you may need to narrow it. For example, the topic *England* is too broad. The topic *London* is narrower than *England*, but even *London* is too broad. Would you write about the scenery, the buses and subways, the flower sellers at Covent Garden, the changing of the guard at Buckingham Palace, the puppet shows in the park, or the restaurant where you ate shepherd's pie? Of course, some topics are too narrow. You might

Composition Skills   411

have trouble writing an entire essay about the postcard you sent home to your grandparents.

If you have chosen a broad topic, think of specific things about your topic that you could develop. Some possible topic ideas from the examples above are the history of the Tower of London or the uniform of a Yeoman of the Guard.

Considering Audience and Determining Purpose

After you choose your topic, identify your audience and purpose. When you write, you are writing to a person and for a reason. Perhaps you are writing a letter to a friend, a science report for your teacher, or a book report to persuade another student to read the book.

The **audience** is the person or group to whom you are writing. Knowing your audience will help you choose effective words and structure as you write. For example, a letter to your friend will be different from a science report for your teacher.

The **purpose** is the reason for which you are writing. Your purpose may be to describe, inform, persuade, or entertain. The reason to write your friend could be to inform him about what has been going on in your life, but the purpose for the science report would be to explain the procedure and outcome of an experiment or to persuade your audience that one product lasts longer than another one.

As you plan, ask yourself these questions:
- Who is my audience?
- What is my purpose?
- What information does my audience already know about my topic?
- What about my topic will interest my audience?
- What information about my topic will help me achieve my purpose?

The answers to these questions will help you make decisions as you gather information and draft your paper.

Look again at the example under "Brainstorming." What information should the writer include if his purpose is to entertain another student? Should he include different information if his purpose is to persuade his teacher to visit London?

Gathering Information

Now that you have decided on a topic, identified your audience, and determined your purpose, you need to gather information about your topic. First, list everything you already know about your topic. You can use the same methods for gathering information that you used to choose a topic: listing, asking questions, brainstorming, clustering, or freewriting. When you have finished, look at the information you have gathered. Do you have enough information to interest your audience and achieve your purpose?

If you need more information, you may want to research your topic. You could look for facts in books and periodicals from the library. Or you could interview someone you know who is an expert on your topic. If you use any information from a source, be sure to state where you found it.

20-1 Practice the Skill

Read the following student example and answer the questions at the end.

 If our castle were attacked, we would easily be conquered. We need to build towers on the walls and dig a moat around the castle. Towers that jut out from the walls would help defending archers who shoot along the walls to push attackers back. A moat would prevent enemies from digging under the walls and coming up on the other side inside the castle walls. Please consider building these additions for the defense of our castle and the safety of our people before the enemy attacks and it is too late.

_____ 1. What is the purpose of this paragraph?

_____ 2. Who is the intended audience for this paragraph?

_____ 3. Who might the writer of this paragraph be?

20-2 Review the Skill

Read the following student example and answer the questions at the end.

 The new drawbridge works very well. It not only looks nice but also keeps away all unwanted salesmen. Your men had the job completed in less than two weeks. They were responsible and undemanding. They agreed to do the job in exchange for food and lodging. Since my castle is well equipped, I was able to keep the men with no problems. I also wanted to send you a little gift of appreciation for all your organization and hard work.

_____ 1. What is the purpose of this paragraph?

_____ 2. Who is the intended audience of this paragraph?

_____ 3. Who is the writer of this paragraph?

Drafting

Paragraphs

 A **paragraph** consists of a group of sentences closely related to one main idea. The main idea of the paragraph is usually stated in the topic sentence. As you write, you indent each new paragraph to show that you are introducing another idea or point.

 Besides the topic sentence, paragraphs contain supporting sentences. These sentences may use details, examples, illustrations, or other methods to support the topic sentence.

 A concluding sentence then joins all the ideas together so that the paragraph will be complete. Many concluding sentences restate the idea in the topic sentence.

topic sentence — During its nine-century history, the famous Tower of London has served several purposes.

supporting sentences — The first building, known as the "White Tower," was erected in 1078 by William the Conqueror as fortification from his enemies. The Tower has been used as a prison almost since its beginning, and it has held church leaders, royalty, and Nazi war criminals alike. Prior to the reign of James I, the Tower sometimes served as a residence for the royal family. Presently, the Tower is a museum and historical site and houses the crown jewels.

concluding sentence — Rich in history, the Tower of London continues to fascinate its students and visitors.

Writing a Topic Sentence

Now that you have chosen a topic, narrowed your subject, identified your audience, determined your purpose, and gathered information, you are ready to write. First, write your topic sentence. The topic sentence states the main idea of a paragraph.

> The present-day Yeomen of the Guard still reflect medieval times. Organized in 1485 by Henry VII, the Yeomen reflect the style of the medieval period through their colorful uniforms. The Yeomen carry medieval weapons like a halberd and sword while they are on duty. The Yeomen of the 1400s originated as royal bodyguards, and their help is still enlisted on ceremonial occasions. These unique soldiers represent their heritage and their sovereign well.

If someone asked you right now what the sample paragraph is about, what would you say? You would probably say something like "medieval Yeomen of the Guard." And you would be correct. If you said only "medieval times" or "Yeomen," you would not be entirely accurate. The paragraph tells about Yeomen, but it more specifically tells how the Yeomen reflect their medieval heritage.

The first sentence is the topic sentence of the paragraph: "The present-day Yeomen of the Guard still reflect medieval times." It tells you both the subject and what will be said about the subject.

The topic sentence is usually, but not always, the first sentence in a paragraph. Because it introduces the topic, putting the topic sentence first is often helpful to the writer as well as to the reader.

20-3 PRACTICE THE SKILL

Write a good topic sentence for the following paragraph. Make the topic of the paragraph the grammatical subject of the sentence.

Peasant women worked in the fields alongside their husbands in order to provide food and clothing for their families. Wives and daughters of craftsmen helped in the family workshop or operated as tradeswomen themselves. Noblewomen organized and ran their large households and sometimes oversaw the family businesses. Hard work was a part of every woman's life during medieval times.

_____

_____

20-4 Review the Skill

Write a good topic sentence for the following paragraph. The sentence should both tell the topic of the paragraph and indicate what will be said about the topic. Make the topic of the paragraph the grammatical subject of the sentence.

Bards had a talent for entertaining. Most bards knew hundreds of songs and poems. Some bards wrote their own songs and poems. The most popular bards were the ones who could hold their audience's attention for long periods of time. Traveling bards were called minstrels. Many kings and knights hired minstrels to perform at a meal, but the minstrel was paid only if his work was considered worthy.

Developing the Supporting Sentences

Now that you have a topic sentence, you need sentences to support your topic. Your supporting sentences use the information that you gathered in the planning stage. Remember your audience and purpose: what kind of support will help you reach your goal?

Paragraph Development

Kind	Definition	Example
Fact	A statement that can be proved	During the Middle Ages, farming was the chief economic activity.
Example	An instance or an event that occurred	The Middle Ages began with the end of the Roman Empire.
Statistic	A fact expressed in numbers	The danger of fire was great in medieval Europe. Rouen, France, burned six times in twenty-five years.
Incident/anecdote	Brief personal account that illustrates the point	My visit to Chepstow Castle in Wales helped me understand the primitive nature of medieval life.
Sensory details	The use of sense words—taste, touch, smell, etc.	Peasants slept on dry, musty, scratchy bags of straw.
Reasons	Explanation of a truth	Because many merchants became peasant farmers during the Middle Ages, the influence of towns diminished.

Composition Skills

Look again at the sample paragraph about the Tower of London (p. 414). Notice that all the sentences coming after the topic sentence support it by giving examples. Fortification, prison, residence, and museum are specific examples of different uses of the Tower. An effective paragraph needs both a clear topic sentence and specific supporting sentences.

20-5 PRACTICE THE SKILL

In the blank write the type of paragraph development the author used in the following paragraph.

In Germany, castle design was influenced by the type of land the castle was built on. For example, some castles took advantage of the natural protection of crags, hills, and mountains and did not need as many walls surrounding them. Others were built on the banks of the Rhine River, which formed a natural barrier on at least one side of the castle. The *Wasserburg,* a type of castle protected by a moat, was common in flatter areas.

_____

20-6 REVIEW THE SKILL

In the blank write the type of paragraph development the author used in the following paragraph.

Many medieval castles still stand today. Last summer when I was in Europe, I was able to see Caerphilly Castle in South Wales. I learned that it is the largest castle in Wales. We also visited Samaur Castle in France. Interestingly, it was at one time used as a prison. I especially enjoyed seeing the Pfalzgrafenstein, which was built on an island in the Rhine by King Ludwig I of Bavaria. Our tour guide told us that it was originally used as a toll station.

_____

Organizing the Supporting Sentences

Now that you have your details, you need to think about the best way to organize the information. As you look at your information, think about the different ways in which you could put your paragraph together. Keep your audience and your purpose in mind. Choose the organizational method that best helps you reach your goals.

Paragraph Organization		
Method	**Definition**	**Good place to use**
Chronological order	A presentation of events in order of their occurrence	Stories, history, biography, news report, process, or instructions
Spatial order	A description according to how something is arranged	Description of a place or an object
Order of importance	A move from least important to most important or vice versa	Persuasive writing, description

Notice how the different organizational methods are used to achieve different purposes in these examples.

- Chronological Order

    What words indicate the order in which things happen?

    > Over the centuries armor became more complex to give knights added protection against enemies. Early knights wore coats of mail, which consisted of many small iron rings that were linked together. During the twelfth century, knights began wearing more mail so that their arms and legs were covered. Many years later in the fourteenth century, knights added plates to both their torsos and limbs. These plates were made of either iron or steel and were riveted to a cloth covering. By the early fifteenth century knights wore full suits of armor. These suits of armor protected the entire body but still were flexible enough to allow the knight to run, to mount his horse, or to lie down without the aid of his squire. As the years progressed, knights' armor grew more effective in protecting them against enemies.

    Words such as *early* and *many years later* indicate that the paragraph is arranged according to the order of occurrence. The time frame is expressed by the phrases *over the centuries, during the twelfth century, by the early fifteenth century,* and *as the years progressed.*

- Spatial Order

    What words indicate that this paragraph's development is spatial?

    > Special features of castles helped them to be easily defended against enemy attacks. An enemy first encountered a ditch that was dug all the way around the castle. Both dry and wet ditches prevented enemies from bringing weapons close to castle walls and from trying to dig under the walls. The next defense an attacker faced was the drawbridge. It was made of flat timber and could be stretched across the ditch to allow entrance or be lifted to a vertical position to deny entrance into the outer gatehouse. The drawbridge was operated from inside the castle and was difficult to overcome. However, if the enemy did manage to conquer it, the portcullis soon stopped their progress. The portcullis was a heavy, grilled, timber wall that could be slid down into grooves for added protection. It was overlaid in iron for added strength. Although entrance was not likely at this point, if the attackers did make it inside the gatehouse, they still had to survive the murder holes. These holes were located in the ceiling of the gatehouse and allowed the defenders to pour scalding water, sand, or other offensive materials on the attackers. All of these defenses helped the lord and his knights defend their castle against enemies.

    Certain features of the castle are described as being located *all the way around the castle, across the ditch,* and *in the ceiling of the gatehouse.* Words such as *first* and *next* also help the reader visualize the placement of the defenses and how an attacker would encounter them.

- Order of Importance

    What words let the reader know what is of most importance and what is of least importance?

Composition Skills 417

The lord of the manor employed several different men to help him run his manor. The most important official was the steward. The steward organized the workers to accomplish the various tasks around the manor. He also kept track of the accounting books and presided at the manor court when the lord was absent. The bailiff was second in rank next to the steward. The bailiff was usually a peasant. However, he was not a serf but a freeholder who owned land. He was in charge of assigning specific tasks to each laborer and hiring skilled craftsmen to make repairs on the lord's castle. The bailiff's assistant was the reeve. The reeve directly supervised the work done on the manor, making sure that the workers began on time and that nothing was stolen from the lord. Each of these men fulfilled a specific task to ensure the smooth running of the manor.

The order of importance in this paragraph moves from *most important* (the steward) to *second in rank* (the bailiff). The sequence finally ends with the least important person in this paragraph, *the bailiff's assistant.*

20-7 Practice the Skill

In the blank write the type of paragraph organization the author used in the following paragraph.

A man became a knight after serving as a page and then a squire. When a boy of noble birth reached the age of seven, he was sent away to a nobleman's household to be a page. He learned the art of courtly manners as well as how to attend noble ladies and how to ride. When a page reached the age of fourteen, he became a squire and was apprenticed to a knight, whom he served. The squire learned how to handle weapons and how to help his master put on his armor. If a squire was successful in his duties, he was knighted when he was around twenty-one years old. He became a knight after learning everything he needed to know as a page and a squire.

_____

20-8 Review the Skill

In the blank write the type of paragraph organization the author used in the following paragraph.

A knight's armor is made up of many pieces, most of which are fastened to the arming doublet. The sabaton, greave, poleyn, and cuisse protect the legs and feet. The mail skirt is worn around the waist. The backplate and breastplate deflect attacks on the torso. The pauldron, couter, vambrace, and besague protect the arms and hands. The bevor shields the chin and lower face. The helmet covers the upper face and head. All of these pieces protect every area of the body and form the knight's full suit of armor.

_____

Coming to a Conclusion

A good paragraph usually contains a good conclusion. As you end your paragraph, you want your audience to have a sense of closure—bringing your discussion to an end. There are several ways to conclude. One common method is to summarize your main idea. However, you also could give a solution to a problem or even ask your audience a question. The purpose of your paragraph will help determine how you end your paragraph.

Look at the sample paragraphs in the previous section. Each of the paragraphs uses the summary method to conclude. Compare the first sentence in each paragraph to the last sentence. Notice that the writer uses the same idea stated in different words.

Now look at the following example. Which method does this writer use to conclude the paragraph?

> As trade continues to increase, our town grows larger. In fact, the past three years have seen our town double in size. However, many tradesmen are becoming discontent with having to answer to and pay taxes to the king. I recently heard of a neighboring town whose dwellers agreed to pay a fixed sum each year to the king in exchange for a royal charter. This royal charter grants them the right to govern themselves, form their own trade guilds, and raise their own taxes. The town is prospering as a result. I suggest that we as a group of tradesmen petition the king to grant us the right to purchase a royal charter that will allow us to have similar privileges.

The sample paragraph presents a problem; the conclusion presents one possible solution to that problem. The writer's purpose (to persuade the tradesmen to petition for a royal charter) determined the type of conclusion that would be most effective. As you write your conclusion, remember to consider your audience and your purpose.

20-9 Practice the Skill

Choose the best conclusion for the following paragraph from the choices provided. In the blank write the letter that corresponds to your answer.

Tournaments were started in the eleventh century so that knights could practice their skills for war. Two teams of knights would fight a mock battle, called a tourney, in a large open area. A good fighter could become very wealthy just by winning tournaments because the victors claimed the armor and horses of the defeated knights. The object was to knock the opponent off his horse by using different weapons. As time went by, sharp weapons were replaced with blunt weapons to reduce injury to the contestants. Tournaments also became popular entertainment as lords and ladies watched from spectator stands. However, tournaments never lost their original purpose.

_____ A. Tournaments were very interesting to watch.
        B. Tournaments kept knights prepared for battle.
        C. Tournaments made many knights wealthy.

20-10 Review the Skill

Choose the best conclusion for the following paragraph from the choices provided. In the blank write the letter that corresponds to your answer.

One famous medieval hero was Robin Hood. Robin Hood was famous for robbing the rich to feed the poor. King John I had taken over the throne of his brother, Richard I, and had taxed the people unmercifully. Robin Hood used all of the resources in his power to stop the evil King John.

_____ A. Robin Hood remains famous for his adventurous exploits.
        B. King John had to give the throne back to his brother.
        C. Richard I was also called Richard the Lionhearted.

Essays

An **essay** consists of several paragraphs about one main idea. Many essays begin with an introduction paragraph that presents the essay's topic. The main idea of the essay is stated in the essay's thesis statement, which usually appears at the end of the introduction. Each supporting paragraph develops the thesis statement in some way. The conclusion paragraph unites all the ideas in the essay. It may begin with a restatement of the thesis statement. As you can see, the paragraphs in an essay are similar to the sentences in an individual paragraph.

Writing a Thesis Statement

The thesis statement in an essay is similar to the topic sentence in a paragraph: it states the main idea of your essay in one sentence. A good thesis statement tells the audience your topic and what you will say about that topic.

> Poor: I would like to talk about stained glass windows.
> Poor: With their many colors, stained glass windows are beautiful.
>
> Good: Although they cannot speak, stained glass windows tell intricate stories.
> Good: Dazzling stained glass windows give the gospel even to those who cannot read.

Developing Supporting Paragraphs

The body of your essay will consist of several paragraphs that support the thesis statement. Look again at the information you gathered during the planning stage. Which facts, examples, statistics, anecdotes, details, and reasons will help you achieve your purpose? Choose the best supporting information and group it with all the related support to create a rough outline for your essay. Look at the example below.

Thesis: In medieval times, dazzling stained glass windows gave the gospel to those who could not read.

I. Windows presented biblical symbols.

II. Windows presented biblical history.
 A. Windows depicted the life of Christ.
  1. Windows showed the Passion of Christ.
  2. Windows showed the miracles of Christ.
 B. Windows depicted stories of Bible characters.

III. Windows presented biblical themes.
 A. Windows depicted the teachings of Christ.
 B. Windows depicted the lives of the martyrs.

Notice that the writer listed specific support under general statements. Notice also that each section of supporting information relates directly to the thesis statement in some way. The group of support statements under the second main point includes information on biblical history, but the group listed under the third main point includes information on biblical themes. Each subpoint in this outline can become a separate supporting paragraph. Use the information in the general statement to write the topic sentence. Then use the specific support for the supporting sentences in the paragraph. Notice how the writer made one of his points into a supporting paragraph.

> Often each of the windows in a church depicted a part of the life of Christ. Christ's death, or Passion, was a favorite topic for stained glass. A detailed plan for the windows was first devised by a church leader and then implemented by a master craftsman. One church's plan might call for the events leading up to Christ's crucifixion being displayed around the sides of the sanctuary. These events might include meetings with the disciples, the prayer in Gethsemane, Roman scourgings, and carrying the cross to Golgotha. For example, the *Hessisches Landesmuseum* in Darmstadt, Germany, contains a stained glass window from the 1200s that shows Judas kissing Jesus to betray Him. At the front of a medieval church might be the largest of the windows showing either Christ's death on the cross or His resurrection.

Organizing Supporting Paragraphs

Just as the supporting sentences in a paragraph follow a logical order, the supporting paragraphs in an essay should follow a logical order too. How can you organize your essay? Choose the method that will help you reach your goals. Here is the earlier example rearranged.

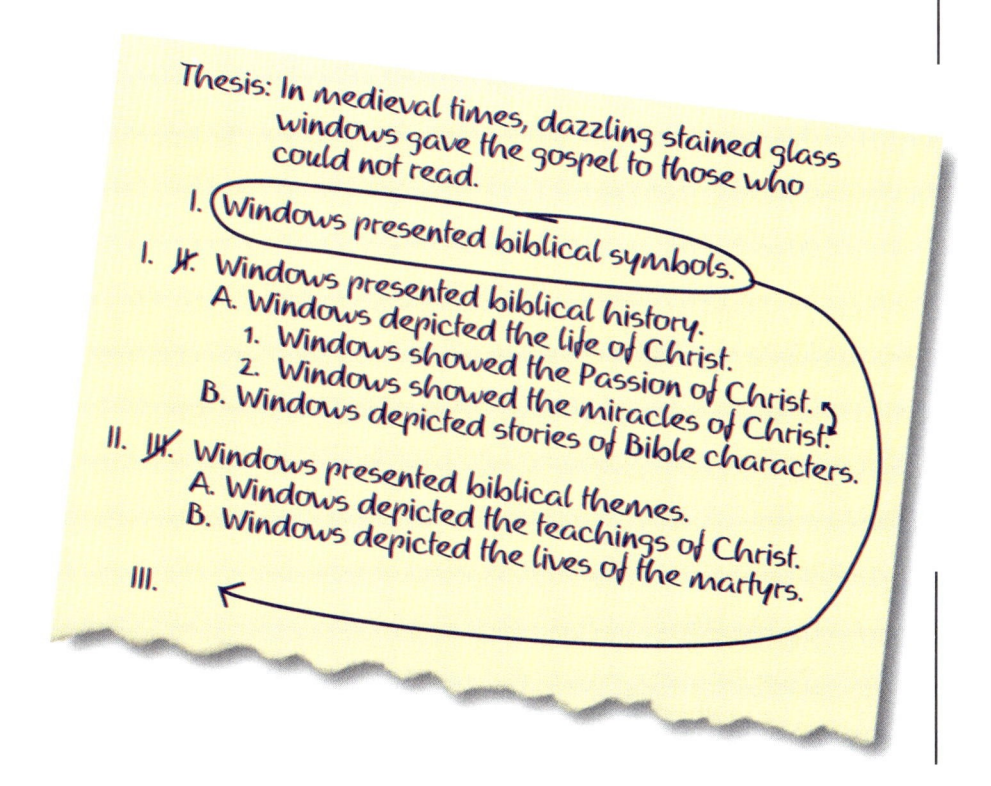

Thesis: In medieval times, dazzling stained glass windows gave the gospel to those who could not read.

I. Windows presented biblical symbols.

I. II. Windows presented biblical history.
   A. Windows depicted the life of Christ.
      1. Windows showed the Passion of Christ.
      2. Windows showed the miracles of Christ.
   B. Windows depicted stories of Bible characters.

II. III. Windows presented biblical themes.
   A. Windows depicted the teachings of Christ.
   B. Windows depicted the lives of the martyrs.

III.

Here is the final outline:

Thesis: In medieval times, dazzling stained glass windows gave the gospel to those who could not read.

I. Windows presented biblical history.
    A. Windows depicted the life of Christ.
        1. Windows showed the miracles of Christ.
        2. Windows showed the Passion of Christ.
    B. Windows depicted stories of Bible characters.

II. Windows presented biblical themes.
    A. Windows depicted the teachings of Christ.
    B. Windows depicted the lives of the martyrs.

III. Windows presented biblical symbols.

The writer rearranged the points of his rough outline to make it more effective. The main points of his essay, as well as the points under the second main point, are now arranged in order of importance. Each supporting paragraph will have its own order. Notice that the subpoints under the life of Christ will be chronological. Use whichever organizational methods will help your essay achieve its purpose.

Writing Introduction and Conclusion Paragraphs

Many essays begin with an introduction paragraph. A good introduction catches the reader's interest, introduces the topic, and draws attention to the main idea in the thesis statement. You may want to begin with an interesting story, a compelling question, or a problem to solve. Think of the introduction paragraph as a funnel: it is wide at the beginning where it introduces the broad topic, and it narrows to the specific thesis statement at the end.

> A hollow sound echoes down the church's aisles. Other notes join the first. The sounds are smooth and rich. In one musical key, men are singing the poetry of the biblical Psalms. This is the beautiful music known as plainsong. Heard primarily in large cathedrals, the plainsong of the early Middle Ages was an important historic form of music.

A good conclusion paragraph draws the essay's many ideas together and leaves the reader thinking about the essay's topic. Your purpose will help determine how to conclude your essay. You may want to summarize your main idea, give a solution to a problem, or ask your audience a question. Whichever method you use, be sure to leave your reader with something that he will remember. Think of the conclusion paragraph as an inverted funnel: it begins narrowly with a restatement of the thesis and broadens to a larger view of the topic.

> The plainsong was influential both on medieval worship and as a predecessor to other forms of music. Without the plainsong, the basis for many early musical forms would be absent, and the worshipers of a thousand years ago might have lacked harmonies for their worship songs. Its influence makes the plainsong important to the history of music in the Middle Ages.

Some short essays do not have separate paragraphs for the introduction and conclusion. An essay without an introduction usually begins with the thesis statement, followed by the topic sentence of the first supporting paragraph. An essay without a conclusion usually ends with a restatement of the thesis as the last sentence of the last supporting paragraph. Many in-class essays on tests follow this shorter format.

Essay Question: Explain how Chaucer was indebted to French and Italian literature.

Geoffrey Chaucer, the most important writer of medieval England, owes a debt to earlier French and Italian writers. First, Chaucer owes a debt to French writers. The French wrote stories known as romances that idealized medieval chivalry and courtly love. The most famous of these romances was *Romance of the Rose* by Guillaume de Lorris and Jean de Meung. Chaucer was quite familiar with the romance, having translated it and studied its views on philosophy and everyday society. Indeed, most scholars believe that *Romance of the Rose* inspired some of Chaucer's early work, much of which focuses on the same social commentary.

Second, Chaucer owes a debt to Italian writers. Chaucer probably used examples from the ancient Roman poet Ovid, who wrote of the many weaknesses of love. Perhaps the best example of Chaucer's borrowing ideas from Italian writers is his use of Giovanni Boccaccio's love story *Troilus and Criseyde* as the basis for his poem of the same name. Because he studied and borrowed from earlier writers, Geoffrey Chaucer was indebted to French and Italian literary traditions.

Revising

No one writes a perfect paper on the first try. No experienced writer skips the process of revision, nor should you. Revision is the way you improve whatever you are writing at the time, and it will help you gradually turn out better first drafts too.

Revising for Ideas

Revision of the first draft should always be re-vision—seeing the material again. That is, you look at the rough draft again to see whether you have said what you wanted to say and to see how you can improve the saying of it. You may want to take the following steps as you revise.

After you have written your first draft, put it aside for a while. Come back to it later. The lapse of time helps you see your draft more objectively, as other people will see it. You will be better able to notice any problems in your paragraph.

Look for ways to improve your rough draft. Use your pencil to indicate changes you want to make. You may circle words you want to change, cross out unrelated sentences, draw arrows to indicate that you want to move a word to another position, insert a caret where you want to add a word, or make other changes.

Read your paper aloud. Just hearing the words will give you a different insight into how you used your words.

The chart summarizes specific areas you need to consider as you revise your paragraph: clarity of purpose, audience interest, unity of ideas, coherence, and emphasis.

Problems	Solutions
Clarity of Purpose Is my purpose clear in my topic sentence? (My topic sentence should clearly state my purpose for my audience.)	Be more specific; zero in on one main idea.
Audience Interest Is my paragraph interesting to my audience? (Let one or more friends read it and give you their reactions.)	Try writing an alternate beginning. Use an interesting fact, question, or anecdote to get your audience interested.
Unity of Ideas Is my paragraph unified? (Every sentence in the paragraph should relate to the topic sentence.)	Leave out any sentence that does not belong or rewrite the sentence to make it pertinent to the topic.
Coherence Is my paragraph coherent? Do my sentences "stick together" well? (The relationships between ideas should be clear and logical.)	Use clear transitional words (*now, then, next, because, in addition, also*). You may need to link some sentences with connecting words.
Emphasis Does my audience know what I am emphasizing? (The best way to show emphasis is by position.)	Put the most important point of a paragraph at the beginning or at the end.

First Draft

add new topic sentence

Many medieval books were decorated beautifully by something called *illumination*. ~~Many people could not read then.~~ One copy of the Bible might take a scribe many months to complete. Illumination [*italicize*] is the name given to the decoration of a manuscript by the addition of paint, gold leaf, and drawings. Gilding [Although it was difficult and time-consuming,] ~~was primarily~~ a means to glorify God. [of the Scriptures continued to be practiced as] [*make concluding sentence*] The process of gold leafing, or gilding, took hours of patient drawing, applying the glue and later the gold leaf, burnishing, and finally painting in the rest of the [*italicize*] [ornamentation] ~~letter. The special glue is called gesso.~~

424   Chapter 20

Second Draft

> The copying by hand of manuscripts and the detailed process of illumination made medieval books extremely expensive and rare. *Illumination* is the name given to the decoration of a manuscript by the addition of paint, gold leaf, and drawings. The process of gold leafing, or *gilding,* took hours of patient drawing, applying the glue and later the gold leaf, burnishing, and finally painting in the rest of the ornamentation. One copy of the Bible might take a scribe many months to complete. Although it was difficult and time-consuming, gilding of the Scriptures continued to be practiced as a means to glorify God.

Revising for Style

After you revise for ideas, look at your paragraph again to revise for style.

Precise Words

As you revise, correct the inaccurate or imprecise words. Precise words help you to get your message across to your reader clearly. Use precise nouns and verbs. Some words may be general (like *city* or *said*) and some words may be specific (like *London* or *shouted*). A thesaurus may help you find the specific word you need.

Showing, Not Telling

Have you ever heard the expression "Don't tell me; show me"? Your paragraph will be more effective if you show, not just tell, your idea. Use words that refer to the senses—tasting, hearing, touching, smelling, seeing—to show your audience what you are describing. Do not rely on adjectives and adverbs alone; try to use precise nouns and verbs too.

Notice the details in the following examples. Which example shows the reader its topic?

> A medieval banquet was crowded and smelly with lots of people who were unable to clean up much. Even animals attended the feast.

> Hundreds of banqueters from all walks of life sat shoulder-to-shoulder on long, low benches while dogs and cats scrabbled for spills on the floor. All diners but the lord of the house shared bowls, with two or three guests per bowl, so hands flew and porridge dripped over the table and onto the clothing of surrounding guests. Often guests came directly from the fields or traveled great distances, arriving at the feast grimy and drenched with sweat in clothing that quite possibly had not been cleaned for months.

20-11 PRACTICE THE SKILL

Rewrite the paragraph on the blanks below, making it more precise. Show the reader what is happening.

People ate a variety of foods during medieval times. Beef, mutton (sheep), and venison (deer) served as the basic meats. Poultry and eggs were common dishes. Various kinds of wild birds also ended up on the menu. Peacocks and cranes were exotic dishes that were served on special occasions. Meat was often eaten with onions, garlic, and herbs from the castle garden. Dried peas and beans were the most common vegetables. Also, fruits, such as apples and pears in the northern areas and figs, grapes, oranges, and lemons in the southern areas, were gathered from the castle orchards and served as delicacies. Puddings made from milk were also favorite dishes. Medieval cooks knew how to make good food.

_____
_____
_____
_____
_____
_____
_____
_____
_____
_____
_____
_____
_____

20-12 REVIEW THE SKILL

Rewrite the paragraph on the blanks below, making it more precise. Show the reader what is happening.

In medieval times, serfs were peasants who farmed on land owned by the feudal lord. Serfs kept a portion of the crops they grew in the fields, but most of the food went to the lord of the manor. In fact, in many cases, the lord owned not only the field but also each family that farmed on his land. This system kept the poor poor and the wealthy wealthy. Serfs had to fight for the right to make something of themselves.

_____
_____
_____
_____
_____
_____
_____
_____

Proofreading

Proofreading your paper is just as important as revising. Make sure that no errors crept in as you wrote your final draft. Mistakes can occur accidentally as you rewrite or type your paper, so you need to find and correct them. Even if someone else types your paper, you are still responsible for any errors.

Good proofreading takes practice, but you can learn to do it well. The most important principle is this: do not expect to find every error (or every kind of error) in a single reading. Read in different ways to find different things.

Use these tactics to proofread your paragraph:

- Slow down by using a blank sheet of paper to cover the part you have not yet read.
- Read the paper aloud. You may hear an error that you did not see when you read the paper silently.
- Look at the words in reverse order; begin reading at the end of the paper and work toward the beginning. This tactic will force you to look at each word individually for spelling or capitalization errors.

Problems	Solutions
Grammar Do I have any fragments, fused sentences, or comma splices?	Figure out what is missing with a fragment and complete the sentence or join it to the adjacent sentence. Divide the fused sentence or comma splice and punctuate it correctly.
Usage Do my subjects and verbs agree and my pronouns and antecedents agree?	Put a singular subject with a singular verb and a plural subject with a plural verb. Follow the correct rules for pronoun-antecedent agreement.
Punctuation Have I omitted any punctuation marks or used any marks incorrectly? Have I used the correct end punctuation or omitted any end punctuation?	Read each sentence carefully. Check the rules in Chapter 16.
Capitalization Does every sentence begin with a capital letter? Are all proper nouns capitalized?	Look for specific places, people, events, and objects. Check each sentence against the rules in Chapter 15.
Spelling Have I misspelled any words?	Look deliberately at every word.

- Finally, you may want to read the paper through more quickly a few times, looking each time for some particular problem area that has been difficult for you in the past. For instance, it is fairly easy to spot comma problems when you read looking only for commas.

Careful proofreading does take some time. It is only a little more time, however, in comparison with what you have already invested in your paragraph. And it can make an important difference in people's impression of your work.

Publishing

Publishing your paper simply means that you are sharing it with others. Before you publish, you need to choose a **title** for your work. Choosing a title is important. The title tells the reader what he is about to read. A good title also captures the reader's attention. For example, "Peasants" is not a good title. It is too broad; it does not let the reader know anything about the paper's specific topic. A better title is "A Medieval Peasant's Daily Life" or "Why Did Peasants Stay Peasants?" Both of these titles let the audience know the paper's topic. The second title even indicates that the paper may give reasons to support its thesis. The second title also grabs the reader's attention by asking a question. Choose a title for your paper that interests your readers and hints at your topic.

These are a few ways you could publish your paragraphs or essays:
- Send them to your local newspaper.
- Put together a class literary collection.
- Use your work for programs (Parent Teacher Fellowships, holiday programs, and so forth).
- Read your work over the school's public address system.
- Share them with your English class.
- Read your work to someone at home.
- Mail them to a friend or relative.

After you finish your final draft, you may want to put it in a folder or notebook where you keep your writing. By the end of the year, you could have a nice collection of your work. You could include your rough drafts and final papers or just the final papers. You and your teacher may find these folders helpful because the folder allows you, your parents, and your teacher to see your progress over the weeks, semesters, or years. The folder also can help you see mistakes you have made in the past so that you will not make them again in your future papers.

20-13 PRACTICE THE SKILL

Choose the best title for the paragraph from the choices provided. In the blank write the letter that corresponds to your answer.

In the twelfth century a standardized system was devised to enable a knight to be identified by the symbols on his shield or full coat of arms. This system is known as heraldry. Heraldry was instituted as a result of the need to identify contestants in tournaments. A knight followed strict rules in obtaining and passing on his coat of arms. For example, one rule was that a knight could carry only one coat of arms. This coat of arms was passed on to the eldest son, the heir, when the knight died. Other children used a form of their father's coat of arms with slight variations. For example, each son in a family would use his own personal symbol to show his order of birth. Heraldry, a unique and ingenious way to distinguish knights in battle, eventually developed into a way to identify families.

_____ A. Heraldry: An Explanation of Its Symbols

B. Heraldry: Why We Should Study It

C. Heraldry: How it Developed

20-14 REVIEW THE SKILL

Choose the best title for the paragraph from the choices provided. In the blank write the letter that corresponds to your answer.

    The church and the clergy dominated Europe in the Middle Ages. The clergy had great power over the common person. The church baptized a person at birth, performed his wedding ceremony, and administered his burial service. The church also owned most of the land during the medieval period because many lords gave the church land in return for favors. Since the lords controlled the land and the people, their giving land to the church gave the church great power. Finally, the church had the power of excommunication. A person who was excommunicated, it was believed, could not go to heaven.

_____   A. The Church: Widespread Control
              B. The Church: Excommunication
              C. The Church: How It Developed

Chapter 1: Sentences

Sentence Types and Punctuation
In the blanks label each sentence as *declarative, interrogative, imperative,* or *exclamatory*. Then insert the correct punctuation mark at the end of the sentence.

_____ 1. What is your favorite month of the year

_____ 2. My favorite month is May

_____ 3. Lilies, May's official flowers, are so beautiful

_____ 4. Tell me which birthstone belongs to the month of May

_____ 5. If you look in the encyclopedia, you will find the answer

Simple Subjects
Find the simple subject, single or compound, in each sentence. In the blank write the letter that corresponds to the correct answer.

_____ 6. The lovely month of May has some of the most pleasant weather of the year.
    A. month
    B. May
    C. weather

_____ 7. During May, the spring flowers are just beginning to bloom.
    A. May, spring
    B. spring, flowers
    C. flowers

_____ 8. White and pink dogwoods and blue and yellow violets are some of May's flowers.
    A. dogwoods, violets
    B. pink dogwoods, yellow violets
    C. white and pink, blue and yellow

_____ 9. Look at the mother birds waiting for their eggs to hatch.
    A. birds
    B. (You)
    C. Look

_____ 10. The green appearance of the landscape and the new flowers are two exciting occurrences in May.
    A. appearance, landscape
    B. landscape, flowers
    C. appearance, flowers

Simple Predicates

Find the simple predicate, single or compound, in each sentence. In the blank write the letter that corresponds to the correct answer.

_____ 11. Mother's Day is officially celebrated on the second Sunday of May.
  A. officially celebrated
  B. is celebrated
  C. is officially

_____ 12. On Mother's Day, give your mother a present and show her your gratefulness.
  A. give, present
  B. give, gratefulness
  C. give, show

_____ 13. Armed Forces Day, the third Saturday of May, recognizes all divisions of the military and honors those in the armed forces.
  A. recognizes, divisions
  B. honors, forces
  C. recognizes, honors

_____ 14. Do you observe Memorial Day on the last Monday of May?
  A. Do you
  B. Do observe
  C. you observe

_____ 15. On Memorial Day, many people place flowers on the graves of soldiers.
  A. place
  B. flowers
  C. graves

Sentence Structure

In the blank, label each group of words *F* (fragment), *CS* (comma splice), *FS* (fused sentence), or *S* (correct sentence).

_____ 16. On May 8, 1884, Harry S. Truman was born, John F. Kennedy was born on May 29, 1917.

_____ 17. Charles Lindbergh flew solo across the Atlantic on May 21, 1927, and Amelia Earhart became the first woman to fly across the Atlantic on May 20, 1932.

_____ 18. The opening of the Brooklyn Bridge on May 24, 1883, and the Golden Gate Bridge on May 27, 1937.

_____ 19. May 10, 1869, marks the completion of the first continental railroad a golden spike was used at the completion point.

_____ 20. The British abandoned the occupation of Palestine on May 14, 1948, Israel was then an independent nation.

Name_____

Chapter 2: Nouns

Identifying Nouns
Questions 1-5: Underline each common noun once and each proper noun twice in the following paragraph.

The last month of the year in the Gregorian calendar is December. In the Roman calendar, it was the tenth month. The name of the month comes from the word *decem* in Latin. Many people around the world celebrate Christmas on the twenty-fifth day. Other holidays in December include Hanukkah and the Feast of Saint Nicholas.

Forms of Nouns
Identify the form of the noun that correctly completes the sentence. In the blank write the letter that corresponds to the correct answer.

  A. snowman
  B. snowman's
  C. snowmen
  D. snowmen's

_____ 6. The morning after it snowed, Kelly and Ian built two _?_.

_____ 7. They looked around for a carrot, but they used a broken pencil for the first _?_ nose instead.

_____ 8. Because they had so much fun building the first two, Kelly and Ian decided to build two more _?_.

_____ 9. Those _?_ mouths were made out of licorice.

_____ 10. Kelly and Ian decided that making a _?_ is their favorite winter pastime.

Forming Possessive Nouns
Identify the correct possessive form of each phrase. In the blank write the letter that corresponds to the correct answer.

_____ 11. the skates of the ice skater
  A. the ice skaters' skates
  B. the ice skater's skates
  C. the ice skaters skates

_____ 12. the snowman of the school
  A. the schools snowman
  B. the schools' snowman
  C. the school's snowman

Chapter 2 Review   433

_____ 13. the snowball fight of the students
   A. the students' snowball fight
   B. the student's snowball fight
   C. the students snowball fight

_____ 14. the skis of his friend
   A. his friends skis
   B. his friend's skis
   C. his friends' skis

_____ 15. the snow day of the county
   A. the county's snow day
   B. the counties' snow day
   C. the counties snow day

Count and Noncount Nouns
Questions 16-20: Look at the italicized common nouns in the following paragraph. Underline the count nouns. Double underline the noncount nouns.

My brother Todd and I used to play in the *snow* all day after a blizzard. We had a hill in our *yard* that made sledding so much fun. Our friends lived right on a lake, and we would ice-skate on the frozen *water* until we were blue with cold. After our *mother* bundled us in our snowsuits, we would spend hours outside making snow angels and snowmen. When we were almost frozen solid, my mother had steaming hot chocolate ready for us when we came in. Winter was one of our favorite times of the *year* because of all the exciting things we could do.

Compound Nouns
Write *Cpd* (compound) in the blank if the italicized noun is a compound noun. Leave the blank empty if the italicized noun is not a compound noun.

_____ 21. In our yard my brothers and I built a *snowman* whom we named Freezy.

_____ 22. Freezy is made of millions of little *snowflakes*.

_____ 23. We decided to make him a *snow wife* so that he wouldn't be lonely.

_____ 24. Her name is *Icicle*.

_____ 25. They are only two of the many *snow people* on my street.

Name_____

Chapter 3: Verbs

Identifying Complete Verbs
Find the complete verb in each sentence. In the blank write the letter that corresponds to the correct answer.

_____ 1. The Mississippi River has been considered one of the most important rivers in the United States.
  A. has been
  B. has been considered
  C. considered

_____ 2. In the 1800s the river was regularly used as a means of transportation.
  A. was used
  B. was regularly used
  C. regularly used as

_____ 3. The Mississippi River is steadily flowing from Minnesota into the Gulf of Mexico.
  A. is steadily flowing
  B. flowing
  C. is flowing

_____ 4. In Missouri, the Illinois River and the Missouri River constantly flow into the Mississippi River.
  A. constantly flow
  B. flow
  C. constantly flow into

_____ 5. Due to the muddiness of the Missouri River, the Mississippi also acquires a muddy appearance.
  A. Mississippi also acquires
  B. also acquires
  C. acquires

Action and State-of-Being Verbs
Underline the complete verb in each sentence. Identify each verb as *action* or *state-of-being*. In the blank write the letter that corresponds to the correct answer.
  A. action
  B. state-of-being

_____ 6. The Mississippi River is a well-known river.

_____ 7. Mark Twain wrote about life on the Mississippi.

_____ 8. Some call the Mississippi "Old Man River."

_____ 9. The river can be one hundred feet deep in some places.

_____ 10. Sometimes the Mississippi floods after heavy rain.

Chapter 3 Review

Sentence Patterns: *S-InV, S-TrV-DO,* and *S-TrV-IO-DO*

Identify the sentence pattern for each sentence. In the blank write the letter that corresponds to the correct answer.

    A. S-InV
    B. S-TrV-DO
    C. S-TrV-IO-DO

_____ 11. Scouts traveled the Mississippi in exploration of the United States.

_____ 12. American Indians gave the Mississippi River its name.

_____ 13. The Mississippi flows in from north to south.

_____ 14. Barges carry commercial products on the river.

_____ 15. The Mississippi provides commercial vessels an efficient transportation route.

Sentence Patterns: *S-LV-PN* and *S-LV-PA*

Identify the sentence pattern for each sentence. In the blank write the letter that corresponds to the correct answer.

    A. S-LV-PN
    B. S-LV-PA

_____ 16. The Mississippi River appears murky in the southern states.

_____ 17. In the northern states, the river is a source of clear water.

_____ 18. The Gulf of Mexico is the final destination of the Mississippi River.

_____ 19. The Mississippi River grows deeper near the Gulf of Mexico.

_____ 20. Because of silt deposits, the land near the Gulf of Mexico has become a delta.

Verb Tenses

Identify the correct verb form to complete each sentence. In the blank write the letter that corresponds to the correct answer.

_____ 21. When he was a boy, Duffee _?_ growing up near the Mississippi River.
    A. enjoyed
    B. is enjoying
    C. will enjoy

_____ 22. When Duffee was twelve, he and his friend Darren already _?_ thousands of proud ships cruise down the rapid waters of the Mississippi.
    A. saw
    B. see
    C. had seen

Name_____

_____ 23. Now that they are teenagers, Duffee and Darren _?_ their own boat for exploring the river.
  A. wanted
  B. want
  C. had wanted

_____ 24. Duffee and Darren _?_ a sturdy raft in the next few days.
  A. will build
  B. building
  C. have built

_____ 25. By next week, the boys _?_ far down the Mississippi in their light raft.
  A. floated
  B. will have floated
  C. will float

In the blank, write the form of the verb indicated in parentheses.

_____ 26. In the sweltering heat of Mississippi, Duffee and Darren _?_ sluggishly on the water. *(past progressive, drift)*

_____ 27. Later they noticed that the waters _?_ more rapidly than before. *(past progressive, rush)*

_____ 28. Duffee exclaimed, "Darren, the water soon _?_ too fast for us to stop." *(future progressive, move)*

_____ 29. A crewman on a large boat _?_ the boys, and he helped pull them from the river to the safety of the boat. *(past perfect progressive, watch)*

_____ 30. By the time dinner was over, Duffee and Darren _?_ their family about their narrow escape for hours. *(past perfect progressive, tell)*

Active and Passive
Label each sentence *active* or *passive*.

_____ 31. The ship moved down the river.

_____ 32. The ship was steered by the captain.

_____ 33. During the night, the captain was given a warning.

_____ 34. The safety of the ship was threatened by the shallow waters.

_____ 35. The captain steered the ship safely through the dangerous area.

Name_____

Chapter 4: Pronouns

Pronouns and Antecedents
In the blank write a pronoun to replace the italicized word or phrase.

_____ 1. Heather says that *Heather's* favorite season of the year is summer.

_____ 2. In the summer, *Heather* enjoys teaching young children to swim.

_____ 3. Her brother Brent loves summertime because *Brent* gets a three-month break from school.

_____ 4. *Brent's* favorite summer activities are camping and hiking.

_____ 5. Brent enjoys hiking and camping only once in a while because *hiking and camping* make his body very sore.

Personal Pronouns
Write five sentences using the personal pronouns referred to in parentheses. Underline the pronoun in your sentence. Use the pronoun chart whenever necessary.

6. Write a sentence about the first day of camp. *(first person singular, subjective case)*

   _____

   _____

7. Write a sentence about meeting the other people in the cabin. *(third person plural, objective case)*

   _____

   _____

8. Tell about a friend's favorite camp game. *(third person singular, possessive case)*

   _____

   _____

9. Ask me about a favorite event at camp. *(second person singular, subjective)*

   _____

   _____

10. List the things needed to build a campfire. *(first person plural, objective case)*

    _____

    _____

Chapter 4 Review

Demonstrative and Interrogative Pronouns

Questions 11-15: Underline the demonstrative and interrogative pronouns in the following paragraph. Above each underlined word, label it *D* (demonstrative) or *I* (interrogative).

One summer, my family took a camping trip in the mountains. That was one of my favorite vacations. We arrived at the campsite after hours of traveling. My sister asked Dad, "Who is going to set up the tents and begin the fire?" My father, however, had everything under control. After everything was set up, my sister and I asked, "Which tent is ours?" He pointed to the one closer to the fire. This was fine with us because it would be easier for us to stay warm if we were near the fire. We did some hiking, swimming, bike riding, and lots of other enjoyable things during our vacation. These are some of the best memories I have of my family and me.

Indefinite Pronouns

In the blank to the left of the number, write an indefinite pronoun that could be a substitute for the underlined word(s).

_____ 16. In the summer, my friends and I play miniature golf; <u>my friends</u> always get lower scores than I get.

_____ 17. Out of all of the players, Kelly is the best <u>player</u>.

_____ 18. <u>My friends and I</u> try to beat Kelly.

_____ 19. <u>My friends' scores</u> total about fifty.

_____ 20. <u>My sister and my best friend</u> defeated me.

More Pronouns

Questions 21-30: Fill in each blank with an appropriate pronoun of the type indicated.

In the weeks before school resumed, _____ *(possessive)* family bought much needed school items. _____ *(indefinite)* of us purchased school clothes and supplies. My brother _____ *(intensive)* enjoyed this time more than the rest of _____ *(personal)*. _____ *(possessive)* list was always longer than ours. _____ *(interrogative)* would have thought a boy would like shopping more than a girl would? Oddly enough, _____ *(demonstrative)* was typical of _____ *(indefinite)* of our school shopping trips. My mother hid _____ *(reflexive)* whenever we told _____ *(personal)* it was time to do some school shopping.

Name_____

Chapter 5: Adjectives

Identifying Adjectives
Questions 1-10: Underline each adjective in the following sentences and draw an arrow to the word it modifies.

1. Many rules for teachers have changed since the days of 1872.

2. In that year teachers had many extra responsibilities.

3. Each teacher was required to bring a full pail of coal for the day's fuel and to clean the classroom chimneys.

4. His students' needs for water and chalk were also the teacher's concern.

5. In addition to his responsibilities, a teacher's free time was different.

6. A normal class day consisted of ten hours in the school classroom before the teacher could relax by reading the Bible or good books at home.

7. A female teacher could not marry.

8. A male teacher could court for one evening in each week.

9. If he attended church, he was allowed two evenings a week for courting.

10. A diligent teacher might get a raise of twenty-five cents for each week's salary after five years of teaching.

Comparing Adjectives
For each sentence, identify the correct form of the adjective in parentheses. In the blank write the letter that corresponds to the correct answer.

_____ 11. *The Last Lesson,* by Alphonse Daudet, is an ? story about a schoolboy's last French lesson. *(expressive, positive)*
  A. expressive
  B. more expressive
  C. most expressive

_____ 12. When little Franz arrives late for class, he is surprised to find that his class is ? than he expected. *(quiet, comparative)*
  A. quiet
  B. quieter
  C. quietest

Chapter 5 Review   441

_____ 13. Everyone looks sad, but the teacher, Monsieur Hamel, is the ? of them all as he informs the class that this will be their last lesson in French. *(sad, superlative)*
   A. sadder
   B. saddest
   C. sad

_____ 14. School, his faithful teacher, and the French language become ? to Franz than ever before. *(important, comparative)*
   A. most important
   B. important
   C. more important

_____ 15. Before Monsieur Hamel dismisses his class for the final time, he writes in his ? handwriting, "Vive la France!" *(large, superlative)*
   A. large
   B. largest
   C. larger

Possessive Adjectives and Independent Possessives

Identify each italicized word as a possessive adjective or independent possessive. In the blank write the letter that corresponds to the correct answer.

   A. possessive adjective
   B. independent possessive

_____ 16. *Adam's* new classmate, Kai, is from Germany.

_____ 17. Kai's German grammar is much better than *his*.

_____ 18. They enjoy singing German songs with *their* German teacher, Frau Adams.

_____ 19. Their German singing is not as good as *hers*.

_____ 20. *Her* voice is clear and melodious.

Other Types of Adjectives

Label the *function* of each italicized word *N* (noun), *P* (pronoun), or *Adj* (adjective).

_____ 21. Most United States citizens probably know Noah Webster as a famous *dictionary* maker.

_____ 22. In 1828 Webster gave *colonial* America the result of his life's work, a dictionary of the English language.

_____ 23. In addition to his *dictionary*, Webster produced the "Blue-backed Speller."

_____ 24. *This* was the common name for one of the three parts of the grammar that Webster wrote.

_____ 25. *This* speller did much to standardize American spelling.

Name_____

Chapter 6: Adverbs

Identifying Adverbs
Questions 1-10: Underline each adverb in the following paragraph.

Jesus told the story of a servant whose lord compassionately forgave him a great sum of money. Out of gratitude for this unusually generous pardon, the servant should have always tried to forgive others. He went instead to another servant who owed him a small amount of money and treated him harshly. When the lord heard of this, he quickly commanded that the servant be held prisoner until he could fully pay what he owed. Jesus was trying to teach the people that they should freely and completely forgive each other since God has graciously forgiven them.

Modifiers
Identify the type of word modified by each italicized adverb. Write in the blank the letter that corresponds to the correct answer.

- A. verb
- B. adverb
- C. adjective

_____ 11. The story of Joseph and his brothers is *very* familiar to most Christians.

_____ 12. After throwing him into a pit, Joseph's brothers sold Joseph to slave traders, whose ways were probably *extremely* foreign to him.

_____ 13. Joseph *rather* quickly became a slave and a prisoner.

_____ 14. Because of his faith in God's providence, Joseph *always* remembered that God had a perfect plan for his life.

_____ 15. Despite their cruel treatment, Joseph *quite* willingly forgave his brothers.

_____ 16. In fact, Joseph *completely* surprised his brothers by his acts of kindness.

_____ 17. They feared his anger, yet he treated them *truly* graciously.

_____ 18. Joseph gave his brothers *much* better treatment than they deserved.

_____ 19. In the same way, God *lovingly* grants forgiveness to anyone who asks.

_____ 20. Though such forgiveness seems *nearly* impossible, with God's help, all Christians can act in a similar way.

Positive, Comparative, and Superlative Adverbs

For each sentence, write the correct form of the adverb in parentheses. Write in the blank the correct answer.

_____ 21. The Lord forgives ?. *(fully, positive)*

_____ 22. David knew ? than most about the Lord's forgiveness. *(well, comparative)*

_____ 23. David sinned ? against the Lord. *(grievously, positive)*

_____ 24. David ? begged the Lord for forgiveness. *(poignantly, positive)*

_____ 25. David prayed ? for cleansing than he ever had before. *(fervently, comparative)*

_____ 26. Though God chastened David in other ways, David perhaps suffered ? when the Lord took his infant son. *(intensely, superlative)*

_____ 27. David ? praised the Lord for restoring his soul. *(joyfully, positive)*

_____ 28. Among the many biblical examples of repentance and forgiveness, David's story probably comes to mind ?. *(frequently, superlative)*

_____ 29. Only Christians rest ? in their forgiveness, because Christians know the one, true God. *(confidently, positive)*

_____ 30. Because God is faithful to forgive penitent sinners, His people should praise Him ?. *(often, comparative)*

Name_____

Chapter 7: Prepositions, Conjunctions, Interjections

Adjectival and Adverbial Prepositional Phrases

Place parentheses around each prepositional phrase in each of the following sentences and write the object of the preposition in the blank. Sentences may include more than one prepositional phrase.

_____ 1. Approximately fifteen million people in the United States have a hearing impairment.

_____ 2. For many disabled people, the hearing impairment is not severe.

_____ 3. Those who suffer from mild hearing loss can often have normal hearing with the use of a hearing aid.

_____ 4. Two million people with some form of hearing impairment are completely deaf.

_____ 5. Because of prenatal defects, some people's auditory systems are damaged before birth.

Identify each italicized phrase as adjectival or adverbial. In the blank write the letter that corresponds to the correct answer.

    A. adjectival prepositional phrase
    B. adverbial prepositional phrase

_____ 6. Others acquire hearing loss *in their teenage or adult years.*

_____ 7. Prolonged exposure *to extremely loud noises* will most likely cause hearing loss.

_____ 8. Most deaf people in America can acquire a good means *of communication* through sign language.

_____ 9. Many people with normal hearing learn sign language so that they can interpret speech *for the hearing impaired.*

_____ 10. A deaf person can send and receive phone messages *over a special Text Telephone.*

Prepositions and Adverbs

Identify each italicized word as a preposition or an adverb. In the blank write the letter that corresponds to the correct answer.

    A. preposition
    B. adverb

_____ 11. Ludwig van Beethoven began losing his hearing in his twenties, and his hearing continually declined *past* his thirtieth birthday.

_____ 12. Most of Beethoven's music was written *before* his total loss of hearing.

_____ 13. He grew more melancholy and reclusive as the years went *past.*

Chapter 7 Review   445

_____ 14. As the end of his life drew *near,* Beethoven became completely deaf.

_____ 15. He did not cease to write music; instead, Beethoven composed some works that were more beautiful than he had ever *before* written.

Conjunctions
Underline the conjunction in each sentence. Determine which parts of the sentence the conjunction joins. In the blank write the letter that corresponds to the correct answer.

_____ 16. People rarely think about their ears or their ears' structure.
A. objects of preposition
B. predicate adjectives
C. predicate nouns

_____ 17. The auricle and the external auditory canal are the visible parts of the outer ear.
A. direct objects
B. subjects
C. prepositional phrases

_____ 18. Some people can move and even wiggle their ears because of the muscles attaching the auricle to the head.
A. direct objects
B. adjectives
C. predicates

_____ 19. The small but visible opening in the ear is the external auditory canal.
A. subjects
B. adjectives
C. adverbs

_____ 20. The canal separates the outer ear from the eardrum and the middle ear.
A. direct objects
B. predicate nouns
C. objects of preposition

Conjunctions and Interjections
In the following sentences underline each coordinating or correlative conjunction once and each interjection twice.

21. My friend Wanda is deaf, but she and I still have much in common.
22. I decided to take sign language classes so that she and I can communicate better.
23. Wow! The class is both interesting and challenging!
24. Sign language is a silent yet expressive form of communication.
25. Well, as a result of taking the class, I hope to begin a deaf ministry in my church or my community.

Name_____

Chapter 8: Phrases and Clauses

Phrases and Clauses
Label each italicized group of words *P* (phrase), *IC* (independent clause), or *DC* (dependent clause).

_____ 1. *Because a rose is one of the most beautiful flowers*, it is a favorite of many flower lovers.

_____ 2. The three main classes of cultivated roses *are old roses, perpetual roses, and the everblooming hybrids*.

_____ 3. Since old roses bloom only once a year, *flower lovers watch carefully for them in early summer*.

_____ 4. Perpetual roses bloom *in early summer and in fall*.

_____ 5. The everblooming hybrids *bloom almost constantly during the growing season*.

_____ 6. *Because roses come in diverse shades of pink, red, yellow, and white*, the perfect color can be found for almost any occasion.

_____ 7. *The most popular garden roses are the hybrid roses*, which are bred from two different varieties.

_____ 8. The climbing and rambler roses were given their names *because they climb trellises and fences*.

_____ 9. Even after they reach full maturity, *some miniature roses have flowers only the size of a nickel*.

_____ 10. Unfortunately, thorns *are attached to the stems of many roses*.

Simple, Compound, Complex Sentences
Label each sentence *S* (simple), *Cd* (compound), or *Cx* (complex). Underline the subjects once and the verbs twice in each clause.

_____ 11. *Daisy* comes from the Old English words for *day's eye*.

_____ 12. It is called this because some daisies, like a human eye, close at night and open at dawn.

_____ 13. While the center of the daisy is made of tiny disk flowers, the outside is made of petal-like ray flowers.

_____ 14. The oxeye daisy is a common plant with a center of tiny yellow flowers, and its center is surrounded by white petals.

_____ 15. The daisy blossom normally measures about two inches.

Chapter 8 Review 447

Adjective Clauses

Place parentheses around the adjective clause in each sentence. Underline the relative pronoun once and the word modified twice.

16. A violet has petals that are heart shaped.
17. Violets, whose blossoms are some of the most beautiful, grow in most of the world.
18. The United States, which is home to one hundred species of violets, contains only one-fifth of the total variety of violets.
19. Violets come in many colors, but blue and purple are the colors that I like best.
20. The violet, which is the flower for March, is also the state flower for four states.

Combining Sentences Using Adjective Clauses

Combine each set of sentences to form a complex sentence. Use the relative pronouns *that, who, whom, whose,* and *which* in your answers.

   Example: Darnita gave her mother a carnation. Darnita loves flowers.
   Answer: Darnita, who loves flowers, gave her mother a carnation.

21. Carnations are colorful flowers. Carnations have many blossoms.

22. Carnations are related to flowers called pinks. Carnations originally came from Europe.

23. A carnation's length can be three feet. A carnation can be pink, red, white, or yellow.

24. My mother gardens extensively. She has many carnation plants.

25. Her garden gets most of its color from the carnation plants. The garden is very beautiful.

Chapter 8 Review

Name_____

Chapter 9: Verbals and Verbal Phrases

Participles
Underline the participles. Draw an arrow to the noun or pronoun the participle modifies. In the blank, identify each participle as a present participle *(present)* or a past participle *(past)*.

_____ 1. Earthquakes are frightful and damaging natural disasters.

_____ 2. Shifting rock plates deep in the earth usually cause the severe shakes that occur during an earthquake.

_____ 3. The result of an earthquake is often ruined homes and collapsed buildings.

_____ 4. Fires begun by the earthquake damage can also be a serious hazard.

_____ 5. The very landscape of an area can be changed by a single ravaging earthquake.

Gerunds
Underline the gerunds in the following sentences. In the blank provided, identify the noun function of the gerund you underlined *(S, DO, IO, PN, OP)*.

_____ 6. An earthquake usually begins near an opening between the earth's rock plates, known as a fault.

_____ 7. Sometimes the sliding of the plates places too much stress on the rocks.

_____ 8. The dangerous result is often the cracking of the rock plates.

_____ 9. The epicenter designates the beginning of an earthquake on the earth's surface.

_____ 10. The breaking of the earth's crust starts at the epicenter and moves outward.

Differentiating Between Participles and Gerunds
Underline the gerunds and present participles. Identify each underlined word as a gerund *(G)* or a participle *(P)*.

_____ 11. Seismographs are used by scientists for earthquake gauging.

_____ 12. The measuring scale scientists use is the Richter scale.

_____ 13. Any earthquake registering over a 7.0 on the Richter scale is potentially very destructive.

_____ 14. The moment magnitude scale is used for earthquakes ranking above a 7.0.

_____ 15. The recording of a 9.5 earthquake on the coast of Chile broke the record for the strongest recorded earthquake on the moment magnitude scale.

Chapter 9 Review

Infinitives
Questions 16-20: Underline the infinitives in the paragraph.

The damage caused by earthquakes can be devastating to towns and cities. During a quake, the ground itself has been known to rise into the air. The shaking causes homes to collapse and buildings to tumble. To add to the destruction, broken power lines may cause fires. Earthquakes in the ocean cause powerful waves called tsunamis to hit on the coasts, causing severe flooding. Earthquakes are among the most severe and terrifying natural disasters.

Participles, Gerunds, Infinitives
Underline the verbals (not the entire verbal phrases) in the following sentences. If the verbal is a modifier, draw an arrow to the word it modifies. If the verbal functions as a noun, identify its function in the blank *(S, DO, IO, PN, OP)*.

_____ 21. The San Andreas Fault, located generally along the coast of California, is the source of numerous earthquakes.

_____ 22. On April 18, 1906, at 5:13 A.M., San Francisco residents were awakened by a dreadful rumbling.

_____ 23. The most destructive action of the 1906 earthquake was the starting of a three-day fire that devastated most of the city.

_____ 24. Minutes before game three of the 1989 World Series, an earthquake struck Candlestick Park. To evacuate was difficult for the thousands of spectators.

_____ 25. Sliding plates along the fault in California are the cause of these destructive earthquakes.

Chapter 10: Subject-Verb Agreement

Agreement
Questions 1-5: Find the errors in agreement in the following paragraph. Rewrite the paragraph correctly in the space provided.

My family moved west last year to help settle the Northwest Territory. We spent many days and weeks building our farm. Our farm contain many different types of animals and buildings. My father add new buildings every time we have a little extra money. Our barns rise high in the sky. They look very large. We keeps hay, animals, and equipment in our barns. Sometimes I sleep in the hayloft, but my mother lets me sleep out there only when it is warm outside. My favorite activity are to gather corn in the fields at harvest time. During the first week after harvest, my mother make corn pudding.

Verbs *Be, Have, Do*
In the blank write the correct form of *be, have,* or *do* to complete the sentence.

_____Does_____ Example: _?_ the Leaning Tower of Pisa really lean? *(do)*

_____ 6. _?_ you know who led the Continental army during the Revolutionary War? *(do)*

_____ 7. George Washington _?_ many farmers and untrained young men under his command. *(have)*

_____ 8. _?_ the colonies win their independence from Great Britain after the Revolutionary War? *(do)*

_____ 9. George Washington _?_ the first president of the United States. *(be)*

_____ 10. _?_ you ever studied Washington or the Revolutionary War? *(have)*

Agreement with Indefinite Pronouns
Underline the verb in parentheses that agrees with the subject of the sentence.

11. One of the first permanent settlements in America *(was, were)* Jamestown.
12. All of the colonists in the new settlement *(was, were)* led by Captain John Smith.
13. Many of the historians *(records, record)* some of the difficulties the first colonists encountered during those first few years.
14. Some of the history books *(show, shows)* that the first representative legislature, the House of Burgesses, met in Jamestown in 1619.
15. Many of the historical facts about our country *(help, helps)* us understand our heritage.

Agreement with Compound Subjects
Underline the verb in parentheses that agrees with the subject of the sentence.

16. Elliot and Harrison *(reviews, review)* their notes before each test.
17. Neither Elliot nor Harrison *(remembers, remember)* that the gold rush began in 1848.
18. Either the test or the quizzes *(contains, contain)* important facts about the colonial period.
19. Pioneers and prospectors *(was, were)* significant in building the towns of the far West.
20. Either a river boat or a covered wagon *(was, were)* used as a settler's main transportation.

Agreement: Intervening Phrases, Predicate Nouns, and Inverted Order
Circle the subject of each sentence. Underline the verb in parentheses that agrees with the subject.

21. The students in the elementary school *(walk, walks)* along the same trail the Cherokees walked in 1838.
22. Many of the students *(imagine, imagines)* the suffering that took place along the Trail of Tears.
23. The Indians' biggest trial *(was, were)* the many deaths that occurred along the trail.
24. Where *(do, does)* the Cherokees live today?
25. There *(is, are)* many American Indians living in the southwestern states.

Chapter 11: Pronoun-Antecedent Agreement

Agreement with Personal Pronouns
Fill in each blank with a pronoun that agrees with its antecedent.

_____ 1. Hannah, a godly woman with no children, prayed desperately that God would give _?_ a son.

_____ 2. The Lord blessed Hannah, and _?_ was given a son.

_____ 3. Hannah named her son Samuel; _?_ name means "asked of God."

_____ 4. Samuel's parents knew that he was a special child, and _?_ dedicated him to the Lord.

_____ 5. When Samuel's parents took him to live in the temple, the separation was not easy for _?_.

_____ 6. Each year, Hannah made a special coat and took _?_ to Samuel.

_____ 7. Samuel understood that God had taken _?_ away from his family to prepare him for a special ministry.

_____ 8. His parents knew that _?_ son would be taught to serve the Lord.

_____ 9. Eli, Eli's three sons, and Samuel worked in the temple, and _?_ also served as their home.

_____ 10. Neither Eli nor his three sons were diligent in _?_ responsibilities.

_____ 11. One night Samuel heard a voice calling _?_.

_____ 12. Perhaps Eli and his sons could not hear the Lord's voice because of sin in _?_ lives.

_____ 13. God said that Eli and his sons would be punished for _?_ sins.

_____ 14. Neither the sons nor Eli turned from _?_ sin.

_____ 15. During _?_ many years in the temple, God was preparing Samuel for an important ministry to the whole nation of Israel.

Agreement with Indefinite Pronouns
Identify the pronoun that agrees with the antecedent. In the blank write the letter that corresponds to the correct answer.

_____ 16. Later in Samuel's life, another of God's calls came, and _?_ was very important.
   A. it
   B. they
   C. them

_____ 17. Samuel's job was to inform someone of _?_ being chosen as the king of Israel.
   A. their
   B. her
   C. his

_____ 18. At first, few in the nation of Israel were dissatisfied with _?_ new king, Saul.
   A. their
   B. his
   C. its

_____ 19. Most of the Israelites were disappointed when _?_ new king began to grow prideful and to turn away from the Lord.
   A. their
   B. his
   C. its

_____ 20. Many in Israel were fearful when Saul disobeyed the Lord by offering sacrifices before _?_ prophet Samuel arrived.
   A. her
   B. its
   C. their

_____ 21. None of the people were surprised when _?_ leader was rebuked by the prophet.
   A. his
   B. its
   C. their

_____ 22. Neither Saul nor his son Jonathan would be able to retain _?_ claim to the throne.
   A. his
   B. their
   C. its

_____ 23. Both Saul and Jonathan would lose _?_ lives in a battle.
   A. his
   B. its
   C. their

_____ 24. No one was more surprised than David about _?_ being chosen as the future king.
   A. his
   B. its
   C. their

_____ 25. Most of the Israelites were excited to see Samuel anoint _?_ new king.
   A. its
   B. their
   C. his

Name_____

Chapter 12: Pronoun Usage

Subjective, Objective, and Possessive Cases
For each sentence, underline the correct pronoun choice in parentheses.

1. The history of the United States is extremely important to *(you and I, you and me)*.
2. Because the people who settled this country came from many different parts of the world, *(they, them)* had to overcome many cultural differences.
3. The people and *(them, their)* descendants had to learn to live together peacefully.
4. Cooperation and patriotism helped the country and *(it, its)* people survive the hardships.
5. *(We, Us)* should imitate their attitude of cooperation and patriotism.
6. Early decisions about government, religion, and other things affect *(we, us)* even today.
7. *(You and I, You and me)* should be thankful for the sacrifice on the part of our ancestors.
8. *(We, Us)* have prospered because of the foresight of our Founding Fathers.

We, Us, Who, or *Whom*
Choose the correct pronoun to complete the sentence. Write in the blank the letter that corresponds to the correct answer.

A. we
B. us
C. who
D. whom

_____ 9. _?_ students learned about Roman history in school this year.

_____ 10. _?_ was one of the greatest Roman military leaders?

_____ 11. For _?_ did Julius Caesar make many improvements?

_____ 12. One of his most valuable improvements for _?_ was his new calendar.

_____ 13. By _?_ was Caesar betrayed?

_____ 14. _?_ was considered to be one of the best Roman orators and writers?

_____ 15. _?_ studied Caesar's direct and clear style of writing.

Problem Pronouns
Underline the correct word from the choices in parentheses.

16. *(Your, You're)* studying the ancient Greek philosophers in your history class, right?
17. *(Their, They're)* philosophies are very interesting!
18. *(Whose, Who's)* philosophy do you find most interesting?
19. *(Its, It's)* the philosophy that combines knowledge and wisdom.
20. *(Theirs, There's)* no completely true philosophy outside of the Bible.

Courtesy Order and Reflexive/Intensive Pronouns
Underline the correct word from the choices in parentheses.

21. The make-up history test was given to *(he, him, himself)* and *(I, me, myself)*.
22. *(She, I, Me)* and *(she, I, me)* had studied ancient history for hours the night before.
23. *(He, You, Him)* and *(he, him, you)* have one hour to complete the exam.
24. *(He, I, me)* and *(He, I, me)* finished at the same time.
25. Only one point differed between the scores of *(he, you, him)* and *(he, you, him)*.

Clear Pronoun Reference
Identify each sentence as having correct or incorrect pronoun reference. Write in the blank the letter that corresponds to the correct answer. If you choose *B*, rewrite the sentence correctly in the space provided.

    A. correct sentence
    B. incorrect pronoun reference

_____ 26. Diannah and Kay studied ancient Greece and Rome. They were full of adventure.

_____ 27. Diannah asked Kay whether she could explain the *Odyssey*.

_____ 28. Although the *Odyssey* tells the adventures of Odysseus and his crew, it also portrays the inner struggle between pride and wisdom.

_____ 29. Odysseus finally returned, but it was not what he expected.

_____ 30. Kay told Diannah that she should learn from the victories and failures of Odysseus.

456   Chapter 12 Review

Name_____

Chapter 13: Using Adjectives and Adverbs Correctly

Adjective or Adverb?
Choose the correct word to complete the sentence. In the blank write the letter that corresponds to the correct answer.

_____ 1. Don Quixote lived ? in La Mancha and owned a scrawny horse.
   A. comfortable
   B. comfortably

_____ 2. Fiction books about knighthood and Don Quixote's own imagination ? caused his complete insanity.
   A. quick
   B. quickly

_____ 3. He left LaMancha with his ? squire, Sancho, and began a new life as a knight.
   A. faithful
   B. faithfully

_____ 4. Cumbersome armor and a cardboard helmet were his ? attire.
   A. knight
   B. knightly

_____ 5. Green ribbons held Don Quixote's helmet together but prevented its ? removal at night.
   A. quick
   B. quickly

_____ 6. As Don Quixote and Sancho traveled the countryside, they became ? with the injustice in the world.
   A. unhappy
   B. unhappily

_____ 7. Don Quixote's scrawny horse and Sancho's donkey were the ? men's knightly transportation.
   A. brave
   B. bravely

_____ 8. Don Quixote imagined an ? village girl as an important lady and renamed her Empress of La Mancha.
   A. ordinary
   B. ordinarily

_____ 9. Thirty or forty windmills seemed to be giants to Don Quixote and appeared ? .
   A. dangerous
   B. dangerously

_____ 10. Students should read all of *Don Quixote* and enjoy his ? humorous adventures.
   A. extreme
   B. extremely

Chapter 13 Review   457

Adjective and Adverb Comparisons
In the blank write the comparative or superlative form of the word in parentheses.

_____ 11. Miguel de Cervantes served in the military, but he is _?_ for writing novels and plays. *(popular)*

_____ 12. *Don Quixote* and *Novelas ejemplares* are two of his works that are read _?_. *(often)*

_____ 13. *Don Quixote* was the _?_ book that brought him fame. *(influential)*

_____ 14. His and his shipmates' capture and enslavement in 1575 in Algiers were _?_ than his writing career. *(perilous)*

_____ 15. The _?_ events of his captivity, such as his escape attempts, contributed to some plot elements in *Don Quixote*. *(exciting)*

Good/Well and *Bad/Badly*
Choose *good, well, bad,* or *badly* to fill in each blank and complete the following sentences.

_____ 16. During the Middle Ages, knights were military men who could fight _?_ with a sword.

_____ 17. In order to be a knight, one was required to have a strong horse and a _?_ suit of armor.

_____ 18. A knight would acquire a _?_ name if he were ever to act in a cowardly or discourteous manner.

_____ 19. Some knights treated the common people _?_, but true knights were expected to be self-sacrificing and generous.

_____ 20. We would do _?_ to imitate the loyalty, bravery, and good manners of the knights of the Middle Ages.

Double Negatives
Correct any double negatives in the following sentences. Write your corrections above the sentence. Write *C* in the blank if the sentence is correct.

_____ 21. Actual armored knights do not exist no more.

_____ 22. In the Middle Ages, no knight would go nowhere without his armor.

_____ 23. The armor was so extensive that often there was no part of the knight's body that was not protected.

_____ 24. Because the armor was so cumbersome, the knights sometimes could not get on their horses if no one didn't help them.

_____ 25. If an enemy could unseat his opponent, the fallen knight probably wouldn't never survive.

Name_____

Chapter 14: Using Troublesome Words Correctly

Troublesome Verbs

Choose the correct verb to complete the sentence. In the blank write the letter that corresponds to the correct answer.

_____ 1. Beautiful mountains all over the world _?_ majestically toward the heavens.
   A. rise
   B. raise

_____ 2. Rock climbing enthusiasts _?_ often view these mountains as challenges to be conquered.
   A. will
   B. shall

_____ 3. Rock climbers often _?_ a specific date for rock climbing.
   A. sit
   B. set

_____ 4. Rock climbing _?_ a climber's level of stamina and endurance.
   A. rises
   B. raises

_____ 5. When beginning the climb, nearly everything has to be _?_ aside so that the climber is not weighed down.
   A. sit
   B. set

_____ 6. More advanced rock climbers choose trails where they have to _?_ flat on their stomachs to finish the course.
   A. lie
   B. lay

_____ 7. I think that competition makes the adventure _?_ to a new level of intensity.
   A. rise
   B. raise

_____ 8. _?_ I help you put your equipment on?
   A. Will
   B. Shall

_____ 9. After this climb I think that I'll go home and _?_ down.
   A. lay
   B. lie

_____ 10. When we finish our work around the house, _?_ we go rock climbing again?
   A. may
   B. can

Chapter 14 Review   459

Troublesome Words
Underline the correct word from the choices in parentheses.

11. Rock climbers *(where, wear)* special climbing equipment.
12. Checking the equipment carefully means the climber will have *(fewer, less)* problems.
13. A good instructor will *(learn, teach)* a beginner to trust his partner and his equipment.
14. The view from the top of the mountain is *(quite, quiet)* amazing.
15. Be careful of *(loose, lose)* rocks and footholds!
16. *(To, Two)* rules to follow when learning to rock climb are to keep going and to be conscientious.
17. Rock climbing is not the only exciting activity; *(alot, a lot)* of people find mountain biking enjoyable as well.
18. Before mountain bikers start on the journey, they make sure everything on their bike is *(alright, all right)*.
19. My sister and I are known as the best mountain bikers *(between, among)* our friends.
20. "Be sure to *(bring, take)* that water bottle back with you," my mother said before we left for a day of mountain biking.
21. I grabbed a peanut butter and jelly sandwich and *(a, an)* apple for my lunch on the trail.
22. The leader of our group rode *(past, passed)* a huge tree trunk in the middle of the trail.
23. My jacket got caught on a *(piece, peace)* of wood sticking out of the ground.
24. *(Accept, Except)* for a skinned knee, the trip went smoothly.
25. *(Why do, How come)* accidents seem always to happen to me?

Name_____

Chapter 15: Capitalization

People and Places
Questions 1-10: Circle the capitalization errors in the following paragraph.

My parents, robert and wendy bodine, are missionaries in Brazil. Since my family is originally from Michigan's upper peninsula, we were unprepared for the hot, humid weather. Since I have lived here in south America, I have hiked in parts of the Andes mountains and rafted down the Amazon river. One of my favorite places to visit is the snow-capped Aconcagua. It is the highest mountain in the western hemisphere. The Moon seems especially bright out in the country where we live. In fact, sometimes my family enjoys camping out under the stars. However, we often visit brasilia, Brazil's capital, when we want to vacation in a city.

Cultural and Historical Terms
Identify the word that is an example of a capitalization error. In the blank write the letter that corresponds to the correct answer.

_____ 11. Venezuela declared its independence from Spain on july 15, 1811.
  A. Independence
  B. July
  C. no error

_____ 12. The official language of Venezuela is spanish.
  A. venezuela
  B. Spanish
  C. no error

_____ 13. Christopher Columbus landed in Venezuela in a.d. 1498.
  A. columbus
  B. venezuela
  C. A.D.

_____ 14. The Venezuelan race is a mixture of Caucasian, African, and American indian blood.
  A. caucasian
  B. african
  C. Indian

_____ 15. The name *Venezuela* is Spanish for *little venice*.
  A. Name
  B. spanish
  C. *Little Venice*

Chapter 15 Review 461

Titles, First Words, Parts of Letters

Identify the word that is an example of a capitalization error. In the blank write the letter that corresponds to the correct answer.

_____ 16. Recently, I read a short article about Chile in *time* magazine.
   A. chile
   B. *Time*
   C. Magazine

_____ 17. The article categorized facts about the Chilean people in the following way:
   I. People
      A. Language
      B. Ancestry
      C. population
   II. Way of Life
      A. Rural life
      B. Urban life

   A. language
   B. Population
   C. rural

_____ 18. one of the most beautiful sections of the country is Chile's southern landscape.
   A. One
   B. Country
   C. Southern

_____ 19. I wrote a letter to missionaries in Chile. "Dear friends" was my greeting to them.
   A. Missionaries
   B. dear
   C. Friends

_____ 20. I asked my mother, "do you think I could go on the missionary trip to Chile?"
   A. Mother
   B. Do
   C. Missionary

Proper Adjectives and Single Letters as Words

Find the capitalization error in each sentence and write the word correctly in the blank. If there is no capitalization error, write *C* in the blank.

_____ 21. De Alencar, a Brazilian author, wrote his book *o Guarani* in 1857.

_____ 22. Did you know that the sculpture of Antonio Lisboa ranks among the earliest examples of Brazil's colonial art?

_____ 23. Before its independence, Brazil was one of portugal's colonies.

_____ 24. I studied hard and received an a on my geography test on Brazil.

_____ 25. Brazil's history interests me; someday i would like to visit there.

Name_____

Chapter 16: Punctuation

End Marks, Periods, and Commas
Insert missing end marks, periods, and commas in each sentence.

1. Idaho has majestic mountains rushing rapids peaceful lakes and steep canyons
2. Boise which is the capital of Idaho is located in the southwestern section
3. Although potatoes are the most profitable crop in Idaho beef and dairy cattle are another source of income
4. Landon Fister Jr gets up at 5:00 AM to watch the beautiful sunrise over the Sawtooth Mountains in Idaho
5. My brother lives at 12 Luray Dr Idaho Falls ID 83415

Semicolons, Colons, and Quotation Marks
Identify the punctuation mark missing from each sentence; identify also quotation marks that should be removed. Write the letter that corresponds to the correct answer.

      A. semicolon
      B. colon
      C. quotation marks
      D. remove quotation marks

_____ 6. "Here's a list of study facts for the test": agricultural resources, mineral resources, and other resources.

_____ 7. Prospectors discovered gold during the 1860s thousands of miners rushed to Idaho to make their fortunes.

_____ 8. Did you know that the state's leading mineral products include the following silver, phosphate rock, and gold?

_____ 9. My teacher told us "that she wanted us to know everything in our notes and our reading."

_____ 10. I think this is your highest grade, my teacher told me.

Quotation Marks, Italics, Apostrophes, and Hyphens
Underline the word in parentheses that is written correctly.

11. The name (Idaho, *Idaho*) became official after the region split from the Oregon territory.
12. Idaho's state song is ("Here We Have Idaho," *Here We Have Idaho*).
13. The (elk's, elks') head on the state flag represents wildlife.
14. Nearly (three-fifths, three fifths) of Idaho's people live in urban areas.
15. Scientists near Idaho Falls built a model reactor for the first nuclear submarine, the (*Nautilus,* "Nautilus").
16. In the early (1900s, 1900's), engineers completed a canal on the Columbia River.
17. All of Idaho's (forty four, forty-four) counties contain valuable mineral deposits.

Chapter 16 Review   463

18. Because of the huge mountains, Idaho is a (skier's, skiers) paradise.
19. The first newspaper in Idaho was the (Golden Age, *Golden Age*).
20. "Did you know that your great-grandfather sold (newspapers"?, newspapers?") my mother asked.

All Punctuation Marks
Add punctuation marks to the following sentences: periods, question marks, exclamation points, commas, semicolons, colons, quotation marks, apostrophes, hyphens, and parentheses. Also add underlining for italics.

21. Many tourists vacation in Idaho because of the skiing camping and white water rafting my favorite activity
22. Water is said to be Idahos most valuable resource it is apparent that Idaho has no water shortage
23. Here is a list of Idahos biggest newspapers Idaho Statesman Post-Register Tribune Times-News and Idaho State Journal
24. Mom do you think we could visit Idaho I asked
25. Idaho is absolutely beautiful

Name_____

Chapter 17: Spelling

Verbs and Nouns
In the blank write the correct singular present-tense form or plural form of each italicized word.

_____ 1. In Miss Bell's literature class, Trent *study* Anne Bradstreet, a seventeenth century poet who lived in early America.

_____ 2. Miss Bell *enjoy* teaching students about poetry and tells them that Bradstreet, born in England in 1612, probably experienced the comforts of a prosperous family, a fine home, and fashionable clothing.

_____ 3. As a young lady, Bradstreet developed her abilities in music and art with the aid of paid *tutor*.

_____ 4. In 1628, she married Simon Bradstreet, who took her away from England to the rocky *beach* of New England.

_____ 5. Trent wonders whether many other young *wife* had similar experiences.

_____ 6. Although Bradstreet sometimes wished she were back in England, Trent *wish* he could travel to a new place.

_____ 7. Trent *fix* his heart to depend on the Lord just as Anne Bradstreet set her mind on God and His goodness.

_____ 8. She grew to love her new home as she lovingly cared for her husband and *child*.

_____ 9. In the unrefined settlements of New England, Bradstreet used her literary *ability* to write sophisticated and powerful poetry.

_____ 10. Bradstreet endured many difficult *loss*, but her confidence in God allowed her to become a successful wife, mother, and poet.

***ie* or *ei* and Suffixes**
Identify the correctly spelled word to complete each sentence. In the blank write the letter that corresponds to the correct answer.

_____ 11. Anne Bradstreet's poetry reveals the ? and hardships of a strong Puritan.
A. happyness
B. happiness

_____ 12. She found time for ? even while maintaining a stable home for her husband and children.
A. writing
B. writeing

Chapter 17 Review 465

_____ 13. Her highly _?_ husband, Simon Bradstreet, was an important figure in the Massachusetts Bay Colony.
   A. esteemmed
   B. esteemed

_____ 14. In 1650, several of Bradstreet's poems were published in London in a collection entitled *The Tenth Muse _?_ Sprung Up in America*.
   A. *Lately*
   B. *Latly*

_____ 15. Some of the best _?_ poems of Anne Bradstreet are about nature and are in a collection called *Contemplations*.
   A. received
   B. recieved

_____ 16. Her best poems are those that relate her own dramatic personal _?_.
   A. expereinces
   B. experiences

_____ 17. Bradstreet's poem "Upon the Burning of Our House" shows not only the _?_ of sorrow but also the calm acceptance after the loss of her home.
   A. wieght
   B. weight

_____ 18. She reveals her love and _?_ for her husband in "To My Dear and Loving Husband."
   A. gratefulness
   B. gratfulness

_____ 19. In _?_ two poems about the death of two of her grandchildren, Bradstreet shows the steadfast yet tender heart of a Puritan.
   A. completeing
   B. completing

_____ 20. In all of her writings, Anne Bradstreet establishes a firm acceptance that all things are _?_ by God.
   A. controlled
   B. controled

Questions 21-25: Underline the spelling errors in the following paragraph. In the spaces above them, correctly spell the words that you underlined.

The source of Anne Bradstreet's peace and happiness was not the absence of hardship and disappointtment. On July 16, 1666, she awoke and percieved that her home was burning. Although this great loss was extremly difficult, she did not despair. Anne Bradstreet knew that her true home was in heaven. She accepted the loss of her belonginges on earth as a loveing reminder that her treasure was in heaven.

Glossary of Terms

Action verb: A verb that tells what someone or something does. (3)

Active voice: Verb usage that creates a sentence in which the subject does the action. (3)

Adjective: A word that modifies a noun or pronoun. An adjective tells *what kind, which one, how many,* or *whose* about the noun it modifies. (5)

Adjective clause: A dependent clause modifying a noun or pronoun. (8)

Adverb: A word that modifies a verb, adjective, or another adverb. An adverb tells *where, when, how,* or *to what extent* about the word it modifies. (6)

Antecedent: The word or phrase that a pronoun replaces; usually comes before the pronoun. (4, 11, 12)

Antonym: A word that means the opposite of another word. (18)

Appendix: Information in a book additional to the regular text; may include charts, diagrams, long lists, and notes of explanation. (19)

Article: An adjective showing a noun's definite or indefinite meaning; the definite article *the* shows specific things; the indefinite articles *a* (precedes a consonant sound) and *an* (precedes a vowel sound) show nonspecific things. (5)

Auxiliary: A verb that helps the main verb express a complete thought or special meaning. (3)

Being verb: A verb that tells what someone or something is; usually acts as a linking verb. (3)

Bibliography: Usually found in the back of a book; lists either books the author used in writing the text or the titles of additional books about the same subject. (19)

Case: The characteristic of a noun or pronoun that reflects the way the word is used in the sentence. Pronouns have three case forms: subjective (sometimes called nominative), objective, and possessive. (4, 12)

Clause: A group of words that has both a subject and a predicate. Two types of clauses are independent and dependent clauses. (8)

Comma splice: The error that results when two sentences are incorrectly joined by only a comma. (1)

Common noun: A general word for a person, place, thing, or idea; the opposite of a proper noun. (2)

Comparative form: An adjective or adverb form used to describe two things being compared; usually formed by adding *er* or *more* to the positive form of the word. (5, 6)

Complete predicate: The complete verb and its modifiers and completers. It describes the subject or tells about the subject's action. (1)

Complete subject: The simple subject and its modifiers. It tells what the sentence is about. (1)

Complete verb: The main verb and any auxiliaries; they work together as the simple predicate in a clause. (3)

Complex sentence: A sentence having one independent clause and at least one dependent clause. (8)

Compound noun: A noun formed by joining two or more words to make a new word; sometimes written as one word and sometimes hyphenated. (2)

Compound predicate: Two or more simple predicates or verbs joined by a conjunction. (1)

Compound sentence: A sentence having two or more independent clauses. (8)

Compound subject: Two or more simple subjects joined by a conjunction. (1)

Conjunction: A connecting word that joins words or groups of words in a sentence. (7, 8)

Contraction: A shortened one-word form made from two separate words; contains an apostrophe instead of the missing letters; examples include *don't, can't,* and *won't.* (6, 14, 16)

Coordinating conjunction: A connecting word that joins sentence parts of the same type; common examples are *and, but, or, nor,* and *yet.* (7)

Correlative conjunctions: Connecting words which always occur in pairs to join parts of equal grammatical type. (7)

Count noun: A common noun that can be made plural to show *how many* and may be introduced with number words such as *one* or *many;* making a singular count noun plural does not change its meaning. (2)

Declarative sentence: A sentence that makes a statement and ends with a period. (1)

Demonstrative pronoun: A pronoun that points out the position of objects, persons, or places. *This, that, these,* and *those* are demonstrative pronouns. (4)

Dependent clause: A clause that cannot stand alone as a sentence. A dependent clause has a subject and a predicate but contains some other word that makes it express an incomplete thought. (8)

Dewey Decimal system: A system of organizing library books; developed by Melvil Dewey; based on the division of knowledge into ten categories. (18)

Direct object: A noun or pronoun in the predicate that receives the action of a transitive verb; answers the question *whom?* or *what?* after the verb. (3)

Double comparison: An error created by using two comparative words together, such as *more better.* (13)

Double negative: An error created by using a negative word and the adverb *not* in the same sentence. (13)

Etymology: The history of a word's origin and the changes it has experienced. (18)

Exclamatory sentence: A sentence that expresses strong emotion or feeling and ends with an exclamation point. (1)

Fiction: Books and other works that are based on imagination. (18)

Fragment: A group of words wrongly punctuated and capitalized as a complete sentence. (1)

Fused sentence: The error that results when two or more sentences are incorrectly joined with no punctuation or conjunction. (1)

Gender: The classification of third-person singular pronouns into masculine, feminine, and neuter. (4, 11)

Gerund: A verb form working as a noun; always ends in *ing,* attached to the first principal part; looks like the present participle. (9)

Gerund phrase: A gerund plus any of its modifiers. (9)

Imperative sentence: A sentence that gives a command or request and ends with a period or exclamation point; usually has understood *you* as its subject. (1)

Indefinite pronoun: A pronoun that refers to persons and things in general terms. It refers to a large category, or part of a large category, without definitely specifying the particular individual or part. (4, 10, 11)

Independent clause: A clause that can stand alone as a sentence and that expresses a complete thought. (8)

Independent possessive: A possessive word that replaces a noun or a pronoun and its adjectives. (5)

Index: An alphabetical listing of key words and phrases with all the page numbers on which they appear in the text. (19)

Indirect object: A noun or pronoun in the predicate that (without a preposition) tells *to whom* or *for whom* the action is done. It always appears after the verb and before the direct object. (3)

Infinitive: A verb form working as a noun, adjective, or adverb; formed by *to* followed by the first principal part of the verb. (9)

Infinitive phrase: An infinitive plus all of its modifiers. (9)

Intensive pronoun: A personal pronoun ending in *self* or *selves* emphasizing an already stated noun or pronoun in the sentence. (4, 12)

Interjection: A word, or sometimes a phrase, that can stand alone, be punctuated as a sentence, or appear along with a regular sentence in which it takes no real part; often expresses strong feeling and is often called an *isolate.* (7)

Interrogative pronoun: A pronoun used to ask a question. *Which, what, who, whom,* and *whose* are examples. (4)

Interrogative sentence: A sentence that asks a question and ends with a question mark; often uses inverted order. (1)

Intervening phrase: A group of words that comes between the subject and the verb of a sentence; common interrupters are negative phrases and prepositional phrases. (10)

Intransitive verb: A verb that does not need an object to express a complete thought. This verb does not send action toward anything or anyone. It occurs in the pattern S-InV. (3)

Inverted order: A sentence organization which places the verb before the subject; found in most interrogative and some declarative sentences and sentences beginning with *there* and *here.* (1, 10)

Linking verb: A verb that functions like an equal sign, linking the subject with a word that renames or describes the subject (a predicate noun or a predicate adjective). It appears in either of these patterns: S-LV-PA or S-LV-PN. (3)

Modifier: A word that describes another word; adjectives and adverbs are examples. (5, 6)

Noncount noun: A common noun that cannot be made plural. (2)

Nonfiction: Books or works not based on imagination; true accounts. (18)

Noun: The name of a person, place, thing, or idea. (2)

Noun of direct address: The name of a person or thing to which a sentence is directed. (16)

Number: The classification of noun forms and personal pronouns telling whether the noun or pronoun is singular or plural. (4, 10, 11)

Object of the preposition: The noun or pronoun (simple object) that follows the preposition and that the preposition relates to the rest of the sentence. The complete object of the preposition is the simple object and its modifiers. (7)

Objective case: The case of nouns or pronouns working as objects; includes uses as direct objects, indirect objects, and objects of prepositions. (4, 12)

Participle: A verb form working as an adjective; carries the action of a verb but modifies a noun or pronoun. (9)

Participial phrase: A participle plus any of its modifiers; followed by a comma when beginning a sentence. (9)

Passive voice: Verb usage which creates a sentence in which the subject is acted upon; passive verbs contain a form of *be* plus a past participle verb form. (3)

Person: The classification of personal pronouns into first person (the speaker), second person (the person spoken to), and third person (the person spoken about). (4)

Personal pronoun: One of the pronouns that are distinguished by person, number, gender, and case. (4)

Phrase: A word group that does not contain both a subject and a predicate. (8)

Positive form: An adjective or adverb form used to describe only one item. (5, 6)

Possessive case: The case of nouns or pronouns used to show ownership; does not use apostrophes. (4)

Predicate: The part of the sentence that asserts something about the subject. It includes the main verb in the sentence. (1, 3)

Predicate adjective: An adjective in the predicate that follows a linking verb and describes the subject. (3, 5)

Predicate noun: A noun or pronoun in the predicate that follows a linking verb and renames or identifies the subject. (3, 10)

Preposition: A word that relates its object (a noun or pronoun) to another word in the sentence; begins prepositional phrases. (7)

Prepositional phrase: A phrase consisting of a preposition and its complete object. Prepositional phrases may function as adjectives or adverbs. (7)

Present participle: The first principal part verb form plus *ing*. (9)

Progressive verb forms: Verbs that show continuing action or action in progress, made from a form of *be* plus an *ing* verb form. (3)

Pronoun: A word that replaces a noun or a noun and its modifiers. (4, 11, 12)

Pronoun-antecedent agreement: The correct use of singular pronouns with singular antecedents and of plural pronouns with plural antecedents. (11)

Pronoun reference: The relation of a pronoun to its antecedent. (12)

Proper adjective: An adjective made from a proper noun. A proper adjective must be capitalized. (5)

Proper noun: A specific name for a person, place, or thing. A proper noun must be capitalized and is a noncount noun. (2)

Reflexive pronoun: A personal pronoun ending in *self* or *selves* that works as an object to refer the verb's action back to the subject. (4, 12)

Relative pronoun: A word introducing an adjective clause and relating the clause to a noun or pronoun in the independent clause. (8)

Run-on sentence: Two or more sentences incorrectly joined with incorrect or no punctuation; usually called a *comma splice* or a *fused sentence*. (1)

Sentence: A group of words forming meaningful communication by expressing a complete thought and having both a subject and a predicate. (1)

Simple predicate: The main verb and any auxiliaries in the predicate of a clause. (1)

Simple sentence: A sentence having one independent clause and no dependent clauses. (8)

Simple subject: The main noun or pronoun in the subject of a clause. (1)

Subject: The part of the sentence that expresses what the sentence is about. It includes the main noun or pronoun in the sentence. (1)

Subjective case: The case of nouns and pronouns doing noun jobs, frequently serving as subjects. (4)

Subject-verb agreement: The correct use of singular subjects with singular verbs and of plural subjects with plural verbs. The first word of the complete verb agrees with the person and number of the subject. (10)

Superlative form: An adjective or adverb form used to describe three or more things being compared; usually formed by adding *-est* or *most* to the positive form of the word. (5, 6)

Synonym: A word which has similar or identical meaning to another word. (18)

Tense: Forms of a verb that indicate time, continuing action, completed action, or state of being. (3)

Transitive verb: A verb that needs a receiver for its action; occurs in the sentence patterns S-TrV-DO and S-TrV-IO-DO. (3)

Verb: A word that expresses action or state of being. (3, 9, 10)

Verbal: A verb form working as a noun, adjective, or adverb; verbals can be modified by adverbs just as verbs can. (9)

Verbal phrase: A verbal plus any of its modifiers. (9)

A

a, use of before consonant (ESL) 102
a/an 102, 287
accept/except 287
adjective
    adjective clause 171, 173-74
    article 102
    comparing with 99-100, 276
    correct usage of 269-72
    definition of 96-97
    diagramming of 96
    irregular, regular 99-100
    possessive noun 103-4
    possessive phrase 104
    possessive pronoun 103-4
    prepositional phrase as 135
    test frame for 96
adjective vs. adverb 269-70
adjectives not made plural (ESL) 109
adverb
    comparing with 122, 276
    correct usage of 269-77
    definition of 116-17
    diagramming of 120
    irregular, regular 122
    prepositional phrase as 135
adverb vs. preposition 137
agreement
    pronoun-antecedent 227-29, 231-32
    subject-verb 209-12, 214, 216, 219-20
ain't 287
almanac 382
alot/a lot 288
alright/all right 288
antecedent
    agreement of pronoun with 227-28, 231-32
    clarity of pronoun reference 256-57, 260-61
    compound 229
    definition of 78
apostrophe 340
article
    definite *(the)* 102
    definition of 102
    indefinite *(a/an)* 102
atlas 382
auxiliary
    definition of 52-53
    examples of 52-53

B

bad/badly 271-72
be, forms of 42, 211-12
between/among 288
book of quotations 382
books, library. *See* library books
brainstorming 410
bring/take 288

C

calvary/cavalry 289
capitalization
    of proper adjectives 313
    of proper nouns 29, 301-2, 304, 306-7, 309, 311
    of titles 309
card catalog
    author card 370-71
    call number 370-71
    subject card 370-71
    title card 370-71
case. *See* pronoun
clause
    adjective 171, 173-74
    definition of 162-63
    dependent 162-63
    independent 162-63
clustering 411
colon 332
comma
    in a compound sentence 326
    in a series 325-26
    to separate 328
    with quotations/dates/addresses/letters 330
comma splice 10-11
complete verb 52-53
complex sentence
    components of 168-69
    definition of 168-69
compound noun 32-33
compound noun, stress in (ESL) 33
compound pronoun. *See* reflexive pronoun *and* intensive pronoun
compound sentence
    components of 166-67
    definition of 166
    diagramming of 167
compound vs. complex 169
computer catalog 370-71
concordance 382

conjunction
    coordinating 139-41
    correlative 144
    definition of 139-41
    diagramming of 140-41, 144
    functions of 139-41, 144
contractions
    possessive pronouns and contractions 252
count and noncount nouns (ESL) 31
count noun 30-31

D

decimal point 323
definition 379
demonstrative pronoun 83
Dewey Decimal System 368
diagramming
    adjective 96
    adverb 120
    compound sentence 167
    conjunction 140-41, 144
    direct object 44
    gerund 194
    indirect object 45
    infinitive 198
    interjection 148
    intransitive 43
    participle 188-89
    predicate adjective 47
    predicate noun 47
    prepositional phrase 135
    transitive 44-45
dictionary
    definition in 379
    entry in 375
    etymology in 380
    function label 379
    guide words in 375
    pronunciation guide 378
    pronunciation in 378
    stress of words in 378
    syllabification in 378
    usage label 379
dictionary skills
    finding the word 375
    pronouncing the word 378
    using the word 379-80
dictionary, type of
    biographical 381
    desk 375
    foreign language 381
    geographic (gazetteer) 381
    thesaurus (dictionary of synonyms/antonyms) 381
    unabridged 375

direct object
    definition of 44-45
    diagramming of 44
    distinguished from predicate noun 49-50
    sentence pattern with 44
do (ESL) 211
do, forms of 211-12
double comparison 277
double negatives 273-74
drafting 413-23

E

encyclopedia 381
entry word 375
ESL notes 3, 5, 21, 22, 31, 33, 87, 102, 109, 192, 197, 211, 274, 298
essay
    conclusion 422-23
    introduction 419, 422
    thesis statement 420
etymology 380
exclamation point 2-3, 321

F

few/little (ESL) 87
fewer/less 289
freewriting 411
fused sentence 10-11
future perfect tense 61
future tense 58-59

G

gender
    feminine 80-81, 227-28, 231-32
    masculine 80-81, 227-28, 231-32
    neuter 80-81, 227-28, 231-32
gerund 191-92
gerund phrase 193-94
gerunds with prepositions (ESL) 192
good/well 271-72
guide words, dictionary 375

H

have, forms of 211-12
hear/here 290
helping verb. *See* auxiliary
how come/why 290
hyphen 342-43

I

idiom, "to stake a claim" (ESL) 22
idiomatic use of "ear" in "ear of corn" (ESL) 21
indefinite pronoun
    agreement with 214, 231-32
    antecedent of 87
    definition of 87
    gender of 231-32
    number of 87, 214, 231
independent possessive 105-6
indirect object
    definition of 45
    diagramming of 45
    sentence pattern with 45
indirect quotation 335
infinitive 196
infinitive, verbs likely to follow (ESL) 197
infinitive phrase 198
intensive pronoun 85, 254-55
interjection
    definition of 148
    diagramming of 148
    function of 148
interrogative pronoun 83
intonation (ESL) 3
intransitive verb 43, 45
inverted order
    with questions 6-7
    with *there* 6
    with *there* or *here* 220
irregular verb 55
italics. *See* underlining/italics

L

learn/teach 290
led/lead 290
library
    audio-visual materials 367
    periodical section 367
    reference section 367
library books
    autobiography 369
    biography 369
    children's 367
    fiction 367-69
    mystery fiction 368
    nonfiction 367-69
    science fiction 368
    young adults/juvenile 367

library books, finding
    call number 370
    card catalog 370-71
    catalog entry 370
    computer catalog 370-71
    Dewey Decimal System 368
    Library of Congress System 369
    section letter 370
Library of Congress System 369
lie/lay 283-84
linking verb 47, 49-50
loose/lose 290

M

may/can 286
memory techniques 393-94
modifier 97. *See also* adjective, adverb

N

noncount noun 30-31
noun
    as direct object 44-45
    as indirect object 45
    as object of the preposition 130
    as predicate noun 47
    as subject 4-5
    common 29
    compound 32-33
    count 30-31
    definition of 22
    distinguishing between PN and DO 49-50
    formation of compounds 32-33
    irregular plural 24
    noncount 30-31
    plural 23-24
    plural possessive 23, 26
    possessive 26, 103-4
    predicate noun 47
    proper 29
    singular 23
    singular possessive 23, 26
    spelling plurals of 23-24, 354-55
number
    of indefinite pronouns 87, 214, 231
    of nouns 23-24
    of personal pronouns 80-81, 227

O

object of the preposition 130
objective case 80-81, 244

P

paragraph
- concluding sentence 418-19
- topic sentence 414

parentheses 345

participial phrase 188-89

participle
- past participle 186
- present participle 184-85

parts of a book, using 387-90

parts of speech. *See* noun, verb, adjective, adverb, pronoun, preposition, conjunction, *and* interjection

passed/past 292

past perfect tense 61

past tense 58-59

peace/piece 292

perfect tense
- future 61
- past 61
- present 60-61

period 2-3, 321, 323

person
- first 80-81
- second 80-81
- third 80-81

personal pronoun
- agreement with 227-28
- characteristics of 80-81
- courtesy order 252
- definition of 80-81
- number of 80-81, 227

personal pronoun, chart 80

phrase
- definition of 162
- gerund 193-94
- infinitive 198
- participial 188-89
- possessive 103-4
- prepositional 132, 135

plane/plain 292

planning 409-12

plural noun
- adding *s* or *es* 23-24

possessive case 80-81

possessive noun
- adding *'* or *'s* 26
- definition of 26
- functions of 26, 103-4

possessive phrase 104

possessive pronoun
- contractions and 252
- forms of 80
- functions of 80, 103-4

possessive, independent. *See* independent possessive

predicate
- complete 5
- compound 5
- simple 5

predicate adjective
- definition of 47
- diagramming of 47

predicate noun
- definition of 47
- diagramming of 47
- distinguished from direct object 49-50

preposition
- definition of 130
- examples of 130
- object of. *See* object of the preposition

preposition vs. adverb 137

prepositional phrase
- adjectival 135
- adverbial 135
- containing compound objects 132
- definition of 132
- diagramming of 135
- functions of 135
- position of 135

present perfect tense 60-61

present tense 58-59

principal parts of verbs
- past 55-57
- past participle 55-57
- present 55-57

progressive verb 63-64

pronoun
- definition of 78
- demonstrative 83
- indefinite 87, 214, 231-32
- intensive 85, 254-55
- interrogative 83
- objective case 80-81, 244
- personal 80-81, 227-28
- possessive 103-4
- possessive case 80-81, 252
- problems with
  - *its/it's* 252
  - *their/they're* 252
  - *theirs/there's* 252
  - *we/us* 248
  - *who/whom* 250
  - *whose/who's* 252
  - *your/you're* 252

Index 473

    reference 85, 87, 256-57, 260-61
    reflexive 85, 254-55
    subjective case 80-81, 242
    usage with compound objects 244
    usage with compound subjects 242
    usage with predicate nouns 242
pronoun reference 85, 87, 256-57, 260-61
pronoun-antecedent agreement
    with indefinite pronouns 231-32
    with personal pronouns 227-28
pronunciation 378
pronunciation guide 378
proofreading 427
proper adjective
    capitalization of 313
    definition of 109
proper noun
    capitalization of 29, 301-2, 304, 306-7, 309, 311
    definition of 29
publishing 428
punctuation. *See* punctuation marks
punctuation marks
    apostrophe 340
    colon 332
    comma 325-26, 328, 330
    decimal point 323
    exclamation point 2-3, 321
    hyphen 342-43
    parentheses 345
    period 2-3, 321, 323
    question mark 2-3, 321
    quotation marks 335
    semicolon 332
    underlining/italics 337-38

Q

question mark 2-3, 321
questions
    inverted order with 6-7
quiet/quite 293
quotation marks 335

R

R.S.V.P., meaning of (ESL) 298
Readers' Guide to Periodical Literature 382
reading comprehension, improving 394-95
reading textbooks 391-92
reference, pronoun 85, 87, 256-57, 260-61
reflexive pronoun 85, 254-55
regular verb 55
relative pronoun 173-74

revising 423-25
rise/raise 284
run-on. *See* comma splice *or* fused sentence

S

semicolon 332
sentence
    definition of 2
    word order 5-6
sentence patterns
    S-InV 43
    S-LV-PA 47
    S-LV-PN 47
    S-TrV-DO 44
    S-TrV-DO-IO 45
sentence problems
    comma splice 10-11
    fragment 8
    fused 10-11
    run-on. *See* comma splice *or* fused sentence
sentence types
    complex 168-69
    compound 166-67
    declarative 2-3
    exclamatory 2-3
    imperative 2-3
    interrogative 2-3
    simple 165-66
shall/will 286
simple sentence
    components of 165-66
    definition of 165, 167
simple tenses
    future 58-59
    past 58-59
    present 58-59
sit/set 284
spelling
    by syllables 353
    of plural forms of nouns 354-55
    of singular present-tense verbs 354-55
stress (pronunciation) 378
study time
    improving 392
    scheduling 392-93
subject
    complete 4-5
    compound 5
    simple 4-5
    understood *you* 5
subject-verb agreement
    with compound subjects 216-17
    with indefinite pronouns 214

with intervening phrases 219-20
with inverted order 220
with linking verbs 212
with personal pronouns 212
with predicate nouns 219-20
subjective case 80-81, 242
subordinating words 162-63
syllabification 378

T

tense, verb. *See* verb
test frame
    for adjectives 96
    for verbs 42
test-taking 400-402
than/then 293
to/too/two 293
transitive verbs 44-45
troublesome words
    a/an 287
    accept/except 287
    ain't 287
    alot/a lot 288
    alright/all right 288
    between/among 288
    bring/take 288
    calvary/cavalry 289
    fewer/less 289
    hear/here 290
    how come/why 290
    learn/teach 290
    led/lead 290
    lie/lay 283-84
    loose/lose 290
    may/can 286
    passed/past 292
    peace/piece 292
    plane/plain 292
    quiet/quite 293
    rise/raise 284
    shall/will 286
    sit/set 284
    than/then 293
    to/too/two 293
    wear/where 293

U

underlining/italics 337-38
understood *you*. *See* subject
usage of *some/any* (ESL) 274

V

verb
    action 42
    active voice 66
    be 42, 211-12
    complete 52-53
    definition of 42
    distinguishing linking verbs from other verbs 49
    do 211-12
    have 211-12
    intransitive 43, 45
    irregular 55
    linking 47, 49-50
    passive voice 66
    perfect tenses 60-61
    principal parts 55-57
    progressive 63-64
    recognition of 42
    regular 55
    simple tenses 58-59
    state-of-being 42
    test frame for 42
    transitive 44-45
verbal 184-85
verbal phrase *See* gerund phrase, infinitive phrase, *or* participial phrase
voice, active and passive. *See* verb

W

wear/where 293
word order (ESL) 5
writing process 409-28
    drafting 413-23
    planning 409-12
    publishing 428
    revising 423-427